Philosophy
and
philosophers

Philosophy and philosophers

An introduction to Western philosophy

John Shand

McGill–Queen's University Press
Montreal & Kingston • London • Buffalo

© John Shand 1993

Published in the United Kingdom by UCL Press Limited.

Published simultaneously in Canada by:
McGill–Queen's University Press
3430 McTavish Street
Montreal
Quebec
H3A 1X9
Canada

Printed in England.

Legal deposit third quarter 1993.

Bibliothèque nationale du Québec.

ISBN: 0-7735-1139-3

CANADIAN CATALOGUING IN PUBLICATION DATA
Shand, John, 1956–
Philosophy and philosophers : an introduction
to Western philosophy

Includes bibliographical references.
ISBN 0-7735-1139-3

1. Philosophy--history.   I. Title.

B791.S43 1993   190   C93-090147-9

CONTENTS

Contents

PREFACE

Several people have helped me write this book.

I should especially like to thank my wife Judith for her unflagging and invaluable encouragement, as well as her practical help; she checked the whole manuscript and proofs and also pointed out anything ambiguous or unclear; without her help this book would not have been completed.

I should like to acknowledge the help of the following people, each of whom read and commented on some part of the manuscript: David Bell, Michael Clark, David E. Cooper, Oswald Hanfling, Desmond P. Henry, David Lamb, Harry Lesser, Kathryn Plant, Robert Wilkinson. Thanks must also go to Ted Honderich and Jonathan Riley. In a general way I should like to thank all my past Open University students, whose actual and hypothetical opinions as to what is comprehensible I constantly bore in mind while writing the book. Invaluable has been the availability of the facilities of the University of Manchester: the Philosophy Department library and especially the John Rylands University Library of Manchester. Any remaining deficiencies in this book are of course entirely my responsibility.

I have not given precise references for quotations in the book, thinking them unnecessary and inappropriate in a work of this kind. However, I direct the reader's attention to the extensive annotated bibliography. The very few short direct quotations used are therefore left without precise references, although I sometimes cite the work from which the quote comes, and in all cases it should be obvious which philosopher is being quoted.

JOHN SHAND

INTRODUCTION

The aim of this book is to give an introduction to Western philosophy through its past, both distant and more recent, and to serve as a useful work for more advanced students of philosophy. The subject of philosophy is presented in this book by studying the thought of major philosophers and by concentrating on what are generally regarded as the central areas of philosophy: the nature of philosophy itself, the theory of knowledge (epistemology) and the essential nature of reality (metaphysics). It is hoped that this work will satisfy the curiosity of those who want to understand what philosophy is and will provide a key to further study of philosophy and philosophers. To aid the reader in further study an extensive annotated bibliography is included, which serves as a guide primarily to works by and about the philosophers considered in this book, although it also includes reference to more general works in philosophy.

The various chapters and sections within the book can be usefully read in isolation, since they are relatively autonomous, although there is an additional cumulative beneficial effect that results from reading right through the book in order.

It is impossible to deal with every controversy over interpretation. However, every attempt has been made to be clear and accurate. The general approach to each philosopher considered is to present an account which tries to make their views hang together convincingly, rather than subject them to intense critical dissection. There are, however, some critical observations which naturally arise from exposition.

It is difficult to give an account of the defining features of philosophy. The reason for the difficulty in answering the question of what philosophy is paradoxically provides an answer of sorts. An essential part of philosophy is the extent to which it reassesses its own nature. Philosophy tends to ask extremely broad and fundamental questions, and it raises problems which are not normally considered problems at all in most other areas of human inquiry. A feature which helps us to understand the nature of philosophy, and is one of the chief attractions of the subject, is its freedom of thought: in philosophy no question is, on the face of it, unaskable.

Philosophy does not have to be especially defensive or coy about its nature or existence. It is sometimes said that the subject matter of philosophy is far removed from anything that could have practical importance in life. Even if this were true it would not follow that philosophy is not worth bothering with, for it might well be intrinsically interesting. In any case, philosophy does examine ideas in ethics and politics that have immediate practical consequences. Moreover, one of the reasons why philosophy is important is that more than any other subject it freely examines presuppositions and assumptions that people have that might otherwise go unquestioned; and many of these very basic beliefs, which people may take for granted, lead to, and underpin, other beliefs which have immediate practical consequences in that they determine what people believe and how they act. Whenever and wherever we live we absorb a world-view which can be so familiar that it can, through going unnoticed, go unexamined. So long as people are not dogmatically locked into, or wedded to, a fixed system of ideas and beliefs there will always be philosophy. Philosophy is not a luxury, indeed it becomes a necessity just as soon as people are able and willing to think freely about their beliefs. The terrible consequences that have followed from dogmatically held beliefs throughout human history bear sufficient testimony to the need to philosophize. Anyone who open-mindedly and critically examines, rather than simply accepts, fundamental ideas, has started doing philosophy. Philosophy cuts very deeply into our beliefs concerning the world and our place in it.

It is characteristic of philosophy that it goes back to where most other subjects begin and then probes still further back in its inquiries. Philosophy discusses enduring problems arising from life and thought. It is one of the attractions of philosophy that it connects thinkers of otherwise different historical ages and finds in them the same fundamental problems.

Reference to the historical and intellectual context in which a philosophical position arose may help us to understand what is meant by that position. However, it is important not to confuse the truth of philosophical positions and the soundness of the arguments presented for them with either their causal, psychological, historical origin or the extent of their causal, psychological, historical influence. Philosophy involves expounding existing ideas, creating new imaginative ideas, and critically assessing the soundness of arguments put forward in support of views claimed to be true. Neither the causal origin of a claim or argument, nor its causal influence on human affairs, has any relevance in assessing the truth of a claim or the soundness of the argument presented for it. One can of course trace origins and influences as well, but that is not the same as, and not a substitute for, assessing the validity of arguments and the truth of beliefs. A given philosophy could have an interesting origin or be very influential, but may still be bad philosophy for all that.

The nature of metaphysics can be characterized as the attempt by reason and argument alone to understand the essential structure of the world on the presupposition that there must be some features that all possible realities must have in common, however else they may differ. The metaphysician claims to be able to determine some general necessary truths about the nature of reality by reason alone independently of observation and the evidence of experience. Epistemology is concerned with what knowledge is, what conditions have to be satisfied for knowledge, what counts as good evidence and justification, and what in that case are the kinds of things we can know. Both metaphysics and epistemology raise questions which cannot be answered by empirical scientific investigation because any such investigation will have metaphysical and epistemological assumptions and presuppositions underpinning it, and so any answers derived from science would beg the questions raised. For example science makes assumptions about the reliability of empirical evidence, the nature of empirical theories, and what conditions have to be satisfied in general for it to be rational to believe one theory rather than another.

References in this book to ethics and politics will be few, although some mention of ethics is unavoidable because it is sometimes inextricably connected to a philosopher's concern with knowledge and the general structure of existence.

Those who are interested and willing to follow the path of philosophical inquiry are embarked on perhaps the greatest adventure of ideas of all. Philosophy is an important part of what Bertrand Russell called "all the noonday brightness of human genius", destined though it may be to ultimate annihilation; it is by such activity that for the time being human beings dignify themselves in the face of a universe that may seem at best indifferent to human concerns.

CHRONOLOGY OF PHILOSOPHERS

This lists the main philosophers considered in this book, apart from those in Chapter Twelve, "Recent philosophy". Sometimes, with figures from the more distant past, the dates are uncertain.

BC	AD
Thales (*c.*624–*c.*546)	Augustine (354–430)
Anaximander (*c.*610–*c.*546)	Aquinas (1225–74)
Anaximenes (*c.*585–*c.*528)	Ockham (*c.*1285–1349)
Pythagoras (*c.*571–*c.*497)	Descartes (1596–1650)
Xenophanes (*fl.*540)	Spinoza (1632–77)
Heraclitus (*fl.*504)	Locke (1632–1704)
Parmenides (*fl.*501–492)	Leibniz (1646–1716)
Zeno (*fl.*464)	Berkeley (1685–1753)
Anaxagoras (*c.*500–428)	Hume (1711–76)
Empedocles (*c.*484–*c.*424)	Kant (1724–1804)
Socrates (470–399)	Hegel (1770–1831)
Democritus (*c.*460–*c.*371)	Nietzsche (1844–1900)
Leucippus (*fl.*450–420)	Husserl (1859–1938)
Melissus (*fl.*441)	Russell (1872–1970)
Plato (427–347)	Wittgenstein (1889–1951)
Aristotle (384–322)	Popper (1902–)
	Sartre (1905–80)
	Ayer (1910–89)

*Philosophy
and
philosophers*

CHAPTER ONE

Presocratic Greek philosophy

The past is not a story; only in retrospect under an interpretation does it unfold as history like a fictional tale in a book. Consequently, in reporting what happened in the past we lack one of the characteristics of a story: a definite beginning. However, in Greece a short time after 600 BC certain changes were taking place in human thought that seemed to have no precedent; and it is on these changes in the way human beings began to think about the world and themselves that the most fundamental aspects of today's Western civilization – its science, ethics, politics, and philosophy – are founded. There were events of significance before this time; but 600 BC onwards marks alterations in human thought sufficient to describe it as a beginning.

The study of ancient philosophy is normally said to extend from 585 BC to AD 529. Of course, philosophical speculation did not cease at that date, but the banning of the teaching of Greek philosophy at the University of Athens by the Roman Christian Emperor Justinian, in AD 529, is thought of as a suitable event to mark a change.

The Presocratic period covers 585 BC to 400 BC and the term "Presocratic" has the obvious literal sense of denoting those philosophers living before Socrates. This meaning is only approximate, as some of the philosophers considered as Presocratics were contemporaries of Socrates who was born in 470 BC and died in 399 BC. Again the decision to divide history in this way is justified by its marking another beginning. A change in direction and style of thought was instigated by Socrates, for knowledge of whom we are almost entirely dependent on Plato (427–347 BC). The labelling of a group of many thinkers, whose work stretched over a period of 185 years, as the Presocratics, can be highly misleading if it is taken to imply a great unity of thought. Nevertheless, comprehension of any one of this group is aided by consideration of the others. Their views were diverse, and

1

their degree of knowledge of the work of others varied greatly.

Considering the enormous claims made for the importance of the Presocratics, it is extraordinary that we have no document dating from that time written by these people. What we know of what they said and wrote comes to us, at best, second-hand, the most substantial contribution being made by Aristotle (384–322 BC), but also a good deal from Simplicius (AD 500–540); and there were many others. Of this derivative information, the most precious is that contained in the "fragments"; this is not actual text that has survived physically down the centuries, but rather all purported direct quotations from the Presocratics. The second source of information is the summaries and comments of those ancient philosophers and historians who did have direct access to Presocratic texts. We must beware of the corruption of Presocratic views by error, misunderstanding, or deliberate point-making.

To understand how these philosophers could have had such an influence on such a wide range of subjects, we have to understand that the early Greeks did not separate out disciplines in the way we do now. "Philosophy" literally means "love of wisdom", and the topics that fell under this name covered what we now pick out as philosophy, logic, science, medicine, ethics, social science, psychology, and religion. The importance of the Presocratic philosophers, particularly the earlier ones, is to be found in their speculations in physics – the study of nature – for it is among these early tentative attempts to provide a complete, simple, unified explanation of the various phenomena of the world, or universe, that the outline of the methods and concepts of modern empirical science were first drawn. From a dissatisfaction with mythical accounts of the world explanations began to emerge that were generalizable and systematic rather than *ad hoc*, naturalistic rather than having recourse to supernatural gods and powers, and that were, most importantly, backed by arguments open to inspection, instead of assertions based on authority or mere durability – although the distinctions between the mythical and the new forms of explanation were not always sharp. The Presocratic philosophers were *phusikoi* (from which comes the word "physics"); speculators on the workings of nature.

It is necessary first to say something about the world in which they lived. Philosophy began not on mainland Greece, still less in Athens where it was later to flourish, but in Ionia – the western seaboard on the Aegean Sea of what is now Turkey, more generally called Asia Minor. Mycenaean civilization developed in mainland Greece between 1580 BC and 1120 BC under the considerable influence of the more ancient Minoan civilization (3000–1000 BC) of Crete. After the collapse of the Mycenaean civilization, Greeks from the mainland after 1000 BC began colonizing the islands of the Aegean, and the west coast of Asia Minor, which became known as Ionia owing to the Ionic form of the Greek language spoken there. The Greeks of the sixth century BC looked back upon the Mycenaean period with nostalgia; the essential features of their myths and religion, told for example through the poems of Homer, were taken from the Mycenaeans. Around 700 BC the Ionians flourished with trade increasing around the Mediterranean. Various peoples influenced the cultural and intellectual growth of Ionia. From the Scythians in the north they received shamanistic beliefs that probably influenced Pythagoras. Other peoples to exert influence on Greek culture were the Lydians and Phrygians in Asia Minor, the Canaanites and Phoenicians – the latter providing the Greeks with the tremendously important matter of an alphabet. Egypt was also a country that fascinated the Greeks, and the effect can be seen in what the Greeks took from Egyptian mathematics and medicine. Perhaps the most significant influence was derived from the Babylonian Empire (which fell to the Persians in 538 BC) where major advances had been made in mathematics and the data collected on astronomical events. The Iranian peoples (which included the Persians) had military domination of Asia Minor by 540 BC.

Against this background Greek city-states began to crystallize out, first on the mainland, then spreading to Ionia by the 7th century BC. The change is significant because it created a sympathetic environment for philosophical thinking and science. The city-states were ruled by oligarchies, but oligarchies which had come to power with the consent, and remained under the influence, of a significant proportion of the population. Although certainly not democracies – since the group with a say excluded women, slaves, and the poor – these states did at least embody some kind of stability through a law invested with some legitimacy through consent, replacing the arbitrary and volatile power of the absolute despot. A relatively stable and increasingly prosperous environment, and an alphabet, were opportune conditions for the rise of scientific and philosophical speculation.

The concerns of Greek philosophy centred on perplexing problems derived from common observation and nascent science: the one (unity) and the many (plurality), permanence and change, reality and appearance, existence (being) and non-existence (non-being). We observe a world of many things over which we require a sense of its unity into one world; we observe also a world of change and movement beyond which we require a sense of its essential stability. Under the heading of permanence and change comes the search for something stable behind the restless world as it appears; something that would either explain the apparent world, or declare it ultimately illusory. We also observe a world containing a plurality of objects; behind this there must be something that binds this diversity into one permanent unified cosmos. Without such a "something", we lack an overall and ultimate explanation for the world. The Greek word *kosmos* (from which we derive "cosmos") implies a universe which is ordered and beautiful in arrangement, and therefore in principle capable of explanation.

Much of Greek philosophy is an attempt to discern underlying similarity between apparently diverse phenomena, which can act as a common explanation of the apparently different phenomena. Similarity is emphasized rather than difference. Thus an explanation of why two differing phenomena occur might be derived from some underlying factor beyond the features by which they differ. This simplifies by eliminating the need for special explanations applicable only to each phenomenon. This approach is one of the foundations of modern science. To use an example from modern science: the way in which, after being dropped from a plane, the phenomena of the falling of a cow and of a hammer are explained does not require two special explanations one applicable only to cows and the other only to hammers, rather the two apparently diverse phenomena are united under the common underlying reality that they are both physical bodies.

There are various possibilities that ensue from the attempt to provide a unified explanation of the phenomena of the universe in the face of its apparent diversity:

(a) To give an account of some material stuff or substance which underlies, and can perhaps be used to explain, all the apparent variety.

(b) To give an account of some universal controlling law which brings unity to the plurality of the apparent world.

(c) To assert that the world as it appears is an illusion because to be really as it appears would be inherently contradictory, and to deduce that the real world must be quite other than it appears.

(d) To be sceptical about our ability to provide a unifying explanation for the world.

In the Presocratics all these possibilities – which are not of course mutually exclusive – are considered.

Among the philosophers called Presocratics there are some minor figures who will not be discussed. Some Presocratics probably wrote nothing. Of the ones who did write, the amount of evidence we have as to what they said varies greatly. Unsurprisingly, although there are difficulties of interpretation in all cases, some are more difficult than others.

It will be useful first to present a list of the most significant Presocratics in the rough order in which they are usually considered and to display the three main phases of Presocratic thought (opposite: I = pre-Parmenidean, II = Parmenidean, III = post-Parmenidean). Any attempt to categorize groups of Presocratic philosophers is more or less arbitrary; the categories must emphasize similarities at the expense of differences. The Milesians sit quite well together as a group; although, as will be seen, Anaximander produces sufficiently

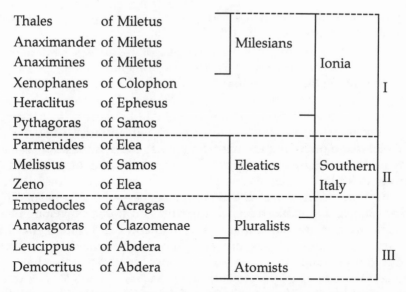

Thales	of Miletus		
Anaximander	of Miletus	Milesians	
Anaximines	of Miletus		Ionia
Xenophanes	of Colophon			I
Heraclitus	of Ephesus		
Pythagoras	of Samos		
Parmenides	of Elea		
Melissus	of Samos	Eleatics	Southern
Zeno	of Elea		Italy	II
Empedocles	of Acragas		
Anaxagoras	of Clazomenae	Pluralists	
Leucippus	of Abdera			III
Democritus	of Abdera	Atomists	

unusual views to make us doubt this grouping. Melissus is included among the Eleatics, although he did not come from Elea, because of his general approach and because he was probably a pupil of Parmenides. It is customary to divide these philosophers into those from Ionia and those from the Greek colonies of southern Italy and Sicily. Pythagoras, who was born in Ionia, comes under southern Italy because of his work and influence in that area.

The customary division of Presocratic philosophy into three phases, as above, is one of which the philosophers themselves would not have been conscious. The first phase (I) indicates (with the exception of Xenophanes) an optimism in the power of empirical explanation; the second (II) denotes a period of the ascendancy of pure reason, separated from empirical explanation and evidence; the third phase (III) can be understood as an attempt to reconcile phases (I) and (II).

Let us now look at the Presocratics in the light of the four approaches, (a), (b), (c), (d), given above, as possible replies which ensue from asking the central early Greek question: how to explain, or reconcile, the permanence (one, unity, being) required for a unifying explanation of the universe, with the appearance of constant change (many, plurality, becoming). Under this notion we find the following groupings:

(a) Thales, Anaximander, Anaximenes, Empedocles, Leucippus, Democritus
(b) Heraclitus, Anaxagoras, Pythagoras
(c) Parmenides, Melissus, Zeno
(d) Xenophanes

To a great extent the guide to putting a particular philosopher in a certain group is merely a matter of emphasis. Plainly those in (a), say, have not only to be concerned with the basic stuff of the universe, but also with the forces that control it, as in (b).

Pre-Parmenidean philosophers

The concept linking the Milesians is that of *arche*. *Arche* is an explanatory concept introduced to understand the Presocratics by Aristotle; it denotes the original and controlling stuff and first principle of the universe, the nature of which provides an explanation of the existing universe, and its origin, as a whole.

Very little is known of the first philosopher-scientist Thales. His chief subject for explanation is the energy of the universe. One answer to this is hylozoism: a view whereby everything in the universe is to some degree animate. This does not mean that stones are conscious, and subject to pain and desire; all-pervasive life is a matter of wide degree. Movement is one of the most powerful intuitive criteria for life, and Thales noticed that magnets were capable of both being moved and moving certain other objects. In the case of Thales the *arche* was water, and seems for Thales to have been self-moving. That water should have been the *arche* need not surprise us greatly since we can immediately reflect upon its life-sustaining properties, and that, when dried out, things die. This provides an explanation for the cosmos which dispenses with the need for *ad hoc* divine intervention; it is this that marks an important step towards rational science. But we should not think that such a view necessarily involves atheism. Indeed, Thales believed that the world as a whole is pervaded with a divine life-force; this accounts for the change and variety of the world. Thales also held the view that the earth floats on a bed of water.

The second, and the most interesting, of the Milesians is Anaximander. Anaximander's *arche* is not any ordinary material stuff, but what he called *apeiron*: the infinite or indefinite. *Apeiron* is a substance and principle of infinite extent and indefinite character; because it explains all the universe it is unlimited in extent, and since from it are evolved all qualities of things, the *apeiron* itself has no qualities. *Apeiron* is neither hot nor cold, wet nor dry; it is qualitatively neutral. The world as we know it is evolved from the entirely homogeneous continuum of *apeiron* by a temporary local imbalance in opposing elements of the *apeiron*; and this passing away and coming to be of worlds is cyclical. Features of the world from the original state are produced by a process of "winnowing out", or shaking, with like qualities gathering with like; this may involve a doctrine of eternal motion. The controlling principle is a form of cosmic justice, whereby if one quality gains dominance there has to be recompense for this by an increase in the opposite quality. The obvious problem surrounding an explanation from imbalance in *apeiron*, is why any kind of imbalance should begin, given its once homogeneous state.

Anaximander held the view that the earth does not move and is cylindrical in shape. The doctrine of an immobile earth was to remain a powerful force in Western cosmology until the time of Copernicus (1473–1543) and Galileo (1564–1642). The reason for supposing that the earth was motionless was based on the equality of forces to which it is subject in its situation equidistant from the edges of the universe.

One of the most interesting aspects of Anaximander is his view on biology and the origins of life, for here he held that life was derived from the action of the sun on moist things, whereby fish developed, and within fish adult humans were originally formed who appeared when the fish form was shed.

Anaximenes, the last of the Milesian philosophers, presents a less bold doctrine of *arche* than Anaximander, for while the *arche* is infinite, Anaximenes returns to a physical substance: air. Air is in constant motion as can be felt, but not seen, from the wind. By a process of rarefaction and condensation air becomes visible in the forms we recognize as fire (rarefaction) and water and stone (condensation); through this process an account is given of how things change. The earth is flat and rides on air, and it is surrounded by heavenly bodies, all of which are centres of fire, but most are so distant from earth that they provide no heat.

With Pythagoras we move to a different phase in Greek philosophy. In the case of Pythagoras it is even more difficult than usual to disentangle those doctrines actually originating with him from those attributed to him by the school of Pythagoreans which appeared later in southern Italy. Pythagoreanism is what is more important to us from the aspect of a philosophical study.

Pythagoras, and those who called themselves his followers, fostered a secret society who kept the doctrines of "The Master" Pythagoras unrevealed, and also formed a political movement; this, and the deliberately exaggerated legend woven around Pythagoras, to the extent of the attribution of magical powers, aroused the suspicion and derision of contemporary thinkers such as Heraclitus, Xenophanes, and the historian Herodotus. The Pythagorean sect seems to have been more concerned with embodying a way of life than encouraging free inquiry. Nevertheless Pythagoras was a brilliant polymath.

The attribution to Pythagoras, or his followers, of significant contributions to mathematics and geometry, including Pythagoras' Theorem, is a matter of dispute among scholars. The activity of Pythagoreans seemed to centre on an obsession with numbers, which derived from a realization that mathematics in the form of expressions in numbers and ratios (proportion) held the key to understanding many disparate aspects of the world, such as musical harmony and architectural proportion. Thus pitch in a stringed instrument may be expressed in numbers as a proportion of total string length. In fact there seems to be an indication that Pythagoreanism did not see numbers merely as a means to an explanation of the world, but thought of the world *as* number in some sense. The identification of numbers and objects may have arisen from the association of numbers with spatial configurations; the number one is a single point in space from which other shapes are built up. If the number one is a point, then it is a short step to identifying the number one with a material point from which material objects are constructed by successive addition. The number one is the point, number two the line, number three the surface, number four the solid. An important Pythagorean doctrine is that a line, or any object with magnitude, is infinitely divisible, and constructed out of an unlimited number of infinitely small magnitudes. The Pythagoreans also asserted the existence of the void and infinite space.

The central importance of the Pythagoreans is that they saw the essence, or real identity, of a thing as determined not by the stuff of which it is made, but by its structure. One only has to think of cases of the same type of object according to structure, made from different stuff, to grasp a crude idea of the thinking here. The doctrine concerned with numbers and structure was deeply influential on Plato's thinking on the Forms, and on Aristotle's identification of substantial individuals with matter plus form or structure. For the Pythagoreans the structure was determined by the numerical concept of ratio or proportion. It has been suggested that Pythagoreanism indirectly encouraged, even if it did not found, the generation of pure, abstract mathematics and geometry from its pragmatic origins in Babylonia.

A major doctrine we can attribute to Pythagoras concerns the soul and its transmigration. The soul is an immortal unity and can be incarnated and reincarnated in a variety of living creatures; whether the soul appears in a creature that is lowly or not is determined by the spiritual purity of the life of that soul in a previous incarnation. Since everything contains soul, this lent itself to an asceticism which involved vegetarianism. The cosmological and moral doctrines were conceived as connected; they were drawn up as displaying the opposing values of the limited (associated with odd numbers) and the unlimited (associated with even numbers) – the former denoted the structured and quantitatively measurable (good), and the latter the chaotic and irrational (bad). The view was also taken that the world went through eternal cycles of recurrence. The Pythagoreans seem to have been the first to suggest that the earth is spherical.

Xenophanes made his contribution to philosophy through poetry, as did Parmenides and Empedocles, although unlike Xenophanes they tended to use poetry merely as a vehicle for expressing their ideas;

Xenophanes was primarily a poet. He was undoubtedly aware of the teachings of Pythagoras, as well as the Milesians. His chief interests were not with nature directly, but with theology and questions about the limits of human knowledge. He criticized the traditional polytheism of Homer, mocking as absurd the unwarranted portrayal of gods in the human image; horses would, if they could, no doubt draw gods like horses. He opposed this view to a rational theology of impersonal monotheism which may have been pantheistic. Although he was probably not an absolute sceptic about knowledge, he did indicate that, while opinion should be granted, the term "knowledge" should be withheld from the total cosmic explanations of the Milesians.

Heraclitus is a figure who stimulates great interest partly because his oracular pronouncements respond flexibly to a variety of interpretations. It is possible to see the conscious influence of Heraclitus' ideas and manner of expression in Hegel (1770–1831) and Nietzsche (1844–1900), although one must be cautious of foisting on thinkers anachronistic interpretation. However, even to his contemporaries Heraclitus had a reputation for obscurity partly because of the oblique rhetorical way he expressed his thought, and partly because of his deliberate eschewal of manifest systematization. For this reason, as well as the usual problems surrounding the study of the Presocratics, a wide variety of interpretations has emerged.

His views suggest an aristocratic contempt for the opinions of other philosophers and the common man. His method of presenting his ideas reflects his belief that the mode of expression needs to fit the deep riddle of the world. Again we see the central problem as that of reconciling change and constancy. Heraclitus adopts the Milesian procedure of identifying an *arche*: fire. Knowledge can be obtained only by combining the information provided by the senses with the discipline of reason. Heraclitus' famous view is that everything is in flux; everything is a process; there is no being, only becoming. But then the problem is to identify a concept of order in this constant change. Heraclitus chooses fire as *arche*; here we have something that is in flux while maintaining its identity; the problem of stability amidst change in this case is solved in so far as the fire is kindled and extinguished in equal measure. This gives the appearance of stability. Air, water, and earth emerge in that order away from likeness to fire through the local quenching of the world-fire.

Things come to be and pass away under the influence of a tension of opposites; if some quality exists, then so must its opposite. The only factor in the world order not subject to change is the *logos*, an objective overall controlling force on the processes which determine the nature of the world, which can be known only to the limited extent to which our soul is part of the divine *logos*. To the extent to which our souls are more spiritual (fiery) and less affected by bodily moisture, we gain understanding of the cosmic *logos*. Sometimes Heraclitus speaks of the *logos* in the abstract terms of a controlling law of measure and proportion, at others it is apparently identified with the cosmic fire.

A striking metaphor is presented by the bow and lyre: a bow, for example, is apparently stable, while it is maintained in its constant state by the equal proportion of opposite forces; the tension of the wood of the bow opposes the equal tension of the string, resulting in a static tension. In another example he points out that we cannot step in the same river twice since the water is in constant flow, nevertheless we identify it as the same river; the being of the river is maintained in its becoming. The *logos* refers to a rational law whereby the existence of a thing is maintained by the strife of pairs of opposites of equal measure to form a harmony or unity. The cosmos is also a unity despite appearances. Indeed, Heraclitus goes further in maintaining an identity of opposites, citing examples like day and night where a thing can convert to its opposite and back again; the process is an *unbroken* circle. God enters Heraclitus' cosmology as embodying all opposites, and as the fire which is the reality behind appearances acting on the world in accordance with the *logos*, which maintains an equal proportion of opposites, so producing all things.

Parmenidean philosophers

With the Eleatic group of philosophers we reach a dramatic change in outlook and method. The Eleatics reveal problems by a process of pure deductive reasoning that threatens to show that the progress made by empirical investigation into nature must be illusory; the world as it appears cannot be real for it is riddled with intrinsic contradictions. The Eleatic conclusions are supported by appeal to reasoned logical argument rather than sensory evidence. By dwelling on the concept of existence as such, deductions by reason show that the world in the form that it appears cannot really exist for it involves factors which contradict deductions from the concept of existence; and where reason and experience contradict each other, reason must oust experience.

With Eleatic philosophers we see the clear emergence of an opposition that persists down through the whole of the subsequent history of philosophy: whether pure reason or the senses reveal most accurately the true nature of reality. There are those rationalists for whom the world as it really is is discovered not by the senses but by reason; the real nature of the world is determined by processes of pure deductive reasoning, and if that view of the world clashes with what is presented by the senses, then what is presented by the senses must be discounted as mere appearance in favour of the world as it really is according to reason. In contrast, for the empiricists only the senses can determine the true nature of the world, if it can be determined at all, and the other supposed true reality of the rationalist, which is likely to be radically different from the world as it appears, will generally be regarded as illusion.

Parmenides was a pupil of Xenophanes, and influenced by Pythagoras; some of what he says sounds like a direct attack on the doctrine of all-pervading becoming found in Heraclitus. The work of Parmenides is divided into two parts: the "Way of Truth", and the "Way of Seeming". The second part, the "Way of Seeming", provides speculations on nature in the usual Ionian manner. Yet he seems to have taken this second part as merely a pragmatic addition, which is ultimately false, to the truth about the world given in the first part. The "Way of Seeming" is false, but has pragmatic value in being designed for dealing with the world as it seems, in contrast with the truth about the world given in the "Way of Truth".

Parmenides' argument proceeds from the premise that "It is": that something exists. The only two alternatives to this are posed: (a) to deny "It is" and assert that there is nothing – this view has had no defenders, and (b) to assert both "It is" and "It is not". The exhaustive choice is between "It is" and "It is not". Non-existence ("It is not") is meaningless, for then we are committed to saying of "It" both that "It is" and that "It is not" which, being a self-contradiction, cannot be formulated as a thought. What cannot be thought cannot exist, and what "is not" cannot enter our thoughts, therefore the existence of non-existence is impossible, being self-contradictory. For something to be thought of and spoken of (recognized) it must exist; it is not possible to speak or think of what is not there – a nothing. Thus what exists, despite the deliverances of our senses, must always have existed as a continuous, unchanging, timeless, indivisible unity. Change and diversity involve the positing of "It is not" – nothing (non-existence) existing – which is contradictory and so impossible.

This view reconciles the problem of the one and the many by demonstrating that the appearance of many is impossible as a reality; permanence is also reconciled with change by denying change. Thus what is is one and cannot change. Coming to be and passing away are impossible. Change and plurality involve becoming; a process from something that is, to something else that is, involves a something becoming a nothing, and a nothing becoming a something; but nothing cannot exist and something cannot come from nothing; and if something comes from something, then what is must already always have existed. Therefore all change and plurality are impossible; apparent change and plurality presented to our senses are an illusion. There is no void (vacuum), just unbroken existence (plenum) that does not admit of degrees, in which, obviously, movement is impossible; a void would mean non-being, which means non-existence, but non-being cannot be (exist). Reality is totally immobile. There is no *kosmos* for Parmenides, for *kosmos* implies structure, and in a true plenum there can be no structure.

The influence of Parmenides can hardly be overestimated; through the respect held for him by Plato he came to affect the course of Western philosophy. (The denial of a void is still found in Descartes (1596–1650)). From Parmenides grew the Platonic metaphysical and epistemological doctrine that what can be known must be real, and what is real, eternal and unchanging cannot be the unstable world given by experience. There must be objects of knowledge to match the immutable status of knowledge proper. From this grew scepticism of empirical knowledge, so that knowledge is taken to apply truly only to mathematics, geometry, and deductive reasoning.

Melissus was a follower of Parmenides and produced some further arguments supporting the absolutely unitary nature of reality as described by Parmenides. His only serious disagreement involved saying that reality must be infinite in space as well as infinite in time. For the question could be raised as to what lay beyond the finite sphere of Parmenidean reality. Parmenides took reality to be a finite sphere because of the necessity for perfection and completeness. It has been suggested that the finitude of Parmenidean reality is such as to rule out the sense of the question "What lies outside the sphere?". But this was not to be understood until the conflicting conceptions of space proposed by Newton (1642–1727) and Einstein (1879–1955) – in particular whether space was Euclidean or non-Euclidean – reached some kind of resolution.

Further support for Parmenides came from Zeno. There is good evidence from Plato to suggest that both Parmenides and Zeno met Socrates. Zeno's deductive arguments produce absurd conclusions derived from taking the world of apparent plurality (divisible), change and motion as real; the only alternative must be that reality is a Parmenidean changeless unity. The apparent world cannot be the real world because analysis of the consequences of its features, if supposed as real, leads to paradox, contradiction and absurdity. There is also an opinion that a target for Zeno's attacks was the Pythagorean thesis that things with magnitude consist of a plurality of infinitesimal magnitudes.

The arguments of Zeno divide into two parts: (a) The paradoxes of plurality, (b) The paradoxes of motion. Each time Zeno's aim in the arguments is to elicit a contradiction from the necessary conditions for plurality and motion. He uses a variety of arguments which have the general form that, from some proposition p about apparent reality, both q and then not-q are deduced, which reveals the absurdity of p, supposing p to be real.

(a) The paradoxes of plurality

(1) Limb (i): If there are many things, then things are infinitely small – things have no magnitude.

Limb (ii): If there are many things, then things are infinitely large – things have unlimited magnitude.

Limb (i): If there are many things, there must be a definite number of things. Otherwise all distinction between one and many is lost. If the number of things is definite, there must be some ultimate parts which are indivisible. If they are indivisible, they cannot have size, for size implies divisibility. Everything is therefore made up of parts with no magnitude. But then no matter how many – even an infinite number – of the infinitely small parts are summed together, they must still add up to something infinitely small.

Limb (ii): What exists must have size. Something with size can be added to, or subtracted from, something else; something that could not add to or subtract from something else would be nothing. Whatever has size must be divisible; and whatever is divisible once must be made up of parts that are always divisible; each part, no matter how small, must have some size, and hence be divisible. Everything is made up of an infinite number of parts, all with some magnitude, therefore everything must be infinitely large.

(2) Limb (i): If there are many things, then they must be finite in number.

Limb (ii): If there are many things, then they must be infinite in number.

Limb (i): If there are many things, they must be countable, for there must be some number that is exactly how many things there are; no more and no less. Then the number of things must be finite or limited in number.

Limb (ii): If there are many things, then they must be separate. Between any juxtaposed but separate items, no matter how close they are, there must be another item; but then there must be some item separating that item, and so on *ad infinitum*. So the number of things must be unlimited.

(3) One further argument is worth mentioning. If the small grains or parts of millet make no noise when dropped on the ground, how can it be the case that when the sum of these, a bushel of millet, is dropped, it does make a sound?

(b) The paradoxes of motion

(1) Motion is impossible because to traverse any distance it is first necessary to travel half the distance; but before that it is necessary

to travel half of half the distance. Since there is an infinite number of such subdivisions in any distance, it is not possible to traverse any distance, or even take the first step.

(2) Achilles and the Tortoise. In a race, despite Achilles being the quicker runner, if he gives the Tortoise any head-start at all, he can never overtake, or even catch up with, the Tortoise. For no matter how fast Achilles runs, by the time Achilles reaches the point where the Tortoise was when Achilles set out, the Tortoise will always have moved on. Achilles would have to pass through an infinite number of points where the Tortoise was before catching the Tortoise, which is impossible.

(3) The flying arrow. An arrow in flight is also stationary, for at any instance it occupies a definite position by filling a volume of space equal to itself.

(4) The stadium. In a stadium there are three rows of men who first stand next to one another, first in one position, then in another position.

$$\text{Position 1}$$
$$A_1 \ A_2 \ A_3 \ A_4$$
$$B_1 \ B_2 \ B_3 \ B_4 \rightarrow$$
$$\leftarrow C_1 \ C_2 \ C_3 \ C_4$$

$$\text{Position 2}$$
$$A_1 \ A_2 \ A_3 \ A_4$$
$$B_1 \ B_2 \ B_3 \ B_4$$
$$C_1 \ C_2 \ C_3 \ C_4$$

Row A is stationary while row B and row C move simultaneously in opposite directions at the same velocity. B_4 passes A_3 to reach A_4 in the same time as it takes B_4 to pass C_1, C_2, C_3, and reach C_4. But bodies travelling at the same velocity must take the same time to pass the same number of bodies of the same size. Here twice the distance was covered in the same time as half the distance. Or alternatively, half of a given time is equal to the whole of that time.

These arguments are meant to support Parmenides' thesis that the world is one and full – a plenum – and therefore incapable of division, motion, or change. This leaves the senses as a source only of illusion and falsehood, since the world as it seems to be according to the senses is impossible and so cannot be real.

Only a few brief remarks can be made on the replies to Zeno's arguments. Some mathematicians and logicians have thought Zeno's arguments of great subtlety, with the solutions forthcoming only with the invention of calculus. Aristotle thought some of the fallacies easy to spot, saying that in the case of the stadium row *A* is stationary, so that rows *B* and *C* move with twice the relative velocity to each other as compared to rows *B* with *A*, or *C* with *A*. Others have thought Aristotle's reply unsatisfactory. Still further problems are created if the change from the two positions is instantaneous, for then there is no time in which the extra men can be passed; this may lead us to conclude that time cannot consist of indivisible instances. It has been pointed out, in reply to the Achilles and the Tortoise case, and similar arguments, that an infinite series such as ½ + ¼ + ⅛ + . . . has the finite sum 1. This too is thought to be a mistaken reply by some: since the first step can never be taken, the series can never begin.

The intellectual situation in Presocratic philosophy now stood like this. (a) One could accept the views of the Eleatics and give up the attempt to explain the world as revealed by the senses; (b) one could accept the Eleatic view, but try to reconcile it with traditional Ionian empirical explanation and knowledge of the world (Empedocles, Anaxagoras, Leucippus, Democritus); (c) one could accept the Eleatic position but take the view that, although we can have *knowledge* only of a world behind and other than appearances, we can have opinion about the world of appearances, and that world is not a mere nothing; at the same time major concern would shift, with Socrates and Plato, from the investigation of nature to that of ethics, meaning, and epistemology.

Post-Parmenidean philosophers

Taking up the challenge of Parmenides to give some place to the world as it appears in reality is the remarkable figure of Empedocles. His surviving work consists of two poems, *On nature* and *Purifications*. Roughly, the first deals with science, and the second with myth and soul; but the distinction is not clear-cut intellectually nor certain in the assignment of certain passages to one poem or the other. The poems are a flawed union of reason, represented to the Greeks by Apollo, with the mystical vision of Dionysus.

Empedocles accepts the Parmenidean view that the world is a plenum, that there is no void, and that nothing in the world could really come into being or be destroyed. But he still maintains that change is possible within the essential imperishable "all" of the universe; the basic substance of the cosmos is immutable, but change occurs through the various interminglings (mixtures) within the plenum. The limitless cosmos is not a unity but a variously mixed plurality of imperishable elements. The Presocratic problem of the one and the many is circumvented by establishing many (four) Parmenidean "ones" in the reality underlying the appearance of many.

Knowledge through the use of the senses is possible if they are used properly. The basic stuff of the world is four "roots" or elements: earth, water, air, fire. These four *archai* are equal and immutable. They mix to create all that there is by the virtue of the opposing forces of Love and Strife. It must be recognized that the cosmos is seen as organic; Empedocles adopts a form of hylozoism, that is, all things are to some degree endowed with life. Love and Strife are active forces within the world which elicit change from things.

The world is adjusted according to the relative dominance of the principles of Love or Strife (attraction and repulsion); this applies both to local areas of the cosmos and to the cosmos as a whole. Within the universe as a whole the process operates in great cyclical epochs. When Love is dominant either locally or globally there is progression towards order and a harmonious blending of the basic elements; when Strife is dominant there is progression towards dissonance of the elements and separation. Strife attracts like to like, thus pulling the mixed elements apart by pulling like elements together; Love attracts unlike to unlike, thus pulling the dissimilar elements together. Within the cosmos where Strife is in overall dominance it is possible to find local areas of harmonious Love, and the reverse is also the case. Empedocles in fact believed he lived in a period of increasing overall Strife.

The development of the world proceeds in four stages in a never-ending cycle; it is therefore incorrect to say the cycle starts anywhere. To begin somewhere: in the first stage Love rules, and the world is a homogeneous sphere of fully blended unlike elements; in the second stage there is a movement from the rule of Love towards that of Strife, during which time the elements begin to separate out like to like; in the third stage Strife rules and the four elements are in separate masses; in the fourth stage the rule of Love begins to gain over Strife and the elements begin to coalesce or fuse unlike to unlike. The cycle is thus completed. Our world is in fact stage two. For the sake of the coherence of this view it is perhaps necessary to admit the first and fourth stages as only momentary watersheds; without this it is impossible to see what could be the engine of change producing destabilization at these times.

There is a biological counterpart to this development which occurs during the transitions between the absolute rule of Love and that of Strife and back again. During the time of Love increasing over Strife, disunited limbs are formed which are gradually brought together by Love, but in monstrous forms. During the time of Strife gaining over Love, "whole-natured forms" arise which are undifferentiated by sex as is the case with plants; this leads on to our own stage where there is differentiation by sex and there is great variety of animate life. Particularly obvious in the first parts of this evolution is the elimination of unviable life forms which are unable either to nurture or to reproduce themselves.

Empedocles explains sensation as a physical interaction. In vision, particles emitted (effluences) from objects fit or fail to fit pores of a certain shape in the eye; this allows the interaction between the element entering the sense organ and the same element within us required for perception. This also accounts for chemical interactions; for example the failure to mix of oil and water. Perception is effected by the balance of elements within the faculty of cognition – like perceiving like. Thought is physical; men think with the blood, and thought is upset by changes in the elements constituting it.

In the *Purifications* the mythical story of man presented by Empedocles is that of the Fall: men are fallen from a higher state of bliss and a golden age when Love was stronger, and the spirit wanders in exile clothed in different physical forms – plants, animals, humans – journeying from a lowly state towards the gods. The soul (*psyche* – distinguishing animate from inanimate) is a microcosm, some combination of the four basic elements. The spirit (*daimon*) is a further divine non-physical element by which we approach the gods. Empedocles gives an account of human biology, including reproduction, in some detail.

With Anaxagoras we also find a philosopher who accepts the Eleatic argument for the absolute conservation of being (no non-being) in reality, but for whom, nevertheless, motion and change are possible. Anaxagoras adopts the interesting thesis that there are no particular basic elements, but that there is an unlimited number of eternal stuffs. The multitudinous stuffs of the world were originally combined in one completely mixed mass, which separated out once and for all under the motive force of the cosmos, Mind (*Nous*: Intellect), which is non-material and infinite. Mind sets things in order, and is the only thing separated out from the stuffs of the world. At the beginning of the cosmos Mind starts the separation out of stuffs by initiating rapid cosmic rotation, causing the cosmos to grow in size; from then on mechanical causation controls change except where Mind animates living things. Heavier stuffs collect at the centre of the vortex, lighter stuffs tend toward the outer edge. The general process accords with the Ionian tradition. Since every stuff and quality were in the original mix, it is not necessary in explaining the world to contradict the Parmenidean principle prohibiting creation or destruction of what is.

The senses are misleading as to the true nature of the world; knowledge is possible only through the understanding contributed by Mind.

Matter is infinitely divisible; a further interesting twist to this thesis is that every stuff contains a mix of *all* stuffs. One of the stuffs is predominant, which gives things their particular character; thus "gold" names that stuff in which gold is predominant. But there can be no pure stuffs. Change occurs when the predominant stuff alters in the remixing of stuffs. The world is built from "seeds" of qualitatively determinate imperceptible stuff, which are not, however, indivisible, and of course themselves still contain a portion of every other stuff.

The combination of an unlimited number of stuffs of unlimited divisibility stands as a direct denial of the conclusions of Zeno; but this does not involve the absurdity of supposing either the unlimited size or unlimited smallness of everything. A thing with an unlimited number of possible divisions always has elements of a determinate size, and can have a finite magnitude.

Leucippus and Democritus are usually considered together because we know almost nothing about Leucippus, although from one remaining fragment we gather that he espoused atomism and may even have been its originator. There is a considerable amount of information on the atomists. The atomic conception of the world as consisting of ultimate indivisible and indestructible particles moving in a void has appeared at intervals repeatedly until the beginning of the twentieth century. So the importance of the Presocratic atomists is immense.

The atomists set out to reconcile an explanation of the empirical world with the arguments of the Eleatics banning the positing of the real destruction or creation of being, or the reality of change and motion. So every atom has Parmenidean being and moves in the void (nothingness). The atomists' conception is the exact opposite of Anaxagoras' and is the genesis of the contrast between explanations which are teleological (purposive) and those which are mechanistic, involving the distinction of primary and secondary qualities. In atomism, ultimate atomic constituents have no intrinsic qualities except size, shape and motion, and they are not divisible. The ultimate constituents are a-tomic: literally cannot be cut. We move from Anaxagoras' world, brimfull of colour, heat, sound, taste, to a world which is in its ultimate real constituents not even grey, but colourless; only derivatively are the "subjective" qualities such as colour experienced owing to the causal effect on us of atoms.

The atomists took the view that atoms had only what were later called objective, "primary qualities": size, shape, motion; "secondary qualities", colour, heat and the others, are subjective – that is, dependent on the experiencing subject – and derived as causal effects on us from the hooking together and rebounding of certain combinations of atoms. The ceaseless motion envisaged does not require a cause, or entail an animistic cosmos, because it has always been present; eternal motion is an inherent characteristic of matter. These views led eventually to the modern mechanics of Galileo, and later Newton, which emerged from the 1,500 years of dominance by Aristotle, who tended to close the gap between appearance and reality. In a view like that of the atomists', which holds both time and space to be infinite, there is time and space enough for our world to have come into being by chance. What forms and events occur are, in fact, determined and depend on the behaviour of the atoms, the action of like drawn to like, and the determinations of size, shape, and weight.

The atomist theory of perception and thought is physicalist (materialist): bodies give off layers or films of atoms, and differently shaped atoms produce, by impinging on us, differently experienced qualitative effects. Soul, like fire, consists of particular small round atoms which can move easily throughout the body. The soul is dispersed after death, and part of the aim of the atomists was to free men of the superstitious fearful belief in an afterlife which might involve punishment.

In one way atomism tends to lead to paradox. The aim of atomism was to counter Eleatic views in providing an account and explanation of the empirical world – the world as it appears to the senses – rather than arguing that the apparent nature of its existence is simply contradictory and thus totally illusory and unreal; however, the atomist view leads to a scepticism about knowledge of the world, for the real nature of the ultimate constituents of the world can only be postulated, as they are in principle unobservable. The atomic theory provides an explanation of the world of our experiences only by being an explanation beyond empirical confirmation. The senses do not ultimately reveal the real nature of the world; the best that can be said is that the empirical world functions *as if* atomism were true. But the next step from this is epistemological scepticism. The atomists attempt to avoid this by saying that sensation can take us a certain way, then rational thought is required to penetrate into the deep nature of the world; and it may be that this slide from sensation to intellection is a matter of degree, not a difference in kind. Thus there is no logically necessary appearance/reality (phenomenon/noumenon) distinction; the inability to sense atoms directly is a contingent and not a logical necessity.

There is an additional problem for the atomists. Are the atoms theoretically indivisible, or only physically indivisible because of their smallness and absolute density (impenetrability)? If the atoms are not theoretically divisible, then this conflicts with the assertion that the atoms have size and shape; if they are theoretically divisible (just not physically so), then the original Eleatic arguments against infinite divisibility apply. Despite the difficulties, it seems that theoretical indivisibility (possession of Parmenidean oneness) must be asserted if the atomists' position is to retain its full force. What the atomists themselves thought is open to scholarly disagreement.

Much later in the history of Greek thought atomism appears in the quietistic scientific and moral teachings of Epicurus (341–270 BC), which in turn were given memorable poetic exposition by Lucretius (*c.*100–*c.*55 BC).

CHAPTER TWO

Greek philosophy: Plato, Aristotle

The period of Greek philosophy that followed the Presocratics begins around 400 BC; the most important figures are Socrates (470–399 BC), Plato (427–347 BC), and Aristotle (384–322 BC). It is possible to discern a shift in interest in Greek philosophy away from explanations of the natural world to moral concerns, in the sense of discovering the best way for men to live. The difficulties of determining what were the objective or real features of the world, as opposed to those only apparent features which depended on a point of view (and hence were subjective), began to undermine the early explanations of natural science. If we are uncertain about what features of the world are real and what are only apparent, then it is unsurprising that such doubt will extend to the objectivity of moral standards. The threat was of moral anarchy.

To understand later Greek philosophy it is necessary to remember some unsolved problems derived from the Presocratics. In one sense Heraclitus stands at one extreme, Parmenides at the other. For Heraclitus everything is in flux; there is no being, only becoming or processes – although this becoming is subject to a cosmic *logos* or law of change. Heraclitus holds a compositional theory of identity whereby something remains the same thing only if the stuff out of which it is made remains exactly the same stuff. The world as it appears to the senses is argued by the Parmenideans to be an illusion: it is a world that appears to involve change and plurality, but these are impossible. The world for the Parmenideans is a plenum (full, or containing no void), and change, movement, plurality and diversity are impossible because they involve an X becoming a not-X (non-being, or a nothing); but even not-X is *something*, therefore not-X is self-contradictory, since it asserts of X both that "It is" and "It is not". Thus the appearance of change and plurality presented to us by the senses is impossible, since it involves a contradiction; it is an illusion. One answer derives from Democritus and the other atomists; the attempt is made to reconcile the explanation of the empirical world with the Parmenidean paradoxes; and the answer is to posit atoms with Parmenidean oneness of being in a void, which lies beyond the world as it appears. In just the way that Parmenidean arguments demand, these atoms do not, in themselves, change or have parts, but the appearance of change and diversity is explained by the coming together and dissolution of aggregates of atoms combined with the effect of these changes on us.

There are, however, problems with atomism. First, there is the difficulty that the atomic world is by definition beyond appearances; its existence cannot be empirically verified, it can only be posited, and cannot be known to exist. Second, the properties that the atoms are supposed to have are said to be objective or real because they are properties which are independent of observers. On inspection the suggested properties, such as size, shape, motion, seem to be equally dependent as properties such as colour and heat on one's point of view. Thus X can be large to you, but small to me; X can be fast moving to you, but slow moving to me; but it would be contradictory to suppose that X has both properties, and since we have no reason for choosing one appearance over the other, X cannot really have either of these properties. No property can be real if its being-what-it-is is dependent on the point of view or state of the observer in this way. Third, mere aggregates of atoms, which might be said to make up some thing (this horse), seem to give no account of the common-sense or pre-theoretical notion of separate or independent individual kinds: an independent "this so-and-so". "This so-and-so" is an independent or separable individual, uniquely distinguished from any other thing, and can undergo certain changes while retaining its individuality or identity as a "so-and-so". The "so-and-so" of an individual "this" is spelt out in its essential nature or "whatness"; the essence is those features which are necessary and sufficient for it to exist as a determinate kind of "so-and-so". This reflects the difference between an individual horse and a mere indeterminate lump of bronze. Without real or substantial separate individuals there is the suggestion that when we say something has become an X ("this so-and-so"), it is purely conventional or relative, and dependent on how our language happens to chop up the world; in reality no new substance has come into being at all, there has just been a rearrangement of the only true substances: the atoms.

These considerations lead to scepticism about our knowledge of the empirical world. One answer, proposed by the Sophist Protagoras (c.483–c.414 BC) is to embrace conventionalism or relativism, and say that reality is not something independent of the way human beings have come to divide things up through their thought and language; there is no reality which is the way things are, independently of the way we talk about it; what we take to be relatively stable factors in the world are derived from facts about how we talk about the world. The danger here to universal ethical standards is obvious. If what in all cases we count as X and as ceasing to be an X is merely a matter of conventional fact or relative to a point of view then it could be thought to be a mere convention, or relative only to a point of view, whether X is morally good or right, bad or wrong. There is no longer any matter of objective fact; it is just a function of the way we happen to talk, it is a relative truth because our criteria for X, reflected in the meaning of the word for X, could change. In the case both of empirical and of moral assertions, we could adopt different conventions; and there would be no grounds to choose between one or the other derived from pointing to objective independent constraints in the world or outside our conventions, for there are none. What *seems* good, from a certain point of view, is good, and we cannot say objectively that one view is more legitimate than another.

Plato

Plato was born into an aristocratic Athenian family. He is, along with Aristotle, perhaps the most important figure in the history of Western philosophy. As a man he is difficult to know, although a strong personality plainly emerges from the many dialogues he wrote. Although he thought of entering politics, he became finally disillusioned with it following the execution of Socrates. Plato's own philosophical views take Socrates' views as their starting-point; and our knowledge of Socrates derives almost entirely from Plato's dialogues, in which Socrates is often the main character. Around 380 BC Plato founded the Academy for the propagation of knowledge and education for the future rulers of Greek city-states. The Academy would have been unlike a modern university, and more akin to a college where there would be ritual communal activities, such as taking meals together. Among the intellectuals of Athens were the Sophists, or "experts", who, unlike Socrates, charged for their teaching services, giving instruction on rhetoric and efficacious behaviour in public office. Socrates, like Plato, considered Sophist claims to knowledge ill-founded, and set out to expose this fact; generally Socrates regarded them as ignorant men who, worst of all, did not even know they were ignorant. The curriculum of the Academy included philosophy, mathematics, astronomy, and some natural science. Later in life, Plato became reluctantly involved in a disastrous visit to Sicily aimed at educating Dionysius II. Plato perhaps felt the need to try to put his political philosophy into action. He returned to Athens, and sheltered from the political storms around him. He died at the age of eighty years old.

It is against the Presocratic background that the views of Socrates and Plato emerge, starting with a concern for ethical matters; but the same overall approach is applied to knowledge generally. Questions are asked, for example, about what is good or what the good is; for surely knowledge must be knowledge of what *is*. We can apply this by taking the example of justice. Socrates does not simply state an answer to the question; rather he admits his ignorance and asks his interlocutors for *hypotheses*, which start with experience and the inductive gathering of particular cases as a first step; he then goes on to test the hypotheses through arguments demonstrating their consequences, and shows that the answers merely give an *example* of the thing he is after, and an example, moreover, that cannot be justice-in-itself, but is merely justice from certain points of view that cannot universally be called justice. What he is after is justice-in-itself (the Just); justice without qualification or unconditionally. For it is in virtue of a fixed justice-in-itself that all things, or all cases, which we correctly call justice are justice. All those things we call just must share some common and peculiar characteristic in virtue of which we are correct to call them all just. To act justly, we need to know what justice truly is. If we talk of X without knowing what X is, we literally do not know what we are talking about. What Socrates is seeking is a true or real definition; that is, not merely an account of how we, in fact, use a word, nor a stipulated use, but a definition that tells us of the true nature of the object or quality to which the word applies; that is, its *essence*. This is similar to asking for an objective account of what is justice, independent of any points of view.

To have knowledge of something, X, involves understanding what we truly mean by the term "X"; and understanding the true meaning of "X" involves saying what X *is* – what the essential fixed nature of X is – what it is for X to be the kind of thing it is. Socrates is concerned not chiefly with the meaning of the word "X", but with the object X, and the real nature of X as determining the true meaning of "X".

Plato holds a realist theory of meaning and knowledge. The meaning of terms and that which we come to know is a process of *discovering* an existing objective reality "out there", not a process of creation which is relative to the apparatus – for example, language, or the senses – we use for the inquiry. This notion of objectivity and invariance of standards – of being able to say what X *is* – applies to ethics and aesthetics, as well as science and mathematics; without fixed reference points for the meanings of classificatory terms, all significant talk about the world would be impossible; the world would be a stream of unique ineffable particulars. The meanings of words are, or can be, determined by the nature of reality – in existing objective references – not the other way around. And if knowledge is possible, it must be knowledge of objects which are real; and this requires that knowledge be knowledge of what *is*; that is, objects that are not in states of becoming, but are eternal, immutable beings. To make our meanings match the world as it really is, is to seek true or real definitions, and requires *objects*, which the definitions are definitions *of*. The meaning of the word "justice" is not, in Plato's view, a mere conception in the mind, but is fixed mind-independently.

In agreeing with Heraclitus that the sensible world is in flux, Plato realizes that the *objects* of such definitions are not going to be found among imperfect and mutable sensible objects, but exist in a supersensible realm of immutable objects "seen" by the intellect beyond sense-experience. In the world we never find justice-in-itself, but only conditional justice. One can always find conditions in which, derived from a changing world or a different point of view, a just action ceases to be a just action. Plato thinks there has to be something that is invariable and common which corresponds to the meaning of universal terms such as "justice" or "bed", that exists over and above the variety of particular instances that terms – such as "justice" or "bed" – cover, and that justifies the classification or grouping of various different things as of the same sort or class. What we mean by "horse" in general, if it is meaningful at all, is something other than any particular horse, each of which differs; each horse is a horse because of its sharing in a nature common to all horses.

It is from the search for definitions of universal, immutable, ethical standards that Plato's theory of Forms emerges as the basis for all knowledge (*epistēmē*) in its full sense. Plato turns Socrates' search for definitions, aimed at understanding the nature of what we are talking about, into an ontological claim whereby the real meaning of classificatory terms requires a reference in a transcendent object or Form (*eidos*). It is not just knowledge of ethical truths that requires the Forms, but all claims to knowledge. Indeed, it applies to knowledge itself, for if we cannot suppose there is some fixed meaning for the term "knowledge", referring to some fixed object, knowledge-in-itself, then surely intellectual chaos must ensue. Plato assumed that for a word to have any fixed objective meaning, this must be in virtue of a fixed and objective entity to which the word refers. This assumption can be questioned.

It is essential for the understanding of the theory of Forms to see why epistemology and metaphysics are so closely connected in Plato's philosophy: the *nature of knowledge* should be matched by an appropriate *ontology*. Knowledge is always *knowledge of* something, and Plato requires these objects of knowledge to bear in their mode of existing (the way they are as objects) the same characteristics as the knowledge we have of those objects. For Plato, two main conditions have to be met for the highest sort of knowledge.

(a) *Universality or objectivity*

Knowledge of something is not relative to a point of view; knowledge should be something that would be true from any point of view.

(b) *Unchangingness, eternality or immutability*

This requires that knowledge is unchanging over time; that if something is knowledge, then it is knowledge once and for all; it cannot cease to be knowledge. Knowledge in its highest sense is infallible: it is absolutely certain. If one really knows something, there cannot be conditions under which what one knows is wrong, and ceases to be knowledge. So one knows only what *must be* true – necessary truths – and cannot be false, and when there is a method of demonstrating conclusively that the known truths are necessary truths.

There are two factors that make the world of sensible objects unsuitable for knowledge.

(a′) That things and properties in the sensible world are not fully real, since they are not unconditionally what they appear, as how they appear depends on a point of view. Sensible things can take on contrary properties for this reason as well if one's point of view changes; the properties sensible things appear to have is therefore determined partly *subjectively*.

(b′) That things in the sensible world are constantly changing. In this way sensible things can take on contrary properties over time; the sensible world is one of *becoming*.

Anything that can take on contrary properties cannot be fully real, since it never unconditionally just *is*, and we cannot be said to be knowing things as they are in themselves. Plato gives strict conditions for knowledge: certainty, universality and immutability. He further needs to show, if knowledge is possible, how we can satisfy those conditions; the Forms of the theory of Forms provide objects which satisfy the conditions for knowledge. Knowledge is knowledge *of* something; that is, it requires an existing object; there must be objects of knowledge that match the characteristics of knowledge proper (knowledge in its full sense) itself if such knowledge is possible at all. These objects are the Forms. The Forms are not objects in the sensible world; sensible objects both are mutable and have properties that vary with one's point of view, and so are not fully objective; nor are the Forms posited entities that underlie appearances in the way that atoms do. Forms subsist beyond the flux of experience and space and time in a transcendent, supersensible realm that is ultimately perceived purely by the *intellect*. The Forms are pure objective essences, and as the objects of knowledge they match the characteristics required of knowledge itself. As opposed to the "thatness" or existence of things (*that* X is), the Forms define the "whatness" or essence of things (*what* X is); the Forms give necessary and sufficient conditions for things to be the kind of things they are. The Forms have the following important characteristics.

(a´´) *Universality or objectivity*
There is no point of view from which the Form of F could be sometimes F and sometimes not-F; if something can be both F and not-F depending on a different point of view or different circumstances, then we cannot have found F-in-itself: the Form of F. The Forms are also what is universally or objectively true from any point of view. Apprehending what things-are-in-themselves is to grasp their Form. As well as being objects of knowledge in themselves, the Forms are the extent to which anything can be said to be universally or objectively true of sensible objects apart from their various appearances.

(b´´) *Unchangingness, eternality or immutability*
Since the Form of F is immutable and indeed eternally what it is, there is no time at which the Form of F can become not-F, it is eternally F. Forms are fully real in that they are not characterized by any becoming; they are being. They are what a sensible object which copies or participates in a Form really *is* apart from its changing states. The Forms are separate *in some sense* from the world of sensible objects and their nature grasped by the sense-independent intellect; their separateness seems to consist of real existence or ontological independence apart from both sensible things and minds.

Taking (a´´) and (b´´) together gives the conditions for the mode of being of fully real existence, and this matches (a) and (b), the conditions for knowledge proper.

Plato seems to hold that the realm of Forms is separate from the realm of sensible objects, but exactly in what this separateness consists is not clear. The sensible world is ontologically secondary; although later in life Plato became more interested in natural science. It is worth noting that since the Forms are not in space or time, it is senseless to ask where the Forms are. It is the ontological separateness of the Forms from particulars which is criticized by Aristotle:

It may not be immediately obvious why we cannot be said to have knowledge of particular truths. Surely I can know that "there is a table in my room"? However, it is worth noting that, regardless of its certainty, we would hardly regard this as a piece of *scientific* knowledge; it is not a universal explanatory law. Plato does not deny that something beyond ignorance is possible in these cases: we can have belief (*doxa*) which is true. But the *highest* form of knowledge, knowledge in its full sense, is of universals or objective essences. Knowledge proper is not of this or that table, but of tables-in-themselves: knowledge of what is involved in something being a table: tableness. Knowledge proper transcends the bounds even of all possible experience, and involves an intellectual "seeing" that reveals things as they are in themselves. If something is known in the highest sense to be true, it cannot become false. If X is known, then necessarily it is true that X. Plato goes further in holding – although it does not follow from the assertion that knowledge entails truth – that if X is known, then X is a necessary truth. Plato holds that what is known must be true in the sense that what is known is only necessary truths; knowledge is of things that could not be otherwise. If what is known ceased to be true, it would cease to be knowledge. Take the example "This water is hot". The problem here for knowledge is that (a) "This water is hot" can be true for one person, but false for another, and (b) the water is something that is in a state of becoming (becoming cold perhaps), so "This water is hot" is true, but will become false. That which has no fixity cannot have true descriptions applied to it, for what is true becomes instantly false.

The model for the ideal of knowledge is to be found not among the mutable and relative truths concerning sensible objects, but among the eternal and universal truths concerning the objects of mathematics and geometry which are known by the intellect. The truths of arithmetic and geometry concern not this or that object (say, a particular triangle), or this or that set of objects (say, two pairs of objects), but rather *triangularity* and $2+2=4$. Knowing the truth $2+2=4$ does not concern any particular two objects, which might through change become one or three objects, or which only look like two objects when viewed in a certain way, or any sensible objects at all. Knowing the truth $2+2=4$ concerns *twoness*, and its relation to other essences, such as equality, addition, and fourness. This is not a truth that varies over time; indeed it is eternal or timeless, and stands outside time; and, as such, this known truth requires an eternal object of which the known truth is true; that object is a Form or combination of Forms. The objects of the sensible world are not suitable objects for such necessary, objective, immutable truths. Take the example of equality: if we have two sticks of equal length, and also observe that they are six feet long, we may be tempted to say that being equal (equality) consists in being six feet long; but there are circumstances in which being six feet long would be both equal (F) and unequal (not-F); so we do not yet know equality-in-itself because we have identified something – being six feet long – that can be both equal and not-equal, whereas to know what equality-in-itself is is to know it irrespective of changes over time, point of view, or conditions. Equality as such must also be what all cases of equality have in common irrespective of their particular differences.

The world of Forms is "perceived" by reason or the intellect, not the senses; the Forms are objects of intellectual vision or looking.

Geometrical truths concern not this or that circle or triangle, nor even generalizations about all empirical circles and triangles which are also approximate and imperfect, but circularity and triangularity as such known by the intellect alone – in short, they deal with essences – with the Xness of objects under the common name "X". It must be noted that mathematical truths are one step down from knowledge of the Forms themselves because mathematics still involves unquestioned assumptions; but since mathematical truths known by the intellect alone are superior in certainty and immutability to the deliverances of the senses, they can be used as a stepping stone toward knowledge of the Forms.

At a lower level than mathematics, we can further understand the Platonic ideal of knowledge, and the requirement that it be objective, through analogy with scientific laws of nature: Newton's first law of motion, "Every body continues in its state of rest, or of uniform motion in a right line, unless it is compelled to change that state by forces impressed upon it", is not a law applicable only to particular bodies, or bodies considered from a certain point of view; it at least applies to all bodies at all times and in all places. Moreover, it may be said to apply to bodies-as-such; that is to say, it is a truth which can be known about the essence of bodies; to be concerned with the essence of bodies is to be concerned with what all and only bodies have in common, that which is necessary and sufficient for them to be bodies, which is correctly called "body".

It may be concluded that if knowledge of the Forms is the only true knowledge, then there can be only ignorance of the objects of the sensible world, and therefore that the sensible world is neglected by Plato. But this is not the case. That the world perceived by the senses is not fully real because it is subject to becoming (it never just "is"), and it cannot be the object of universal, immutable, unconditional truths, does not mean that it does not exist. The existence of immutable Forms divides the world into various fixed kinds of things as they are in themselves, and is the formal and final *cause* of the sensible objects in the world (the world of becoming) having whatever limited degree of being of which they are capable. "Cause" should be understood here in a more general sense than that to which we are accustomed: causation is an answer to a "Why?" by a "Because...". The Forms are "formal causes" in giving definite character to things which we bring under common names ("man"); the Forms are "final causes" as the perfection towards which that kind of thing aims as an end. As formal causes, the Forms are a precondition for our saying of anything that it *is* something of a specific kind; they define and make definite things as objects of a certain type; they are thereby causes by giving definite character and a limited degree of type-identity to the flux of the sensible world.

Although Plato never answers the point, one assumes there must be some limit to the number of classificatory divisions; if every positive common name has a Form, then the danger is of an unlimited and unknowable world of Forms. Relative terms such as "large" are also problematic. Although the Forms do not give us eternal, immutable particular sensible objects – for only universal kinds or types are eternal and immutable – they give to sensible objects a stability somewhere in between the being and non-being of Parmenides, avoiding thereby the universal becoming of Heraclitus; and of these sensible objects of relative stability we are able to have true beliefs, if not knowledge. Plato points out that "is" does not always mean "exists". The exhaustive choice is not being X (existence) and non-being X (non-existence or nothing); for we can say that X can be an X while losing some properties and gaining others. To say that a person X was hairy and is now bald is to say there has been a change in X not from existence to non-existence, but from being hairy to X being not hairy (bald). At the same time, Plato attacks Protagoras' relativism, which claims that universal objective knowledge is not possible at all, and that we are merely left with *particular* knowledge claims about immediate experience, which are perhaps infallible (cannot be mistaken) in themselves, but which are true only from a certain point of view at a certain time, with no claim to *universality* or generality at all.

Plato's answer to both Heraclitus and Parmenides is the Forms. Plato agrees with Heraclitus that the world of sensible objects is ultimately in flux, and he agrees with Parmenides that the intellect alone knows the true nature of reality. Knowledge proper is of immutable and eternal truths and must concern the nature of immutable, eternal objects that really exist; but the sensible world reveals only mutable, non-eternal objects; therefore, if knowledge is possible, it must concern a realm of immutable, eternal objects that really exist, beyond sense-experience, that are intuited or seen by the intellect alone; those objects are the Forms.

Plato's epistemology and metaphysics mirror each other: the Forms which have only being are fully knowable; of utter non-being there can only be ignorance; but in between these is the sensible world of becoming of which there can be true belief which lies between full knowability and complete ignorance. This gives the following picture.

Being (Forms)   – knowledge
Becoming (sensible world)   – true belief
Non-being (nothing)   – ignorance

The way to approach true knowledge is by the method of dialectic: giving, improving, and eventually destroying, hypotheses – assumptions used for justification in the sense of reasoned grounds for what we claim to know. Claims to knowledge are thereby based on fewer and fewer, and different, assumptions. For it to be said that I know X, it has to be the case not only that I have beliefs, even if they are true, concerning X, but also that I can give an account of why it is true that X, or what X is; a proper account or justification marks the beginning of the distinction between belief and knowledge. Giving an account of X is saying what it is that makes it X. The account that I give may be based on assumptions which are not themselves beyond question. If I try to account for X being true by deducing X from certain premises, then it can be asked what justification I have for these premises. I can answer this challenge by deducing the initial premises themselves from more general premises. The method of hypothesis is a process of questioning and testing deduced consequences of hypotheses. The intellect or thought transcends, in mathematics, hypotheses about the imperfect, approximate, objects of experience. We successively ascend from hypothesis to hypothesis, until we eventually reach the Forms, and ultimately the "First Principle" or highest Form the "Good" or "Being" or the "One", which is said to transcend even being, and which is self-authenticating (unhypothesized) and destroys the need for hypotheses.

Another related description of the dialectic found in the later work of Plato is the method of division and collection: this is the process of collection and division into genera and species, and it suggests a hierarchy of Forms; the Forms are complex wholes which are divided through genus and difference by species. The logic of the dialectic is matched by an ontological process; the logical collection of species under genus is like the blending into one another (in the manner of colours) of different Forms. The aim of division in the dialectic is to give real definitions of terms referring to indivisible "atomic Forms" (*infima species*) such as "man", "horse", "tree", that have no subspecies and designate species or universals, not particulars or individuals. The "atomic Forms" cannot combine at all: so the expression "man horses" makes no sense at all. The hierarchy of Forms is describes a hierarchy of reality or degrees of being proportional to permanence and generality. Below the "atomic Forms" there are only individuals (for example, individual men), not further species. Alternatively we can, by collecting species, ascend in the hierarchy to ever more pervasively general categories of being, to Forms of ever richer content and greater degrees of being. It has also been suggested that Plato envisioned some kind of mystical road to the highest Forms, as well as the rational dialectic.

Plato's view on epistemology and metaphysics can be summarized, although not entirely in his terminology, in the following way. Reality should determine language to give objective concepts which are not our creation, but rather fixed, and imposed upon us. The highest sort of knowledge is of objective necessary truths, which are discovered by the intellectual inspection of the ways that non-conventional objective universal concepts – discovered and not arbitrarily created – are connected or not connected to each other. The necessary connections concerning the highest sort of knowledge are found by intellectually seeing the inclusion or non-inclusion of the true meanings of common words – concepts – in each other. These concepts are objective in describing the real eternal immutable nature of the Forms, which are real eternal immutable objects. Some Forms are the essential features of the objects to which common names refer, and determine and tell us what each thing is in itself. The essential nature of a thing includes only those features which are necessary and jointly sufficient for it to be the kind of thing it is. The essential features are revealed in a true or real definition of what it is for a thing to be of a determinate kind.

It is important to see that for Plato the concern is not with the necessary connection of propositions, or merely with the meaning of words, but with the nature of the objects the words stand for: real immutable eternal objects – the Forms with the required characteristic of being – understood by the sense-independent intellect through their descriptive concepts revealed in definitions or formulae. These ontological connections are revealed by linking the true meaning of terms which name Forms, given by a true description of essences in real definitions (providing a correct account or *logos*), which give concepts of eternal existing objective Forms. The connection of these concepts which name Forms is seen by the intellect in the inclusion or non-inclusion of the meaning of one concept in another. This produces, in the case of inclusion, a logically necessary truth concerning the connection of the objects referred to. Such necessary connections, which depend only on the inspection of correct meanings, produce truths logically independent of experience. We can know necessary truths by showing conceptual connections; and such necessary truths are necessary because the terms in these truths have as their reference eternal immutable objects – Forms – which are not, and cannot be, objects of sense-experience, but are objects of the intellect. The dialectic method is deductive, ensuring that knowledge is infallible (non-revisable) and certain; a truth known by the correct use of the method cannot be shaken by new evidence. The dialectical method for justifying truths cannot be valid by degree. It provides a way of making the justification element in our knowledge a conclusive logical proof: it is a valid argument deduced from necessary truths. In this way the necessary truths which are known are conclusively shown to be necessary, and hence to have the absolute certainty and immutability required of knowledge proper.

The Platonic dialectic of collection and division approximates to the modern notion of analyticity, and the discovery of analytic truths; but Plato thinks that these are objective truths (they are true of the Forms) and independent of the factual conventions of linguistic usage.

The inclusion and non-inclusion of meanings can be illustrated as follows: "man" is included in the concept "animal"; and under the concept "animal" falls the array of different animals; so "man is an animal" is a necessary truth; whereas plainly "man" does not, and indeed cannot, include the concept "fox". Man and trousers are connected, if at all, only contingently because the concept "man" (real meaning or definition of "man") does not include "trousers"; so "man wears trousers" is not an eternal truth, and is not an object of the highest knowledge (*epistēmē*), but a matter of belief (*doxa*), perhaps true belief, about a contingent fact in the sensible world.

No necessary truths picking out necessary connections can be discovered in the sensible world; yet this is required if knowledge of the sensible world is possible – in the highest sense of being absolutely certain or infallible and eternal. Otherwise there are only correct beliefs concerning contingent truths in the sensible world. If what is known is a necessary truth, and can be shown to be a necessary truth, then it is absolutely certainly known, since it is impossible that it could be false. In any case, knowledge of the sensible world is dependent on the availability of the absolute objective fixity of the concepts we bring to the world, and this is guaranteed only by the absolute objective fixity of concepts' references in a real, supersensible realm of Forms "perceived" by the intellect. Whether, and how, such Forms, articulated in concepts, can be connected with the sensible world is a difficult question. But even to say of anything that it "is X" ("is yellow") is to use the concept of being (being X) that goes beyond the particular yellow percept, which may change. In the same way being able meaningfully to say "that is a man" presupposes the conceptual fixity of "man". Plato thinks that meaningful talk about the world must involve both that there must be absolute conceptual fixity of meaning and also that such meaning is derived from a special object: a Form.

There is an ascent to the Forms, and through the hierarchy of Forms, until what we claim to know is a truth, where the justification is deduced, by way of the relation of real definitions, from a starting-point which is self-authenticating, completely certain, and involves no assumptions. We aim to ascend to this "First Principle", from which we see the whole of reality as a connected rational system based on the absolute objectivity of the Forms. To the extent that anything like knowledge of the sensible world is possible – and Plato's interest in natural science increased in later life – it involves a downward dialectical process in the hierarchy of Forms: in this, one initially proposes the most general class to which the thing to be defined (the *definiendum*) belongs, until through division by similarity (by genus) and difference (by species) we have specified the narrowest class the thing defined belongs to; then we shall have knowledge in the fullest sense of what the *definiendum* is: this gives the necessary and sufficient conditions for a thing being the kind of thing it is. For example, the definition of "triangle" combines the genus of "triangle" as "polygon" with the species of polygon "having three sides" into "polygon having three sides". This fixes *what* a triangle is.

The taxonomy of the unchanging hierarchy of Forms is the true object of knowledge. Through the Forms is revealed, in the terminal definitions by genus and difference, the essence of things sharing a positive common name. We also come to know the rules of combination or blending of those Forms, since not all Forms can blend together. An assertion suggesting the blending of incompatible Forms – "motion is rest" – is a contradiction.

False judgements are not about *nothing*, but concern elements which exist – say, the particular Theaetetus and the Form flying – but which, in combination, are judged to assert falsely "Theaetetus flies". Indeed, every meaningful statement involves at least one universal or Form.

Through studying the interrelation of the Forms we come to know the true unchanging or eternal structure of reality. The highest Form – the "Good" or "Being" – is the genus of all that is real; a real whole covering – common to – all and only that which is real. That is, the highest Form is the essence of reality as such. The Forms exist in a world that transcends both the physical and mental, while they are somehow related to particulars. The Form of the "Good" or "Being" is the aim and aspiration of all things, the ultimate ground of the world's intelligible reality through defining the nature of being or reality itself or as such.

Our ability to have knowledge of the Forms, transcending the sensible world, is explained by Plato's theory of recollection. One way of interpreting this theory is to see it as Plato's attempt to account for the possibility of *a priori* knowledge; that is, truths known by the intellect alone independently of sense-experience. At some time before we were born, our immortal soul was disembodied and was thereby not confused and distracted by sensible particulars. Our soul is part of the eternal realm, and so able through pure reason to grasp the nature of the Forms themselves. Indeed, the possibility of knowledge of essences – the Forms – is taken as proof of our immortality. Sensible objects remind us of the perfect Forms we have forgotten, of which sensible objects are imperfect copies, and which have being only in so far as they partake of the immutable divisions of reality or being of the Forms. The extraction of universals by comparing sensible objects with a common name can be a starting-point for reminding us of the Forms, but it is not sufficient for knowledge of the Forms; rather, a productive starting-point of classification assumes that it is an objective classification contained in the Forms of which the classification of particulars reminds us.

It is tempting to think of the Forms as perfect particular instances of sensible objects. But this cannot be so. Plato was aware of this in the "third man" argument: if all the instances of X are instances of X by having in common some feature embodied in the Form X (Xness), and the Form of X is itself an instance of X, then all the instances of X and the Form of X taken together are instances of X only in virtue of some further Form embodying common features in virtue of which all the instances of X and the Form of X itself are X. And so on to infinity. There is no doubt that the nature of the relation of the Forms to sensible particulars presents Plato with difficulties, whether this relation is said to be one of copying or resemblance, or one of participation. If the relation is one of resemblance, there is the problem revealed in the "third man" argument. If the relation is one of participation, then we have the dilemma of deciding whether the Form is present in each instance in its entirety or whether each has a different part of the Form: in the first case the Form which is supposed to be one or unitary is yet in its entirety in many individuals, in the second case we lose anything common to, or the same in, all the instances, and the Form is both one and many or divisible.

One way of thinking about the Forms is to consider them not as entities which are perfect instances of sensible particulars, but more as akin to formulae known by the intellect. This brings to mind the Pythagoreans, for whom Plato had some sympathy. There is a completely general formula for a circle, but the formula is not itself circular or an instance of circularity; the formula may be verbal as "a plane figure bounded by one line every point of which is equally distant from a fixed point called the centre", or as an algebraic equation. In the same way the formula or definition of man or bed is not itself an instance – even a perfect instance – of a man or a bed.

The main feature of Plato's achievement is perhaps the way he laid down the highest standards for knowledge as absolutely universal, certain and necessary – a standard for which scientific knowledge has striven. The standard is too high for natural science. Nevertheless, it points scientific knowledge away from the particular case toward unifying and inclusive truths of greater general explanatory power and scope. Science does not deal with particulars, which in their full particularity are unknowable, since the inevitable use of universal terms means they can never be pinned down in their unique particularity. Scientific knowledge deals with generally applicable unifying truths concerning the underlying common or general features of an apparently enormously diverse world. Thus it will concern itself, at one level, not with this table and that table, or tables and cows, in so far as they differ and are particular, but with giving a unified explanation for their behaviour under their common nature or feature of all being bodies or material objects. Science is concerned with the structure or nature of an underlying general explanatory reality which is fully objective and rationally understandable.

Aristotle

Aristotle (384–322 BC) was born the son of a prominent physician, in

Macedon in north east Greece. The medical interests of his family encouraged his own later detailed empirical works in biology, which influenced his philosophical outlook. At the age of seventeen he became a student of Plato's Academy, and later a teacher there. In the early days he was generally in agreement with Platonic philosophy, paying particular attention to the *Phaedo*, and only later, in important respects, did he reject Plato's philosophy. Nevertheless, he continued to share Plato's opposition to scepticism, and agreed that knowledge is possible; it is on how the sceptical problem is to be solved that they differed. Aristotle was predisposed to take a greater interest than Plato in the natural world, of which Aristotle thought knowledge is possible. Following the death of Plato, Aristotle left the Athenian Academy, and was eventually tutor to the heir to the Macedonian throne, Alexander the Great. Aristotle returned to Athens in 335 BC, and taught at the Lyceum; but following the early death of the all-conquering Alexander, resentment arose at the Macedonian domination of Greece and the city-states; this made Aristotle's position in Athens, as an alien with Macedonian connections, increasingly uncomfortable. A charge of impiety was brought against Aristotle; rather than be the central character in a replay of the fate of Socrates, he left Athens in 323 BC. Unable to return home to Stagira, the city of his birth, which had been destroyed, he went to the remote city of Chalcis, where he died in lonely exile in 322 BC at the age of sixty-two. He married twice, having been once widowed; by his second marriage he had a son, Nicomachus.

The philosophy of Aristotle owes a great deal to Plato. First, although Aristotle rejected Plato's theory of real separately existing Forms, he held on to the notion of forms as the unchanging reality providing the basis for knowledge proper of what things are. Plato's intelligible Forms are essences or defining formulae that really exist as separate entities transcending the sensible world and minds. Aristotle's intelligible forms are immanent (in-dwelling) in sensible particulars, and cannot, unlike Platonic Forms, exist apart from particulars; the Aristotelean forms can be separated from particulars only in thought, although they are objective and not subjective or mind-dependent. Second, Aristotle supports anti-mechanical, teleological methods of explanation. Teleology is not so much an empirical hypothesis as a decision to adopt a certain method of explanation. It aims to explain why things are as they are by referring to the ends to which they aim; the end is being perfect, or fully developed, specimens of the kind of things they are. It is reasonable to see Aristotle as synthesizing Platonic realistic abstraction with a concern to explain the natural world found among the Presocratics.

Aristotle agrees with Plato that knowledge proper or scientific knowledge (*epistēmē*) must be certain and necessary; knowledge is of invariant or unchanging universal necessary truths. Knowledge must be knowledge *of* something. Aristotle shares with Plato the notion that if knowledge is possible, knowledge must be of what is real, and what is real is eternal and unchanging. In short, the necessary truths we know must be matched by their referring to ontologically suitable objects.

Aristotle rejects Plato's solution of positing as the true objects of knowledge a realm of separately existing essences, the Forms: first, because he thinks it only duplicates our problems concerning knowledge of the world, and second, because Plato gives no clear account of how individual objects in the world are supposed to participate in, or resemble, the Forms.

Knowledge for Aristotle consists in a systematically connected set of disciplines. Metaphysics (First Philosophy) is the most general and fundamental aspect of all knowledge because it studies being *qua* being. Unlike each individual science, metaphysics examines not this or that sort of thing, but existing things, or being, as such; it restricts itself to understanding that which is common to all and only things which are real and have being; it studies those features of things which they have merely in virtue of their existing as real things at all.

If the world is in constant flux, as Heraclitus suggests, then it cannot contain eternal unchanging objects suitable for knowledge. If we adopt, on the other hand, a Parmenidean view, all change and plurality in the world are illusions, for they involve logical contradictions: F becoming not-F; hotness becoming coldness. Atomism may seem to point to a way out, for atoms remain the same (have being) through change; indeed change is simply a rearrangement of the same atoms. Aristotle rejects atomism (or materialism) because collections of atoms do not do justice to our common-sense, or pre-theoretical, notion that there really are separately existing individual instances of kinds of things. Atomism allows no distinction in kind between a mere heap of bricks and a horse which is a genuine substantial separable, hence bounded, kind of thing. Although a brick may be an instance of a "so-and-so", a heap of bricks is not identifiable as a new "this so-and-so". Matter alone is not a "this so-and-so" (it does not pick out, say, *this horse*), for it is common in its nature to different kinds of particulars, and thus cannot differentiate between them as particulars of different types.

The important point is that the talk of the kinds of things there are in the world which concerns Aristotle corresponds to real or natural kinds; the way things are grouped together by kind, if properly carried out, marks real objective divisions in the world made by nature herself, not merely the arbitrary or subjective classification into groups imposed by us on individuals which are in some way similar.

For these reasons Aristotle posits *substance* as that which has identity or stability through change. Aristotle notices that when we talk about the world we distinguish between certain factors that alter and certain factors *to which* the alterations occur which can remain the same. Substances are, in a sense, pivots around which change occurs.

This is supported by the logical analysis of the carrier of all true or false assertions about the world: the proposition. In Aristotle's view propositions always contain two elements: the subject and the predicate. Predicates are what is said to be true or false of subjects. Subjects can remain the same while having different, or indeed contrary, predicates applied to them, and predicates logically depend on there being subjects.

Predicates, whereby we say things about subjects, can be grouped in different sorts or *categories* that are the highest *genera* or classes of being and together may cover all modes of being. Aristotle gives the ten genus categories as: substance, quality, quantity, relation (which are the chief categories), place, time, less temporary condition/state, more temporary condition/state, activity, passivity. Under the genus category of relation, how something is related to other things, there is among others the *species* of spatial relation, an example of which is: X is to the left of Y. The metaphysical counterparts of subjects and predicates are what these terms stand for. The most fundamental category is that of substance; predication in this category tells us, concerning the subject of a proposition, what kind of thing it is: X is a horse. To say *what* kind of thing X is, is to give its *essence*; the other categories of predication are of *accidents*, and these depend ontologically on, and are always predicated of, substances. The essence or "whatness" of a thing is given in a real definition or formula which provides the necessary and sufficient conditions for a thing to be *what* it is; an essence is what is common to all and only things of a specific sort in virtue of which they are the sort of things they are. This is a logically separate question from whether there exist things of that sort: the existence or "thatness" of a thing. In short, the essence refers to *what* it is to be an X; the existence refers to the fact *that* there is an X; and one can know what an X is without knowing that an X is. The essence of X therefore defines what we *mean* by an "X".

A term such as "horse" is a species substance term identifying a species of a substantial separable way-of-being; a species quality term such as "pale" is a non-substance term identifying a species of a non-substantial non-separable way-of-being. In either case, contrary to Plato's theory of Forms, there cannot, metaphysically speaking, be universal attributes such as horseness without horses or paleness without some object or other that is pale. But whereas an instance of the way-of-being of a substance never depends for its way-of-being on its predication of any other way-of-being, the way-of-being of a non-substance always depends for its way-of-being on its predication of some other way-of-being. This indicates that the relation between substances and accidental attributes is asymmetrical. It always makes sense to ask, if any non-substance term such as "pale" is applied, "What is it that is pale?". It makes no sense to ask, if a substance term such as "horse" is applied, "What is it that is horse?". The logical point about subjects and predicates, and the corresponding metaphysical dependence of some ways-of-being on others, led Aristotle to formulate two senses of *substance*.

(a) It must be that which is always a subject of predication, and never predicated of any subject.
(b) It must be that which has an independent or separate way-of-being or mode of existence.

What satisfies these formulations, and is substance in the *primary* sense, is concrete individuals of various identifiable kinds that can exist separately: they are those instances of whatness or ways-of-being that have a separable existence. These are independent subjects which can undergo certain changes while they remain identifiable as the same kinds of individuals. Substances are still pools of being in a sea of accidental becoming which avoid the conclusion that every change *of* a subject of change is a change *in* the subject of change. The subject Socrates can change from young to old, pale to flushed, and yet he remains the same individual: an instance of a man. The Greek word Aristotle uses for substance, *ousia*, is derived from "to be": substances are the *most primary* ways-to-be identifiable as "this so-and-so" (the Greek is *tode ti*), of which all other ways-to-be are predicated modes, and on which those other ways-to-be are dependent for their existence as ways-to-be. Paleness as a way-of-being depends for its existence both on some instances of paleness and on objects of some kind or other being pale; but the instances of kinds of objects which are pale, if they are substances such as this man, are not dependent on their being predicated of instances of any other kinds of being.

Primary substances are not, however, the objects of science. Science studies universal necessary features of the objects of the world, not this or that object in its particularity. Aristotle supports the common-sense or pre-theoretical view that individuals fall into determinate *natural kinds* of things. Thus individual men fall into, and are instances of, the natural kind man, and individual horses fall into, and are instances of, the natural kind horse. Aristotle refers to the universal predicates that define the properties that individual instances of a natural kind must have in order to be the kind they are as substance in the *secondary* sense: *substance* because they are the objects of science, *secondary* because the being of a certain kind as such is dependent on there existing individuals or instances of that kind. There cannot be independent "so-and-sos", or bare types as such, "floating" around, unattached to particular "thises"; there cannot be the universal essence horseness existing without there being particular horses existing. So we have *two* meanings of *substance*:

(1) Primary substances: individual instances of the class of universals, designated by a certain category of predicates, which can exist separately being what they are – "this so-and-so", this *X*, this man, this horse.

(2) Secondary substances: the universals, designated by a certain category of predicates, which are the properties defining real or natural kinds or what something is, of which primary substances are instances: "so-and-so", Xness, man, horse.

Logically speaking, secondary substances are a special class of predicates. The secondary substance predicates designate certain sorts of property, the sorts of property which are the *essential* defining properties of a thing that tell us what a primary substance is, and which it cannot lose without ceasing to exist as the kind of thing it is.

In addition there are non-substances:

(3) Non-substances: the classes of universals and particulars, designated by certain categories of predicates, which are not capable of independent existence as identifiable instances of kinds or ways-of-being – *X*, a heap of bricks; Xness, paleness.

The categories of universal predicates which identify non-substantial dependent ways-of-being are *accidental* properties; these are properties which a primary substance can gain or lose while continuing to exist as the kind that it is, that is, while remaining the same identifiable kind of individual.

In the case of (3), non-substances are not primary substances, either because they are not capable of separate existence as instances of what they are (for example, paleness) even though they may designate a universal, or because they are not identifiable individual kinds or ways-of-being at all (for example, a heap of bricks) even though they are capable of independent existence.

A genuine *substance* must for Aristotle satisfy two conditions: it must be *both* a determinate instance of a "so-and-so" or "whatness" of some identifiable sort *and also* capable of separate existence as that way-of-being such that it is not a modification or qualification of the way-of-being of any other thing. A substance is both an individual instance of a universal – an identifiable "this so-and-so" – and a way-of-being that can exist separately, not as a mode of any other identifiable "this so-and-so". This man or Socrates satisfies both the conditions for being a substance: it is both identifiable as a "what" – an individual instance of man – and has a separate or independent existence, is not a way-of-being dependent on the modification of any other thing. In short, substances are the class of *particular whatnesses* or ways-of-being that do not depend for their existence on being modifications of any other thing or way-of-being.

Thus Socrates is a primary substance *both* because he is an instance of the identifiable universal way-of-being man (unlike a heap of bricks, which is not an instance of a universal way-of-being at all), *and* because the way-of-being which is a man does not depend for its existence on the modification of any other thing or way-of-being (unlike an instance of paleness which depends for its existence on being a mode of *some* other thing). An instance of paleness depends, in a way that an instance of man does not, on there being *some* other thing – for example, this man or Socrates – which is pale; logically there cannot be an unattached instance of paleness without a subject which is pale; there can logically be unattached instances of Socrates.

Primary substances are compounded of two elements.

(a´)   matter (*hylē*)

(b´)   form (*eidos, morphē*).

By "matter" here is meant something more general than the physical stuff out of which it is made; what is meant by "matter" is whatever it is that takes on a certain determinate form, which thereby turns a "this" into a "this so-and-so". The form of a thing is immaterial and structural, and it is what gives matter a determinate character as a certain kind of thing. The form is the structure or shape the matter has which makes it a determinate kind of individual or instance of a kind – rather as there might be two brass keys (they are of the same matter: brass), but only one fits my front door (they are of different forms: shape). So matter is that which is "informed" as an identifiable kind of thing, and form is that which makes some matter something of a certain kind: the whatness, or being-what-it-is, of each individual. In this sense any matter as such is *potential* substance, which is actualized as substance when it takes on a form and becomes a "this so-and-so". The meaning of "matter" here is not restricted to physical stuff: "matter" might be a man's general character that takes on the form "bad" so he has a "bad character".

The connection between the secondary substances and the forms – (2) and (b´) above – is that secondary substances are instantiated in particular instances in matter as the form of that matter; the "so-and--so" of a "this", giving a separately existing individual, "this so-and-so" of a certain kind or sort. The form or essence is what all and only individuals sharing a common name and falling into a natural kind (marking a natural division in nature such as horse) have in common in virtue of which they are the kind of things they are. It perhaps helps to understand what is meant by matter taking on a determinate form, while also seeing that form is not a separate entity, to think of stone as a petrifying of matter, and of a horse as an equinizing of matter.

Matter and form are the logical parts of substance (apart from God who is pure actualized form); they always occur together and can be separated only in thought; we never find "prime matter" devoid of all specific determinations. Anything said of something posited as prime matter would show it not to be prime, because the ability to talk about it and say what it is would necessarily involve saying that it has some specific characteristics or whatness. Prime matter is literally ineffable. Specific compounds of matter and form are in a hierarchy of matter and form; for what takes on a certain form will already have form at some level. For example, a lump of bronze is matter with the determinate form of bronze, and a bronze statue is matter with the determinate form of bronze taking on the form of a statue. The same bronze statue may be melted down and take on a new form, turning it into a bronze bowl. With the progressive addition of form to matter we can move "upward" from clay, to bricks, to walls, to house. That matter and form are logically distinct is shown by the fact that we can have the same form giving an instance of a kind of thing (a hammer) but different matter (some metal, some wood), and have the same matter (some metal) but a different form giving an instance of a kind of thing (a hammer, a chisel).

These distinctions allow Aristotle to give an account of change. He distinguishes two sorts of change:

(a´´)   substantial change
(b´´)   non-substantial change, or accidental change.

These mark the distinction between (a´´) cases where a new kind of individual comes into being and (b´´) cases where the same kind of individual thing persists in being through change. As a man moves from being young to being old we have a case of non-substantial change; the subject of change remains, through the change, the same individual or instance of what kind of thing it is: a man. But when a man dies, we have a case of substantial change – the individual becomes a different kind of thing. What it is is something else: a mere pile of flesh and bones. The form or essence of a thing X is a core set of properties a, b, c, which are together necessary and sufficient for X to be the kind of thing it is; that is, properties that jointly all and only things of kind X have that thereby determine what they are. What remains the same through substantial change (a´´) is the matter (a´) which has lost one form (b´) and taken on another form. What remains constant through non-substantial change (b´´) is the form (b´) or essence, formulated in a definition, that gives those properties that make a thing the kind of thing it is.

Another way of looking at this analysis of change is to make the distinction between the *essential* properties ((2) above) of things and the *accidental* properties ((3) above) of things; so these correspond to the secondary substances and the non-substances respectively. The essential properties are those properties that remain the same through accidental change whereby an individual remains in existence as the same kind of thing or what it is. Essential properties are the properties which are necessary and sufficient for an individual to continue to be an individual of a certain kind. The essential properties are given by the true or real definition of the term designating the kind of thing an individual is: so something is of kind X if, and only if, it has properties *a, b, c*; and this is the same as giving its form. The form of a thing is its essence given by a real definition, and this remains the same through accidental change. Thus a man can be hairy and go bald; he can change his blue shirt for a green shirt; but he still remains a *man*, since hairiness is not part of the definition of man. What is part of the essence of a man, given by the real definition of man, is the set of properties common to all and only individual men that makes it correct to include them under the term "man". Thus the real definition of man, revealing his essential nature, may be "mortal animal capable of discourse", which is definition by genus (animal) and difference by species (capable of discourse). The essential nature, or form, of a determinate kind is the residue of features which remain after the differences between individuals of the same kind have been removed, and we are left with a set of properties that all and only individuals of that kind have in common; in that way we say what some thing is.

How individuals of the *same* natural kind are to be distinguished is a difficult question. They cannot be distinguished by their kind, since that is common to them. One suggestion is that they are distinguished by their parcels of matter, which will be different parcels in each individual. Another suggestion is that we should admit *individual* essences as well as essences *by kind*. Later philosophers have said that only a complete enumeration of attributes of a given individual, denying any distinction between those that are essential and those that are accidental, can give a satisfactory principle of individuation. Generally it is held that, for a principle of individuation to guarantee unique reference, some appeal to space, time and motion is required.

To complete Aristotle's analysis of the nature of change, we have to make the distinction between "actuality" and "potentiality". When matter takes on a certain form, there is contained within the nature of the form not only what the actual form is at any given time, but also the potential further actualizations. For example, an acorn has a certain determinate actuality (actual state) at any given time; but it is also potentially an oak tree. Thus a complete characterization of the form of a thing – determining what kind of thing it is – will include a description of various progressive stages of actualization, and the full actualization towards which that kind of thing aims, which it contains only potentially until it reaches that end point. So a specimen of a certain kind will be a compound of matter and form, and the form will include what is actualized at any given time, plus its future potential states. This process is particularly obvious in the case of a living organism; but what it means in the case of non-living things is less clear. The point to be noted is that the form limits the way that a particular kind of thing goes on; acorns do not develop into horses, but have a certain natural course of development. An eye that is blind suffers from "privation", because it is not actualizing its potential;

whereas to say that a tree cannot see is not to say it suffers from privation, since to actualize seeing is not a potential part of the form of a tree.

Natural kinds are divisions of nature herself, not divisions imposed arbitrarily by us in language; the divisions are discovered, not created. How many different natural kinds there are is a difficult question for Aristotle, and his answers are not always consistent. (i) The criterion sometimes emphasized for natural kinds is that they are those things that persist through change. In this case it seems to make sense to include artefacts like beds in the list of kinds; a bed remains a bed after it has been painted green instead of blue. (ii) At other times the criterion emphasized is that of independence from external causes. Thus sometimes Aristotle includes in the natural world only things which can reproduce themselves "after their kind": horses naturally beget other horses, whereas if you plant a bed, you do not get another bed produced, it has to be made. Also bits of stuff like pieces of wood are excluded from the list of natural kinds since they are indeterminate – they are subject to destruction by degree; whereas it makes no sense to say of a horse that it is more or less a horse – it is either a horse or not a horse.

The explanation of change is, however, sometimes very unclear. This is partly due to difficulties as to what natural kinds there actually are. It is also due to the obscurity of the distinction between essential and accidental properties. This produces the problem of distinguishing substantial from accidental change. If, for example, we have a change of property from f to g, it may not be clear if it is correct to say, "Xf has become Xg" (an accidental change), or if it is correct to say, "Xf has become Yg" (a substantial change). If sweet wine turns sour, it is unclear whether it is correct to say that the sweet wine has become sour wine (an accidental change), or that the wine has become vinegar (a substantial change). How are we to distinguish a change in substance, a change from "this so-and-so" to a different "this so-and-so", from a merely accidental change in the same "this so-and-so"? There is a danger that if the number of instances of secondary substances increases, the explanatory power of explanations which depend on referring to the kind of thing something is will be diminished. If, at the limit, every change of properties involved a change in kind, then we would be unable to explain the change in terms of its being a consequence of the properties of the constant kind of thing in question developing in its natural ways, according to its form or nature.

The point that this talk of natural kinds is leading to is that the explanation for why a thing is as it is can be derived from discovering the kind of thing that it is and its connection with more general natural kinds of things. The form of a thing is an *intelligible* form; it is ultimately perceived not by the senses, but by the intellect or reason – by *intellectual intuition* (*nous*). It is this reference to the kinds or sorts of things there are in the world that is the basis for scientific knowledge and explanations of the world.

Knowledge is knowledge of "causes", and Aristotle gives four senses to the notion of "cause". It is important to see that "cause" here has a wider connotation than our mechanical notion, and none of Aristotle's four senses really matches our use of the concept. When he is referring to understanding the causes of things, he is concerned with providing an answer to a "why" question: "Why is X as it is?" There are various ways of answering this question through different "becauses". This is not at all mysterious if we consider the way we use non-mechanical explanations every day. Question: "Why was Durham Cathedral built?" Answer: "Because people wanted to praise God." So Aristotle distinguishes four "becauses" answering "Why is X as it is?":

(a) Material
(b) Formal
(c) Efficient
(d) Final or Teleological

The (a) here refers to the matter or stuff (not necessarily physical stuff) out of which X is made. (b) refers to what kind of thing X is; it is a "so-and-so". (c) refers to the agent (not what the agent does) that brings X about. (d) refers to what X is for, or what its goal or end state will be; what its purpose is. If we take the case of a house, we can see that (a) is the bricks out of which it is made; (b) is the kind of house it is (Victorian style terrace); (c) is the men who built it; (d) points to its purpose of providing shelter. It should be noted with reference to (c) that causal links, or "becauses", hold for Aristotle not between events, but between things. Taken together, these four causes provide a complete explanation for why X is as it is.

In the case of things with final causes, the formal and final causes will be closely linked; in giving the form of something, it will be necessary to refer in a definition to what that something is for. The use of form and function in explanations allows us to see why something can remain the same thing, even when certain changes are made to it. If a green bed is painted blue, it remains the same as an individual instance of *bed*, in that its form and final "becauses" are unchanged. We can plainly see that formal and final explanations are more obviously applicable to artefacts and living organisms than to inanimate objects. Aristotle suggests that stones fall down because their natural place – their natural final state spelt out in their form or essence – is as near to the earth as possible. But we would hardly regard this explanation as satisfactory today. There is the danger that explanations derived from the kind of thing X is in this way become uninformative and lead us to fail to seek the real internal causal mechanisms that bring about a specific change. We have not identifying the object before us as a clock. The explanations are at risk of being uninformative because they become tautological: X is as it is because of the real definition of X, and any counter-evidence is immediately excluded because if a putative X is found to act in a way contrary to its definition then it is not a case of X at all. We cannot define a thing if we exclude its causal powers; we thereby risk circular explanations if causal consequences are deduced from definitions.

All substantial change involves matter taking on a new form, which is, in some way, passed on from an agent. In the case of a house, the efficient cause operates by the form of the house that exists as an idea in the mind of the builder being passed on to the matter of the house. In the case of natural objects, the efficient cause is the natural parent in which the form of the offspring is latent. This logically rules out both creation from nothing – where there is no matter – and any possibility of Darwinian evolution of the kinds of things there are, since the forms manifested in natural kinds do not change in themselves. God is the supreme source of all change; He transcends the world as pure form devoid of matter, fully actualized, possessing no potential. God is not the creator of the world out of nothing, but the "unmoved mover" in the sense of a final cause which is the ultimate cause of whatever form the world has.

Knowledge proper requires that its objects must be both really existing, and eternal and unchanging. If nothing in the sensible world is eternal and unchanging, then it follows that knowledge of the sensible world is not possible. If it is also the case that the sensible world is the only really existing world, then knowledge is not possible at all. If knowledge is possible, but it is accepted that the sensible world is not eternal and unchanging, then knowledge must be of a really existing transcendent supersensible world of eternal and unchanging objects: the Forms or essences of Plato. If knowledge is possible, but it is accepted that the sensible world is the only real world, then knowledge must be of really existing eternal and unchanging features of the sensible world: the forms or real kinds of Aristotle. That is, if knowledge proper is possible, it must be the case either that there is a world of eternal and unchanging real objects beyond the sensible world (the position of Plato), or that there are eternal and unchanging real features of the sensible world (the position of Aristotle).

Aristotle holds that there is something about the sensible world that is eternal and unchanging and graspable ultimately by the *intellect* and is a suitable object for scientific knowledge: the natural kinds of things there are and the relations between them. These natural kinds are objective really existing features of the world, not mere arbitrary conventional classifications imposed by us. The common-sense view of the world is that it divides itself up into many distinct kinds or sorts of individuals; and we have knowledge proper or scientific knowledge (*epistēmē*), as opposed to mere belief or opinion (*doxa*), of those individuals through knowing the kind of thing an individual is. It is natural or real kinds that are the proper objects of knowledge.

Aristotle made great contributions to logic, which he sees as the tool (*organon*) of philosophy. Through the notion of the syllogism he sought to identify all the valid forms of deductive reasoning. In fact there are other forms of deductive reasoning that Aristotle does not consider. Deductive logic is a vital tool of philosophy, and of inquiry generally, in providing a way to get infallibly from true premises to true conclusions. If the premises are true in a valid deductive argument, then we know that it must be the case that the conclusion is true. Aristotle introduced the important notion of variables – letters such as *A*, *B*, and *C* – to stand for classes of things; this reveals that deductive arguments are valid or invalid regardless of their content and in virtue of their argument-form. For example:

All *A*s are *B*s.
All *B*s are *C*s.

All *A*s are *C*s.
This is a valid argument-form: an inference which would be valid regardless of what classes of things are substituted for *A*, *B*, *C*.

Aristotle ideally sees knowledge as forming a system that is a deductively connected body of truths. Scientific knowledge is knowledge of causes: giving the reason why *X* is as it is, and must be as it is. We have first to know what kind of thing *X* is, and then to show why, given the kind of thing it is, *X* must be as it is. Thus knowledge of some truth about *X* would consist of deducing the truth about *X* from premises which we know are true, thereby proving by a valid deductive argument that what we say is true about *X* is necessarily true of *X*.

Aristotle was aware of an important problem connected with this: *all* knowledge cannot be a matter of providing a deductive proof or demonstration, because this leads to an infinite regress of proofs: any premises we suggested would themselves stand in need of further proof. If the regress is infinite, then nothing can actually be proved, and nothing therefore known. This leads Aristotle to the view that there must be self-evident first principles or axioms that can be known *immediately* by intellectual intuition (*nous*), which neither require nor are capable of proof. The most general and firmest of these principles is the law of non-contradiction, which in the *Metaphysics* Aristotle states thus: "For the same thing to hold good and not to hold good simultaneously of the same thing and in the same respect is impossible." This can also be expressed in a more modern way: "It is not the case that both *p* and not-*p*", where *p* can be any proposition. This principle is presupposed in all rational thought; thus any attempt to prove it by rational thought is hopelessly circular. We can, however, prove it by rational thought is hopelessly circular. We can, however, simply see intrinsically that it is a true principle.

Ideally the deductions of science would take place from the most fundamental first principles; but, in fact, this is not possible; science cannot proceed purely *a priori*, independently of experience, because the most general first principles are too general for studying particular kinds of things. The deductions of science are based on real forms (the essences, real natures) of things and true universal principles (all *A*s are *B*s) connecting these forms; and the process of apprehending both of these is initiated by induction. We observe by sense-perception many particulars of the same kind, and through reason or intellectual intuition (*nous*) we "perceive" the form or essence of that kind of thing as a real definition or concept given by genus and difference. We then form a hierarchy of different degrees of generality, of kinds of things, descending to *infima specie*: those specific kinds of things below which there are no further kinds, but only individuals of a specific kind. Such a species would be man, and above it, and including man, is the genus animal. We also derive in the same way, by sense-perception and intellectual intuition, universal principles logically connecting the forms or essences. We are able to have knowledge proper since, by taking the forms and universal principles together, we are able to deduce universal certain necessary truths about the kind of things we are interested in.

In this way it is shown why things are as they are, and why they must be as they are, and not otherwise. If a certain truth about the world is the conclusion of a valid deductive argument whose premises we know to be true, we have shown: (a) why that conclusion is a truth, because it follows logically from known premises, and (b) that the conclusion is a universal necessary truth, in virtue of the argument being deductive. To follow a valid deductive argument from true premises is to follow a causal connection in the world. We explain some feature of the world by deducing it from the definition of the kind of thing it is and from principles universally true of a general kind of which it is a part.

We might ask why X is f. If we know the kind of thing X is – it is of kind Y – and the universal principle that "all Ys are f", then we can deduce and explain, why X must be f.

An X is a Y.
All Ys are f.

All Xs are f.
For example: "Why does a horse suckle its young?"
A horse is a mammal.
All mammals suckle their young.

All horses suckle their young.

The principle in the second line is what science seeks to use in explanations, and it is known only by inductive observation of many animals combined with the use of reason or the intellect. The first line is known in the same way.

Science – knowledge in its highest sense – deals with universal eternal necessary truths, not with particulars as particulars. The forms or essences of kinds of things, and the universal principles derived from the connection of those forms or essences, are the real eternal unchanging intelligible aspects of the world. For science to study what is real there must be kinds or sorts of things that mark real, objective, fixed cleavages in the world, which are not the imposition of human conventional classification. That they are real is an assumption Aristotle makes on the basis of our common-sense ways of talking about the world. Our explanations derive from the ways that the vast plurality of things of certain real kinds behave, given that their forms or essential natures determine the kinds they fall into. The positing of such fixed intelligible forms is what makes a scientific knowledge of nature possible, in the sense of knowing universal necessary truths about universal necessary features of the world. Scientific knowledge gives deductive proof that specific kinds of things are necessarily as they are. The common principles of all reasoning, plus known universal principles, plus knowledge of the kind of specimen we have before us, together enable us to prove necessary truths about that specimen. It is possible for us to have scientific knowledge of the world, since the world can be understood according to general principles and real definitions which do not alter and are eternal, and which the intellect can apprehend.

It must be noted that this means that science can deal with particulars only in so far as it considers them instances of universals; it considers only objective universal properties common to all and only particulars of the same kind. Science is concerned not with what makes a thing particular, but with what makes it an instance of a general kind. Science can have as its object only genera, species or universals – the specific defining form that individuals share – and not particulars as such. Individuals are in the scientific sense unknowable; in their unique particularity they are perhaps ineffable, since to talk of them at all is to use common classifying terms which apply to other individuals.

While we might grant that the proper principles or laws that science aims to discover are *universal* in application, we do not thereby have to agree they are *necessary*. The inductive inferences as envisioned by Aristotle to derive general principles concerning kinds of things would at best be known to be universally true. Even this is clearly not possible if the number of kinds in the class to be investigated is infinite. However, Aristotle thinks that such induction produces evidence supporting universal *necessary* truths which intellectual intuition apprehends as necessary. The problem is that this tends to confuse contingent universal truths – which might be supported, if not conclusively, by experience – with necessary universal truths which are necessary just because their truth is independent of all experience and which rely for their necessity only on logic and the meaning of their terms. Aristotle relies on the justification of intellectual perception – going beyond the limited possibilities of experience – to establish finally the features of the inmost nature or essence of things, the correctness of our real definitions of those things, and the necessity of principles. But it is not clear that an account of there being necessary truths depends on the subjective intuitive self-evidence of some truths, rather than on the purely objective logical form of such truths, such as the denial of a necessary truth implying a contradiction. Moreover, if the necessity of a truth is entirely a result of its denial implying a contradiction, then it does not say anything about an actual world if the nature of that world is not logically necessary but contingent; then truths about that world cannot be known to be true merely by showing that their denial implies a logical contradiction, because none of them does.

Plato and Aristotle think that science should attain knowledge of universal necessary truths. Aristotle thinks we can have scientific knowledge of the sensible world because eternal unchanging forms are immanent in the world of sensible objects. The sensible world thus has two aspects: its sensible aspect, and its intelligible aspect (the forms), and we can, through the intelligible aspect, know necessary truths about the sensible world. That such provable universal necessary truths – propositions whose falsity is impossible – are restricted to mathematics and logic is now something generally accepted to be the case. Plato, we might say, was more aware of this point in thinking that if knowledge (*epistēmē*) of necessary truths were possible it must be of a supersensible world, not of the empirical world. Plato thinks that the universal necessity of the truths of highest forms of knowledge depends upon their being about eternal transcendent supersensible objects beyond the natural world: Forms, essences, or objective concepts. Whether such realism is required to account for knowledge of universal necessary truths is certainly disputable. It might be possible to account for necessary truths without saying that they are about any world of real objects at all, perhaps by saying that they are merely those propositions whose denial implies a contradiction. Plato disagreed with Aristotle who thought that knowledge, even in the highest sense of knowledge of universal necessary truths, must be about aspects of the world of sensible or empirical objects. The point at issue here is whether there is such a thing as natural necessity: whether there are necessary features and connections in the natural world expressible in necessary truths, or whether such necessity is restricted to logical truths which say nothing about the natural world, although they may say something about a world of real objects apprehended by pure intellectual thought beyond the natural world.

CHAPTER THREE

Medieval philosophy: Augustine, Aquinas, Ockham

In thinking of medieval philosophy, we must consider that we are covering a vast time of around a thousand years including St Augustine of Hippo (AD 354–430) and William of Ockham (c.1285–1349) and extending until at least the time of the Renaissance. What links the diversity of this period in Western philosophy is the rise to dominance of Christian beliefs.

It would be wrong to conclude that thinkers in the medieval period merely slavishly reiterated Christian dogma. There exists a tension in medieval philosophy between reason and faith (from the Latin *fidere*, to trust). The distinction, if there is admitted to be one at all, between the reason of philosophy and the faith of theology is that between, respectively, the insights of natural knowledge derived from the natural cognitive powers of the intellect and senses, and the insights of supernatural knowledge derived from divine revelation. The distinction between philosophy and theology in the Middle Ages was often not clear; generally it can be said that whereas philosophy embodied rational arguments based on premises derivable from naturally occurring powers of thought and the logical working out of those premises (particularly from the philosophers of the ancient world, especially Aristotle), theological arguments were based on divine Christian premises derived from God – in particular from the Bible and the opinions of the Church Fathers as collected in Peter Lombard (c.1100–60), *Four books of sentences*. Christian thought insisted that reason must succumb to the deliverances of faith or religious belief where the two are irreconcilable.

It is characteristic of the dominant intellectual framework of the scholars of the universities of the medieval period – called scholasticism – to try to reconcile the demands of rational philosophy and the demands of theological faith. The dissolution of scholasticism at the end of the Middle Ages really amounts to the increasing triumph of reason over faith; instead of Christian faith being the standard by which rational arguments were to be judged, arguments were increasingly followed wherever they led. Reason in scholasticism was often used as a tool for supporting and deepening the understanding of what was already believed to be true as a matter of religious faith. After all, it is reasonable to suppose that even if some true beliefs are accepted as true without sufficient argument, it might still be possible to provide a rational justification for those true beliefs.

It was also thought that some truths were beyond the reach of rational demonstration, but that this was not detrimental to these truths, since their acceptance depended on religious faith. Belief in truths of faith influenced rational arguments by affecting the premises considered, and by judging the truth of the conclusions reached. If a valid argument leads to a conclusion which is false – false, in this case, according to religious faith – we know that at least one of the premises must be false. However, the strain of combining reason and faith eventually led to the separation of philosophy and theology; the attempt had been made to fit philosophy in as a rational, but limited, path to religious truth, but in the end it tended to undermine the body of theological dogma.

The source of medieval theological doctrine was the Bible and the Church Fathers; the problem presented to medieval thinkers was how to reconcile beliefs from these sources with the beliefs and logical arguments derived from Plato and Aristotle, and the attempts of Arabic and Jewish thinkers from the tenth century to the twelfth century to combine Plato and Aristotle. This reflects the high opinion which was held of work from the ancient world; throughout the medieval period, ancient philosophy was a source of authority which toward the end of the period was used to oppose new arguments in philosophy and science. Nearly all medieval philosophical literature takes the form of either commentaries on previous works (especially Aristotle), or disputes (*quaestio disputata*), where a question would be raised and opposing solutions and objections considered and eventually reconciled.

During the period from the second century to the fifth century AD, while the Roman Empire remained intact, Platonism and Neoplatonism had the upper hand in Christian thought; this is apparent in the works of St Augustine. The greatest Neoplatonists were Plotinus (AD 205–270), his disciple Porphyry (AD 233–304), and later Proclus (c. AD 410–485). St Augustine adopted, but profoundly modified, Platonism in the service of Christianity, to which he converted in AD 386 at the age of thirty-two. But with the break-up of the Roman Empire in the fifth century, Western Europe and the eastern parts became separated, and from the sixth century to the eleventh century we enter the Dark Ages.

During the Dark Ages nearly all serious intellectual activity ceased in Western Europe, although it continued in the eastern provinces

conquered by the Arabs. From the fifth century onwards little of Plato
was known directly in Western Europe, and the full corpus of his
works did not re-emerge until the end of the Middle Ages; apart from
in the work of John Scotus Erigena (*c.*810–*c.*877) Neoplatonism as such
was also not rediscovered until the late twelfth and thirteenth
centuries, but its influence seeped in from around the fifth century
from the Arabs and the works of Pseudo-Dionysius, who was falsely
thought to be the Athenian converted by St Paul. Only the works of
Aristotle on logic remained known throughout the Middle Ages,
thanks largely to translations and commentaries by the Roman philosopher Boethius (*c.* AD 480–524); but in the latter part of the twelfth
century other works of Aristotle were rediscovered, revealing the
ambitious system of metaphysics, science, and ethics.

In contrast to the period before the lacuna of the Dark Ages, after
that period it was Aristotelian philosophy, rather than Platonic
philosophy, which dominated Western European thinking. It was
during the period from the twelfth century to the fourteenth century
that the tensions between reason and faith intensified, and this gave
way to the progressive weakening, from the fourteenth century, of
the scholastic attempts to harmonize the two. The spread of new
ideas continued, aided by the invention of printing in the fifteenth
century. Intellectual changes were matched by the disintegration of
the medieval social order; the increased disrespect for ecclesiastical
authority and the rise of the rival power of the nation state undermined the unity of Christendom. The door was open for the Protestant Reformation of the sixteenth century and the greater importance
of the conscience of the individual and direct understanding of
Christianity. Philosophy became increasingly autonomous after the
fourteenth century, and the gap between philosophy and theology
was never again closed. By the end of the medieval period both
Christianity and Aristotelianism, as the authoritative storehouses of
correct opinions, were being replaced by a different vision of
intellectual and moral advancement in the light of new philosophical
and scientific ideas.

Given such a long period as the Middle Ages, it is unsurprising that
it is possible here to make only a small selection of its thinkers. Apart
from the thinkers discussed, among other important figures are
Abelard (1079–1142), St Anselm (1033–1109), St Bonaventure (1221–74)
and Duns Scotus (*c.* 1266–1308). Augustine, Aquinas and Ockham are
chosen here as representative of different important aspects of the
period; they might be said to embody respectively medieval philosophy's inception, its consolidation, and the beginning of its dissolution. Their views on the place of reason and faith can roughly be
summarized as follows: for Augustine there is no fundamental distinction because reason depends on divine help to grasp eternal truths;
for Aquinas there is a distinction on the basis of the natural and the

divine but the two are complementary and to a degree overlapping; for Ockham reason and faith are distinct and have no overlap.

Augustine

Augustine (AD 354–430) was born in Thagaste and died in Hippo, both places in North Africa. Intellectually he straddles the gap between the philosophers of ancient Greece and those of medieval Christian Europe; he lived through the decline of the Roman Empire, which led to the Dark Ages. The eventual historical outcome in the eleventh century was the increased dominance of Christianity. Augustine's mother, Monica, was a Christian, but initially he did not accept the faith and adopted Manichaeanism, which embodied some elements of Christianity among elements from other religions. At the age of seventeen he became a student of the University of Carthage where he became a teacher of rhetoric and, while there, lived a life of extravagant pleasure – including sexual pleasure – which was to contrast starkly with his later monkish life. In AD 383 he moved to teach in Rome; following financial problems, he accepted a teaching post in Milan, where he greatly augmented his knowledge of ancient Greek philosophy, in particular Neoplatonism. In Milan he was impressed by the teachings of Ambrose, Bishop of Milan.

Augustine converted to Christianity in AD 386, and was baptized the following year. He was then determined to enter the Church and renounced worldly pleasures. Initially Augustine found no difficulty in reconciling the dominant intellectual position of his day, Neoplatonism, with the demands of Christian scripture; later he began to see greater problems in reconciling their basic concepts. He soon founded his own monastic community in Thagaste; but this lasted only a couple of years through his being forced into the Catholic priesthood. Augustine eventually became Bishop of Hippo in AD 396. He never left North Africa for the last thirty-nine years of his life. In AD 410, Rome was sacked by the Goths; in 429 the Vandals crossed to North Africa from Spain and laid siege to Hippo; Augustine died in 430, aged seventy-five, a short time before Hippo fell.

The character of Augustine's thought is distinctly religious, rather than purely philosophical; the discussion of certain philosophical problems is not that of the disinterested academic, but has the overriding purpose of identifying the path to the attainment of blessedness or beatitude. This does not mean that what is true is crudely identified with whatever makes one happy; it is rather the other way around: knowledge of truths will make one happy. It is assumed that the wise man and the happy man are one, and knowledge of truths is part of the attainment of wisdom. The question of whether we can know truths is generally assumed to be answered positively; the chief question is how we can attain that knowledge. The overall religious purpose is twofold: first, to show how we can become closer to God; secondly, to emphasize the importance of God by showing how everything is closely dependent on God.

A problem of particular concern to Augustine is how we come to know the universal necessary eternal truths described by Plato and the Neoplatonists. First, however, Augustine sets about demolishing the sceptic who asserts that no knowledge at all is possible. He points to a range of things we clearly know to be true, which the sceptic cannot possibly deny. He is not aiming to use these known truths as the axiomatic foundation of the rest of knowledge, rather, if any of the examples are admitted as known truths, then knowledge is possible, and the absolute sceptic refuted.

(a)   We know the law of non-contradiction, whereby if something is true, it cannot also be the case at the same time that the opposite is true.

(b)   I know that I exist. "If I err, I exist" (*"Si fallor, sum"*). This anticipates Descartes' *cogito*; but it is not used in the same way; Augustine is not concerned to use it to prove the existence of the external world.

(c)   Appearances cannot in themselves be false; I know infallibly what my subjective experiences are, how things appear to me: my "seemings". I can know infallibly what *seems* to be the case; it is my judgement, which goes beyond what seems to be the case, which introduces the possibility of falsehoods.

(d)   We clearly, even from the sceptic's point of view, have the capacity to doubt; so we know at least one truth: there is doubting.

(e)   We obviously know with certainty mathematical and geometrical truths.

(f)   We do not just know abstract principles, we also know real existences. We know that we exist, that we are alive, and that we understand these facts. Augustine points out that even if our experience is really a dream, we nevertheless still know we were alive. We are also conscious that we will certain things.

These bulwarks against scepticism are in one way or another derived from introspection independently of the errors of the senses.

Augustine does not dismiss the senses as wholly deceptive. From the fact that we can sometimes err in our sense-based judgements (for example if we judge that a stick which appears bent in the water really is bent), and can on any particular occasion err, it does not follow that the senses cannot ever support true beliefs. That the senses deliver truths less certain than those of mathematics does not mean the senses do not deliver truths at all. However, Augustine supports the Platonic view that the lack of certainty and the relativity of judgement (the same thing can appear different to different people) that beset the senses make the objects of sense not suitable objects for true knowledge or knowledge proper. The true objects of knowledge – the truths we can know with greatest certainty – are truths that are universal, necessary, and eternal; this is the highest form of knowledge, and sensory knowledge the lowest. This means that these eternal truths have to be found within the mind independently of sensory experience.

The problem arises of how eternal truths and our knowledge of eternal truths are to be accounted for. The sensible world does not provide us with the required immutable concepts and truths; the human mind or soul, although immortal, is also temporal and mutable. Augustine agrees with Plato that, just as transient truths are accounted for by the mutable objects of the sensible world, so universal necessary eternal truths are accounted for by their being truths about eternal and immutable real objects. Moreover, these eternal objects, and the truths concerning the relations of the concepts of these objects, are independent of the human mind; they are truths that we discover, which we cannot alter, and which are thereby objective and common to all capable of reasoning. Such objects – immaterial impersonal essences – referred to by Plato as Forms, are identified by Augustine as ideas in the eternal, immutable mind of God – they are the content of the divine mind. Such divine ideas provide both truly objective fixed concepts and necessary truths by being the objects of necessary judgements. Augustine, like Plato, has no facility to account for the necessity of some truths which does not involve realism, requiring there to be eternal objects to which those truths correspond; he is unable to account for such necessary truths merely on the basis of the logical relations between concepts, but thinks that such truths require eternal objects which the eternal truths are true of eternally.

Such necessary truths are available to us in the areas of mathematics and geometry, but they are also possible in moral and aesthetic judgements. The divine ideas provide perfect objects for the concepts of number and geometrical forms; they also provide objective standards for moral judgements concerning good and evil, and aesthetic judgements concerning what is, or is not, beautiful. We do not find perfect unity in our experience (we always find things with parts which are thereby both one and many); we do not find absolute goodness or evil or perfect beauty in our experience. We do not find these things in themselves exemplified in the sensible world; but nor are they mere constructions of the human mind. Rather, the divine ideas in God's mind are the absolute eternal standards by which all else is judged, and which are assumed in our judgements.

The problem remains of how such eternal truths are accessible to the non-eternal human mind. We have certainly been granted reason by which we are able to form true or false judgements not derivable from sense-experience. But reason alone is not enough to account for our knowledge of eternal truths. The human mind, in seeking eternal truths, is seeking something beyond, and superior to, the mutable and temporal mind, and to know such truths we need help. Such help emanates from God in the form of "divine illumination"; and as an illuminator God is present in us as He is present in all things. All knowledge in Augustine is seen as a form of seeing. Just as the senses see independent objects when they are illuminated by the sun, so reason or intellect "sees" eternal truths when illuminated by the divine light. This does not mean that in apprehending eternal truths we have direct access to God's nature – that is possible only after death, if at all. We do not intellectually see God or the mind of God when we know eternal truths. It is unclear whether the illumination implants the concepts constituting necessary truths in our minds, or whether it simply enables us to recognize which judgements are eternal and necessary – it could indeed function in both ways. Perhaps the best interpretation is to say that God does not directly infuse our minds with the absolute concepts which constitute eternal truths, rather such concepts are latent in the mind as copies of the archetypes in God's mind; divine illumination enables us to see intellectually which are the eternal and necessary truths that are latent in our souls, and so to recognize them as eternal and necessary. The latent concepts, and the eternal truths connecting them, are in *memoria*; in this way ideas can be in the mind without the mind being aware of those ideas. This accords with our use of "memory" only in that it refers to ideas that can be in the mind without our being always aware of them; it refers in Augustine, most importantly, to the *a priori* content of minds, which is not literally a remembrance of things past. Nevertheless the theory is close to Plato's account of our possessing *a priori* knowledge through reminiscence.

Eternal truths are, of course, independent of and irrefutable by sense-experience. So the true objects of knowledge are objective eternal objects which depend on there being ontologically appropriate eternal objects in the divine mind. Knowledge of eternal truths is granted by a combination of natural human reason and supernatural divine illumination. To benefit from such illumination we have to turn towards God. This precludes the possibility of making a distinction between natural reason and divine faith, for both are always needed and mixed in the search for knowledge. This again emphasizes the dependence of all things on God, in this case our capacity to know eternal necessary truths.

The immateriality of the soul and its superiority to the body mean that Augustine has great difficulty accounting for perceptions through the corporeal organs. The superior nature of the soul's mode of existence involves the view that it cannot be affected by the inferior corporeal organs. At first he suggests that the mind uses the sense organs as a tool. Later he tries to account for our awareness of changes in our corporeal senses by the mind attending to or noticing such changes; but it is difficult to see how, in this case, some causal influence of the corporeal sense organs on the mind can be avoided.

Augustine uses the existence of eternal truths as proof of the existence of God. Leibniz in the seventeenth century presents a similar argument. The argument starts by getting one to admit that there are eternal truths – immutable necessary truths, forced on human beings. The only way to account for there being such necessary inescapable truths is their objective existence as truths in an eternal mind. We serve and are closer to God in so far as we contemplate eternal ideas in the mind of God. This, however, is not all that is required; we also need a spiritual purification – goodness – in order to approach God.

Aquinas

Thomas Aquinas (1225–74) was born of a noble family at Roccasecca, Italy. From the age of five he began studying at the Benedictine abbey of Monte Cassino. In 1239 he went on to the University of Naples, where he studied the seven liberal arts of grammar, logic, rhetoric, arithmetic, geometry, music, and astronomy; while at Naples he entered the Dominican Order. His entry into this Order, with its emphasis on poverty and evangelism, was opposed by his family to such an extent that he felt the need to escape to Paris; but while on the road to Paris, he was abducted by his elder brother and locked up in the family castle at Monte San Giovanni. He was later held prisoner in Roccasecca for over a year. His family was unable either to strip him literally of his Dominican robes, or to persuade him to renounce the Order. While he was imprisoned his brothers sent him a seductress; but he drove her from the room with a burning brand, and the event merely reinforced his commitment to chastity. Eventually his family relented and he returned to the Dominican Order, first at the University of Paris in 1248, then at Cologne under Albert the Great. During this time he became deeply versed in the works of Aristotle.

He returned to Paris in 1252 for advanced study, and he lectured there in theology until 1259. The next ten years of his life were spent at various Dominican monasteries near Rome; in 1268 he returned to teach again at the University of Paris. In 1272 he went to teach at the University of Naples; but ill-health forced him to stop work. In 1273 he had a mystical vision which caused him to regard his intellectual work as worthless – he consequently ceased work on the massive

Summa theologiae. In 1274 he was journeying to Lyon for a meeting of the church council, but had to rest at Fossanova, not far from his place of birth, owing to illness; there he died in 1274.

Aquinas' character seems to have been one of imperturbability, and there is no doubting his sharpness of intellect. After his death the teaching of Aquinas and Thomism formed the official doctrine of the Dominicans, and this was adopted by some other Orders, but it was in general relatively neglected by the Catholic Church. However, in the nineteenth century Aquinas was commended by Pope Pius IX as the premier figure of Catholic philosophy and theology.

Aquinas' thought owes a great deal to Aristotle, and he attempts to reconcile the central tenets of Aristotelian philosophy with Christian dogma; these attempts deal with issues like the nature of God, our means to salvation, and our understanding of the nature of creation. Aquinas' thought begins with the presupposition that the universe is, at least partly, intelligible to finite human intellects: the structures and laws of the universe can be understood.

Aquinas hatches a compromise between the conclusions derived from our natural cognitive faculties (the senses and reason of secular philosophy), and conclusions derived from divine revelation (the faith of divine theology). One could dismiss one or the other as worthless, or say that each one ultimately depends on the other, as Augustine does; Aquinas however maintains the distinction, and says that they are two generally autonomous ways of looking at the same object, namely God. Whereas our natural cognition works "from below" to know God through His effects as the creator of the world, divine revelation – supernatural cognition – works "from above" to know God as cause. Thus faith (*fides*) and scientific knowledge (*scientia*) are sharply distinguished not by object, but by method. Both are cognitive processes involving the assent of the intellect to truths; but whereas faith requires the addition of the will in order to believe truths with certainty, scientific knowledge requires no such application of will since the intellect either intuitively "sees" truths immediately, or argues validly to establish truths from intuitively known premises.

Within theology we can make a distinction between supernatural and natural theology: respectively, truths revealed about God and other elements of Christian doctrine which depend on divine revelation (grace, which derives from the Latin *gratia*, meaning favour), and those that can be known through natural powers of cognition. There is also an overlap of truths: some truths are both revealed and known through being provable by natural cognition. In this sense natural theology is part of supernatural theology. So the totality of truths grasped by the human mind has three parts.

(A)   That which is believed *only* in virtue of divine illumination or revelation.

(B)   That which is believed by divine revelation *and* is known by being provable by natural cognition.

(C)   That which is known by natural cognition.

Ideally a conflict will never arise between the deliverances of the revelations of faith, and the proofs of natural reason; but in the latter we are fallible, and a conclusion derived from reasoning that conflicts irreconcilably with a properly understood truth of faith shows that we have made a mistake in our reasoning. But we have, ideally, a twofold route to some Christian truths.

Natural cognition is made up of the senses and the intellect, and of these the senses are primary both genetically and logically for knowledge of existing things and for possession of abstract ideas; all the materials of our intellectual faculty – our ideas – are abstracted ultimately from the senses. The intellect is involved in forming judgements about what we perceive: that what we perceive really exists, that it has certain properties and that it is a certain kind of thing. The intellect also engages in abstract reasoning. The senses see X; the intellect actively judges X as X; the intellect goes on to understand and think of X when it is not perceived. The intellect goes beyond the sensory experience in forming a judgement, which is an affirmation or denial of some truth; this goes beyond the mere fact of one's having a certain experience. The sensible aspects of particular things (red, sweet, warm, etc.) are given through sense-perception alone; but the intelligible aspects of particular things (that they exist, that they actually have certain properties and are certain kinds of things) are derived not from the passive association of the ideas of senses alone, but in conjunction with an active synthesizing and interpretative intellect, which forms from the ideas of sense complex conceptions and hypotheses. The intellect forms concepts – universal ideas – of things by abstracting general ideas from sense-experience; the intellect thinks of the nature of those things and how they are connected to other things by understanding those general concepts.

Aquinas follows Aristotle closely in not supposing that essences (the "whatness" of things) can exist apart from individual things; philosophically speaking, there is no *universale ante rem*, that is, essence before or apart from individual things; rather, essence is *universale in re*, present in individual things, in the sense that real things are real substances and are always compounded of two elements.

(a)   Essence (*essentia, quidditas, natura*). This is "whatness"; viewed epistemologically through a definition it tells us *what* a thing is.

(b)   Existence (*esse*, which is a form of the Latin verb "to be"; but *esse* is also used as a noun). This is the fact *that* a thing is.

The difference between a mere essence (*quidditas*) and real substance is existence (*esse*); existence is what turns, by being "added" to it, a merely potential essence into an actual individual substance. This is the primary move from potentiality to actuality: mere potential existence to actual existence. Once a certain essence is actualized, there is a further process of change from potential to actualization as the essence brought into existence strives to fulfil its potential within its kind; an acorn (an actual acorn, but potential tree) will grow into a tree (an actual tree). The terms above in (a) and (b) roughly correlate with the following.

(a´)   potential (*potentia*, potency)

(b´)   actuality (*actus*, act).

The difference between essence and potentiality is partly one of generality; to speak of essence is to imply some determinate potentiality: a certain "so-and-so"; whereas to speak of potentiality is to suggest mere possibility: some "so-and-so" or other. Anything that is not logically impossible has potentiality in the second sense.

To know the *essence* of something is to know its real definition, the essential features without which a thing would cease to be the kind or sort of thing it is. The *accidental* features that an individual kind of thing has are those features which it can lose or gain while remaining the same kind of thing. It is most important to note that Aquinas thinks that in giving a definition of the essential nature of an individual, he is giving a *real* definition; that is, the definitions are not a function of the way we conceptually happen to divide up the world, rather the definitions, if true, reflect accurately the way the world divides itself up.

The distinction between essence and existence is also a *real* distinction. That is not to say we ever encounter in the world pure existence or pure essence, but the distinction is real in the sense of being independent of human cognition; it is not a distinction projected onto the world by the mind. For to say *what* something is is one thing, but to say *that* it is, is another; we can know what a dog is – the essence "dogness" – without committing ourselves to affirming either the existence or non-existence of dogs. Another way of putting this is to say that essences have no existential import. This is true for all entities except God; He alone has existence as part of His essence. For all other beings, existence (*esse*) is something added to essence – added to a mere determinate potentiality – by God; thus all things depend ultimately on God. Essence and existence are never found in separation; nothing simply *is*, a thing always is a *determinate kind* of thing; to be is to be a "so-and-so"; to be is always a determinate *way* of being. The obvious limitation of individual substances is explained by essences receiving *esse* and at the same time limiting that *esse* to a certain way of being. In God the *esse* is unlimited, and also eternal; there are no limits to God's being; He has "fullness of being".

For Aquinas as a Christian, unlike for Aristotle, the existence of things cannot be taken for granted but requires explanation. Aristotle thought that the world exists eternally, and that any change in the world is not a change from absolute non-existence (nothing) to absolute existence or vice versa, but a change either of an accident, or from one form of substantial being to another. For example a substantial change occurs when a tree ceases to be a tree and becomes ash when it is burnt. For Aquinas the very fact of existence itself is a problem; given that nothing, except God, has existence as part of its essence, an explanation beyond the essences of things is required to explain why anything *is* at all; that explanation derives from God the creator who adds *esse* to essences.

Apart from God, no essence is fully actualized. In God's case, the positive essence is fully actualized. God does not merely actualize His divine essence; He actualizes it all the way, so to speak. If we take any other entity, we will always have an entity which has potential within its kind – its essence will not be fully actualized; there will be aspects of its essence that it does not fully exemplify. God's absolute perfection is to be identified with His complete actualization of His positive divine essence – He is pure act (*actus purus*); He contains no unactualized potential of His positive divine essence.

The relation between essence and existence, and between potency and actuality, applies to any substance whatsoever. It must not be supposed that all real substances must be material or corporeal; not only material things have *esse*. The analysis of material things introduces another pair of terms.

(i)   form (*morphe*)
(ii) matter (*hyle*).

This gives a hylemorphic theory of material substance. In the case of material substances, potential corresponds to matter; the matter is potentially a "so-and-so", and is actualized as an individual separable thing of a certain kind by taking on a certain form; that form is actualized in that matter. However, pure matter (*materia prima*) would be completely ineffable; it would by definition possess no character, no whatness. Only by the addition of form in act in the matter does it become a determinate "so-and-so"; matter as a mere determinable is not possible, although we can understand what we mean when we talk of it. The notion of pure potentiality as pure matter is impossible as something that exists – it would indeed be a contradiction – but it is intelligible conceptually. Indeed, pure potentiality cannot in any case exist. The soul is the form of human beings; and souls are individuated by the matter of the body of which they are the soul. But pure forms can exist, as well as material substances, when certain non-material essences receive *esse*. What Aquinas has in mind here seems to be a three-level hierarchy of being.

(1) Corporeal substances. These are matter and form; they are perishable and finite.
(2) Incorporeal limited substances. These are pure form – spiritual entities, which although imperishable are finite. The kinds of entities Aquinas has in mind here are the separated soul and angels.

(3) Incorporeal unlimited substance. This is pure act; all aspects of the positive essence receive existence (*esse*). This is, in fact, God who alone exists necessarily, since in Him alone His way of being must be conceived as including existence; in Him no distinction can be made between the essence He has and His existence, for He necessarily completely actualizes His essence, all the positive aspects of the divine essence there are; there is nothing He is only potentially; there is nothing divinely positive He is not.

The object of human knowledge in intellectual cognition is the discovery of what essence is actualized in any individual. We understand substances in so far as we come to know the essence that is in act – is *esse* – in substances. Aquinas holds that for each known truth there must always be something existing (*esse*) that corresponds to that truth. Individual substances are understood by us not as individuals *qua* individuals (individual things as such: features which constitute their particularity), but through knowing that which is general or common in them that defines the nature of the kind in which all the individuals of a certain kind share. Thus we know a dog in so far as we know the real definition of "dog", and hence understand it in its essential dogness; we do not know the dog in its full particularity because the terms we apply always have some generality of application.

An essence is what must be the case for a thing to be *what* it is: that which a thing cannot lack and still be what it is. Thus understanding *what* a thing is – its essence – is logically independent of the fact *that* a thing is, its existence. I can understand *what* a dog or a Phoenix is independently of *whether* it is. The essence of X is given in a set of necessary and sufficient conditions *a, b, c* for X to be the kind of thing it is. In this way we can form a real definition: X is of a specific kind if, and only if, *a, b, c* are true of X. When we are correctly said to know X, the aspect of X we know is that set of features X has in common with all and only other Xs of the same kind. We would not understand a clock as a *clock* by referring to its colour or the scratch on the face, but in so far as we understand that in virtue of which a clock is a clock: what makes it distinctively a clock and not another kind of thing. We understand the nature of the clock by understanding those common features shared by all and only clocks which define them as clocks. Then what makes a clock or a dog a particular clock or dog cannot be its essence or form, since that is common to all instances of the same kind, but must, Aquinas argues, be its being formed of a quantitatively or numerically different parcel of matter.

With incorporeal or spiritual substances such a method of individuation is clearly inapplicable; he suggests that each incorporeal substance must be individuated by essence; that is, the essence of each soul or angel must be different, so each angel differs in essence as a dog does from a cat; each angel is of a different, and unique, kind.

Aquinas strikes a middle course on the question of the reality of universals. Universals are general concepts or categories with which we talk about the world and with which we classify particulars into kinds or sorts. Aquinas adopts a form of moderate realism. He rejects the full realism of Plato, whereby universals exist as real entities in a world of intelligible Forms independently of the world of sensible things. He also rejects conventionalism, whereby universal concepts are mere arbitrary, subjective mental constructs, for which the most that can perhaps be said is that they are made for our convenience. Aquinas compromises: universals are *objective* in being real, extramental and immutable, but they exist in instances of individual kinds of things and cannot exist apart from those instances. Universals or kinds as such exist only in virtue of there being individual actual instances of those kinds. Only individuals exist, but the natures of those individuals radically resemble each other and are understood from this essential common resembling nature as being members of universal classes or species – for example, humanity, dogness, justice. Individual material things of the same kind are the same kind in virtue of sharing a substantial form; but that substantial form, although it cannot exist apart from the individuals who share it, is nevertheless something objective in the world, and derives its objectivity from the really existing common nature shared by individuals of the same class. The world divides itself into kinds, so to speak; the kinds are real and there to be discovered, and are independent of our subjective mental classifications. Abstracted forms are derived from individual instances; the logical rules of the combination of such forms are revealed in real definitions; the forms, through real definitions, give concepts which have fixed immutable objective meaning; the forms and their logical combination, known through their concepts, are the proper objects of knowledge. Knowledge of the forms, through real definitions, is derived from sensory experience and the intellectual faculty of abstracting general concepts from the resembling essential nature of instances of individuals of the same sort. Thus although universals do not exist as separate entities, they are objective in reflecting the extramental common defining real natures of individuals.

Ockham

William of Ockham (*c.* 1285–1349) was born in the village of Ockham outside Guildford near London. The details of his life are obscure, and often a matter of conjecture. Of his early life nothing definite is known. We know that he was ordained subdeacon in 1306. He became a student at the University of Oxford around 1309 and soon a member of the Franciscan Order. He pursued his studies at Oxford until 1315; from 1315 to 1317 he gave lectures on the Bible and, from 1317 to 1319, lectures on the hugely influential *Four books of sentences* by Peter Lombard. The *Four books of sentences* was compiled around 1150; it brought together the teachings of the early Church Fathers – especially St Augustine – and it was a cornerstone of Christian theology.

Ockham completed the requirements for the degree of *Magister theologiae*, but he never became a Master occupying the Chair of Theology. This was probably due to the opposition of Lutterell, a keen Thomist, to the appointment of Ockham; Lutterell had been removed from the post of Chancellor of the University by 1322. Lutterell left in 1323 for Avignon, the residence of Pope John XXII; there he set about blackening Ockham's name by accusing him of holding in his *Commentary on the Sentences* heretical and dangerous views. Ockham was summoned to Avignon in 1324 to have his views examined; the examination lasted for three years. Ockham refused to retract his views.

Michael of Cesena, the General of the Franciscan Order, also faced the condemnation of the Pope for his Order's espousal of absolute apostolic poverty. Ockham joined forces with Michael, his superior, and, together with another Franciscan, Bonogratia, they fled from Avignon in 1328, seeking the protection of the German Emperor, Louis of Bavaria. Louis had installed in Rome an antipope who had in return crowned him head of the Roman Empire. Ockham, Michael and Bonogratia joined the new Emperor in Munich, and were excommunicated from the Catholic Church and their own Order. In 1342 Michael died; in 1347 Louis also died. This left Ockham in an extremely vulnerable position; he sought reconciliation with the Church and his Order. Before any reconciliation could be decided upon, Ockham died in 1349, probably of the prevalent Black Death. He was buried in the old Franciscan church in Munich; but in 1802 his remains were moved to a place that is still unknown.

Ockham may be seen as something of a philosophical Janus, since like that god, his philosophy looks in two opposite directions; it looks back to the Middle Ages, and it looks forward to some of the ideas of the Enlightenment – to the empiricism of John Locke (1632–1704) and David Hume (1711–76), and aspects of materialism – but the forward-looking characteristics must not be overemphasized; Ockham would have seen himself not as a philosophical revolutionary, but merely as reinterpreting an already established tradition. The chief problem was still to reconcile Aristotle and Christianity. A sharp distinction is found in Ockham's thought between reason and faith. The truths of theology are based on revelation and are a matter of faith, and they are neither provable nor refutable by any process of natural cognition in secular philosophy. Theology retreats to a domain of truths about which natural reason can have nothing to say.

The chief characteristic of the tradition to which Ockham was heir was realism in its various forms: that the human intellect can discover, in the particular things perceived by sense-experience, a real objective system of universal common essences which become somehow individualized, and which can either have an independent existence from, or exist as a real part of, particular individuals. These essences have an extralinguistic reality over and above – *really distinct* from – the particular features of individuals which are classified in virtue of the essence as being the same kind. Then from the linguistic connections in meaning between the terms that refer to these real essences we can know necessary truths about an extralinguistic reality. Necessary truths can be known about the world we perceive and about God. The universals we intellectually abstract – humanity or horse – from particular individuals are not merely arbitrary subjective mental or linguistic constructs, or merely derived from objective particular features of individual things, but have a real ontologically distinct reference in or beyond the world, independent of individuals, or their particular features, whereby such individuals fall into the general class designated by universal terms. In short, the linguistic distinction we make between universal and particular terms has a real ontological counterpart.

The problem of universals – what if anything universal terms stand for – to which realism is one answer, centres on the problem of the relationship between the universality of concepts and our apparently encountering as independent objects only particulars. Realists would argue that, without a suitable system of real entities for universal terms to refer to, our system of universal terms will be entirely arbitrary, conventional and subjective. This would make any science, which will inevitably be couched in general or universal terms (such as "body", "animal", "heavy"), an arbitrary mental construction among other possible constructions with no objective validity derived from its reflecting an extramental reality; this leaves open the rationally anarchic possibility of a variety of different incommensurable conceptual systems of scientific explanation between which we can have no common grounds or independent standard for a rational choice.

Moderate medieval realism does not go all the way with Platonism, which suggests that universal essences or "whatness" – such as humanity, horseness, justice – can exist as Forms quite independently of all particular individuals which are grouped together in virtue of those universal essences. Moderate realism follows Aristotle in maintaining that in some way there is a real distinction in the world between the common universal essence and the individuating characteristics of particular things sharing that essence. Moderate realism holds that, although the common universal essences of individuals and those individuals cannot be found existing in separation, the distinction between universal essences and particular individuals which can be made in thought nevertheless reflects a real distinction in things in the world. The same common nature or essence is really distinct from things in respect of what makes them particular, as it exists in all the particulars of the same sort, and it is this that makes them the kind of things they are.

The forward-looking aspect of Ockham's philosophy resides in his rejection of realism and his alternative explanation: his rejection of the reality of a world of intelligible, literally common, essences or forms ontologically or really distinct from the characteristics that pick out individuals, and his consequent propagation of nominalism and empiricism. His nominalism and empiricism are closely linked.

Ockham objects to the idea of some literally common nature shared by all and only individuals of the same kind; if this common nature is singular and indivisible, then it cannot be shared by many individuals, and if the common nature is many, then each instance of the many must be singular and itself individual and cannot be shared in common between various individuals.

Ockham does not deny that the world falls into a mind-independent system of natural kinds – in this sense he is still a realist. What he denies in his nominalism is that a condition for its being correct to talk about a natural order of kinds of individual things is the positing of common natures or essences, ontologically or really distinct from the individualizing characteristics, and shared by all and only the individual things of the same kind. Moreover, he thinks that such a view is an unnecessary misinterpretation of Aristotle. He denies in this nominalism that universals subsist as ideas in the mind of God prior to their actualization (their receiving *esse*); God is not necessitated even to this extent; He is not constrained to create, if He creates at all, a particular world-system of kinds. There is, therefore, no system of essences whose necessary relations could be known *a priori*.

For Ockham, universality is a property primarily of thoughts, secondarily of language which expresses thoughts, and not of entities or natures distinct from the individual characteristics of things in the world. Universality is the property of a thought, a generalized abstractive cognition, which is entertained in such a way as to be equally truly predicable of, or usable of, more than one individual. Thus the term "city" is used of London, Paris, New York. Ockham's view is roughly equivalent to saying that universals are concepts, along with the commitment that the being of the concepts is as mental states. Nominalism holds that the only thing strictly in common between individuals falling under a universal name is that they all fall under that name.

The question arises as to why we apply the same universal name to many individuals. Ockham's empiricism complements his nominalism by maintaining that there are no literally common real essences graspable by the intellect, but only individuals apprehended by the senses between which we perceive *similarities* in the individuating characteristics, and it is from these albeit objective but nevertheless contingent similarities that we derive the meanings of universal terms and their range of application to a determinate class of individuals. Thus the connotation or meaning of a universal term such as "humanity" is whatever characteristics we perceive as similar between all those individuals whereby we classify them as human. This list of characteristics defines "humanity" and gives us criteria for deciding whether any given individual should be included under that heading; the denotation or reference of the term "humanity" is then just all individual human beings. The meaning of a universal term such as "humanity" is not explained by its denoting a common essence distinct from the characteristics of particular human beings; its meaning is explained by the similar characteristics of a number of individual men, in virtue of which we call them all "men". Talk of something "similar" between many individuals may seem to evoke a common nature again; but Ockham would say that we perceive similarity not by perceiving some literally identical common nature distinct from the individuating characteristics, but in virtue of a resemblance between the characteristics which are part of the natures or features of the individuals themselves.

Thus Ockham denies that there is a metaphysical problem of determining in virtue of what universals are individualized, since there are no such universals to be individuated. Aquinas had suggested that universals are individuated in virtue of their being exemplified in a different parcel of stuff or matter; Duns Scotus (*c.* 1266–1308) rejected this and suggested that beside universal essences – what features a thing cannot lack and still be the kind of thing it is – there is an individuating essence, the *haecceitas* or individualizing "thisness" of a kind, which gives *this* horse. Ockham, however, has the logical problem of showing how to reduce universal concepts to terms that signify what he regards as the only existents, individuals; and he has the epistemological problem of saying how from experiencing only individuals we form universal concepts.

It should be pointed out that for Ockham the primary carriers of meanings are mental expressions – states of mind – with which written and spoken expressions become associated by convention. Mental signs mean what they stand for directly; linguistic expressions are signs only conventionally; thus the mental sign for rain is the same for the speaker of any language, but its linguistic expression may be different.

Terms are elements in propositions and they take on different functions depending on the proposition they are in; in particular they acquire a determinate "standing for" (*suppositio*) function. Here we are talking of natural terms or concepts, not the conventional terms of any particular language; the terms "*homme*" and "man" are conventional terms for the same natural sign or concept. Ockham distinguishes between "terms of the first intention" and "terms of the second intention". For example, a singular term such as "Socrates" stands as a natural sign for the *thing* Socrates and is of the "first intention". A universal term such as "species" is of the "second intention" and stands not immediately for things that are not themselves signs, but for other signs that do stand immediately as signs for things. Thus, "Socrates" is a sign for the individual man Socrates; "species" stands not immediately for individual things, but for terms of the "first intention" such as "man", "horse" and "dog"; the term "species" can be predicated of the terms "man", "horse" and "dog", each of which stands for all the members of a different class of individuals, and says of these *terms* that they are all species-terms which are the names of many things. Ockham contends that the realist belief in universal terms standing, albeit obliquely or indirectly, for entities distinct from individual entities is a consequence of confusing the two levels of intentions: terms that stand for things, and terms that stand for terms; that is, talk about things in an object language, and talk about the object language in a metalanguage. If we confuse these two we are tempted to suppose mistakenly that metalinguistic talk is about things.

Nominalism is in accord with the most famous feature of Ockham's thought, "Ockham's razor"; this is a methodological principle designed to keep the number of kinds of entities posited as distinct in the world to a minimum – it is a principle of parsimony. Ockham's objection to realism and the positing of real ontologically distinct essences is partly just that they are unnecessary to explain how we come to classify things in a universal manner. Logically what this means is that apparent reference to real abstract entities by universal terms can in principle always be replaced by an analysis of universal terms, so that they refer only to individuals. Thus "man" signifies merely the total disjunction: Socrates, or Plato, or Aquinas, and so on. Relational terms such as "taller" do not denote entities distinct from the individuals to which they apply; in referring to *A* being taller than *B*, we are referring to only two entities, and the truth "*A* is taller than *B*" is reduced to a truth about *A* (*A* is six feet tall) and a truth about *B* (*B* is five feet tall). The only sorts of thing that exist are individuals: individual substances and their individual qualities.

It has been objected that Ockham's criticism of the real distinction between essences and individuals misses the point, for he attacks a position which the most important medieval thinkers such as Aquinas and Duns Scotus never sought to defend. The accusation is that Ockham thought that if the distinction between the common essence of individuals and what constitutes their individuality were to be a *real* distinction, then it must be a distinction between *things* of the same sort, such as exists between any two existing individuals, and that Ockham was led to this assumption by thinking of the attribution of essences as noun-like rather than verb-like. If we think of the attribution of essences or forms as more verb-like than noun-like – as in "humanizing", "equinizing" – we will see that there is a formal objective extralinguistic distinction being made which is separable in thought and is nevertheless not a distinction between separable individual entities. It is not clear whether this pointing up of the distinction between the grammatically verb-like use of ascribed essences to things, as opposed to naming those same things, is sufficient to maintain that there is a corresponding metaphysical extralinguistic distinction between the common natures and the particular features of individuals.

Moving to Ockham's epistemology, we find that he distinguishes between intellectual acts of apprehension and judgement: apprehension or cognition is awareness on the basis of which a judgement can be made, which is an intellectual assent to the truth or falsity of a proposition. He further contrasts an *intuitive* cognition, on the basis of which one is in a position to make a judgement of contingent fact which is *evident*, and an *abstract* cognition, on the basis of which we are *not* in a position to make an *evident* judgement of contingent fact – such contingent judgement will concern whether an object exists or whether it has some contingent property. The objects of these cognitions are the same; what differs is the manner in which they are apprehended; in an intuitive cognition the apprehension of the object is caused immediately by the object apprehended; in an abstract cognition the apprehension of the object is not caused immediately by the object apprehended, but it always presupposes an intuitive cognition of the object at some previous time. From an intuitive cognition of X, or X as f, we can judge *evidently* that it is true that X exists, or that X is f. Once we have an intuitive cognition of X, or X as f, it can be stored in the memory as an acquired capacity (*habitus*) so we can then form an abstract cognition of X, or X as f, which is divorced from X existing or not existing, or X actually being f or not being f; but this abstract cognition of X, or X as f, does not put us in the position to make the judgement we might make concerning X *evident*. If I saw you sitting in my study, I would be in a position to form an evident judgement that it is true that you are sitting in my study; if, however, I did not see you, but nevertheless formed from an abstractive cognition the judgement that you were sitting in my study, then the judgement, although it *may* be true, may also be false, and is not in any case evident. Ockham is realist with respect to individual objects and their individual properties in the external world: he does not doubt that in mental acts of intuitive cognition what we directly apprehend is constituted by objects and their properties just as they really are in the external world outside the mind. In intuitive cognition there is no distinction between the way things seem to us and the way they really are; the way they seem is how they are. Ockham holds that we can also have intuitive cognition of introspectively apprehended mental states.

In the natural course of events, if we have an intuitive cognition of X, then X exists, since X is a part of the cause of the cognition of X; thus the judgement that X exists is evident. However, since it is logically possible, God could produce supernaturally in us the same mental state as a cognitive intuition – that is, phenomenologically the same intuition, which is *as if* we were having a real intuitive cognition – without the object existing, which would in natural circumstances suffice for the evident judgement that the object exists. But, in fact, God does not normally act like this, although He did so in the case of the prophets.

Ockham's empiricism surfaces in his account of explanations of the natural world. Strictly speaking, science is concerned with necessary universal truths concerning that which must be and cannot be otherwise, expressed in propositions that are proved from self-evident propositions by syllogistic deductive reasoning. But one needs experience even to understand the meaning of the terms in propositions – at least those that stand for things – even when, once understood, they are self-evident propositions; for to understand the meaning of the terms we need a primary experience of what the terms stand for. For Ockham, as for Locke, there are no innate ideas which could account for this; all our ideas, by association with which words get their meaning, are derived from experience.

Science in a narrow sense includes only necessary provable propositions; and since the existence and nature of the world are in all ways contingent (that which may be true or may be false), it would seem that a science of the world is not strictly possible. In mathematics, geometry, metaphysics and theology, there are truths which are quite independent of whether any world exists or not and these are suitable subjects for scientific knowledge. However, Ockham extends science (*scientia*) to include hypothetical or conditional premises of demonstrations or proofs, and evident contingent judgements made on the basis of intuitive cognitions.

Ockham maintains that God must be supremely unnecessitated, being completely free and completely omnipotent. This leads him to assert that the world is radically contingent in its existence and nature; necessity applies only within thought and language, not to events or things in the world. All that is not self-contradictory is possible; what is actual but not necessary cannot be determined by *a priori* reason or logic alone; reason and logic can determine only what is necessary, impossible and possible, not what is actual and contingent among what is possible. Logically speaking in the world anything could follow from anything else, and the only way to determine what things there are, and how things are connected, is by experience. Ockham does not deny that there are real objective causal connections in nature; the order we appear to see is not merely derived from the conventional use of expressions; he does not deny that there is a natural order in the world that can form the basis for the discovery of universal connections which are the aim of science; what he denies is that these universal connections in fact have any metaphysical necessity which could be discovered through deductive reasoning alone. All those connections between things and events that are not merely analytically true by the definitions which give identifying criteria are radically contingent and can be known to hold only from intuitive cognitions. Thus to have new knowledge of connections which goes beyond what is already assumed in definitions, as is the case with causal connections, we rely on experience. If all connections between things and events were analytic and merely followed from definitions, then working them out would be a purely linguistic matter. Clearly we suppose that most connections are not definitional in this way, in which case the connections can be known to hold only by experience.

Ockham does not tackle the question which was to concern Hume much later, in the eighteenth century, of how we can rationally justify the belief that there is any objective natural system of laws at all – the problem of the "uniformity of nature" – or how the evidence from the experience of a finite number of singular instances can ever justify the assertion of universal laws of the form "All *As* are *Bs*" or causal connections of the form "If *A* occurs, then *B* must occur". Ockham thinks that God has, as a matter of fact, so arranged things that we can discover objective regular natural laws; but these laws are only contingently – in fact – true, and God could have arranged the laws quite differently; He was not bound by any kind of necessity to arrange things the way He actually arranged them. It follows that if the arrangement of things is not a matter of necessity, the discovery of the arranged regularities is not knowable by *a priori* deductive reasoning alone, which can give us knowledge only of necessities (that which must be), impossibilities (that which cannot be) and possibilities (that which may or may not be); rather, we require experience in order to discover what actual contingent (that which is, but need not be) arrangement exists. God maintains the natural order so that we can rely (barring miracles) on *B* always following *A*; *A* is a sign that *B* will follow, and we can be confident, thanks to God, that *B* will follow. This is not to say that God, and not *A*, is the real cause of *B*, but merely that God chooses to maintain a natural order whereby, albeit contingently, *A* causes *B*.

CHAPTER FOUR

Rationalism: Descartes, Spinoza, Leibniz

The philosophers of the seventeenth and eighteenth centuries are often separated into rationalists and empiricists. While this distinction certainly blurs similarities between philosophers of both "schools", this retrospective classification has some value at least in bringing out tendencies of the philosophers grouped under these headings. The contrast chiefly lies in what is said to be knowable by pure reason alone. Some factors consistently underlie rationalist philosophy.

Rationalism holds that the human mind has the capacity, logically speaking, to establish truths about the nature of reality (including ourselves) by reason alone independently of experience; indeed, if knowledge of the fundamental structure of the world in the proper scientific sense is possible, then it must be derived from reason, which alone has access to the required certain, necessary, universally valid, timeless truths; the senses inform us only of what is uncertain, contingent, particular, perspectival and transient. These necessary truths about the world can be known to be true merely through our properly understanding the concepts they involve or are deduced from such truths, and ideally they form a single deductive system. Truths known *a priori* by pure understanding, if they do not concern the world as it appears in perception, instead concern a really existing intelligible world that underlies the appearance of changing particulars that we experience; this underlying reality makes intelligible, and ultimately explains, the appearances. The intellect has access to concepts, and the terms that express them, whose meaning does not depend on being referred to some feature of our experience. Thus there is, according to the rationalists, a reality whose nature is comprehended by the intellect (reason or understanding) alone and which stands behind the mere appearance of things; it is this ultimate reality which delivers the conceptions which bring the explanation of the way the world is to an end.

The rationalists do not disregard the senses, but they share the characteristic of thinking that knowledge based on experience is inferior to that derived from reason. The rationalist contention is that the world has an underlying real structure of natural necessary connections, which is logically understandable by reason and deduction alone; this does not inevitably lead to the advocation of an *a priori* methodology in science – as if all scientific truths can actually be discovered just by sitting and thinking – for although in principle or ideally the world is understandable *a priori* by the intellect alone, in fact we as humans have a limited capacity to determine the nature of the world independently of experience; scientific truths are often in fact discovered by us through experience. Moreover, the necessary *a priori* truths of metaphysics concern not the world of appearances, which is the subject matter of science, but a reality beyond appearances.

There is the conviction among the rationalists that everything is in principle rationally explicable; one can never rest content with features of the world for which a reason cannot be given as to why they necessarily are a certain way and not otherwise. The tendency of empiricism is to admit that there are *a priori* necessary truths knowable with certainty independently of experience, but to deny that such truths can determine anything about what really exists or the real nature of the world, because in all such cases we are dealing with the contingent features of the world we experience, and not what is necessary concerning a supposed world beyond possible experience.

Descartes

The importance of Descartes in Western philosophy can hardly be overestimated; he shaped the kinds of questions and answers which were to dominate Western philosophy for many years; and, with some notable exceptions, this approach has only seriously been questioned in the twentieth century.

René Descartes (1596–1650) was born in France, in a small village near Tours that is now called La Haye-Descartes. His constitution as a child was poor. He was educated at a Jesuit college at La Flèche in Anjou. Here he encountered scholastic doctrines that his philosophy was to reject; but he also discovered his love for and great proficiency at mathematics; and he remained a Catholic all his life. Descartes had the desire to travel and experience the world of practical affairs, and to this end he joined, unpaid, the army of the Dutch Prince Maurice of Orange and later the army of the Duke of Bavaria.

While in Holland he encountered Isaac Beeckman, who encouraged Descartes to consider questions in mathematics, physics and philosophy. On 10 November 1619, he spent the night by a large stove in Ulm; there he had a vision, and later three dreams, concerning how he might lay the foundations for a unified science which would include all human learning. From 1625 he spent two years in Paris, where he lived the life of a gentleman; he gambled, and was involved in a duel over a love affair. In 1628 he began writing, in Latin, *Rules for the direction of the mind*, which was unfinished and unpublished in his life time. This states the overall projects that were to preoccupy all of Descartes' philosophy: that of founding science on absolute certainty, free from sceptical doubts, and that of devising a method of inquiry which, if properly followed, would lead science inexorably to certain truth.

Descartes spent most of the period from 1628 to 1649 in the relatively liberal atmosphere of Holland. The death of his five-year-old illegitimate daughter Francine in 1640 was his life's great grief. He was secretive about his whereabouts, and lived in many different houses; he also had a great desire for solitude, although he was not always without company. In 1647 Descartes had dinner with the philosophers Gassendi (1592–1655) and Hobbes (1588–1679), both of whom were critics of Descartes' *Meditations*.

Descartes received criticism of the *Meditations* from various theologians, and most fruitfully from Antoine Arnauld (1612–94). All these criticisms are printed as *Objections* and *Replies*; the latter of these being Descartes' responses. We are fortunate that as well as producing his major writings, he engaged in extensive correspondence with many people about his ideas. Towards the end of his life Descartes developed a friendship with the exiled Princess Elizabeth, daughter of Elector Frederick; he replied in letters to her acute questions. He acquired royal patronage from Queen Christina of Sweden, and was persuaded in 1649 to go to Stockholm. There he continued his long-standing habit of rising late, having spent some hours in the morning reading and writing in bed. In Sweden he led a lonely life, and in 1650, in the winter, he contracted pneumonia and died. His last words are said to have been "My soul, we must leave". Although initially buried in Sweden, his body was eventually transferred to the church of Saint-Germain-des-Prés, and his skull is to be found in the Musée de l'Homme, in Paris.

The overall aim of Descartes' philosophy might be said to be the attempt to free explanations of the nature of the world from confusions and conflicts, and set them on a path that would lead to a unified explanation of things that was true, and, because it was also certain, free from scepticism. Descartes made a significant contribution to the revolution of how man viewed his place in the universe, and the proper way of pursuing truths. His particular contribution to this revolution in thought is the egocentricity of his approach: the foundation of truth and knowledge begins by working from what is most evident to the mind of the individual.

In the dedication to the *Meditations* Descartes seems to have other aims: proofs of both the immortality of the soul and the existence of God. It would be wrong to suppose that he was insincere in his expressed concern for these matters. However, the concern of enduring importance for modern readers lies in his aim and method in securing a scientific, in particular mathematical, understanding of the world that is secure against even exaggerated sceptical doubts. More generally this involved a search for a method of ridding ourselves of beliefs not known to be true, and maximizing those which are known to be true. Descartes presents such a search to us in the *Meditations* in the form of a personal odyssey. This is a kind of intellectual record so that anyone might follow the same procedure at least once in his life, and by it strip his mind of the accumulated rubbish of uncritically accepted beliefs. Descartes sets out in the *Meditations* not merely the arguments for his philosophy, but also a convincing route we can follow which will enable us to overcome the psychological resistance we may have to such a journey. It is the path which should be followed by the seeker after the ultimate foundations of knowledge; in particular it involves showing that a mathematical physics of the world is attainable by creatures with our intellectual capacities and faculties.

Descartes sets out on an extraordinary procedure of answering the most extreme scepticism about knowledge and rationality by embracing that scepticism; he then attempts to show that something remains that cannot conceivably be doubted even after scepticism has been applied in its most stringent form, and that what remains is sufficient to secure the foundations for knowledge. The tool used to this end is the "method of doubt".

The final position at which Descartes wishes to arrive is that we can have *objective* knowledge of the world; knowledge independent of the way we happen to be biologically constituted; disinterested knowledge that aims to divest itself of our perspective, and that tells us how things really are in the world. Descartes thinks that such an objective conception must be independent of our contingent sensory faculties, since we have no guarantee that our senses present to us the world in its fundamental form; after all, if our senses changed, the world would appear differently. So the aim is to produce a way of describing the world based on conceptions which would not change if our senses changed; a world whose laws we could fraternally share with any rational beings. To be objective our science must be sense-independent, and derived from reason or the faculty of understanding. Descartes sets out to show that when the mind is emptied of all sense-dependent beliefs, it is not empty of ideas or concepts, and that the ideas that remain are sufficient to form the basis for science. This involves a belief that we have innate ideas independent of the senses;

we have such ideas concerning mathematics and geometry. By "ideas" here Descartes does not mean images; he means concepts. Descartes attempts to show that the fundamental explanations of all phenomena can be derived from a mathematical and geometric conception of reality independent of sense-experience. Descartes aims to demonstrate that mathematical geometry can be applied to the explanation of the world of material things because, contrary to the appearance of a vast array of natural kinds of things in the world, the only essential properties of matter are geometric; that is, matter stripped of all properties other than the ones which geometry deals with will still be matter, and will be matter if and only if it has those properties; those properties are extension, shape and motion, of which extension is primary. The essential properties are those properties which a thing cannot lack and still be the kind of thing it is.

Descartes in many ways can be seen as opposing the Aristotelian science; Aristotle takes at face value the division of the world into what appear to be natural kinds of things. An Aristotelian scientific explanation of some phenomenon associated with a thing is then obtained by deducing the phenomenon from an intellectual examination of the essential nature of that thing given by a real definition, or from a more general category of which the thing is a part. The identification of genuine natural kinds, from which explanations are to be deduced, is very difficult. However, Descartes does not reject essentialism, which is the view that we eventually reach a certain category of stuff beyond which we cannot go since we have reached that which is most ontologically self-sufficient, and from which we derive explanations of everything else that appears to us in the world. But instead of a vast array of the natural kinds there appear to be, Descartes, in the case of the material world, reduces this to one fundamental kind: matter as extension. It is in terms of this underlying reality behind appearances that the variety of features making up appearances are to be explained. The explanation of a vast array of different phenomena is thus simplified and unified under a more general conception which reflects the fundamental nature of reality. The tendency of Descartes' philosophy, and the revolution of which his philosophy is a part, is to reopen the gap between how things appear to us in perception, and how they really are in themselves; moreover, how things really are, which should form the basis of the explanation of appearances, has to be comprehended by *intellectual* contemplation or thinking, not experience. This marks the distinction between primary qualities, which are the real qualities things have independently of perceivers, and secondary qualities, which are in objects as arrangements of primary qualities (say particles in motion), but which produce in perceivers quite different ideas, like the experience of heat and red.

First, Descartes has to deal with radical scepticism. The method of doubt seeks to eliminate all beliefs not known to be true which may taint and infect the truth; it does this by rejecting as *false* all beliefs it is *possible* to doubt; that is, it rejects all beliefs whose falsity is possible. In this way Descartes meets the sceptic head-on. This is done not because he thinks all those beliefs it is possible to doubt the truth of are false; rather, it is a way of making certain in one go that no false beliefs slip through and are mistakenly accepted as true. It is important to note that Descartes is not suggesting that we adopt such scepticism in our everyday life; Descartes' doubt is a method adopted for the pure project or special purpose of securing the first principles or foundations of all knowledge, disregarding all practical concerns. Straight away we can note that we do, after all, find cases of things we once believed to be true turning out to be false. Even without sceptical doubt, Descartes' view that we should make a fresh start makes sense; we have over our lifetime accumulated uncritically a mass of beliefs from which we make all sorts of inferences; but any falsity among these beliefs is likely to infect any inferences we make and conclusions we draw from those beliefs. If we then arrive at true conclusions, even in valid inferences, it can only be by a sort of luck.

What remains after this process of sceptical doubt is not a massively rich axiom from which all that we would wish to claim we can know can be deduced, but something which, when examined for the reason for its immunity from doubt, will give us a *criterion* to distinguish truth from falsity. That criterion is clarity and distinctness. Descartes does not wish the criterion to be merely a notion of subjective obviousness, but he is unable to formulate it in terms of primary truths or logical truths whose denial implies a contradiction, in the way that Leibniz does; rather, Descartes explains it as our possessing intellectual intuition giving us an ability simply to see that certain propositions or beliefs, once fully understood, must be true. After this we can begin to reinstate many of those beliefs we previously supposed false. In this search we take time off from practical concerns and constraints, and apply the criterion single-mindedly.

Descartes embarks on his method of doubt by disposing of the range of beliefs in three classes: first, we abandon sense-based beliefs by accepting that the senses may deceive us; second, we abandon the belief that we can have knowledge of real "simple natures"; third, we abandon the belief that God exists. A belief in the existence of God is simply dropped, both because Descartes has no wish to assume one of the things he sets out to prove, and because if the existence of a beneficent God were granted the radical scepticism Descartes envisions would not be plausible. Descartes also wishes to show that there are degrees of doubt involved in these classes of beliefs, and to indicate the order of trustworthiness in which we should reinstate them; he also wishes to make the method of doubt psychologically convincing. To these ends he suggests two hypotheses: the "dream hypothesis" and the "evil demon hypothesis".

The first of these – the dream hypothesis – points to those occasions on which I thought I was awake when in fact I was dreaming. Our sleeping dreams may also be phenomenally or qualitatively indistinguishable from our waking states: I may be convinced I am awake and seeing real things when I am in fact asleep. This suffices to undermine the trust we may have in the senses as representing to us something real. This doubt extends to the existence of my own body, which brings us to the second class of beliefs: the existence of "simple natures". When we dream we dream about something, and that something must conform to the most simple and universal categories such as extension, shape, duration, number, movement. Even if what we dream of does not exist exactly as we dream about it, it is still possible, and less doubtful, that simple and universal natures exist; for example, objects with extension. Thus an object of a specific shape might not exist because we might dream about an imaginary unreal object of that shape; but that is not the same as showing there are no objects with shape: shape as such does not exist. Even dreaming involves objects considered under the simplest categories and concepts which are surely real. Horses, and bodies of particular shapes, may not exist, but it is less doubtful that there exists a world of extended material things at all. Moreover, the greater security of mathematics and geometry derives from its dealing with simple natures (such as number and shape) and their necessary relations regardless of whether those general things exist or not. Geometrical proofs done in a dream would still be valid since their validity is independent of whether geometric objects exist. The evil demon, however, who has the active power to deceive us has the ability to lead us to believe falsely that there exist in the world even the most general sorts of things characterized by simple natures. The evil demon finally makes it conceivable that no external world exists corresponding to our idea of a world of extended substance; the evil demon could cause our idea of an extended world although that world does not exist. It is not always clear if simple mathematical and geometric truths can be doubted under the influence of the evil demon. It must be remembered that it is not within the power even of the demon to alter logical truths and to make $2+2=4$ false and $2+2=5$ true; however, the demon can make us *believe* that $2+2=5$. Descartes thinks it is within God's power to alter such logical truths. Even if we accept that beliefs in basic mathematical and geometric truths survive the demon, we have not established that anything exists corresponding to the simple natures; doubt as to their existence is *conceivable*, so their existence is therefore not free from scepticism. We have at best a pure mathematics and geometry which has not been shown to apply to anything existing, for the simple natures are what it would deal with.

What remains that cannot be doubted is *cogito ergo sum*: I think, therefore I am. For however the demon may twist and turn in his attempt to trap and deceive us, and lead us to accept doubtful and false beliefs, there is one belief I cannot doubt: that whenever I think, I exist. This belief is somehow self-verifying; the mark of truth is intrinsic to it and does not depend on accepting any other truth. Even if the content of that thinking is itself an act of doubting, this too could not take place unless I existed. The *cogito* is the necessary condition for all reasoning – even all deception. Each time I entertain the *cogito* it is certainly true.

What is more, I am essentially a thing that thinks, for, although I can doubt that I have a body and still exist, I cannot cease to think and still exist. Descartes believes that he is essentially a thinking thing: he is necessarily immaterial (incorporeal) if he exists at all, and only contingently embodied. The question of whether he is entitled to this conclusion is much disputed; but one obvious objection has been that it does not follow from the premise "I necessarily exist whenever I think" that "I am necessarily only a thing that thinks". We might accept that "I think" entails "I exist" without agreeing that "I exist" entails "I think"; I may still exist in some other way when I do not think. Therefore I may not be essentially only a thinking thing. There is indeed some doubt as to how much weight Descartes puts on this argument. Whatever we think of this, Descartes is committed to the view that he is essentially a thinking thing, and that thought is his only essential property. Descartes of course presents more than one argument for this view.

By essence Descartes means some property, or set of properties, f, such that if f is an essential property of X, then X cannot be an X without possessing property f; if f is the essence of X, then X cannot be what it is or the sort of thing it is without f. Thus, f is a necessary and sufficient condition for X to be *what* it is independently of the fact *that* it is. In a case where there is only one essential property, as with mind and matter, that property is alone both necessary and sufficient. Descartes thinks we can know – that is, have clear and distinct conceptions of – what mind and matter are before we know whether any exists or not. For Descartes, as for other rationalists, only God has existence as part of His necessary and sufficient conditions for what He is: God. In this way Descartes draws the distinction, criticized by Spinoza, between true substance, God, and the finite or created substances mind and matter.

As it stands, the *cogito* is merely a subjectively certain truth; it is time-bound; its certainty is restricted to those times when it is actually being entertained. Descartes obviously wishes to move beyond the perpetual reiteration of this one truth. What makes the *cogito* a certain truth is that it is clearly and distinctly perceived. Descartes makes use of an analogy with sense-perceptions: an idea is clear in so far as we attend to features of which we are forcefully and immediately aware, and an idea is distinct when we attend only to those features which are clear, and thus do not make inferences beyond that of which we are immediately aware. This turns out to be awareness of the essential nature of the objects of one's awareness; and awareness of an object's essence means that the object of awareness could not be confused with anything else. The thinking behind clear and distinct ideas is that there must be a "natural light" of reason that allows a direct grasp or intuition of some truths with certainty, independently of the acceptance of any other truths. They are grasped by anyone who can reason and can understand at all. If some truths are not immediately manifestly true on intrinsic grounds alone, following our full understanding of them, without any further ("external") justification, then all reasoning would be impossible, since it could never get started. Those propositions which we can clearly and distinctly conceive, or intuit, can be known to be true because we can see they must be true merely from completely understanding them. Such truths can be seen as analytic: they can be known to be true merely from understanding the meaning of the terms they involve.

One problem with the *cogito* is that in it Descartes does seem to go beyond what he is immediately aware of; what he is aware of is particular acts of thinking; but this falls short of establishing a durable "I" or self as a mental substance on which the thinking depends.

Descartes' plan is then to move from the two features of the *cogito*, thinking and existence, to prove the existence of God. Having established the existence of God, Descartes relies on our understanding of the nature of God as an all powerful, perfect and benevolent being to say that, as deception is an imperfection, God would not deceive us in that which we most clearly and distinctly conceive: that is, truths that are knowable through the understanding alone. If I do not go beyond judging as true that which I clearly and distinctly perceive, then I will always judge truly, and I will not entertain falsehoods.

What I clearly and distinctly understand about things is the essential properties of those things; those properties without which those things cannot be the kind of things they are; those properties which, if I think about those things at all, cannot be separated from, and so must be part of, my conception of those things. These are the defining properties of substances, on which all the other apparent qualities of things rely. There are three substances according to Descartes: matter, whose essential property is extension; mind, whose essential property is thought; and God, whose essential properties are perfection, omnipotence, benevolence, infiniteness, and existence. Only God contains *existence* as part of His essence; that is, among the necessary and sufficient conditions for being God is existence. But the created substances of matter and mind are distinguished by relying on nothing else apart from God for their existence. The same cannot be said for colour, for example, which relies on there being an extended physical object which is coloured.

If we examine the essential properties of mind and matter, we discover that it is the intellect, independently of the senses, which gives us our understanding of them. If we conceive of mind and matter, and we imagine away all those properties which seem unnecessary to their being either mind or matter, we find that we are left with the essential properties; thought in the case of mind, and extension in the case of matter. Without these properties neither could have any other properties at all; the essential properties are what all other properties depend on. All the other properties can change, but without extension and thought, matter and minds respectively would not be what they are. These essential natures remain constant to give identity to matter and minds through the changes they appear to undergo according to our senses, and even when all the sensory qualities have changed; the intellect reveals the underlying reality upon which sensory appearances are a kind of clothing. If the senses are eliminated by sceptical doubt, it is by the sense-independent conception of the understanding that the essential properties or intelligible properties remain known to us. The essential properties these substances have are what remains constant through change, and makes sense of the continued identity of a thing over time through *accidental* change. If essential properties change, we do not say that X has acquired property g and lost property f, we say, rather, that X has ceased to be X; it ceases to be the same substance if it loses its essence. What makes a material thing (for example, a piece of wax) a piece of matter through its various appearances is not sensible qualities (something we perceive by sense), for these can all alter; the conception of a material thing revealing its essence, by which we identify it as the same material thing through its various appearances, is therefore given through inspection by the intellect.

The thinker who has reached the intuitive certainty of his own existence and the essential nature of that existence has still to get beyond this. Descartes distinguishes between levels of reality, or being, by degree of ontological dependence; the more independently a thing exists, the more formal (actual) reality it has. Descartes distinguishes between objective and formal reality. An idea has a certain degree of formal reality as an entity in itself; but it also has an objective reality – its content, what the idea is about – which may differ from its formal reality as an idea. The cause of an idea must have at least as much *formal* reality as the idea has *objective* reality; that is, the actual cause of an idea must have as much reality as the content of the idea. One idea we have is the idea of God. In the case of the idea of God we have an idea with infinite objective reality since the object of that idea has infinite formal reality. An idea with such a content (such an object) could not be caused by something merely finite, with less formal reality than the content, like ourselves, but must have as its cause something of equal or greater actual or formal reality; so only God can be the cause of our idea of God. This is a cosmological argument for God's existence. The notion of levels of reality can be summarized in the following diagram; the arrows show the direction of decreasing formal (actual) reality.

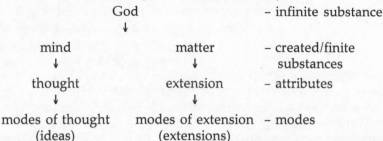

The other argument Descartes uses to prove God's existence is the ontological argument. God contains, by definition, all perfections, and one of these perfections is existence itself. Therefore God exists. One problem here is involved in suggesting that existence is a predicate rather than a term confirming that predicates are actualized. Another problem is that, although it may be part of God's definition that *if* He exists, then He exists necessarily, it may still be questioned whether anything actually satisfies that definition.

A serious problem for Descartes' arguments which aim to escape the exaggerated doubt is the charge of circularity: the Cartesian Circle. If we are dependent on the existence of God to free us from scepticism, it is important to see how far this dependence extends. If the dependence extends to God being our only guarantee of the truth of even that which we most clearly and distinctly perceive, then it is impossible to see how there can be any rational proof of God's existence; in that case the truth of any of the premises and the reliability of any of the inferential steps in the proof would logically depend on the outcome of the proof: God's existence. We cannot, without circularity, prove God's existence by means of propositions and arguments whose truth and validity depend on assuming God's existence. It is not clear what Descartes' final view is on this. One suggestion has been that God's role is not to guarantee clear and distinct ideas themselves as we intuit them – since they are in that case as certain as they could ever be – but to obviate the necessity of our running constantly through proofs to reassure ourselves. The central problem then with the proofs of the existence of God is not their circularity but their questionable validity and the dubiousness of their premises.

Descartes, however, thinks he has proved the existence of God. Having done this he can begin to reinstate some of the things cast aside by the method of doubt by invoking the nature of God. In the case of the material world, what we clearly and distinctly perceive about it is that it is extended; and this is something grasped by the intellect, not the senses; it follows from our merely properly understanding the concept of matter. God would not deceive us about what we most clearly and distinctly perceive. Those ideas that we most clearly and distinctly conceive are innate; and once God's existence is proved, the truth of those ideas we identify as innate by subtracting the sense-derived ideas is also guaranteed by their being directly planted in us by God. This then gives us a pure physics of the world, but it is one that is hypothetical: we have a clear and distinct idea of what matter is as being essentially extended, but the question remains as to whether such matter actually exists. God is required again in order to demonstrate the possibility of an applied physics. The ideas I receive when I perceive a material world, which I suppose are caused by external bodies, could indeed have as their cause external bodies, but their cause might also be myself, or derive directly from God. These ideas come to me unbidden so I cannot be their cause, and I have a strong belief that they derive from material bodies; if the source of the ideas was other than what I strongly believe it to be, God would be allowing me to be deceived; but God is no deceiver; therefore bodies exist. This argument aims to prove the existence of the material world. This establishes the possibility of applied physics within what I clearly and distinctly perceive about bodies. If we judge as true only that which we clearly and distinctly perceive, God guarantees that those judgements correspond to actual states of affairs in the world.

All that has been established in Descartes' argument has been established by pure reason alone independently of information derived from the senses; the senses have been denied any role by the sceptical doubt. Truths must be tested by reason, not by the unreliable senses.

If God is no deceiver, why does he let us make mistakes at all? Letting us make mistakes is not the same as actively deceiving us. Descartes is clear that such mistakes as we make are our responsibility, not God's. The mind is made up of two chief faculties: intellect and will. We make mistakes when we allow the will to push beyond what is clearly and distinctly perceived by the intellect. God gives us the possibility of avoiding error: we merely have to stick within what we clearly and distinctly perceive: propositions we can know to be true purely by fully understanding them.

If this is the case, it tends to undermine Descartes' proof of the existence of the material world. His argument depends on the notion that God cannot be a deceiver and would be deceiving us if he allowed us to believe strongly that material objects were the cause of our perceptions of material objects when they are not the cause. But

God could only be accused of deception if in those circumstances He either implanted the belief in us, or such a belief was a clear and distinct one. Descartes does not attempt to demonstrate the former, and the latter is obviously not the case. So it is perfectly possible that God is not a deceiver and that material objects do not exist as the cause of our perceptions of material objects. Descartes has already admitted that God lets us make our own mistakes in judgement and these are likely to occur when we make judgements beyond what we clearly and distinctly perceive to be the case.

Descartes gives a dualistic conception of reality; there are two basic substances in the world, mind and matter. These two give at least the appearance of interaction: things in the world act on my sensory organs and result in perceptions; I will my arm to move, and it moves. But the problem arises for Descartes of how a non-spatial (unextended) substance, which cannot thereby be in motion, can cause the motion of extended substance, or how motions in our bodies can cause changes in consciousness. Mind and matter have no properties in common, and it is difficult to see how their interaction can be rendered intelligible. They are created substances dependent on God for their existence, but apart from that the explanation of their states should be independent of any causes "external" to their own type of substance. Descartes' motivation for dualism derives from his belief in both the immortality of the soul and the possibility of free will. The immortality of the soul is maintained by the soul being an independent substance which might survive the dissolution of the body. Free will is maintained by making the soul independent of the deterministic mechanical laws which govern matter; then our behaviour is not governed by mechanical compulsion, but can be acts done out of choice in knowledge of good and evil.

It is important to summarize some of Descartes' achievements. They are mainly seen in his attempt to gain a more objective point of view of the world, and this requires a conception of the world which is non-sense-based; an objective conception is non-species specific, and independent of the way we happen, contingently, to be biologically constituted. Some of our view of how the world is is contributed by our natures; and to get a view of how the world really is (how it is in itself), it is necessary to strip away as much as possible of the elements in our conception contributed by the particularities of our perceptual apparatus and perspective. Certainly the sense organs we happen to have could alter to give us a different view of the world, but the world would not thereby be different. The objective conception of the world is a conception which is universally valid, revealing the world as it is in itself, a conception devoid of features that depend, as apparent features of the world, on the contingent peculiarities of our point of view, such as those derived from our particular sensory apparatus. Reason provides a conception, as a source of disinterested universally valid concepts and truths, independent of our, or indeed any, point of view. Take an extreme example: the truth $2+2=4$ would presumably be a truth for Martians no matter what sensory apparatus they had – they might see X-rays but not light-rays. The idea is that our view of the world could be objective and universally valid in the same way. We cannot perhaps attain this ultimately objective point of view – a God's-eye, or no-eye view – but it is something at which we can aim; only God sees things as they are in themselves independent of any point of view; for God there is no appearance/reality distinction, for His view is non-perspectival.

We can obtain objective knowledge of the physical world, according to Descartes, by concentrating exclusively on conceiving it to have only mathematical and geometric properties. Descartes needs to start from the point of disinterested pure consciousness, which is outside nature; using only the resources of reason or intellect that are found within the incorporeal consciousness, Descartes hopes to build a unified and universal conception of nature which would be common to all beings capable of reasoning at all.

Spinoza

Benedict (Baruch) de Spinoza (1632–77) was the son of a Jewish merchant who fled to the Netherlands from persecution in Portugal. The Jews who entered Amsterdam met a close-knit and strict Jewish community to which they had to accommodate themselves by manifesting doctrinal purity. Spinoza was taught at a school run by a rabbi, and he became familiar with Hebrew sacred books and Jewish theology. But in 1656 he was excommunicated from the Amsterdam synagogue for being unable to assent to important aspects of Judaic orthodoxy; the root of this lay in Spinoza's increasingly critical attitude towards the Bible. His life as an outcast from the Jewish community necessitated that he become financially independent; so Spinoza came to make his living as a lens grinder. Although towards the end of his life he was offered a professorship at the University of Heidelberg, he declined it as a threat to his intellectual freedom – he thus never held an academic post.

The advocacy of toleration, particularly the opposition to religious fanaticism, was a mark of Spinoza's outlook, surrounded as he was by violent schisms of every sort. Spinoza was held in great affection by his friends – friendship between those who in common seek truth being something, in the Aristotelian tradition, he valued highly. Something of Spinoza's inner strength and personal bravery is indicated by two incidents toward the end of his life. In 1670, while living in The Hague, Spinoza received a small annuity from Jan de Witt, Grand Pensionary of the Netherlands and an enlightened advocate of religious freedom. De Witt was accused of treachery in 1671 when England joined forces with France against the Netherlands; an angry mob seized de Witt and his brother and beat them to death. In an uncharacteristic display of recklessness, Spinoza was prepared to confront the mob and denounce their barbarism, but he was dissuaded from this course of action. Later, in 1677, following his appointment to a peace mission to France, Spinoza too came under suspicion as a spy; his house in The Hague was besieged by an enraged mob; again Spinoza was prepared to try and face down the crowd despite the possibility that he might be killed in the same manner as de Witt.

However, these are incidents untypical of Spinoza's life, most of which was spent in independence and simplicity; he was stoical in outlook, and dedicated to intellectual and scholarly pursuits. Fortunately he was able to discuss his philosophical views with tolerant Protestant friends. He was uncomplaining, and cautious; suspicious of violent emotions (which is not to say he was unfamiliar with them), knowing well their destructive power; but he did not thereby lack either charm or warmth. He smoked a pipe, and liked to drink beer. He was unmarried, thinking that such emotional attachment would disrupt his scholarly study; although it seems that he had been disappointed in love early in life. The consumption from which he had suffered for many years, aggravated perhaps by the glass dust he breathed in his work as a lens grinder, claimed his life in 1677. Spinoza's interests wandered freely across mathematics and the various sciences. Among Spinoza's modest library there was the Bible, books of Euclidean geometry, works on optics, and astronomy. This apparently likable man was vilified both during and after his life, variously as heretic and atheist.

Spinoza's correspondence aids our understanding of his philosophy: that with Henry Oldenburg, who became secretary of the new Royal Society in London, but most important that with the scientist Tschirnhaus. In 1676 Spinoza was visited by Leibniz; he overcame Spinoza's initial wariness to the extent that Spinoza allowed him access to the unpublished *Ethics*. Spinoza also became acquainted with Christiaan Huygens who originated the modern theories of optics, and corresponded with Robert Boyle, the founder of chemistry.

There are probably three main influences on Spinoza's philosophical views: scholastic Aristotelianism transmitted through the early Jewish thinker Maimonides (1135–1204); Cartesian philosophy; and the works of Hobbes. Spinoza came to reject, or modify massively, all of these influences.

To gain full understanding of Spinoza, it is the *Ethics* on which one must concentrate. The *Ethics* is a work of stupendous ambition. Spinoza aims to connect how the world necessarily really is at its deepest level with the practical concern of how we should live our lives and attain a blessed peace (*acquiescentia*) of mind. This project has a good deal to do with ways of controlling, but not eliminating, the emotions; emotional states and reactions are inextricably linked to beliefs; if we see that certain of the beliefs we hold are false, we can thereby change the emotions connected with those beliefs. This suggests that through a form of cognitive therapy there can be some control over emotions.

The *Ethics* is set out in a form which follows the methods of geometric proof: using axioms, definitions, and postulates, from which propositions are inferred by deductive reasoning. It uses a highly abstract and technical language, much of which derives from the medieval scholastic tradition – although its views are quite opposed to scholastic metaphysics. Spinoza aims to start from first principles which he thinks self-evidently true, and then logically deduce what consequences follow; thus the propositions that follow are proved and necessarily true. The definitions are not merely stipulative (arbitrarily laying down how a word will be used); they are meant to be true of the objects to which they refer; they are "real definitions" which can be true or false because they aim to give the necessary and sufficient conditions for their reference being what it is; that is, such definitions give a thing's essential features. Nevertheless, the definitions often depart greatly from common usage. The axioms are both self-evident and primitive: they are obviously true, and not derivable from anything simpler.

The heart of Spinoza's philosophy is the nature of *substance*. Certain aspects of the world seem to be dependent on other aspects for their nature and existence; if anything in the world is ultimately real in being fully independent – and we are not to embark on an infinite regress – we must reach something that does not depend for its nature and existence on anything else. The rationalist contention is that by chasing down the ladder of dependence, our *intellect* or *reason* will reveal what satisfies the conditions for ultimately independent being which is fully self-explanatory and explains everything else, so nothing whatsoever is left unexplained. The universe as a whole must have no superfluous features in its nature or existence that are inexplicable in being not deducible from its total concept. Spinoza is dissatisfied with Descartes' analysis of substance; Descartes' notion of the "created substances" mind and matter is for Spinoza a mistake because they are not fully self-explanatory. There are, for Spinoza, two main conditions which must be satisfied for something to be regarded as a substance:

(a) Whether that thing is self-subsistent or self-caused (*causa sui*): that which has the most independent sort of nature and existence and does not owe its nature and existence to anything else.

(b)   Whether that thing can be totally conceived – understood or explained – through itself alone, without involving any conception of another thing outside it.

And there is a third point to be borne in mind which ultimately derives from Aristotle:

(c)   A substance is that which is a subject (ultimately: *always* a subject) and not a predicate (ultimately: *never* a predicate). It is the subject of predication, and not predicated of anything; it is what remains the same through changes in predication.

So substance is that which is self-caused, self-explanatory, and the ultimate subject of all predication. This amounts to saying that true substance must be such that all of its features are deducible from its essence.

Spinoza is committed to some form of the ontological argument: God, and only God, exists necessarily, since God's essence involves existence; it would therefore be a contradiction to suppose God did not exist. So God exists and, moreover, only God can fulfil the conditions for substance, therefore there can be only one substance. It is a mistake to regard mind and matter as substances: they are not fully self-subsistent, but are dependent modes or manifestations of God. Only God includes existence among the necessary and sufficient conditions defining His nature. A true substance must be that which contains within itself, as part of its essence, the *complete* explanation of its nature and existence.

This complete causal autonomy and explanatory autonomy amount to the same thing. If we have a clear and distinct conception of things, which we derive from self-evident truths intuited by the intellect, then the consequent logical deductive links between the concepts will correspond to causal links between things. In this way, the underlying structure of the world is seen to be one reflected in necessary deductive links. This conflates (in a way unsatisfactory to empiricists such as Hume) causal connections with logical necessity so that: if A causes B, then B is logically deducible from A.

It is vital to understand that Spinoza thinks that the intellect can ideally attain a system of concepts which represents the underlying nature of the world as a whole; and that a complete explanation of the world would be constituted by laying out all the deductive logical interrelations between these concepts.

Spinoza's concept of God is not one of a transcendent God who stands outside the world; Spinoza writes of "God or Nature" (*Deus sive Natura*); God is to be identified with the totality of the universe. Spinoza's view of God is sometimes regarded as pantheistic. The totality of the universe includes more than that which is material. God is infinite and unlimited; unless one contradicts this, there can be nothing which is not "in" God; that is, there is nothing which is not dependent on God both ontologically and for its explanation. There can only be a single substance; there cannot be a plurality of substances. Substance in Spinoza has upon it the extremely restricting definition that it must be completely self-caused (*causa sui*) and must be entirely self-explanatory; and this eliminates the traditional distinction with respect to *true substance* between having necessary and contingent properties; that is, necessary properties given by an essence or definition, and accidental or contingent properties, derived from the conception of another thing that is an external cause; to be a true substance all its states must follow necessarily or deductively from its essence or definition, otherwise it would not be completely independent in being its own complete explanation. Spinoza identifies true substance with God or the totality of nature because only that can satisfy the conditions of a true substance by being fully the cause and explanation of itself; it satisfies these conditions simply because, by being the totality of what there is, there is nothing else that is required to be, or could be, its cause or involved in its explanation.

To suggest that there could be two or more substances would be to suppose the following.

(i)   To suppose something – assuming that everything has to be rationally explicable – outside the plurality of putative substances which explains the plurality; but then this contradicts the definition that true substance must be entirely self-explanatory.

(ii)   To suppose that a substance could be limited; but limitation entails that part of the explanation, and thus of the cause, for the substance being as it is does not lie within it, but depends on another thing outside it explaining its limitation; but then something limited like that could not be a true substance because true substance is by definition fully self-explanatory.

There are two alternatives here in talking of a plurality of substances: there could be two or more substances with *different* attributes or essences, or two or more substances with the *same* attribute or essence.

(a)   The possibility of there being two substances with different attributes is ruled out by the definition of God as having all attributes; God, as it were, uses up all possible attributes, so if there is a substance other than God, it must have the same attributes as God.

(b)   So if there is more than one substance, then those substances must have the same attributes.

Spinoza therefore aims to show that there cannot be two or more substances with the same attributes – the same essence. If they differ in attributes, then we have two substances with different attributes, which is not what we are looking for. If two things differ only in mode, and modes are modes of substance and not themselves substances, then a difference merely in modes does not mark a difference in substance; since we are by hypothesis dealing with a difference only in mode, and not in attribute, the modes must be modes of the same substance; two things that differ only in mode are therefore essentially the same, and are not therefore different substances.

Moreover, we would have no reason to regard "two things" with the same attributes – differing merely numerically – as two; for there is no sense in which they could be distinguished, since all their features are dependent upon their attributes, or essence, which are here posited to be the same; a difference in modes would involve a difference in attributes in the case of true substance, since all its features must depend only on itself; this means there cannot be two true substances differing only in mode and not in attribute as well.

There cannot be a difference in substance apart from a difference in attributes, so there cannot be two substances with the same attributes. But there cannot be two substances with different attributes either, because of the definition of God as a being of infinite attributes. So there cannot be more than one substance.

Hence, true substance is utterly *causa sui*, cause of itself, and for this to hold true, there can be only one substance. This unique unlimited substance must have infinite attributes – that is, all possible attributes – each of which is infinite in its kind. True substance is God or Nature, and is theoretically conceivable in an infinity of ways, of which our intellect truly grasps just two: we conceive the world under the attribute of *thought* or under the attribute of *extension*; these are what the intellect perceives of substance as constituting its essence. Thus Descartes' two "created substances", mind and matter, are properly seen as attributes of the one substance, not themselves two substances.

The notion of something being the cause of itself (*causa sui*) may seem incomprehensible. For A to cause itself to exist would seem to involve A existing before A exists. But the notion of causation involved here is that of logical deduction; the existence and nature of A is caused by A in the same sense as the theorems of a geometry follow from the axioms; and here the sense of *following from* is entirely non-temporal; it does involves not succession in time, but rather a non-temporal logical relation.

The notion of two attributes is partly understood as two perspectives on the same thing – analogous to two sides of the same coin – but here the "perspectives" are intellectual, not spatial, points of view. There are two systems of concepts which represent or express the order of the same thing in two ways, such that each way of talking is irreducible to the other; explanations in both systems or schemes take place by logical deduction using the concepts within that system only;

the two systems of concepts, within each of which there are logical links, are irreducible one to the other; they are incommensurable. They are two completely autonomous ways of looking at the same thing.

All that we observe in the world as particular things are either modes of the attribute of extension (physical things) or modes of the attribute of thought (ideas, which make up minds); all things are thus a determinate expression of the essence of God. Infinite modes are those features that are common to all modes that fall under a certain attribute: motion and rest in the case of physical particles, and ideas in the case of thoughts. Finite modes are the more particular features of the world. Thus an infinite mode under the attribute of extension would be described by a law of nature that applied to all physical things, whereas a finite mode such as the red of this book is a particular feature of the book and is not a feature common to all physical things. The explanation of the existence and nature of particular modes derives either from the essence of that mode, something that lies within it "in so far as it is in itself", or something external to that mode, something that lies outside it. God or nature as a totality is the only thing which has within it the complete explanation of its existence and nature; all other things are modes which are determinate cases of God expressed under the attribute of either thought or extension, and to varying degrees their explanation lies outside such modes; but in any case the full explanation must ultimately be traced back to the nature or essence of God.

This begins to move us from metaphysics to epistemology. Spinoza thinks that the logical order of ideas (their logical relations) is the same as the connection of things (their causal relations). The perfect, or fully "adequate", understanding of the world would be attained if we could see how everything was deducible from the essence of God. We would then see how everything in the world follows by *logical necessity* from God's eternally fixed nature. This is more than determinism: it is necessitarianism. One might have a variety of sets of axioms from which different theorems could be deduced, which would constitute their explanation or proof. But these proofs are conditional or hypothetical in that they depend on the acceptance of the axioms: *if* one accepts the axioms, *then* the theorems follow by logical necessity, so that to accept the axioms (premises) and deny the theorems (conclusions) would imply a logical contradiction. In the completely adequate science of the world (falling under the attributes of extension and thought) there is only one possible axiom set: the essence of God. So the world is not explained in conditional truths deduced from a set of basic truths which we might reject in favour of some alternative set; the world follows unconditionally from God's nature, which it would be absurd to suppose could be different from what it is. God is perfect, so any change in God would produce imperfection in God; God cannot be other than what He is. On similar grounds Spinoza opposes final cause or purposive or teleological explanations. God's nature stands immutably and eternally the same; it stands outside time. So this world not only follows in every detail, when properly understood, with logical necessity from God's nature, this world is also the only logically possible world. Not only is each link in the series deductively connected with other links, the series itself is the only logically possible series – the series itself as a whole is logically necessary. Presumably this means any other series, and hence world, would produce within it a logical contradiction.

The notion of a completely perfect conception of the world derives from Spinoza's doctrine of "adequate ideas". The world, and features of it, are always viewable under its two expressions of thought and extension; these two worlds run in irreducible parallel; they are isomorphic. From this metaphysics it follows that for every idea there is a corresponding physical correlate, an *ideatum*. This does not mean there cannot be false ideas, since truth involves more than mere correspondence of an idea to some *ideatum*; the idea must also be an adequate idea; this involves more than the external correspondence to the object the idea purports to be an idea of; it must also represent the true nature of the object represented. It is clear that Spinoza is using the term "true" in a way different from common usage. For an idea to be true in Spinoza's sense it must not only correspond to the facts, but must also be known to be true and one must know the nature of the object to which the idea corresponds; only then is an idea said to be adequate and true. Thus falsity is a privation of knowledge; although an idea that failed to correspond to the facts would also be false. To have an adequate idea of X involves understanding X, that is, knowing the causes of X being as it is; this involves explaining X by deducing it from other adequate ideas. Ultimately the chain of adequate ideas is traced back to axiomatic necessary truths and concepts called "common notions". An inadequate idea is like a conclusion without premises. An idea is more or less adequate in so far as it fits into a more or less general system of explanation; the system will be more general and powerful to the extent that features of the world can be unified and deduced from it by deductive reasoning. An idea becomes more adequate – thus adequacy is a matter of degree – by fitting as a deducible conception within an ever wider, and more inclusive, unifying, explanatory system. Complete adequacy would involve fitting in the idea or conception deductively with the system describing the order of the totality of things; ultimately this is the ideal system contemplated by God. The completely adequate system of ideas will ultimately be deducible from universally acceptable "common notions" that are seen as evident by intuitive reason: these are the axiomatic necessary truths and basic concepts of Spinoza's science and metaphysics that comprehend or constitute the logically necessary and essential features of the universe.

An adequate idea gives an intrinsic mark of truth, as distinct from the extrinsic mark whereby an idea merely corresponds to its object; a completely adequate idea does not merely correspond to its *ideatum*; it presents to us the true nature of, or understanding of, its *ideatum*. A false idea is one that is inadequate; we know it corresponds to an *ideatum*, but it will misrepresent, and fail to explain, the nature of that *ideatum*, by failing to place the idea in the deductive system of explanation which is constituted by a coherent system of ideas that represents the true order of things. To have an adequate or true idea of X is to understand X, which is to explain X, which is to know the causes of X. The criterion of truth is given by features of ideas or propositions themselves and the logical relation of proof between them, and not by a mere comparison of ideas and the world; the determination of what is true and what we know about the world is available to us within the circle of ideas themselves in the form of intuitions of reason giving "common notions" and necessary logical deductions from these notions. At the level of completely adequate ideas there turns out to be an exact agreement between ideas and reality.

We can use a spatial perspectival example to understand the notion of the completely adequate science. What I now see is in a way true only from my perspective, my point of view; if I moved, or if I were different biologically, what I see would be different – my view is in this way particular. The aim of an adequate understanding is to see things from no point of view; that is, to subtract all those features which make my point of view mine or a mere point of view. The intellect already provides us with such radically non-perspectival truths: $2+2=4$, for example. This is true from all points of view; its truth is unconditional in not depending on any qualifying reference to a perspective. Such is the nature of fully adequate ideas of the world; these are found in rationally universally valid "common notions" and deductions from them.

This rules out sense-perception as a means of attaining adequate ideas of the world; we are to aim for an intellectual conception of the world freed from the mixing of things in the world with their effect upon us in terms of bodily processes. When we observe the sun, the *ideatum* of the idea we have we confusedly think is the sun itself, whereas the *ideatum* is really, in the sense of its physical correlate, that bodily process corresponding to the perception of the sun, which is a result of the effect of the sun on us. This is not a great problem provided we come to understand the nature of our perceptions themselves; in isolation the ideas of perception are not false, but may become so – hence they are inadequate or untrue – when placed within a wider explanatory context. A true, and thus adequate, idea, of the sun as it is in itself will be approached by its deduction from other ideas as part of a general science of physical things, the concepts of which are grasped by the intellect, and this will replace the "false", inadequate, idea of sense-perception. The completely adequate system of ideas places each idea in a totality of ideas such that the deductive relation of the ideas represents the true order of causes in the world. This is the world as understood by the intellect of God, who is identical with the world.

Ultimately Spinoza's completely adequate view of the world is *sub specie aeternitatis* – the view from eternity, from outside time, from no point of view. This is opposed to *sub specie durationis* – the view of things as happening in time. God has such an eternal, non-temporal view of the world; it should be our aim to participate in such a view. We already have such non-temporal universal truths in mathematics and geometry; it is senseless to apply time or duration to the truth $2+2=4$; it is more than always true, its truth lies outside time altogether, in eternity; the concept of duration has no application here at all. Spinoza thinks that a true, hence completely adequate, explanation of the world can be attained only through a view which is similarly *sub specie aeternitatis*; the view outside time is the final step in ridding a conception of all perspectives; one would then have the eternal, necessary, *a priori* deductive explanation for everything. Some of these truths we can grasp; but our finite minds enable us to grasp only a small fraction of them.

There are three levels or kinds of knowledge. The first kind of knowledge is sense-experience, the second kind of knowledge is deductive reasoning, the third kind of knowledge is immediate intuition of reason.

Sense-perceptions can be useful in giving us limited knowledge of particular facts and in the forming of inductive generalizations. Our finite minds cannot trace the infinity of causes that would give us fully adequate ideas of the objects of sense-perception. Our finite minds cannot cope with the infinite complexity of deducing truths concerning finite modes ("A red book is on my desk") all the way back to the essence of God. Knowledge of the third kind, intuitions of reason, is the highest form of understanding. There we not only have ideas giving logical explanations by being related deductively to premises, as in the second kind of knowledge, we also simply grasp the proof complete in one intellectual act by seeing the rule in the instance. In the case of sense-perceptions, we are presented with one inadequate, fragmentary, logically unconnected idea after another (which is correlated with inadequately understood states of the body) with no real possibility of the order of presentation reflecting the true order of causes. Sense-perception is not needed and cannot give knowledge of the essence of things; in so far as we do not distinguish a thing from its essence, we can deduce its nature from its definition.

Sense-perception can give knowledge *that* but not knowledge *why*, which involves deducing the necessity of that perceived to be the case. Nevertheless, sense-perception presents a low-level sort of knowledge since it can satisfy what seem to be Spinoza's three conditions for knowledge that *p*:
(a)   *p* corresponds to what is the case
(b)   there is no reason to doubt that *p* (that is not to say *p* cannot be doubted)
(c)   there is a good reason to assert that *p* is the case (it is not a guess).
Sense-experience as the ground for the assertion of either particular facts or inductive generalizations seems to satisfy these conditions. Knowledge in its highest senses of the second and third kind, which involve deductive proof or logical necessity, clearly satisfies the above conditions for knowledge, but to a higher degree.

The third kind of knowledge is the kind of understanding God has of things in their totality derived from "common notions". God's view of the world *sub specie aeternitatis* telescopes down the process of deductive reasoning involved in comprehension of the totality of the world to one intellectual "point". Time is thus ultimately unreal from a God's-eye point of view. The ultimate explanation of the world lies within the world; the world is fully explicable as a self-contained system.

The general metaphysical conclusions are reflected in the Spinozian response to the mind–body problem: ontological monism (a single substance) is combined with a conceptual dualism (double-aspect). A human being is viewed as mind or as body – these are two aspects of the same thing; indeed, the *ideatum* of the mind is the human body. This does not mean one is always conscious of one's body; it alerts us to a dual use of "idea of" in Spinoza. First, there is that derived from ideas being expressions in thought of that which is expressed under the attribute of extension; second there is the sense in which I have an idea *about* some object. In the case of an idea of a table there is the first meaning of the "idea of" the table, in the sense of the idea being an expression in thought of some state of my body affected by the table (that which may be involved in seeing the table); there is the second, different, meaning of "idea of" in the sense of my idea being about the table – its content or object is the table. In this second sense ideas are said to be active and to exhibit intentionality: they point beyond themselves to an intended object.

There can be no *causal* relation between mind and body; mind concepts and body concepts are incommensurable so that logical deductions, and hence causal laws, which included talk from both ways of conceptualizing substance would be senseless. The relation between the two systems of concepts is like that between two autonomous languages which can say or express the same things each in its different way. There is some relation between mind and body: it is the correlation between determinate states of two attributes of one substance. The complexity of thought of which a mind is capable is therefore directly matched by the complexity of the body; a human being is capable of complex thought processes, and this has its correlate in the complexity of the human body. This means that although every physical mode (*ideatum*) under the aspect of extension has its corresponding idea, most things lack the necessary complexity to be capable of conscious thought. Spinoza is not committed to stones or chairs thinking; but the difference between them and us is only one of great degree.

A human being is one kind of finite mode of the one infinite substance. What gives meaning to the notion of any finite mode having limited individuality is our *conatus* (striving, endeavour or power): the endeavour to maintain its integrity or persist in being against the effects of external causes. The nature or essence of a finite mode is that without which it would cease to exist as what it is even as a qualified individual, and would collapse under external causes. In so far as the states of a thing are deducible from its nature or essence, that is the *conatus* or power of that thing in self-preservation. This will vary in degree and kind. The greater the *conatus*, the more self-dependent it is and the more that through its essence, it expresses power of self-preservation, power which is ultimately derived from and expresses the power of the only truly independent individual, God. Higher level finite modes such as organisms obviously exhibit *conatus*: they try to persist in being what they are – a man, a dog – with some degree of individuality. The greater our *conatus* the more we realize our essence as rational beings; but this seems to produce a conflict with our individuality, for we then have a view from which we appreciate our connectedness with the whole of nature. No finite mode can be ultimately self-explanatory of course, but the degree of independence is determined by the balance between the derived "active" (internal) explanation of its states and the "passive" (external) explanation of its states.

A result of this is that no thing can be the cause of its own destruction; the destruction of a thing is always through an external cause. This is because the *conatus* of a thing is its essence, and its essence revealed in a definition affirms what it is; thus in so far as a thing is considered only in itself, in virtue of its essence, it cannot be destroyed as that thing. This seems to make suicide impossible. But Spinoza can answer that suicide is a case of being overwhelmed by external causes. However, cases of rationally defensible self-sacrifice complicate matters; the answer relates to Spinoza's conception of freedom as acting in accordance with universal rational principles.

Freedom does not consist in our being able to do otherwise than we do; it is not contrasted with necessity; it is understood in opposition to constraint. Everything that exists is necessary either by reason of its essence or by reason of an external cause (another finite mode); everything that does not exist is impossible either by reason of its essence containing a contradiction, or for want of an external (efficient) cause. The external chain of causation is ultimately necessary by deriving from God's essence; the impression we have of contingency is merely the consequence of ignorance of causes. We are free in so far as the explanation of what we do derives from our conative disposition to behave in certain ways, as our essential natures meet each situation. The exact nature of the *conatus* will vary between organisms. There is nothing that is good or bad in itself; things are good or bad only in relation to some conative disposition; things are good or bad for someone or some kind of thing. Everything is free "in so far as it is in itself': that is, in so far as the explanation for what it does is derived from its essence, which determines what it is. In this sense God is absolutely free; not because what follows from His nature could be any different from what it is – not because He could have "acted" otherwise – but because God is totally self-determined, and thus totally unconstrained. We are in a state of bondage in so far as we are the slaves of external determinations and circumstances. This does not mean we should live without emotion, but we should, in order to be free, have *active* emotions following from reasoning; we should control our *passive* emotions which are derived from external causes. In so far as a man is externally caused, he acts under the influence of inadequate ideas, failing to see how events must follow by logical necessity from one another. The free man acts under the dictates of reason, by the active causal determination of an internal logic; the principles of reason are *universal*, thus in so far as we act because of reason we make ourselves free in virtue of acting from causes independent of particular circumstances.

This returns us to adequate ideas and their metaphysical connection with Spinoza's search for human happiness, contentment and freedom. To understand this we have to remember that Spinoza conflates logical and causal necessity. In so far as we entertain adequate ideas, our ideas follow one another by their internal logic, a logic that is independent of external causes. The explanation for the occurrence of one idea, in so far as it is adequate, will be found in its logical deduction from previous ideas; this gives a logical and causal integrity, a self-sufficient, self-contained system based on universal rational principles independent of external explanations and hence external causes. There will be some bodily equivalent to this mental aspect of human beings and in this sense we are free. What human *conatus* ultimately seeks to preserve is this power of self-determination itself. It reaches its highest degree when ideas are *sub specie aeternitatis* because such ideas are absolutely necessary and universally true.

We are free when we act according to reason because the dictates

of reason are necessary, universal, categorical and thus independent
of context or particular situation. We act independently of contingent
particular external causes and circumstances if we act by reason: we
are then free.

Passive human emotions are controlled by reason to the highest
degree under the third kind of knowledge; for then the truth I grasp
is not an abstract deduction, but is intuited irresistibly in the particular case; thereby it becomes not a truth I merely rationally accept, but
one that has *force* or *power* to effect changes in my emotional states.
The inference has force as well as validity. But since Spinoza is a strict
determinist, it is difficult to see what someone can *do* to bring about
the attitudes Spinoza thinks desirable; either one will be determined
to have them or one will not.

Our aim should be the attainment of a view of the world that is
detached and eternal. By striving for the completely adequate view
which is *sub specie aeternitatis*, of which only God is fully capable, one
comes to see the strict logical necessity of all that happens; all follows
from God's immutable nature by logical necessity. We can thus reconcile ourselves to the necessity of things. It no more makes sense to
hate a man who hits us than it makes sense to hate a tree that falls on
us; although in both cases this does not preclude our trying to do
anything about it, like getting out of the way – but we understand the
necessity of what happens through reason.

Although there seems nothing we can do to bring about human
happiness and peace of mind, they nevertheless consist in having a
certain attitude toward the world. The wise man engages in a life of
philosophical contemplation studying the rational and eternal: a life
of relative independence from the buffeting vicissitudes and unreli-
ability of particular circumstance, one which gives enduring pleasure
and grants peace of mind; the troubled mind is alleviated when one
views the world and events in one's life *sub specie aeternitatis*. The
rational understanding that God is the ultimate eternal cause of all
things is what Spinoza calls the "intellectual love of God". To the
extent that we entertain conceptions or ideas *sub specie aeternitatis*, we
free ourselves from the bondage of time, since such conceptions are
absolutely necessary and have no temporal reference; and it is in this
that our ultimate happiness lies; to the extent that we do this, we
participate in God's eternal vision and the eternal existence which is
God's existence.

Leibniz

Gottfried Wilhelm Leibniz (1646–1716) was the son of a Professor of
Moral Philosophy at the University of Leipzig. Leibniz's early

education, with a Lutheran religious background, would have involved the study of Latin, Greek, theology, and Aristotelian logic. He graduated from the University of Leipzig in 1663, and gained his doctorate in 1666 from the University of Altdorf near Nuremberg. He began his employment with the Baron of Boineburg who was first minister to the Elector and Archbishop of Mainz, but in 1667, following the death of Boineburg, he moved into the service of the Duke of Brunswick in Hanover. One of his major duties was that of librarian. Between 1672 and 1676, Leibniz was on a diplomatic mission in Paris, which was at that time the centre of European intellectual activity. There he met important thinkers such as Malebranche, Arnauld (with whom Leibniz corresponded extensively), and the physicist Huygens. Huygens, recognizing the talent of Leibniz, set about improving Leibniz's mathematical knowledge. In Paris Leibniz would have been fully apprised of Cartesian philosophy. In 1673 Leibniz visited London, where he met the chemist Boyle and the Secretary of the Royal Society, Oldenburg; on this visit he also became acquainted with the materialism of Hobbes. In 1676 Leibniz went to Amsterdam in the hope that he would find, in the work of Spinoza, answers to some of the problems he perceived in Cartesian philosophy. He spent a month there; some of the time was spent reading Spinoza's *Ethics*, some in discussion with the ailing Spinoza.

There were many influences on Leibniz's philosophy; apart from those already mentioned, he was impressed by Plato's *Phaedo* and *Theaetetus* and well acquainted with scholastic philosophy (derived from Aristotle) – for example the notion of substantial forms.

Leibniz was a stupendous polymath, active in almost every imaginable area of inquiry, from geology and mining engineering to philosophy, mathematics and logic. He was indeed a mathematician of genius, and discovered independently, and simultaneously with Newton, the infinitesimal calculus. His fertility of mind left an array of unfinished projects. Leibniz was a man capable of bouts of intense intellectual activity; he is said to have spent several days at a time sitting working at his desk – even sleeping in his chair. He suffered from intellectual isolation in Hanover, where he spent most of his time. During Leibniz's lifetime there were few academic journals, and letters were the chief means of exchanging ideas. Leibniz's correspondence is massive involving over 1,000 correspondents; in any single year he frequently wrote to more than 150 people. He hoped that one day all reasoning in various fields of inquiry could be united in one system, a universal calculus of all reasoning, which would eliminate fruitless disputes; answers to disagreements could be settled simply by calculation.

Leibniz never married; he proposed, but the woman hesitated long enough for him to think better of it. He was of medium height, with sharply intelligent eyes; he had broad shoulders, but stooped and had weak lungs. The last years of his life were ones of loneliness and neglect. No member of the House of Brunswick bothered to attend his funeral.

The philosophy of Leibniz is not like a building based on unshakable foundations, it is more like a platform kept in balance by constant adjustments to the weight put upon various fundamental logical principles. These basic principles in Leibniz's philosophy are logically interconnected; and for this reason it has no definitive starting place.

In Leibniz's philosophy there is an intimate connection between metaphysics and the fundamental nature of logic. This is a view which has ancestors and heirs: it suggests that conclusions in and about the basic structures of logic lay bare the basic structures of the world. Certain important truths derived from logic are seen by Leibniz as having consequences for any attempt to explain the *fundamental* nature of the world which is studied in metaphysics. Probably the best approach to Leibniz is to state what the basic truths of his thinking are, and then proceed to see how he uses them to solve certain philosophical problems. There are five major basic principles in the philosophy of Leibniz.

(1)   *The predicate-in-subject principle: the nature of the proposition*
      This "*inesse* principle" holds that, in *all* true propositions that which is predicated of a subject is contained within the concept of the subject. All propositions are ultimately reducible to the subject–predicate form. This gives a theory of truth in which in all and only true propositions the predicates are contained in the concept of the subject; all analytic propositions are true and all true propositions are analytic.

(2)   *The principle of non-contradiction*
      This asserts that propositions p and not-p cannot both be true, and that any proposition that implies a contradiction is necessarily false; and any proposition whose denial implies a contradiction is necessarily true.

(3)   *The identity of indiscernibles*
      This says that there cannot be two entities which have *all* their properties in common. Entities which are identical in their lists of qualities are the same entity; they are indiscernible.

(4)   *The principle of sufficient reason*
      There must be a sufficient reason (complete explanation) why everything in the world is just so and not otherwise, even if we cannot know what that reason is. There are to be admitted no inexplicable truths about the world.

(5)   *The principle of perfection*
      Those propositions which describe the most perfect world – the best of all possible worlds – are true. This amounts to saying that God creates the most perfect world He can and it involves the notion that the most perfect world is "simplest in hypoth-

eses and richest in phenomena"; God maximizes both plenitude or variety of phenomena and order or simplicity of explanatory hypotheses.

Leibniz makes a fundamental distinction in his logic between "truths of reason" (necessary or eternal truths) and "truths of fact" (contingent truths). Truths of reason are those truths which, by a finite analysis, show that their denial produces a contradiction, that is, an assertion of (p and not-p). To assert a necessary truth is, on analysis, to assert an identity. The analysis is a process of definitional substitution: for example, $1+1$ being substituted by definition for 2. Thus, to assert $2+2=4$ is ultimately to assert $1+1+1+1=1+1+1+1$; to deny $2+2=4$ would obviously produce the contradiction that $1+1+1+1 \neq 1+1+1+1$. To allow that (p and not-p) could be true would be to threaten the possibility of all meaningful talk, since we would fail to make the most basic distinction required for any such talk, that between assertion and denial. The assertion that p, and its denial, not-p, cannot simultaneously be true. Truths of fact do not, if denied, entail a contradiction; to deny "Alan is wearing a green shirt" does not seem to involve any contradiction. Truths of reason are necessary truths in that they could not be otherwise; they must be true; in any possible world these truths must hold. Truths of fact are contingent, they could have been otherwise; they might not have been true; there could be possible worlds in which these truths do not hold. Leibniz accepts that truths of reason can be known independently of any sense-experience, *a priori*; whereas truths of fact can be known only through examining the world, *a posteriori*.

Leibniz argues that although the meanings of the terms of a language may to some degree be a matter of arbitrary definition, this does not mean that either the contingent or the necessary truths expressed in a language are dependent on contingent facts about language; the only thing that is contingent is the particular form the *expression* of such truths takes, not the logical status of the truths themselves as either necessary or contingent. This distinction between the truth expressed and the form of expression of a truth is particularly important in the case of necessary truths, which he sees as eternal and objective.

At first sight Leibniz's philosophy can seem obviously false; some of the basic principles listed above, far from being universal truths, seem plainly false when applied to the world. For example, surely it is *possible* (probable even) to have two identical objects? Surely it is far from obvious that all truths are true in virtue of the predicates being contained in the concept of their subject? It becomes clear, however, that what Leibniz is applying the basic principles to is the *underlying structure of reality*; this reality is a metaphysical reality that stands behind the world as it *appears*; it is grasped by the intellect by an inexorable logic as the way the world is and *must* (necessarily) be at its most fundamental level if the most basic truths of reason are to hold. If we accept Leibniz's basic principles, then he argues that the nature of reality is not how it appears to be, but really quite different. This is to characterize substance, or the really real.

The examination of this underlying structure can begin by considering substance. In Cartesian philosophy there are two "created substances": mind and matter. In Spinoza there is just a single substance: "God or Nature". What the Cartesian view seems to leave out is an account of the individual, or identity. As we look around us it seems obvious that some things are separate individuals capable of remaining the same *individual kind* of thing while undergoing change, whereas other things are merely "heaps" or collections of qualities with no intrinsic unity. Compare a pile of pebbles, which is not a kind of thing, with a crab found on a beach. Scholastic philosophy, derived from Aristotle, had sought to take account of this through the notion of "substantial forms". Thus, the soul is the substantial form of the body, for whatever may befall someone, so long as that person exists the soul remains the same soul; without some such notion we cannot make sense of someone being young and that same someone being old; any change would, strictly speaking, produce a new entity, not the same entity with a new property. The notion of individuals here aims to do justice to the distinction we make between things which have an intrinsic organic unity as *kinds* of thing, such as men and dogs have, and things which are mere heaps of stuff, such as a pile of pebbles. But in pursuing things that are true unities or true individuals, Leibniz moves a long way beyond the Aristotelian common-sense substantial forms which are natural kinds such as man or horse.

In the case of physical things the identification of real unities (things that remain the *same kind* through change) is relatively unimportant; it is possible to say that all physical things are portions of a single extended substance. In the case of the person as mind, individuality becomes of pressing concern; identity in this case is of vital importance. Spinoza challenges the Cartesians to provide a principle of individuating minds; if the only essential attribute of mind is thought, it is difficult to see how there can be a plurality of distinct mental substances or minds differentiated by essence. Spinoza's conclusion is to deny any sense of individuality as substances to either physical things or minds; they have a limited individuality at the level of modes, but are all modifications (modes) of the one substance, without any ultimate substantial independent unity of their own. Leibniz sides with the Cartesians in agreeing to a plurality of substantial individuals, but makes the claim all-encompassing; for anything in the world to be real, there must be at some deep level true unities or individuals: completely autonomous entities.

This brings us to what Leibniz calls the "labyrinth of the composition of the continuum", which leads him to his conception of substance, and thus to the ultimate nature of reality. Leibniz has the same general conditions for substance as were found in Descartes and Spinoza: that in considering the nature of the world and our explanations of that world, we must, if we are not to enter into an infinite regress, reach something which is (a) ontologically independent or autonomous, and (b) self-explanatory. Substance is the permanent stuff which stands behind appearances which are secondary or derivative. Things appear to change in the world; the explanation of these changes comes to an end at something that remains the same, otherwise the explanation would go on for ever. What is fully real is completely independent and self-explanatory; the fully real is the ultimate logically unchanging constituent of change and plurality. The explanation for anything, if we are not to regress infinitely by always having to look to another thing for an explanation outside that which we are explaining, must end in something that is fully causally autonomous and fully the explanation for its own states.

Spinoza says that within true substance must lie the full explanation of not only its nature but also its existence; and he contends that there can only be one substance, and that is the totality of reality. Leibniz demands not that a true substance should contain within itself the reason for its own existence, but only that it should contain the reason for its entire nature, that is, all its states.

In Leibniz's view, in giving a rational account of the world, we must give an account of what it is that is the ultimate constituent of reality; that which does not alter through natural change, but is, rather, the constituent of that change and, to avoid a regress of ontological dependence, is not itself subject to natural alteration. Leibniz is searching for that which, with respect to all natural means of change, cannot be destroyed and is without parts, and so is indivisible; the aggregation and dissolution of aggregates of such entities constitute all perceived change and plurality. Leibniz identifies this true substance as a *monad* (a word which derives from Greek meaning "unit alone"). Ultimately we must reach such really independent substantial unities, and each one is a unique kind, not merely a collection of parts; they do not change by natural means, but exist or do not exist all at once. They are perfectly determinate. Such entities are the only way to ensure that we have identified genuine substance; something not ontologically or rationally dependent on any further constituent elements because its existence is all or nothing; each is a unique kind that either exists complete, or ceases to exist completely; as a unique kind, if it changed in any detail, it would cease to exist altogether. The ultimate constituents of reality are an infinity of unique individual kinds called monads.

The "labyrinth of the continuum" problem involves considering the ultimate nature of the world, in particular the nature of matter. If the world is a continuous whole, then its parts would seem to be unreal arbitrary divisions; if, on the other hand, the parts are real, then the world is not a continuum, but a collection of unrelated discontinuous parts. The aim is to reconcile real wholes which are continuous with real parts that are indivisible. We can consider this as the relation of wholes to parts, and present it as a dilemma: extended whole things are either finitely or infinitely divisible. If extended wholes are finitely divisible, we reach atoms, which are real parts in being indivisible; but then the whole that they make up becomes unreal because it is discontinuous, a mere arbitrary heap of atoms between which there is no intrinsic connection. The suggestion that there are, in addition, forces between the atoms runs counter to atoms being the ultimate constituents of reality in terms of which *all* else is explained and constituted. Nor can the coherence of atoms be explained through an interlocking system of hooks and eyes; anything capable of having hooks and eyes would itself be capable of having parts in need of some internal principle of cohesion. If extended wholes are infinitely divisible, as the Cartesians thought, then the parts are unreal because we have an infinite regress of divisibility; and this gives us a whole with unreal parts. Leibniz argues, against physical atomism, that anything extended must be divisible in principle. The solution in this search for a substance which reconciles the real continuity of the world with the real indivisibility of parts is to exclude *extension* from among the qualities ascribed to substances: the most basic entities of the world. Anything that can be divided would cease to exist as one thing, and thus would be subject to external causes, and could not be a true substance.

Ultimate substances are monads which have no extension; they are purely qualitative (intensive), and have no quantitative (extensive) properties; they are independent in all respects except for their existence, for which they depend on God, and they are simple in being without parts; they can be destroyed only by total annihilation (or miracle), not natural change, for natural change is the constantly changing aggregation of monads. This notion of substance is derived by analogy from the non-spatial "I" or "soul", for it is this that remains the same through all the changes in our lives, so that we retain our identity. Monads are the unchanging constituents of all natural change, in that anything that happens in a monad is a product of its own indwelling nature. There is an infinity of monads, each of which is a unique individual kind in virtue of being identified by a unique infinite list of predicates giving all its properties.

Leibniz conjoins the contingency of existence with the principle of sufficient reason to give a proof of the existence of God. For every fact or truth there must be a sufficient reason. Granted that something exists, there must be a reason why something exists rather than nothing; this reason cannot lie within the series of existing finite things, for we would never among existing things find something whose existence did not itself require further explanation. We must find such a reason outside the world in a logically or metaphysically necessary being – a being whose existence is not contingent – which is the sufficient reason for its own existence. Another way of putting this is to say that although the state of A is explained sufficiently by reference to state B, so that we can explain this or that state from within contingent events within the world, we cannot from within the world of things with states explain why there are things with states at all, why there are any states whatsoever. This argument relies on the principle of sufficient reason having unlimited application; we might instead be prepared to argue that "Why is there something rather than nothing?" or "Why should there be anything at all?" is a question which does not have an answer; it is a brute fact beyond which we cannot go.

The world as it appears to us as matter in space and time is a set of "well-founded phenomena" (*phenomena bene fundata*); the world as it appears is our misperception of qualitative changes in the world of monads; the world of appearances is secondary, and derived from the underlying reality of an infinity of self-subsistent, self-explanatory monads which are without parts. This solves the problem of reconciling the continuity of the whole with the indivisible (simple) reality of the parts: the whole is a plenum or continuum in virtue of the adjacent monads differing infinitesimally from each other, and the parts are real in that monads, being unextended, are indivisible.

Given the conception of true substance as monads, we can now begin to apply to the world the basic principles of Leibniz's philosophy listed above. Monads, as true substances, must – except for their dependence on God for their existence – be independent of all other things, and must be completely self-explanatory; monads can be both these things by all that is true of them being true analytically. Each monad is its own *complete concept* in that it contains within its essence the list of *all* the predicates, past, present and future, which are true of that individual monad, apart from its existence. God is the only substance that exists in conjunction with all possible worlds, for unlike all other substances, that God exists is analytically part of His complete concept or essence. Although the existence of all monads except God is contingent, Leibniz sees no sense in the distinction between accidental and essential properties of substantial individuals; all properties are equally essential in being deducible from the complete concept of the monad; and substantial individuals are individuated only through considering their whole being or complete concept.

Leibniz thinks that Spinoza confuses determinism and extreme necessitarianism. While, according to the principle of sufficient reason, everything in the world must be fully determined – there must be something which is sufficiently the reason for the way it is

– this does not mean that this or any other deterministic world is the only possible deterministic world. That would involve confusing necessary and contingent truths. Leibniz makes the distinction, and derives it from the idea that all propositions are ultimately reducible to the subject-predicate form; a true proposition is such that the predicate is contained in the concept of the subject.

Necessary truths (truths of reason), such as 2+2=4, are those whose denial, in itself, implies a contradiction; they are unconditionally true in all possible worlds; they have an absolute or metaphysical necessity. Contingent truths (truths of fact) are those whose denial does not in itself imply a logical contradiction; they are, however, conditionally or hypothetically necessary when they are logically implied by some other true proposition from which it would therefore be a contradiction to deny they follow. Contingent truths (such as "Caesar crossed the Rubicon") are conditionally necessary truths, given that the individual monadic substance (Caesar), of whom the truths are predicated (crossed the Rubicon), *exists*. A proposition is *conditionally* necessary (contingent) if its denial is not a contradiction in itself, but there is some other proposition from which it logically follows. A proposition is *unconditionally* necessary if, by finite analysis, its denial is a contradiction in itself.

Unconditionally necessary truths (truths of reason) hold across all possible worlds, and cannot determine which of the infinity of possible worlds is actual. The principle of non-contradiction is sufficient to account for metaphysically necessary truths, although Leibniz also thinks such truths are eternal objective truths in being in the mind of God. But in the case of contingent truths a further reason is needed to account for why certain truths are actualized and not others. Truths are contingent because God was not ultimately logically compelled by the principle of non-contradiction to actualize those truths. The *further sufficient reason* for contingent truths – what among the non-necessary possibilities God actualizes – is found in the principle of perfection. God creates the best, or most perfect, of possible worlds from a choice of infinite possible worlds; the actual world is the one that maximizes copossibles. All possible truths strive to be actual truths in that they will be actual truths if their being true does not contradict the actualization of some other possible truth. The principle of perfection is the general test for truths of fact: the actual world is the one that maximizes both plentiful variety (diversity) and order (simplest laws). Existence is taken to be a perfection by Leibniz. All truths ultimately refer to truths about the underlying monads, so all truths are eventually analytic in that the predicates are contained in their subject; but in the case of contingent truths this analysis is infinite, because to show analyticity is equivalent to showing how that truth fits into the most perfect world.

The principle of perfection gives us a criterion of truth for choosing scientific laws: we should choose the law that explains the greatest variety of phenomena with the greatest unifying simplicity.

Being true substances, monads are their own complete explanation, except for the explanation of their existence; thus everything that is true of them is true analytically; they are fully independent; so there can be no causal interaction between them. Nevertheless, things in nature appear to interact. This appearance is accounted for by Leibniz's notion of *pre-established harmony*. Leibniz denies causal relations involving necessary connections between phenomena or between the monads; he replaces these with pre-established harmony and causal laws with functional relationships; in science we are simply concerned with the determinate way one phenomenon varies in relation to another. It is these functional relations that constitute laws of nature, not some mysterious further notion of necessary connection. Just as the existence of any monad is always contingent, and there is an infinity of possible worlds, so there is an infinity of possible laws or orders of nature. The only true causes, apart from God, in the sense of producing deductive explanations, are the states of the monads derived from within each monad itself.

Each monad is completely self-contained, but in a more or less confused way every monad mirrors the entire universe. The mirroring of the universe gives each monad a unique point of view; these constitute active states of the monads which are "perceptions"; the tendency to change between these perceptions is termed "apperception". The spontaneity of changing states of the monads reflects Leibniz's concern for dynamics; that an essential property of substance must be force or activity, contrary to the inert extended matter of Descartes. The monads have "no windows" through which anything can come in or go out; monads are substances and there can be no interaction between substances. God's initial choice of what set of monads to create arranges things so that the subsequent states of the monads are perfectly coordinated or harmonized in accordance with certain laws. This is analogous to two clocks being set at the same time: they always strike correctly together at twelve o'clock and at all other times on the hour even though they do not interact. God, in choosing this world, arranges a perfect coordination of all its monadic elements. Each monad has within it an active force whereby its states unfold. This harmonious coordination of the monads involves a mirroring by each monad of the states of *all* the other monads, which means that a change in any one monad would entail a completely different universe, for adjustments would have to be made in the systematic arrangement everywhere else. The universe is a plenum; the plenum of space corresponds to the infinitesimal qualitative differences between monads which are perfectly compacted.

The world as it appears to us in space and time is a set of "well-founded phenomena" rather than a mere illusion; that is, the world of appearances is *systematically* underpinned by states of the monads. Appearances are correlated with something that is ultimately real. Great distances in space are correlated with great qualitative differences between monads, small distances with the reverse. Time is correlated with our perceiving the unfolding of the states of the monads. All apparent relations are reducible to truths about individual monads. So we can say that the relation of A being heavier than B is reducible to a truth about A weighing five tonnes and a truth about B weighing one tonne.

We can now see why the identity of indiscernibles applies universally, as Leibniz suggests. Leibniz's principles apply to the ultimate nature of the world, not to things as they merely appear. It may be suggested that we could have two substances with identical sets of true predicates, but at different places in space. But space, as well as time, is itself something derived from truths predicated of the monads. Once we see that *all* true predicates describing all states whatsoever are contained within the ultimate monadic elements in the universe, we see that there could not be two substances with identical lists of predicates; there would be nothing left in virtue of which they could be distinguished.

Leibniz's view of the world can be summarized as follows. All reality is made up of an infinity of soul-like monads; these are true substances; they are ontologically independent of everything except God, as they depend on Him for their existence, and no two monads are alike. They are independent in the sense that all that is true of them is deducible from their full concept or essential nature. Logically necessary truths are true of all possible worlds in virtue of the principle of non-contradiction alone. Only God is such that a denial of His existence would be a contradiction; the existence of all other things is contingent. Each monad when it comes into existence goes from being an unactualized possibility to being an actualized possibility. But given that God chooses to create particular monads (basic substantial individuals), everything proceeds from the complete conception of those individuals with necessity. Thus some truths are contingent because, although given the creation of individual A all that happens to A follows with necessity, it is only hypothetical necessity, since the creation of A was not itself necessary.

The monads actualized are the reality that underlies appearances which are systematically related to those monads so that the appearances are well-founded phenomena. We explain the appearance of causation and causal laws between phenomena, which all derive from monads, by there being an analogue of strict rules governing the non-causal coordination of the states of the monads.

God cannot choose what is impossible, and any universe must include what is necessary; but among contingent truths – those truths that are neither necessary nor impossible – God chooses from among the possible, pure essences that are not actualized. There must, however, be a sufficient reason for what God chooses if the universe is to be fully rationally explicable; the reason why God chooses to actualize some contingent possibilities rather than others cannot be found in the principle of non-contradiction, since their non-actualization would not imply a contradiction; the sufficient reason is derived from the goodness of God, which means that, from an infinity of possible worlds, He chooses the best of all possible worlds; a world of maximum plenitude or variety tempered with greatest order or simplicity of explanation.

It should not be supposed from Leibniz's talk of soul-like monads inhabiting everything that everything is thereby conscious. Nevertheless, the distinction between different levels of monads is a matter of degree and is dependent on their level of activity and the clarity of their perceptions. It is in virtue of these factors being at a high level in our case that we have the capacity for reason.

We are monads. The human body is a collection of monads which is dominated by the powerful monad of the human mind: the "I" in us. Leibniz's doctrine of pre-established harmony solves the Cartesian mind–body interaction problem; there is now no mystery concerning interaction for it is only an appearance, but one that is well-founded in the coordination of the monads. The appearance of mind–body interaction is the coordination of the mind-monad and the body-monads, and this is just a special case of monad harmonization. There is no more difficulty in explaining this than there is the coordination between any other monads in the universe; God so arranges things from their inception. The monads that correspond to the telephone ringing are perfectly harmonized with the monad which is myself having the experience of the telephone ringing, without the experience of the ringing being caused by the ringing itself. The intimate nature of the relation between the mind/self-monad and its body-monads, is accounted for by the special characteristics of my perceptions in relation to my body-monads. I am a structured aggregate of monads, structured by the degree of activity and clarity of perception of the monads. The dominant monad is that which has the greatest degree of activity and clarity. Leibniz distinguishes three levels of monads: self-conscious monads; conscious monads; unconscious or bare monads.

A remaining question concerns human freedom. The notion of human freedom in the sense of choosing otherwise at a particular moment seems irreconcilable with all truths concerning substantial individuals, such as particular people, being analytic truths. Although the predicates true of an existing individual are only hypothetically necessary, since they depend upon God's original decree to create *that individual* of which the predicates are true, this does not seem sufficient for freedom. It makes all that I do contingent in the sense that there is no logical contradiction in supposing that the specific individual that is me might not have been created at all to do what I do. But, given God's decision to actualize the possible pure essence A_1, and thereby create monad A_1 in particular, then its states, $(a, b, c \ldots)$ follow necessarily or deductively from the complete concept of A_1. The existence of monad A_1 is itself contingent – it is not contradictory to deny that A_1 was brought into being or actualized – so any particular state of A_1, say c, is contingent in that "not-A_1c" is not a logical contradiction. There are possible worlds in which A_1c might not be true because A_1 might not have been actualized – brought into existence – at all, but instead A_2. But we do not say that people are free if it is a mere logical possibility that what they do might not have been done because *they* may not have existed at all. When God decides to create an individual monad A, this means creating the complete concept from which all truths predicated of the subject A follow deductively from analysis of – are contained in – the concept of that subject; thus to change any of these truths would be to change the complete concept and thereby destroy that individual as *that* particular individual and create another individual. It seems that I could only be free by controlling my complete concept; but only God has this control at the inception of that monad. All that is true of – happens to – an individual in total defines that individual. That Leibniz died in 1716 is a truth that follows necessarily, given the initial creation of that particular individual, that Leibniz had to die in 1716; if this had not happened, we must be talking of a different individual.

A worrying question remains for Leibniz, connected with the problem of freedom. Does the *inesse* (predicate-in-subject) principle apply to God? Does whatever God does follow deductively from His complete concept, including His decrees as to which world to create? If this is so, then the distinction between necessary and contingent truths is in danger of collapsing, because God's decree to create the most perfect world itself follows deductively from God's complete concept; and then what follows could not be otherwise unless God ceased to be God, destroying His own complete concept. It would then be a logical contradiction to suppose God could have chosen otherwise. This threatens a return to Spinoza's extreme necessitarianism.

Leibniz is a rationalist in the sense that he thinks reason can grasp the true nature of reality that lies behind appearances; he is also a rationalist in the sense that it ought *in principle* to be possible to deduce all the states of the world from an analysis of the complete concepts of actualized monadic substances. This *a priori* analysis is also infinite, and not completable by human beings, and moreover refers to an intelligible reality that lies behind appearances and accounts for those appearances, not to the appearances themselves.

However, Leibniz's metaphysics provides only a framework of principles which are vastly too general to allow the deduction of specific scientific laws; and in this sense Leibniz is an empiricist; we can discover specific scientific laws concerning the connection and order of appearances only from observation and experimentation.

CHAPTER FIVE

Empiricism:
Locke, Berkeley, Hume

The empiricists in general have tendencies which contrast with those of the rationalists. Empiricists hold that all the material for knowledge, our ideas or concepts, and all knowledge of actual matters of fact, as opposed to logical or conceptual truths, must be derived from, or be reducible to, aspects of our experience: features of the information provided by the content of our senses and introspection. Empiricists deny that it is possible to know by reason alone the nature of what exists; rather, the nature of what exists can be known only through experience. We should reject as meaningless ideas or concepts which cannot be specified as corresponding to any possible experiences. We should reject knowledge claims concerning matters of fact about the nature of the world which are not supportable by the evidence of experience. This leads to a tendency among empiricists to emphasize that the limit of human knowledge and imagination is bounded by the limit of our experience. Empiricists reject the rationalist claim that it is possible to come to know by *a priori* reason alone the nature of an intelligible real world inaccessible to experience that stands beyond appearances. The empiricist may argue that concepts (such as substance), and the terms that express them, are meaningless or else must relate to some possible experience, since concepts and terms get their meaning by reference to some possible experience, but a world beyond experience cannot be a world that might possibly be experienced; in either case it is not possible to use meaningful concepts to talk of a world beyond possible experiences.

The tendency in empiricism is also to deny the existence of natural necessity: necessity is a property only of logical relations between concepts, or of logical relations between ideas or thoughts, not between things or events in the world whose existence, nature and connections are all contingent; such natural contingent connections can be discovered not by reason, which can establish only necessary truths and necessary connections, but only by experience.

Empiricism is inclined to argue that there are two exclusive and together exhaustive types of proposition.

(a) Propositions whose truth, logically speaking, can be known merely by understanding them, or by deductive reasoning alone, independently of the evidence of experience: truths of reason.

(b) Propositions whose truth, logically speaking, cannot be known merely by understanding them, or by deductive reasoning alone, but which depend on the evidence of experience: truths of fact.

All propositions which tell us anything about the real or actual world are truths of fact. Propositions stating matters of fact cannot be known to be true merely by our understanding them, or by our deducing them from other propositions known to be true by the understanding alone; if we can know them to be true at all, they must be known through consulting experience. It should be noted that the distinction is not the genetic one of how we come to have, acquire, or understand these different sorts of proposition, but a logical question concerning on what, once acquired or understood, the truth or falsity of a proposition depends, and on what knowledge of the truth or falsity of a proposition depends. If the truth or falsity of a proposition depends only on the meaning of the terms in it, then it is an *a priori* proposition whose truth or falsity can be known *a priori* by reason alone independently of empirical evidence. If the truth or falsity of a proposition does not depend only on the meaning of the terms in it, then it is an *a posteriori* proposition whose truth or falsity can only be known *a posteriori* by empirical evidence, not by reason alone.

The basic contrast between rationalism and empiricism is an argument about the extent and nature of what truths it is logically possible to know *a priori* by the understanding independently of experience, by intellectual intuition and pure logical reasoning alone, and what truths it is logically possible to know *a posteriori* by the senses, by experience and observation alone. The rationalist argues that certain things can be known with certainty to be necessarily true about the nature of reality, what exists, by *a priori* reason alone, even if such truths refer to a reality that lies behind appearances. This the empiricist denies, arguing that claims to knowledge of truths concerning the nature of reality or the actual world must seek their justification, if such justification is possible at all, in experience; *a priori* reason alone cannot reveal the real or actual nature or existence of the world. Reason alone can give knowledge only of what is necessary (that which must be because its denial is contradictory), impossible (that which cannot be because its assertion is contradictory), and possible (that which may or may not be because its denial is not contradictory), but *not what is actual* among what is merely possible or contingent (not impossible and not necessary). If the premises of a valid deductive argument are true, then the conclusion must be true. A deductively valid argument is one in which to assert the premises and deny the conclusion would be a contradiction. Conclusions can be validly deduced from premises independently of the evidence of experience; but if the conclusions are factual, then such deductions must involve factual premises which can be known to be true not by reason alone but only by the evidence of experience; without the evidence of experience any factual conclusion of a deduction is at best hypothetical and not yet known to be true.

The spectre raised by empiricism is of two exclusive and together exhaustive sets of truths: one set is necessary, certain and known *a priori*, but says nothing about the actual nature of the world; the other set is contingent, not certain and known, if at all, *a posteriori*, but can say something about the actual nature of the world; this undermines the search for necessary and certain knowledge about the actual nature of the world by leaving all truths about the actual nature of the world both contingent and not certain.

Locke

John Locke (1632–1704) was born in Wrington in Somerset and died at Oates in Essex. Locke was far from being the caricature of the philosophical recluse; he was, on the contrary, a man well known in public affairs, sometimes involving considerable danger; but, despite his close involvement with controversial political affairs, Locke was a prudent man. Locke's father was a lawyer and a staunch Puritan and Parliamentarian who fought with the Parliamentarian army in the English Civil War; this began in 1642 against Charles I, who was beheaded in 1649. Locke attended Westminster School, and in 1652 he went to Christ Church, Oxford. At Oxford he studied the arts course of logic, grammar, rhetoric, Greek and moral philosophy. After obtaining his BA he was elected in 1658 to a Senior Studentship at Christ Church which was tenable for life. He taught Greek and moral philosophy, but soon became interested in medicine, and attained the BM (Bachelor of Medicine) degree from the University of Oxford in 1674.

It was during his time at Oxford that Locke became dissatisfied with the philosophy of scholasticism and first became acquainted with, and derived inspiration from, the works of Descartes. Locke was elected a Fellow of the Royal Society in 1668; there he came to know the chemist and physicist Robert Boyle (1627–92), whose emphasis on experimental method and the corpuscular theory of the constitution of matter impressed and decisively affected Locke: it influenced his philosophical thought, particularly in its rejection of Aristotelian modes of physical explanation. Sympathetic to Locke's views is the

motto of the Royal Society, *Nullius in verba*: "Nothing by mere authority". Locke's thought, both in its purely philosophical as well as in its
political interests, is consistently marked by the advocation of
tolerance and resistance to dogmatism in the face of the limits and
uncertainties of human knowledge. His political thought, as embodied
in the *Two treatises on government* (1690), became a philosophical
foundation of liberal democracy.

After Cromwell's Commonwealth, the monarchy was restored in
1660 under Charles II. Through his interest in medicine, Locke had
initially become in 1667 a medical adviser to Lord Ashley, later the
Earl of Shaftesbury. Locke in fact left his college, never to teach there
again, and instead entered into a series of official appointments.
Between 1675 and 1679, Locke spent time in France mainly for the
sake of his poor health. His travels in Europe fostered his keen
interest in all aspects of contemporary scientific work. This association
and friendship with Shaftesbury was to bring Locke problems;
Shaftesbury was party to the failed attempt to overthrow and replace
Charles II with Charles's illegitimate offspring, the Protestant Duke
of Monmouth. Shaftesbury, fearing impeachment for treason, fled to
Holland in 1682, and died the next year; Locke also wisely, because
of his support of Shaftesbury and Monmouth, moved to, and for a
time hid in, Holland under a false name, until returning to England
after the Glorious Revolution of 1688, when the Catholic Stuart King,
James II, fled the English throne, to be replaced by the Protestant
William of Orange, which led to the Hanoverian Succession. From
1691 Locke lived at Oates in Essex in the house of Sir Francis and
Lady Masham until his death in 1704.

It is important to understand the overall aim of Locke's philosophy:
it is concerned mainly with determining the nature, scope, and limits
of knowledge and with giving an account of the nature of reality.
Locke's position stands in contrast to that of many of his philosophical predecessors and, indeed, some of his philosophical successors. The heart of the matter lies in the interplay between
scepticism and the scope of human knowledge; and it can be summed
up by the aim of discovering what it is human beings are and are not
fitted to know. Locke accepts that knowledge, properly speaking, is
of truths which are *certain* and *universal*. Our inability to refute
scepticism in various areas of human inquiry where we wish to claim
to know truths might lead us to the despairing view that only
scepticism can remain in those areas. Locke emphasizes the limits of
human knowledge proper, but in a way that allows for areas where,
although we do not have knowledge in the strict sense, we are not
thereby forced into scepticism because in many of these areas of
inquiry we are still capable of probable belief; and, indeed, the belief
is sometimes so probable that it is virtually as good as knowledge.
What Locke is advocating might be called degrees of appropriate

certainty. This presents us with something other than a choice between strict knowledge and total ignorance. In those areas where we cannot strictly speaking know, Locke argues that we should acknowledge that we have reached our limitations; but knowledge in the strict sense is usually not required; the probable belief we may have instead is sufficient for our purposes, and this, although not a refutation, is the answer to the sceptic. Locke advocates the view that absolute certainty in many important areas of human inquiry is not possible for us but nor is it required or even appropriate; an example is our degree of certainty about the existence of an external world.

Locke's strategy in delimiting human knowledge is to examine the power of the human mind and the objects of thought: ideas. The philosophy of Locke stands on two main foundations: first, that all knowledge derives from reasoning about our ideas and, secondly, that all ideas originate in experience. We cannot in our thinking and knowledge go beyond the ideas or concepts we actually have – ideas are the materials of thought and knowledge – and the ideas we have are bounded by what ideas can be attained through experience.

From this it is not surprising to find that Locke opposes what he regards as a prevalent notion that we have innate, or inborn, ideas in the mind independently of experience. It soon becomes clear that what Locke is most concerned to oppose is the existence in the mind of innate principles and knowledge; although in denying the existence of innate ideas – ideas being the building blocks of knowledge – Locke is also denying innate knowledge of truths. One of the chief motives for Locke's denial of innate knowledge is that the identification of a principle as innate or inborn is sometimes used, especially in moral matters, as a block to any questioning of the truth of that principle. But we must, Locke says, think through what we claim to know, and make knowledge our own. This goes along with Locke's general suspicion of authority as a valid ground for accepting something as true.

Apart from certain moral principles alleged to be innate, there were also said by advocates of innate ideas to be innate basic logical principles, such as "Whatever is is". One of the arguments used in favour of innate principles is that there are some principles that are universally assented to as true, and this shows them to be innate rather than acquired. Locke flatly denies that there is such universal assent; children and idiots just do not assent to abstract principles; but he goes on to say that even if universal assent were a fact, this would not show that the universal assent could not be explained in some other way than by saying that what is assented to is innate. In fact Locke thinks the argument from immediate universal assent to the conclusion that particular principles are innate confuses innateness and cases of self-evidence; the universal assent, on encountering a self-evident proposition, is fully accounted for by the relation of the terms in the proposition, meaning we cannot think otherwise if we understand it at all. Locke rejects the idea that there might be innate principles implicitly in the mind which are not explicitly understood. Moral rules, which are supposedly innate, are not even self-evident and they therefore demand reasons to be given for their acceptance. Moreover, the abstracted ideas or concept terms of abstract principles suggested as innate can be acquired only after experience of the particular cases and the gaining of particular ideas.

Locke does not deny the existence of innate *capacities* – the power to perceive, believe, recognize truth and falsity, judge, assent to principles – but none of these capacities actually amounts in itself to possessing innate ideas, principles or knowledge of truths. If innateness merely amounted to the capacity to recognize and assent to truths when presented, then all knowledge, since it involves this, would be innate – which Locke thinks is absurd.

Locke never questions whether even if there were innate principles this would make any difference to whether those principles were true; he never questions the truth of putative innate principles. The reason for this is Locke's piety; if there were innate principles they would have to be true because they could be implanted directly in us only by God. Locke argues that there are, in fact, no innate ideas and principles, so the question of their truth or falsity does not arise, and the positing of them is unnecessary to explain the knowledge we have. The explanation for all the ideas we have is that they originate in experience: experience is made up of *sensation* derived from external material objects, and *reflection* derived from awareness of the workings of our own mind. Examples of ideas of sense-experience are yellow, elephant, cold, army; examples of ideas of reflective-experience are thinking, believing, willing, doubting.

Locke is not free from the charge of confusing psychological or genetic empiricism with philosophical or logical empiricism. Genetic empiricism is a psychological theory accounting for the way we actually come to have, or acquire, ideas and knowledge of which propositions are true and which false; philosophical empiricism is concerned only with that on which the truth or falsity of propositions depends and what is logically required in order to justify the claim to know whether the propositions are true or false. This makes the distinction between knowledge of truths being psychologically innate and its being logically *a priori*. Showing that a certain proposition is, psychologically speaking, entertained in the mind at a time prior to any experience would not show whether that proposition were true or false or have any relevance to justifying logically a claim to know it to be true or false. Whether a proposition can be known to be true or false logically independently of experience is not shown by discovering whether it was in the mind innately or not, but by deciding of what logical type the proposition is.

Take the following two propositions:

(a)   The internal angles of a plane triangle add up to 180 degrees.
(b)   There are lions in Africa.

If the truth of (a), which is a necessary truth, were questioned, we would prove it to be true by showing it is deducible from the axioms of Euclidean geometry; if (b), which is a contingent truth, were questioned we could only establish its truth by going to Africa and looking. The truth of (a), and knowledge of that truth, is, logically speaking, independent of evidence of experience, whereas the truth of (b), and knowledge of that truth, is, logically speaking, knowable only through the evidence of experience. Whether a truth is knowable *a priori* or *a posteriori* is determined by whether the truth can possibly be established empirically or non-empirically; and this is different from the truth being actually innate or acquired. We might possess no non-empirical truths such as (a) innately; but that would not alter the fact that these propositions are true regardless of any states of affairs in the world, and they can be known to be true independently of experience and by pure logical reasoning. We might possess a whole stack of what turn out to be empirical truths such as (b) innately, and although this might be psychologically surprising it would not alter the fact that the truth of these propositions depends on certain states of affairs in the world obtaining, and they can be known to obtain only through experience, not by pure logical reasoning alone. A truth such as "Either it is raining or it is not raining" ("*p* or not-*p*") is an *a priori* truth because it is true independently of any states of affairs in the world, and it logically can be known to be true independently of inspecting the weather; but it tells us nothing about the weather; it does not help us to decide if we should take an umbrella. All propositional beliefs, even if true, which are not logically *a priori* can be known to be true only by checking them against the evidence of experience, regardless of whether we have the beliefs innately or not. Those truths known independently of experience are said to be necessary in that their denial implies a contradiction; those truths known only by experience are said to be contingent, as their denial does not imply a contradiction. The philosophical concern should be to distinguish between *a priori* propositions, which are all those propositions where the logical justification of knowledge of whether they are true or false is independent of empirical evidence, and *a posteriori* propositions, which are all those propositions where the logical justification of knowledge of whether they are true or false is dependent on empirical evidence.

There is considerable uncertainty and controversy over what Locke means by "idea". Locke defines an idea as "whatsoever is the object of the understanding when a man thinks". Some have taken Locke to mean by "idea" some kind of mental entity – mental images which are objects in the mind. The consequence of this (a point raised by Berkeley) is that it immediately leads to scepticism about knowledge through perception of the external world. If the "veil of perception" or "picture-original" view is correct, and we only ever perceive ideas in the mind, then there can be no way of checking if the ideas represent the external world truthfully, or even if there is an external world at all corresponding to the ideas. We are locked in a circle of ideas, with the knower logically blocked off from what is known; our ideas are a barrier between us and what the ideas are ideas of. Partly because of this point, which seems too obvious for Locke to have missed, and which he even seems to point out, other interpreters of his work suggest an alternative view in which the reification of ideas is resisted. Locke, it is said, means by "idea" in "idea of *X*" a mental or perceptual *act*, not a thing; "idea" refers to our understanding of *X*, or our perception of *X*, as distinct from *X* itself; "idea of *X*" means "*X*-as-it-is-perceived/understood/known/appears"; and it expresses the epistemological relation between the knower and the thing known. To avoid a regress, what must ultimately be caused in the perceptual process is an act of perceptual awareness itself, not another object of which to be aware. An "idea of *X*" involves two entities, knower and object known, not three by including an entity "idea of *X*". The expression "idea of" points out that our conception or perception of an object is *our* conception or perception; it is how it appears to us, as opposed to how the object is in itself, which may differ from our idea. This emphasizes the assertion that we inevitably view things under the constraint or qualification of their being seen from our point of view – how things appear to us – and that we cannot attain the God's-eye view of knowing objects as they are in themselves quite independently of all reference to its being our perspective. To say I have an idea of *X* is just to say I have some understanding of the object *X*. On this interpretation, when Locke speaks in a variety of ways about a relation of resemblance or non-resemblance between ideas and what they are ideas of, he is not committing himself to this being like the relation between a picture or image and an original – literal picturing – but rather the kind of relation that holds between an accurate and inaccurate description and the object described.

Locke divides ideas into *simple* and *complex*. Complex ideas are compounds of simple ideas. We may experience ideas in complexes, or even only in complexes, but they must be reducible to simple atomic unanalyzable ideas. The thinking behind this is that at some point there are ideas which cannot be broken down into anything simpler and to have the ideas at all one must derive them directly from experience. If one has never experienced the simple idea of red, there is no way that having the idea can be explained by showing how it is compounded of simpler ideas one has experienced; whereas the idea of a mermaid, even if one has not encountered mermaids in one's experience, is made up of ideas one has encountered in experience. Locke is not saying that we always experience simple ideas first, and then build up compounds, merely that all compounds must be analyzable into simple ideas of which we have had direct experience. Locke's position places restrictions on the scope of imagination: whatever we make up we will only ever be compounding simple ideas that ultimately originate in experience.

For Locke the meaning of a word derives from its standing for, and its association with, an idea or complex of ideas; we know the meaning of a word when we know the idea it stands for. If someone has not experienced the simple idea X, then he will not understand the meaning of the word standing for X. We will, in attempting to speak about that which is, strictly speaking, beyond our experience and is in no way analogous to anything in our experience, be using meaningless expressions and talking nonsense because we will be unable to specify any idea for which the word stands.

If it is the case that we only ever encounter particulars in our experience from whence we derive particular ideas, the problem arises as to how we come by abstract general ideas, for which general words stand as signs – such as "redness", "man", "nurse" – which can apply equally to many particulars. Such general terms are necessary for communication and knowledge. Pure nominalism holds that all that any group of particulars under a general name have literally in common is the sharing of that name; but this leaves unanswered the problem of universals: namely how we know which particulars come under that general name in the first place. Locke has more than one answer. His first answer is that we are blessed with a faculty of abstraction: by a process of omission the abstract general idea is formed by leaving out of each idea of particular members of a similar class all those characteristics in which they differ, thereby including only that which is common. The general idea will itself be a particular; but it is not clear what the resultant idea amounts to. Berkeley argues that Locke's procedure is impossible: if we take away all particular features we are left with an impossible idea; we could not represent to ourselves a red which is no particular shade of red at all; there cannot be an idea which is merely determinable. Locke's second answer is that the meaning of abstract general ideas and words is fixed by "nominal essences": we notice similar characteristics between particulars, and we decide on some set of defining objective particular characteristics by which we then have the ability to recognize whether any particular is correctly admitted to a specific general class.

Locke explains the relation between our ideas in the mind of sensible qualities of external objects and those sensible qualities as they exist in external objects themselves by making a distinction between primary qualities and secondary qualities.

(a) Primary qualities: our ideas of primary qualities resemble those qualities as they are in bodies. Primary qualities are size, extension, shape, movement, solidity.

(b) Secondary qualities: our ideas of secondary qualities do not resemble those qualities as they are in bodies. Secondary qualities are hot, cold, sound, colour, taste, odour, etc.

Locke was greatly influenced by the atomic theory of matter propounded by Boyle; the basic stuff of the natural world consists of material objects which are made up of an insensible structure or configuration of atoms or corpuscles which themselves have no internal structure; these microscopic atoms have only primary qualities. Locke thinks, however, that the soul is immaterial, although he does not think it impossible that God could have made thought an attribute of matter. Macroscopic material objects we perceive appear to have both primary and secondary qualities, but both qualities at the macroscopic level depend on configurations of insensible particles which themselves have only primary qualities. The secondary qualities we perceive are not in objects *as-we-perceive-secondary-qualities* to be; this does not mean the secondary qualities are *nothing* in objects; rather, the secondary qualities are *in objects* some *determinate* fine corpuscular structure; our ideas of secondary qualities are a result of the power of qualities as they exist in objects, as insensible corpuscles, which produce certain sensations in us. The ideas of secondary qualities are an effect on us of those qualities in objects as insensible corpuscles with only primary qualities. The ideas caused in us of secondary qualities never resemble that which in objects causes us to have those ideas, but are in objects nothing but a certain configuration of corpuscles.

Take, for example, the secondary quality red: it is true to say that object X is red if what is meant is that X has a corpuscular structure such that under normal conditions it has the power to produce in us the idea or sensation of red, and thus the object X is seen as red; but it is false to say that object X is red if what is meant is that red exists in X in the same way as I have the idea or sensation of red. Locke also distinguishes a third quality which he simply calls "powers", which is the capacity of bodies to cause changes in other bodies such that they then appear different to us, as when the sun melts wax.

Another way of explaining the distinction between primary and secondary qualities is through the notion of resemblance and accurate descriptions. Our ideas of primary qualities can resemble (can be accurate or correct representations/descriptions of) those qualities as they are in objects. Our ideas of secondary qualities never resemble (cannot be accurate or correct representations/descriptions of) those qualities as they are in objects. This is not to say we cannot be mistaken about what determinate primary quality an object has; but we *can* be right in the sense that the quality exists in the object as the same kind as that which is perceived. We might misperceive the determinate shape of X as triangular when it is square, but we are not mistaken that it really has some determinable shape or other; in this sense our ideas of primary qualities resemble the qualities as they are in objects. We will always be wrong about the object having any secondary qualities if we mean that the secondary qualities ever exist in the object in the same way as we perceive qualities; secondary qualities do not exist in bodies in the same way as we perceive them at all. This does not mean we are incorrect to describe X as red if we mean by this that it has that determinate corpuscular structure which causes one to have the idea of red under specific conditions.

God has chosen to connect specific corpuscular configurations in bodies with the power to produce the specific sensations or ideas we experience; why a certain corpuscular configuration should produce just those experiences within us is something Locke regards as mysterious.

Recent thinking suggests that Locke was not *making* the distinction between primary and secondary qualities, but was *accepting* the distinction, which he took over from the scientific work of Boyle. Berkeley objects to Locke's apparent argument for the distinction that the primary qualities are invariant and secondary qualities variant with respect to observers: primary qualities are just as variant with the changing perspective of the observer as secondary ones. But if Locke did not try by argument to justify making a distinction between primary and secondary qualities, then Berkeley's counter argument is beside the point. Locke's chief point in accepting the corpuscular hypothesis is that it provides an economical unifying explanation of a great variety of phenomena; and whereas we can conceive of an explanation of changes in secondary qualities in terms of changes in primary qualities, the reverse seems inconceivable.

How is Locke entitled to have an idea of, and talk meaningfully about, the insensible configuration of particles which are too small for us to experience them, given his empiricism about the origin of all ideas? Locke's answer is that our inability to experience such particles is purely contingent, and did we but have microscopical eyes, we would see them. Moreover, corpuscular explanations involve insensible particles which are entities which have properties of the same kind as, or are analogous to, the properties of macroscopic things we do experience, namely, primary qualities. We speak intelligibly in referring to the particles because we have ideas of the kind of properties they have and therefore understand what we mean by the words describing them.

Locke's account of substance, the most fundamental independent stuff in the world, is subject to different interpretations. On one view Locke notoriously means by substance "naked substance", a something I know not what: a "something", or *substratum* in general, beside all the qualities we predicate of objects which "support" all those qualities. We have ideas of things having various qualities, and since we suppose that these qualities cannot subsist by themselves, we suppose there to be a something which they are the qualities of, and that that something is something beside the qualities themselves. But if a *substratum* is imagined to be that which is stripped of *all* qualities, one is left not with a special, if mysterious, something, but with an ineffable nothing. Thus the reason that this substance is not known is that a propertyless substance is logically or necessarily unknowable.

Other interpretations have suggested that Locke's remarks concerning pure substance in general – *substratum* – are ironic. The suggestion is that Locke rejects the confused notion of a pure substance in general and aims to replace such talk with positive talk of something else, while also wishing to explain how we are led to think of it as underlying aggregates of sensible qualities. He thinks we are led to belief in substance through: (a) the grammar of subject-predicate talk; (b) seeking something to explain the cause of the union of apparently unrelated aggregates of different sorts of qualities; (c) our notion that qualities – for example, the yellow, malleable, heavy qualities of gold – cannot exist separately from something in which the qualities can exist. Locke's reinterpretation of substance originates in substance as the sought-after cause explaining why some particular substance such as gold should always have the qualities of being yellow, malleable, and heavy, when there seems to be no connection between the qualities. The explanation for the connection or union of these apparently unconnected qualities in all instances of a particular kind of substance in fact lies in the common real determinate internal corpuscular structure.

Locke describes the nominal essence of a thing as simply the qualities or properties we decide to gather under a sortal name, such as "gold", for the purpose of classifying particulars into kinds. The nominal essence gives us a criterion for identification. Although there are natural constraints on us, the sorting of things into kinds in this way is created and linguistic.

Locke talks of real essence in two senses. First, the traditional scholastic sense of real essence as a thing's substantial form which makes a thing the kind of thing it is; Locke rejects this as obscure and having no explanatory use; to explain the properties of gold by saying that it has those properties because it possesses the substantial form of gold is just to say gold has the properties of gold; talk of substantial forms stops us seeking the underlying causes. Talk of underlying causes refers us to Locke's second sense of real essence; that is, Lockean real essence which is the real determinate internal corpuscular constitution on which the apparent properties depend.

We cannot strictly know the inner atomic structure of things because our senses are not fitted to perceive them; nevertheless, the notion, unlike substantial forms, is an intelligible hypothesis which has genuine explanatory power. Moreover, our lack of knowledge of the inner atomic constitution of things is, unlike the lack of knowledge of "pure substance in general", merely a contingent matter.

Locke defines knowledge as "nothing but the perception of the connection and agreement, or disagreement and repugnancy, of any of our ideas". Propositions are true when the ideas constituting the propositions are connected in such a way as to make them true; we can know propositions to be true in so far as we can "perceive" this connection. Add to this the condition that knowledge must be of truths that are certain and universal, and what we can be said strictly to know turns out to be extremely meagre. But we are not left only with doubt where we cannot have knowledge since we can also have probable belief. Locke's overall aim is to commend to us the view that the lover of truth should not hold a proposition more firmly than the proof or evidence for it warrants. Locke lists four sorts of agreement and disagreement of ideas.

(1) *Identity or diversity*
    Here he seems to have in mind logical identity and contradiction.
(2) *Relation*
    Here he is referring to demonstrative logical or mathematical relations.
(3) *Coexistence or necessary connection*
    Here is meant connection of ideas which reflect the manner of connection of properties of things occurring together in nature.
(4) *Real existence*
    Here he means what really exists in the world.

Our limited ability actually to perceive the appropriate connection between ideas in a large range of cases immediately restricts what we can know, strictly speaking. There is no problem in claiming to know as true propositions whose ideas can be immediately perceived as connected or disagreeing, such as "blue is blue" or "blue is not yellow"; these are intuitive truths. Such truths Locke refers to as trifling. Locke more dubiously claims some moral truths can be known intuitively. There is also little difficulty in making a plausible case for our knowing truths which result from logical deductive reasoning, such as geometric and mathematical truths, which can be thought of as made up of intuitive steps or connected chains of intuitive truths which form the process of demonstrative reasoning. After this difficulties arise.

Locke himself admits that to have an idea is one thing, but it does not follow, when not actually receiving the idea, that anything exists corresponding to that idea. The problem is the lack of any connection to be perceived between our having an idea and the real existence of that which the idea is an idea of. A possible exception is the existence of God and that the idea of God entails that God is – which amounts to a compressed ontological argument. Locke equivocates on what we can be said to *know* exists. He thinks that we have intuitive knowledge of our own existence; he thinks that we can have demonstrative knowledge of God's existence; and he thinks that, while we are actually perceiving objects, we have a belief of such great assurance and certainty that those objects exist without us that it "deserves the name knowledge". He is clear, however, that strictly speaking we cannot know the truths expressing actual factual connections between the properties we experience objects to have or know the scientific hypotheses with which we describe their behaviour (for example the connection of the idea of "gold" and "soluble in *aqua regia*" in the proposition "Gold is soluble in *aqua regia*"); we cannot know truths in these cases because we cannot perceive any intrinsic connection between the constituent ideas reflecting those properties such that it would make them true; we cannot perceive any necessary connection between the ideas; all that we perceive is the juxtaposition or conjunction of the ideas. So in the case of natural science we are not capable of knowledge, but we can believe with some degree of probability in the truth of scientific propositions, and the probability of truth will increase in proportion as it conforms to my past experience and that of others.

Locke's view suggests a hierarchy of certainty, here given in descending order of certainty:
(A) intuition
(B) deductions or demonstrations
(C) sensitive knowledge
(D) natural science.

(A) and (B) strictly constitute areas of knowledge; (C) is knowledge of the existence of particular objects in the external world as we actually perceive them, although it is not so certain as (A) and (B); but with (D) we have only probable belief. Knowledge of our own existence is included in (A), and that of the existence of God in (B). With these exceptions, Locke is in danger of leaving us with knowledge almost entirely of propositions which are hypothetical non-existential (stating what follows if we accept certain propositions, regardless of whether those initial propositions are actually true) and verifiable *a priori*, and little knowledge of propositions which are categorical existential (asserting the actual existence and nature of things) and verifiable *a posteriori*. There is certainly a problem in claiming to know the general or universal existential propositions and the existence of objects not actually perceived which are required for natural science. In short, knowledge is restricted to necessary certain truths, in which case knowledge is limited to logical relations and excludes relations of fact which are neither necessarily nor certainly true.

Locke is Cartesian, or at least rationalist, in giving a necessitarian account of reality: knowledge of reality would ideally be one of revealing the natural necessity and connection of things. He differs from the rationalists in his scepticism over whether natural necessities

can actually be known; but he also differs from empiricists in holding
that there nevertheless are natural necessities – necessities between
matters of fact about the world – which could be known. Thus he
does not fit the traditional empiricist mould for two important
reasons:

(a) Locke does not share the empiricist view that all knowledge
which we can know independently of experience by reason alone
is thereby trivial and unable to tell us anything about the actual
nature of reality. Mathematical and geometrical truths are cases
of non-trivial *a priori* knowledge in which we discover new
truths.

(b) Locke believes, unlike Hume, in natural or metaphysical necessity. The epistemological problem that we cannot know natural
connections to be necessary and with certainty does not show
the necessary connections are not there. Locke says in addition
that our inability to perceive the connections as necessary is a
purely contingent matter which depends merely on our inability
to perceive the inner microscopic corpuscular structure of
material objects; could we see this structure, we would perceive
that the connection between the qualities objects have is
necessary. If we could see the microscopic structure, we would
see that the sensible qualities or properties of X which depend
on that microscopic structure must occur together necessarily.

Locke does not see the problem Hume uncovers, that no matter
how acute our senses we would only ever perceive one idea A in
conjunction with, or followed by, another idea B, but would never
perceive between them a necessary connection such that B must be in
conjunction with, or must follow, A, and things cannot be otherwise.
If the connection were necessary, then the assertion of (A and not-B)
would be a logical contradiction, but it never is when describing
actual matters of fact. There is no analogous connection between
natural matters of fact for necessary deductive connections or logical
relations. It is never a logical contradiction to suppose that A occurs,
but B does not follow, or that property A is not found with property
B, no matter how many times the conjunction of A and B has been
observed. Necessity based on logical contradiction is the only sort
possible. The universal generalization "All A is B" and the necessary
causal connection "If A occurs, then B *must* occur", where A and B
describe matters of fact, cannot be known to hold, or the beliefs
rationally justified, through the evidence of experience or by
deductive reasoning; thus they cannot be known or rationally justified
at all; this is the logical problem of induction and causation.

Berkeley

George Berkeley (1685–1753) was born near Kilkenny, Ireland. At the age of fifteen he entered Trinity College, Dublin, and graduated with his BA in 1704 at the age of nineteen; he became a fellow of the College in 1707. The spur to his philosophical writing probably derived from reading Locke, Newton (1642–1727), and Malebranche (1638–1715). Berkeley's *New theory of vision* appeared in 1709, with a fourth edition in 1732. His major philosophical works, *A treatise concerning the principles of human knowledge* (1710) and the *Three dialogues between Hylas and Philonous* (1713), were both published by the time he was twenty-eight. In 1724 he resigned from his fellowship to become Dean of Derry. In 1728 Berkeley left, with his wife, for America in an attempt to found a college in Bermuda to educate the native Indians and the sons of local planters, but the money for the project failed to materialize from the government in England. Thus in 1731 Berkeley returned to England, and eventually to Ireland where he became Bishop of Cloyne in 1734. In 1752 he moved to Oxford, and died there suddenly in 1753 at the age of sixty-eight.

It is perhaps more than usually necessary in understanding the philosophy of Berkeley to place it in its intellectual context; otherwise Berkeley's philosophy can seem too obviously false to require serious examination; his philosophy has been called immaterialism or idealism, although the two terms are not exactly equivalent.

Berkeley exemplifies one way of stringently applying empiricism: he conjoins the view that all we can ever know is our immediate ideas with the view that words and other expressions in our language derive their meaning only from association with specific ideas; this leads to the ontological doctrine that only ideas subsisting in minds and minds themselves can be said to exist because to talk of things existing in any other way is meaningless as the expressions used in the talk are necessarily unconnected to any ideas. Expressions not translatable into, or associated with, some experience are meaningless.

The essential background to the understanding of Berkeley's philosophy is formed by a combination of the new scientific materialism and the representative theory of perception. Scientific materialism, mainly derived from Newton, proposes a mechanistic conception of the universe which functions like the works of a giant clock and a corpuscular hypothesis as to the constitution of matter. The representative theory of perception, mainly derived from an interpretation of Locke, is here the thesis that the immediate objects of perception are always ideas. There are also connected problems arising from Descartes and Malebranche concerning the relation between the incorporeal mind and the corporeal body. Berkeley saw the scepticism that could arise from these beliefs as a scandalous affront to common sense and a threat to religious belief; but all the forms of scepticism, Berkeley thinks, can be eliminated at one blow by rejecting their common assumptions.

The scepticism to which the materialistic philosophy gave rise took three main forms:
(a)   the existence of sensible things
(b)   the nature of sensible things
(c)   the existence and nature of God.
The main additional sceptical problem posed by Cartesianism is:
(d)   how matter and spirit can interact.
Materialism gives rise to all the first three forms of scepticism when combined with the doctrine that we only ever perceive immediately ideas in our minds by opening an unbridgeable gap between how things appear to us and how they really are in themselves: a gap between our ideas and what our ideas are ideas of. Material objects, specifically their corpuscular structures, are seen as the cause of our ideas; but material objects do not have, in the same way that we perceive them, all the qualities that they appear to have. The gap between the ideas that we immediately perceive and their supposed causes, which we do not directly but only ever mediately perceive by way of ideas, opens up the possibility of an insoluble scepticism concerning our knowledge of the nature and even existence of the objects of the external world. We can never gain immediate access to the something, whatever it is, that is the cause of our ideas to check whether the ideas which supposedly represent the nature of that something are accurate, or even whether the supposed something exists at all; we can never perceive the something that is the supposed cause of our ideas immediately but only mediately in virtue of perceiving immediately intermediate mental objects: ideas. Materialism also leads to atheism according to Berkeley, since the posited material substance is to a high degree, or perhaps completely, independent of God in its operations and existence. Many materialists supposed that God was ultimately still required as the creator and first mover of the universe; but if we suppose that the universe has existed for ever, then God's existence again becomes dispensable. The existence of God is still possible, but His existence is not logically required, nor even obviously important.

An additional, but connected, source of scepticism derives from Descartes and Malebranche. In the Cartesian view there are two distinct substances, mind and matter, whose essential attributes are thought and extension respectively. The problem then arises as to how their interaction is to be made intelligible: how can the non-extended mind cause changes in motion of extended bodily parts, such as the brain, and how can motions of the extended bodily parts cause changes in non-spatial mental substance which produces thoughts? This problem led Malebranche to the doctrine of occasionalism: this holds that although mind and body do not interact, God on the appropriate occasions systematically intervenes to produce the same result as if they did interact; on the occasion of my willing the movement of my body God causes the correct bodily movement; on the occasion of my observing a physical object God causes me to have the appropriate perception by sharing in His ideas.

Berkeley thinks that materialism is:

(i) *Unjustified*

The arguments presented for the adoption of materialism are insufficient.

(ii) *Unnecessary*

The thesis is extravagant since it posits the existence of material entities that are not required to give an explanation of the course of our experiences.

(iii) *False and must be false*

Matter is not, and indeed cannot be, the cause of our experiences.

(iv) *Meaningless*

It requires us to give meaning to the term "matter" or "material substance" which is something we never directly experience, which is the cause of our ideas; but as the meaning of a term is the idea for which it stands, and there can be no idea of that which we cannot experience, then all terms referring to entities such as material substance, which are beyond experience, must be meaningless.

(v) *Contradictory*

It requires that ideas may exist when not perceived by us in an unthinking corporeal substance or matter.

In several important ways Berkeley is a very strict empiricist. Generally he holds that the limits of what it is intelligible or meaningful to talk about must refer to something in the content of our experience. If we are making some distinction in the world, it must, to be genuine, refer to some perceivable difference; if a proposition is intelligible, it must refer to something perceivable. It is surely part of the persuasiveness, even attractiveness, of Berkeley's idealism that it asks us to concentrate only on the actual character of the content of our own minds.

Berkeley's overall strategy in opposing all the forms ((a), (b), (c), (d), above) of scepticism derives from closing the gap between our ideas and what our ideas are ideas of; thus preventing the sceptic from driving a wedge between the two. Berkeley advocates negatively immaterialism and positively idealism; he also assumes that if materialism can be shown to be false, then his form of idealism must be true in virtue of its being the only alternative to that materialism.

Talk of material objects, in Berkeley's philosophy, is not a reference to some material substance which can exist unperceived as the supposed cause of our ideas but which, since the objects of perception are always ideas, we never actually perceive. To talk of material or sensible objects is to talk about actual or possible objects of perception, and that is to talk of ideas or bundles/collections of ideas themselves which must, as ideas, exist in a mind or spiritual substance. To talk of material objects or sensible things is not to refer to something other than the ideas we perceive, it is to talk of those ideas themselves; what we mean by material objects is just certain ideas or sets of ideas. Any reference to the nature or character of the world is a reference to, and is only intelligible as a reference to, actual or possible experiences. What we immediately perceive in vision is a flat, two-dimensional array of colours and shapes. In the *New theory of vision* Berkeley presents arguments to show that distance is not something immediately perceived but something constructed from certain orderly relations of the ideas of different senses in the mind. Thus to say an object is one mile away is just to say that a certain sequence of ideas – for example, those constituting the experience of walking forward – would have to go through the mind before we received such-and-such ideas of touch. This lays the groundwork for the view that what is perceived (the object of perception), because it is in no case an immediate perception of something at a distance from us, is therefore always something in the mind.

The equating of ideas with sensible things, which thereby makes sensible things mind-dependent, eliminates each of the previously mentioned forms of scepticism ((a), (b), (c), (d), above) produced by materialism and Cartesianism in the following way.

(a) The existence of sensible things. This problem is eliminated because the sceptic cannot drive a wedge between ideas and things; if the objects of sense *are* ideas, and we cannot doubt that we have ideas and thus ideas exist, we cannot doubt the existence of the objects of sense or sensible things.

(b) The nature of sensible things. This is just the sum of a thing's sensible qualities. In addition science no longer purports to reveal the essential nature of things in the external world whereby it can establish the necessary connections required for true causal relations between the sensible properties of things we can perceive; rather, it aspires only to map the regular correlations between ideas, that is, between phenomena.

(c) The existence and nature of God. This problem is eliminated by making God metaphysically indispensable: once material substance is eliminated, it is necessary to affirm that God exists as the immediate real cause of those ideas that are not caused by our imaginations and as the sustainer of those ideas we do not actually perceive; thus God's existence is manifest at all times as the immediate cause of the vast majority of that which we experience; the supposition that God does not exist is refuted by almost every experience we have.

(d) How matter and spirit can interact. This problem is eliminated by denying the existence of material substance; then the problem of interaction between spirit and matter simply does not arise. Berkeley also rejects occasionalism, arguing that we cause those ideas which constitute what we can legitimately will, such as moving our legs.

Berkeley presents various arguments opposing materialism.

(1) Berkeley thinks that the conception of matter as really having only primary qualities, such as extension, shape, solidity, movement, is an impossible one; he questions whether it is possible for us to conceive of a shape which is no colour whatsoever; the conception of matter required for materialism is impossible, for it involves matter devoid of all secondary qualities, which are types of qualities which it could not lack, and from which primary qualities cannot be separated.

(2) Berkeley argues that it is a logical contradiction to talk of conceiving of a thing which exists unconceived, for to conceive of the possibility of something existing unconceived is necessarily to conceive of that thing. But this argument, although tempting, is fallacious. It is true that it is not possible for *A* to be conceived of, and at the same time both exist and be a thing unconceived; but that does not mean that at some other time *A* could not exist as an unconceived-of-*A*; thus there is nothing contradictory in *A* existing unthought about.

(3) Berkeley turns Locke's argument concerning the relativity of perceptions against Locke's materialism. Berkeley takes Locke to be arguing for the distinction between primary qualities (shape, size, motion, solidity) and secondary qualities (colour, taste, heat, sound, etc.) on the basis that those qualities, not really in objects as we perceive them to be, are those that vary with the disposition of the perceiver; such qualities are, as they are perceived, subjective or in the mind (Locke does not in fact argue that secondary qualities are therefore *merely* subjective) and result from the effect of the insensible particles on us. But Berkeley points out that if this argument proves that secondary qualities are ideas in the mind, the same argument proves that primary qualities are also only ideas in the mind, for these too vary with the observer. In fact, there is no reason to suppose that in either case we have shown the qualities to be subjective, for there is no reason to believe that for a kind of quality to be really in objects, or be attributed as a real objective property of objects, it must be invariant with all changes in the observer. Moreover, we would actually expect the real properties of things to vary with the observer; for example, size as we get closer to an object.

(4) This argument concerns pain and heat. When we approach a fire closely the heat is felt as a pain in the mind; when we are at a

further distance from the fire the heat is felt merely as warmth.
We are not tempted to say that the heat felt as pain is in the fire;
so we should also say the same for the lesser degrees of heat felt
as warmth, that heat is an idea in the mind.

(5) In this Berkeley runs together the notion of matter with what
Locke has to say about substance in general. He attributes to
Locke an account of substance which he thinks unintelligible, and
then takes this to be Locke's account of material substance or
matter, so that is also unintelligible. Locke's discussion of
substance in general seems to suggest that it is characterized by
being the "support" of all qualities; the qualities cannot subsist
alone, so substance is that in which the qualities subsist. But if
substance is the support of *all* qualities whatsoever, then any
attempt to give it a positive characterization is impossible, since to
do so would be to attribute qualities to it; thus substance becomes
an unknowable qualityless "something". While this argument is
perfectly flawless as an attack on a qualityless *substratum*, it is
wide of the mark as an attack on matter because no materialist
would suggest that matter is qualityless.

The general form of Berkeley's positive argument for idealism is as
follows. Sensible things (ordinary objects) are those things perceived
by the senses, and those things perceived by the senses are ideas. It
follows that sensible things are ideas or collections of ideas. In addition, ideas can exist only if perceived by minds. With this additional
premise it follows that sensible things cannot exist unperceived.

Repeatedly Berkeley asks how the supposed "material substance"
should be characterized: what qualities or properties does it have?
Indeed any concept, apart from that of mind, if it is to be given a
meaning at all, must be translated into talk about some possible or
actual experiences. Whatever is suggested as the nature of "material
substance", he points out that, if we can make what we are talking of
intelligible at all, the quality referred to is something that we
experience; but what we experience immediately is ideas, and hence
the existence of the quality is as an idea in the mind; and if we refer
to something that we do not experience, then he does not understand
what we mean when we refer to it.

Berkeley makes a distinction between immediate and mediate perception; respectively between the immediate sensations of the various
senses, which involve no inference and about which we cannot be
mistaken, and that which is suggested by these perceptions. The
proper objects of perception are strictly speaking only those things we
perceive immediately, and all else that we claim to perceive is a construct or inference from immediate perceptions.

Thus Berkeley identifies the normal everyday objects or sensible
things that we talk about with ideas or bundles of ideas; but in
making things into ideas he thinks he can show that he has not made

them any less real. Berkeley's idealism is opposed only to the philosopher's conception of material substance as that in which sensible qualities that we perceive through the mediation of ideas subsist when we do not perceive them. Berkeley concludes that the very meaning of saying that sensible objects exist is that they are perceived – although at times he suggests that an object's existence consists in its being perceivable. Berkeley moves from the common-sense belief that sensible things are simply what we perceive, to idealism which holds that the existence or being of sensible things consists in their being perceived or at least perceivable. In the end Berkeley holds to the view that to be or exist as a sensible object is to be actually perceived, and not to the phenomenalist view that to be is to be perceived or *perceivable* – to be perceivable is to exist as a mere permanent possibility of sensation. Thus, in Berkeley, with respect to sensible things, *esse est percipi*: to be is to be perceived. This is not the only meaning that can be given to existence, however: minds or spiritual substance, which have ideas, also exist. To exist is thus also to perceive: *esse est percipere*: to be is to perceive or be a perceiver. So in full we can say *esse est aut percipi aut percipere*: to be (exist) is either to be perceived or to perceive. Spirits are not, like sensible things, constructed as phenomena out of perceived collections of ideas; they are that substance in which ideas inhere.

This position might seem to suggest implausibly that when sensible things are not perceived by us they cease to exist: that they would come and go out of existence. This would be true if only our own or only human minds did the perceiving. But Berkeley's view is only that to exist is to be perceived by some mind or other. This is part of God's place in Berkeley's world, although strictly speaking God does not perceive ideas since He lacks senses, He nevertheless sustains in existence by His mind those ideas of sensible objects not actually perceived by us. Ideas that do not subsist in our finite minds subsist in the infinite, omnipresent, omnipotent mind of God. God is essential to Berkeley's system; and if the system is true God is indispensable to all of us. God is required for two main reasons. First, God is required to give the continuity of a sustained existence to sensible things unperceived by us. Second, God is required as the cause of those ideas we experience which are not caused by us. The only entities capable of being real efficient causes are minds, which alone are active as they are capable of willing; ideas themselves are inert and incapable of being real efficient causes. Berkeley agrees with Locke that causality can only be understood through the experience of willing, but goes further in saying that the only intelligible cases of causation are those that involve willing. We are to a limited extent capable of creating ideas through the faculty of imagination, but most of the ideas we have are not caused by us; they must therefore be caused by some other mind; nothing but the infinite mind of God could account for the richness, stability and orderliness of the ideas we perceive. God *directly* causes us, without the unnecessary mediation of any material substance, to have those ideas which we call ideas or perceptions of sensible things, which are those ideas not caused by ourselves.

Berkeley maintains the distinction between perception of reality and the imagination, and denies the suggestion that he has turned the world into mere fancy. Initially the distinction is made by pointing to those ideas that come before our mind that are not products of our will and imagination; these ideas are ideas of reality and have some other cause, and that cause is God. In short, the real is characterized by being those ideas caused by God. However, dreams also are involuntary although caused by us. Also the problem remains of how we identify which ideas are God-caused. There is, argues Berkeley, a greater strength (force and vivacity), order and coherence among ideas we refer to as being of reality.

There remains too the problem of distinguishing veridical perceptions from illusions. A stick appearing bent in water is a genuine perception, since it is not caused by us; it is an illusion, not in isolation, but in virtue of its relation to the sequence of other ideas we have, such as whether it is followed or not followed by the experience of a straight stick if we feel the stick in the water or the sight of a straight stick if we take it out of the water.

Berkeley seems to say there is an "archetype" (original) idea in the mind of God which God wills us to perceive. We perceive ideas as well as imagining ideas. God imagines and wills ideas only; if this were not the case, we would have to posit an infinity of Gods as the cause of each other's perceptions. God wills that we perceive "ectypes" (copies) of aspects of the archetype ideas in His mind. The notion of two or more people perceiving the same thing, although their ideas may be qualitatively different, seems to depend on there being a common archetype.

We can summarize Berkeley's ontology in the following way:

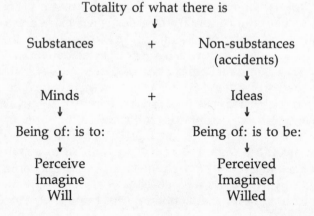

Totality of what there is
↓

Substances	+	Non-substances (accidents)
↓		↓
Minds	+	Ideas
↓		↓
Being of: is to:		Being of: is to be:
↓		↓
Perceive		Perceived
Imagine		Imagined
Will		Willed

Reference here to "Minds", of course, includes the mind of God.

Berkeley's idealism claims not to question the truth of the judge-ments of common sense; rather it claims to affirm them and to make clear what affirming those truths really means. Berkeley's world will *appear* exactly the same as the world containing matter; it makes no difference to the course or order of our experiences. Nevertheless Berkeley's world *is* different even if it looks the same.

This brings us to Berkeley's views on the meaning of words or terms. The meaning of terms is the ideas for which they stand; if there is no identifiable idea corresponding to, or associated with, a term, then it is meaningless; if the term has a meaning at all, it must refer to some feature of experience: to a particular idea or collection of ideas.

This leads us to examine Berkeley's objection to abstract ideas as the meaning of general terms. Locke had suggested, according to Berkeley, that it was possible to form abstract ideas from particular ideas and that this explained the meaning of general terms and their ability to apply to any particular of a class of particulars similar in some respect; thus we form the abstract idea of triangularity, which is what the term "triangularity" stands for, and so it applies indiffer-ently to every triangle. A general term such as "man" applies to all things of the same kind, namely men. The abstract idea applies indifferently to all particulars of a certain class by virtue of including only that which all the particulars have in common and nothing in which they differ. Berkeley thinks that Locke's notion of our forming abstract ideas is both impossible and unnecessary. It is impossible because the process of abstraction involves separating qualities that cannot be separated, and running together qualities that are incompat-ible. In the case of triangularity we have to separate off just the property of being a triangle from that triangle being, for example, any particular or determinate size or colour; it is also an idea of a triangle which is no particular kind of triangle, so it must, to be general, be an idea which is at once all and none of the differents kinds of triangle. Berkeley thinks that we cannot form such an idea. Abstract ideas are unnecessary because terms can be general without their meaning deriving from their standing for abstract ideas: terms become general through their being *used* to stand for a class of particulars which are similar in some relevant respect.

The connection of this with Berkeley's objection to materialism is that he sees the route to positing material substance as dependent on the possibility of abstraction. If we can form abstract ideas, it is possible to argue that we can speak meaningfully, through the formation of an appropriate abstract idea, about something that exists which is not, and could not be, an actual object or content of experience; we can thereby give meaning to terms such as "matter" or "material substance" and so refer to something other than what we can actually experience – which is particular ideas – and then posit its existence independently of its being perceived. If Berkeley has shown that abstract ideas are impossible, and if abstract ideas are required to give meaning to terms such as "matter" or "material substance" which refer to that which can exist unperceived, then he has shown that all talk of matter or material substance in this sense is meaningless or unintelligible.

Berkeley is, however, strangely inconsistent in his empiricism, since he sees fit to talk, and claims to talk meaningfully, about mental substance and God, of both of which we can never actually have ideas, so talk of them should strictly be meaningless. Ideas can only be like other ideas; ideas are passive or inert whereas minds are active; ideas are thereby debarred from representing spiritual substance. Berkeley tries to get round this by claiming that although we cannot, strictly speaking, have ideas of spirit, we can have a *notion* of it. He intends by this to contrast spirit with matter: whereas the latter has been shown to be impossible or contradictory, mind is at least possible and intelligible, and we can therefore form some notion of its operations.

The only sense that Berkeley gives to causation is that of active willing. Ideas themselves are inert and passive, incapable of willing, and therefore incapable of causal influence. The supposed material substance in which qualities are said to inhere is also lifeless and passive, and would therefore be incapable of causal influence. Only spirits are active; it follows from this that the cause of all ideas must be some spirit or mind. Some ideas are caused by our own finite minds, as when we imagine ideas; but the vast richness of our other experiences must be caused by the infinite mind of God.

When it comes to his analysis of natural science, in particular physics, Berkeley's views find powerful echoes in modern instrumentalism. Berkeley argues against essentialism in physics: essentialism suggests that beyond the phenomena or appearances that we observe, the phenomena are caused by and united in an ultimate reality whose essential nature (such as atomic structure, extension, or substantial form) finally explains all phenomena and the necessary connection between phenomena observed to be constantly conjoined. This necessary connection takes the form of logical deducibility. The positing of some kind of essential nature is required to give a foundation to unifying causal laws which are the characteristic aim of science. A causal law of the form "If A then B", or "All As are Bs" does not merely describe the accidental juxtaposition of A and B in our experience, but aims to identify a necessary connection between A and B such that we say if A happens, then B *must* follow, and if something is A, it *must* also be B; in short A and B are connected in a way that could not be otherwise. That there exist such necessary connections between ideas we experience is denied by Berkeley; no such necessary connection is perceived between phenomena. There are no essential natures in things beyond experience; indeed, it is senseless to posit an essential nature in a reality of things beyond phenomena which would account for the necessary connection of our ideas; all that we ever experience is a succession of ideas among which we perceive patterns, associations and regularities. The search for such unattainable necessary connections only breeds scepticism about the achievements of science when science fails to show that it can establish how the world *must* be. Scientific theories do not present us with the truth about reality – metaphysics and theology do that – rather their value lies in their usefulness as general rules by which we can predict phenomena: what ideas will follow what, and what ideas are invariably found together. By limiting the aspirations of science Berkeley hopes to secure science from scepticism, and at the same time make room for the indispensability of theology.

Ideas are seen by Berkeley as natural signs; the experience of idea X is a sign that idea Y is about to follow; and it is our job to learn what these regularities are and to come to know the rules which correctly map the patterns of ideas; but we must not suppose that we have thereby discovered necessary connections between the ideas that could not be otherwise. That the ideas follow each other in regular order is entirely dependent on the will of God who chooses to present to us ideas in definite regular patterns, the rules of which we can learn. In learning the order of natural signs in science we learn the "language of God": the signs He systematically presents us with. The experience of getting closer to a fire will be followed by the experience of pain; but the two experiences are not necessarily connected; the relation between the two experiences is contingent; there is nothing about the experiences themselves, or about any further thing which is the cause of the experiences, which means that the juxtaposition of the experiences could not be otherwise. Yet we can trust in God that He will invariably maintain a regular order which it is possible for us to learn. In this way science is seen merely as a more systematic attempt to chart our experience than our everyday understanding, but not different in the kind of knowledge it produces.

It is, however, not true to say that Berkeley gives a regularity theory of causation. Although the mapping of regularities between non-causally associated ideas is the aim of science, real efficient causal influences take place between spiritual substances and ideas.

On Berkeley's view, the use in science of various terms such as "force", "gravity", "attraction", "cause", "effect", and "insensible particles" is harmless provided we do not think that these terms name real entities in the world which explain the causal necessary connection of phenomena or events we experience; such terms should be seen as merely useful suppositions or hypothetical posits which may aid us in making predictions. They do not describe facts about the world; but we can use them to help us predict phenomena; the phenomena can be understood as occurring *as if* they were facts about reality. From the point of view of facilitating the discovery of the general rules describing the order of phenomena, the truth of what one supposes as a mechanism is to be valued purely for its convenience, and its truth is irrelevant, for its truth as a mere useful supposition does not arise at all. More positively we can say that anti-essentialism encourages us always to seek further explanations because it does not assume there will be, and we might find, some point at which explanations are exhausted and complete.

Nevertheless, the sense in which we can be said to learn the *language* of God gives some residual meaning to scientific theories or laws being true; not every invariable correlation will constitute a law of science; the use of the terms *language* and *signs* suggests a structure that, although not necessary, does have an order of meaning and syntax analogous to that of a language.

Many problems reside in Berkeley's system. It is difficult to see how his proof that God exists can be valid if based on the premise that ideas that are not perceived by our minds must, if they are ideas of real things, continue to exist, and can do so only in the mind of God. No possible empirical evidence could verify the proposition that the ideas constituting object *A* exist unperceived by us. We are precluded from establishing by experience the ontological continuity of ideas constituting sensible objects when we do not experience them by the fact that any attempt to gather appropriate empirical evidence would be self-defeating: we cannot get a sly glance at things unperceived. This is rather like trying to determine whether the fridge light goes off when one closes the door, except that in the case of ideas constituting sensible objects it is a logical impossibility, not an empirical difficulty involving empirically determining if things exist unperceived. If the only guarantee we could have for knowing real things exist unperceived is following a proof that God exists, then a proof of the existence of God cannot, without being circular, use as a known premise that real things exist unperceived when not perceived by us.

The basis for idealism is that all that we ever perceive is ideas or sensations – light, colours, sounds, smells, tastes and the like – which can only be conceived of as existing in the mind. It is this that must be denied in an effective refutation of idealism. We must say that we can be immediately aware of physical objects in perception; what we perceive is appearances or aspects of objects themselves, not other entities called ideas that mediate between us and objects perceived.

If Berkeley were to stick strictly to his empiricism in using as evidence only the immediate content of our own minds, then it is difficult to see how he could avoid extreme solipsism: there is nothing he can be sure of except the nature and existence of the ideas of which he is immediately or currently conscious.

Hume

David Hume (1711-76) was born in Edinburgh, into a family of the minor gentry near the Scottish Border; the family home was the estate of Ninewells, close to the village of Chirnside near Berwick. David Hume's father died in 1713, leaving his mother to bring up David and two siblings, of whom David was the youngest. Their religious education was Calvinist in character with regular attendance at kirk.

Hume entered Edinburgh University in 1723 when not quite twelve. Here he received instruction in Latin, Greek, mathematics, physics and philosophy, and became acquainted with the work of John Locke and Isaac Newton; but he left the university around 1726 without taking his degree. By this time he had arrived at the atheism that was to last for the rest of his life. He returned to Ninewells where, following the family tradition, it was proposed that he turn to law as a profession; but Hume had no appetite for the law and instead spent time studying great classical literature. In 1734 Hume entered the offices of the West India company in Bristol, but his stay here was very short-lived, and he went to France where he could live more cheaply, first in Rheims, and then at the small town of La Flèche in Anjou; here he wrote A treatise of human nature. He returned to London in 1737 and after some difficulty eventually found a publisher; the Treatise appeared in 1739 and 1740, by which time he had returned to Ninewells. The book did not receive the high level of attention he had hoped, although he exaggerated when he said that "It fell dead-born from the Press." In 1745 Hume's application for the professorship of philosophy at Edinburgh University was rejected. From 1747 onwards Hume earned his living chiefly as a diplomatic secretary, which involved travel abroad. During this time he continued to publish short essays on various topics, and began work on the Enquiries concerning human understanding and concerning the principles of morals, in which he sought to rectify the presentational and stylistic deficiencies which he thought had led to the modest acclaim awarded to the Treatise; the Enquiries was published in 1748. In 1752 Hume became librarian to the Faculty of Advocates in Edinburgh, having been turned down in 1751 for the Chair of Logic at Glasgow despite the support of the vacating professor, Hume's friend, the economist Adam Smith (1723-90); it was as a librarian that Hume began his History of England. In 1761 he became a personal secretary at the Embassy in Paris and was extremely popular in Paris society. In 1766 Hume returned to England with the philosopher Jean-Jacques Rousseau (1712-78); however, Rousseau's chronic paranoia and unreasonableness soon caused them to fall out. Hume retired from work in 1769 and lived in Edinburgh. In 1775 he was struck by a fatal wasting disease of the bowels and he died the following year.

Hume's affable disposition while terminally ill was typical of his general character; he also remained unshaken in his rejection of any kind of survival in an afterlife. Although lean in his youth, in later years he had a rotund physique, and he took pleasure in food and good conversation. Despite having a formidably sharp intellect, he seems to have had a generally amiable, sociable, cheerful personality.

There is a tension which runs through Hume's philosophy between scepticism and naturalism. The sceptical side involves the employment of various arguments showing that we lack any rational justification for beliefs usually regarded as fundamental to our view of the world. There are three beliefs of particular importance that come in for this treatment:

(a) existence of causation and the rationality of induction
(b) existence of the external world: bodies continue to exist independently of us in the external world
(c) existence of a permanent self.

In each case Hume sets out to show that we have no rational justification for the belief, but also how the belief is a fundamental product of the faculty of imagination in human nature. Hume's purpose in revealing the lack of rational warrant is to show the limits of what human reason can account for. The naturalist strand in Hume's philosophy now enters for he does not draw the conclusion that because we lack rational justification for these beliefs we ought therefore to reject the beliefs. It is a fact that we do irresistibly, invariably and universally hold these beliefs, which are the foundation of thought and necessary for our survival; if our holding of these beliefs cannot be accounted for through our possessing sufficient rational grounds for the beliefs, then it is still to be explained why nevertheless we hold these beliefs, think the way we do, and remain unshaken by sceptical arguments directed against them. In short, one possible explanation for why we hold these beliefs is that we have rational grounds for doing so, but where we do not have rational grounds there must be some other explanation for why we have these entrenched beliefs. The explanation is to be found in the science of human nature. This science reveals that the way we come to form these beliefs is the same kind of way as other animals form beliefs; it is therefore quite proper to say that animals reason.

Sceptical arguments or reasoning can operate only against other arguments or reasons; but given that the explanation of our holding certain fundamental beliefs or thinking in certain ways is not to be found in our having reasons at all, the sceptical arguments or reasons against these fundamental beliefs or fundamental ways of thinking find no purchase; rational arguments are simply irrelevant. There is no question that we ought to think differently because we lack rational grounds in these cases, as the sceptic suggests, since nature, specifically human nature, ensures that we cannot help thinking in these ways; these ways of thinking are *fundamental facts about human nature* which are explained by *non*-rational laws describing how we go on or function; the beliefs thus produced are not thereby *irrational*; they would be irrational only if we supposed that the explanation of our having the beliefs is based on insufficient rational justification and that rational justification is required. We are psychologically constituted in such a way that, given a certain course of experiences, we will inevitably come to hold certain kinds of beliefs.

In our philosophical search for the ultimate foundations for our beliefs we come to see that certain of our most basic or fundamental beliefs are rationally groundless or unjustified; but we also come to understand that they are not the kind of beliefs that can be rationally grounded or justified; therefore the lack of rational justification is not to be thought of as a deficiency in these beliefs. They are not the kind of beliefs which we can be rationally justified or unjustified in holding; so showing there is no rational justification for the beliefs does not show them to be irrational or confused; rather, they are *non*-rational, but beliefs that we must have resulting from the way our natures fundamentally are. This position can be further defended by pointing out that if we enter into the process of giving reasons at all and suppose that it can ever be successfully brought to an end, there must be some beliefs for which reasons neither can be given nor are required; justification has to end somewhere.

An analogy may help. If we take the notion of *love* we can clearly understand that cases may arise where L giving reasons to M why M should love L rather than N is simply out of place; it is not that L's reasons are bad reasons; reasons of any sort are simply irrelevant and make no difference; it may just be a fact that M loves N and not L, and that is an end to it. One might as well argue with a tree that it is unusually early to come into leaf, or with an avalanche that it is wrong to fall on villages.

This naturalism has serious consequences for anything like Descartes' project for an absolute, non-species specific, objective conception or understanding of the world based on pure reason, not on concepts dependent on our contingent biological or psychological constitution. For it turns out that some of our most basic conceptions and beliefs are not transcendent and eternal, but depend on contingent facts about human nature. Descartes supposes that the fundamental conceptions involved in a truly scientific view of the world are are either intuitively obvious or rationally justifiable, and thereby are true universally for any intelligence whatsoever. Hume argues that these conceptions are dependent on human nature being what it is and functioning in certain ways, and without a nature which reacts in certain ways to experience such conceptions or ideas would not arise at all, since they cannot be derived from or justified by universal and valid deductive reasoning or experience. Our fundamental concepts and beliefs, which we apply to, and regard as real features of, the world, are species-dependent, not non-perspectival and absolute. That we have an idea of, and belief in, causality and induction, a belief in external physical bodies and in a relatively permanent self, depends on our reacting to certain experiences in certain ways; such ideas are neither a product of the pure necessity of reasoning nor derivable from passive observation of the world; our having these ideas depends on experience combining with the way human nature functions.

The tension between scepticism and naturalism arises from the uncertainty as to whether any particular case of a belief lacking rational justification should lead us to reject the belief or lead us to conclude that it is vain and unnecessary to ask for justification. The answer would seem to involve assessing how fundamental the belief is to human nature; that is, to what extent it is universal, irresistible and permanent.

Hume maintains the view common to other philosophers of his period that we are only ever immediately acquainted with the contents of our mind: perceptions. He divides perceptions in the mind into *impressions* and *ideas*. These are to be distinguished not by their origin, but by their degree of force and liveliness; impressions are lively perceptions or experiences and ideas less lively. Impressions are the primary or first appearance in the mind of any mental content, ideas are secondary and derivative weaker copies of impressions. Roughly the distinction is between actually experiencing X, and thinking about X. Fundamental to Hume's philosophy is that ideas, which are, generally speaking, the materials of thought, are faint copies of impressions and that we cannot have a *simple* idea of which we have not had a simple impression. Every simple idea has a corresponding simple impression that resembles it, and every simple impression a corresponding idea; that is, every simple perception appears both as impression and idea. This account has the odd consequence that to think about X (say, a pain) is mildly to experience X (a pain), which is surely false. We can have complex ideas of which we have no corresponding complex impressions, but only if they are made up of simple ideas copied from simple impressions we have had. The reason for this view is that Hume wishes to identify the correct impressions from which we derive ideas. There are two possible sources of ideas: impressions of sensation and impressions of reflection. Impressions of sensation are basically sense-experiences; impressions of reflection are often new impressions which derive from the natural way we react to certain impressions of sensation. If we have an idea which is derived from an impression of reflection in this way, then the existence and nature of the resultant idea partly depend on the workings and nature of our mind, and the idea is not something derived wholly passively from experience of the world.

The question is whether we are then justified in regarding the resultant idea as corresponding to a real feature of the world, or whether the idea does not correspond to a real feature of the world since it is simply a product of the way we react naturally to certain impressions of sensation, which in themselves do not contain that idea. For example we find that the idea of evil and evil acts is not derived from anything observed purely in acts, but results from the impression of reflection, *abhorrence*, we naturally feel, because of the reaction of human nature, at seeing certain acts; that we then regard evil as really in the world, and certain acts as abhorrent, results from the idea of evil being projected onto certain acts in the world, although it is not derived from something observed passively as really being in the world. If we did not react in certain natural ways to produce these impressions of reflection we would not, from observing the world, find any passive impressions of sensation from which the idea of evil could derive.

The meaning of a term is to be found in associating the term with the correct idea. If we cannot find any impression of either sensation or reflection as the origin of an idea which is presupposed in the corresponding term having meaning, then we must conclude that we are deluded when we say we have the idea, and the term which publicly articulates the supposed idea is in fact meaningless. But we must look carefully; if we cannot find an impression of sensation (perceptions of red, chairs, mountains, as well as sensations such as hot, cold, pain) we may well find an impression of reflection (feelings, passions, emotions, basic appetites, such as anger, sadness, hunger) from which an idea we have derives; but this has the important consequence that the true meaning and implications of the term corresponding to the idea may be quite different from what we thought them to be. We will have to conclude that if an idea derives from an impression of reflection or inner sentiment only, then it is not an objective feature of the world, but one that depends on our natural propensity to react to experiences in certain ways according to our human nature.

Hume distinguishes between memory and imagination on the basis of the distinction between impressions and ideas. Memory: the order/sequence and combination of ideas is the same as the original order/sequence and combination of the impressions. Imagination: the order/sequence and combination of ideas can be different from the original order/sequence of the impressions.

The *imagination* is of fundamental importance for Hume's account of why we have the beliefs we do have. The order/sequence and combination with which ideas feature in our imagination is not random but has rules governing that order; there are forces of attraction, which, although not intrinsic to the ideas by themselves, govern the way simple atomic ideas and complex ideas are associated as a result of fundamental propensities of human nature.

Hume argues that all perceptions are really distinct from each other; they can exist at different times; they can thus be conceived existing separately without any contradiction; therefore any connection, if it exists at all, between perceptions is contingent and not necessary. It is the *human mind* that, according to certain natural propensities, associates perceptions which have logically distinct existences and between which no necessary connections are ever discovered by reason or observation; but it is from this *feeling of being determined* to associate ideas in certain ways, which is an impression of *reflection*, that the idea originates of the perceptions themselves being necessarily connected.

Hume sees part of his function as explaining why we hold certain fundamental beliefs; this he does through discovering and calling upon the laws governing the order of perceptions in our minds. The basis of Hume's explanation is the "principle of association of ideas"; this explains why we in fact think as we do, although we may have no rational justification for doing so. Ideas become associated in our minds in specific ways and this controls the order or sequence of thoughts through our minds. There are three main factors that determine which ideas are associated in the human mind:

 (i) resemblance: qualitative similarity
 (ii) contiguity: proximity in space and/or time
(iii) cause and effect: the thought of one idea leads to the thought of
       a causally connected idea.

The mind naturally moves smoothly from one idea to another in accordance with these principles of association. If we have an impression of *A*, or entertain an idea *A*, we naturally move to the idea *B* related to it in the highest degree by some or all of the above principles. Ideas are mental atoms among which Hume attempts to describe the rules governing their behaviour.

The objects of human understanding and inquiry fall into two exclusive and exhaustive classes. The distinction is sometimes called "Hume's fork": this contends that all meaningful propositions can be divided into one of two types:

 (I) relations of ideas
 (II) matters of fact and real existence.

All propositions of type (I) concern the abstract relation of ideas, and can be known to be true *a priori* because their denial would involve a contradiction and they are thus necessary. Examples are truths in mathematics and logic. They are intuitively or deductively certain. The examination of the meaning of the constituent ideas of the propositions alone is sufficient to establish their truth or falsity. All propositions of type (II) concern connections between matters of fact and the actual existence of things, and can be known to be true, if at all, only *a posteriori* by experience, and not through examining the meaning of the constituent ideas alone because their denial does not involve a contradiction and they are thus contingent. Examples are the propositions of natural science and common-sense statements of fact. The price of our knowing propositions of type (I), however, is that they are trivial truths that can tell us nothing about what is actual and contingent, but only what is possible (not contradictory), impossible (contradictory) or necessary (denial is contradictory). Thus we cannot know any truths about the actual contingent or real world *a priori* by pure logical reasoning alone; if we can know truths about the world at all, we must rely on the evidence of experience. Propositions that do not concern either relations of ideas or empirical matters of fact are meaningless.

Closely connected with this is the way Hume shows that we lack reasons for our fundamental beliefs by showing that the only two possible sources of rational justification do not provide reasons for those fundamental beliefs.

(I′) *Reason*

Justification by intuitive, demonstrative, deductive or logical *a priori* reasoning.

(II′) *Senses*

Justification by the evidence of observation or *a posteriori* experience.

These are exhaustive of the sources of rational justification. Hume purports to show that rational justification from either source, demonstrative reasoning or experience, is lacking for our fundamental beliefs in causation in the world and inductive inference, in the existence of physical objects in the external world, and in a persistent self; thus they cannot be rationally justified at all; nevertheless, the mechanics of the mind are such that we *hold irresistibly* these beliefs so necessary for our survival. Hume's positive contribution is to give an account of why, in fact, given that rational justification cannot account for it, we do hold these basic beliefs.

Why, in particular, do we form beliefs about matters of fact that we have not observed on the basis of what we have observed? Characteristically this takes the form of an inductive inference of the form:

$$\frac{\text{All observed } As \text{ are } Bs.}{\text{Therefore all } As \text{ are } Bs.}$$

or

Therefore the next A will be a B.

But is there any rational justification for this inference? Take, for example, the propositions "All unsupported bodies fall", "The sun will rise tomorrow", or the propositions "All A is B" and "If A occurs, then B must occur". These are characteristic of the propositions of natural science and common sense. Is there any rational justification for our assertion of these propositions? As it stands the above

inductive inference, which might be used to support such propositions, is clearly deductively invalid: it is possible for the premise to be
true but the conclusion false. In all such instances we move from
cases we have observed to cases we have not observed on the
supposed basis of there being a *causal relation*. That is, *A* is the cause
of *B*, which supposes that *A* occurring is necessarily connected with
B occurring.

If the inference from *A* we have observed to *B* we have not
observed, and the belief that they are necessarily connected, is to be
rationally justifiable, it must be because of (I´) reason or (II´) the
senses. Hume thinks both fail to provide such rational justification.

Hume is clear that the causal connection between *A* and *B*, which
describe events in the world, is not explained and rationally justified
by (I´): its being logical or deductive. The relation between event *A*
and event *B* is not like the relation in a deductive argument between
premises and conclusions. If the connection were deductive, and
hence logically necessary, then the assertion of *A* and the denial of *B*
would involve a contradiction. But in the case of connections of events
or matters of fact this seems never to be the case; the assertion of a
matter-of-fact connection and its denial seem equally conceivable. The
logical relation which holds between a plane figure being three-sided
and its being triangular, or its internal angles being equal to 180
degrees, is the kind of relation that would, if it applied, make a
connection necessary and enable us to justify rationally the inference
to cases we have not observed from cases we have observed; but such
a relation does not hold between events in the world corresponding
to our ideas of them *A* and *B*. *A* and *B* can exist at separate times,
therefore *A* and *B* are separable in thought; the existence of *A* can be
supposed without supposing the existence of *B*, and the assertion that
A is always found with *B* is therefore a contingent, not a necessary,
truth. In short, if it is ever the case that *A* and *B* can exist at different
times, we can conceive of *A* and *B* as separate, and any connection
between them cannot be necessary.

It might seem as though the causal relation is deductive, and thus
we can know *a priori* the connection between *A* and its causal
consequences *B* because we know the kind of thing *A* is: say a billiard
ball. But the question arises as to how we know what kind of thing
A is. Hume argues that in the case where *A* is something entirely new
to us, we can know that *B*, or anything else, will follow only by
experience. Logically speaking, apart from what would be logically
contradictory anything could happen. If it seems as though we can
deduce *B* from *A*, this is because we have already observed the
behaviour of *A*-like things and included in the definition identifying
A as *A* (what is an *A*) the relation to *B*. We cannot from examining *A*-
in-itself or alone prior to any experience of *A*, before a characterizing
definition of it that may include *B* as a causal consequence, deduce

what will follow. In identifying A as an A – as something of a certain sort – we already have to include certain potential causal consequences; we cannot separate what we mean by an A – what A is – from all its causal consequences. To show that we could by pure reason alone deduce B from A, and yet by this produce new non-trivial knowledge, we would have to define A independently of its causal consequences, but this is impossible if what we mean by an A – and hence use to identify something as an A in the first place – must include the range of A's causal effects. That certain causal consequences are connected with A is not something that can be known *a priori*.

Alternatively it might be the case that we make the inference from A to B, and are rationally justified in doing so in accordance with (II′), because we observe in experience a necessary connection between A and B when observing the conjunction of an instance of A and B, or B following A; but in fact we observe no such necessary connection between A and B, but simply observe A and B occurring together. The hammer is thrown, hits the window, and then the window breaks; there is no necessary connection observed as part of this, but rather a sequence of logically distinct events. We observe no necessary connection between observed matters of fact themselves, but only events conjoined with or following one another. Nevertheless, we still believe some events and ideas to be necessarily connected, and it remains to be explained why we do so.

Partly the formation of beliefs about the unobserved on the basis of the observed is founded on the principle that "Every event has a cause". But Hume shows that this principle lacks rational justification by showing that it cannot be justified either by (I′) or by (II′); this applies Hume's fork. First, it is not a necessary logical truth, since its negation does not imply a contradiction; the assertion of an uncaused event is conceivable. He notes that the assertion of an uncaused event does not involve the contradictory assertion that the uncaused event is *caused* by "nothing", rather it asserts that the event has no cause at all. Second, it is not a truth that can be known empirically, since it can be neither established nor refuted by experience; logically there is no hope of examining all cases. It cannot be confirmed because we cannot examine all cases to show every case has a cause; it cannot be refuted because in any given case we cannot examine and exclude everything that might be a cause.

If the causal relation between A and B is not deductive, then the move from the observed to the unobserved on the basis of observed As and Bs is an inductive inference, and if the assertion of general propositions such as "All A is B", or "If A occurs, then B must occur", is to be rationally justified, then they depend on some kind of "uniformity of nature principle": that conjoined events that we have observed will hold in cases we have not observed. Thus, events that we have observed to be constantly conjoined in the past will continue to be so in the future. In short, the uniformity principle asserts that the laws of nature will hold in cases we have not observed, and the future will resemble the past. The acceptance of the uniformity principle would make the inference, from cases we have observed to those we have not, rationally justified – the inference would be valid – by acting as a required premise in the inference from instances we have observed to those we have not observed.

All observed *A*s are *B*s.
Uniformity principle: past conjunctions will continue in future.
_____
Therefore all *A*s are *B*s.

or

Therefore the next *A* will be a *B*.

But what is the rational justification for the truth of the uniformity principle itself? Again Hume's fork is applied, this time in testing the uniformity principle. First, if the uniformity principle were a logical truth, then its negation would be a contradiction, its denial inconceivable; this is clearly not the case; it is certainly conceivable that any law which has operated in all cases until now should cease to operate in the future and should fail to operate in cases we have not observed. The uniformity principle cannot be known *a priori*. Secondly, the uniformity principle, if it is itself merely a further matter of fact, cannot be justified by experience for any such attempt will be irredeemably circular. We might try to justify the uniformity principle by experience *a posteriori* by saying: the uniformity principle itself has always operated or held in the past, and so it will continue to operate or hold in the future, therefore the uniformity principle is justified by experience. In applying this to the uniformity principle itself such a justifying inference is circular, since it is exactly the kind of inference which depends for its validity on accepting the uniformity principle: that past observations *are* evidence that the future will operate in the same way.

The startling conclusion that Hume draws from his analysis of our belief in unobserved matters of fact is that such beliefs lack all rational justification, and thus having a rational justification is not responsible for our making the inference from observed *A* to unobserved *B* following the observation of *A* and *B* conjoined in the past. We do not make the inference from *A* which we observe to *B* which we do not observe because we are rationally justified in doing so. Nevertheless we *do* make the inference, so there must be some other explanation for why we make it.

Hume gives on the one hand an account of causation and what is involved in the idea that events are causally connected, on which all moves to unobserved matters of fact depend; and on the other hand an account of the conditions under which we hold the belief that events are causally connected.

C′ (a) spatial and temporal contiguity
    (b) temporal priority: cause comes before effect
    (c) necessary connection between cause and effect
C′′ (a) observed spatial and temporal contiguity
    (b) observed temporal priority: cause comes before effect
    (c) observed repeated constant conjunction.

The reason for these accounts is that Hume wishes to argue that C′ describes the necessary and sufficient conditions for events being causally linked and what is involved in the idea that they are, but we come to hold the belief that they are causally connected in just those conditions or circumstances described in C′′, and those conditions or circumstances do not rationally justify the belief as true, nor is there any other way of doing so.

When we believe A and B in sense C′ to be causally connected:

(1) We make the inference from observed As and Bs to unobserved As and Bs.

(2) We believe or expect, not merely think, that B will occur following a fresh observation of A.

(3) We believe the connection between A and B to be a necessary connection: that it could not be otherwise.

We do not have any rational justification for the inference involved in (1), for the relation between A and B is neither logical nor justified by experience. We have no rational justification for the belief (2), since it cannot be based on either logic or experience. We do not have any rational justification for the belief (3), since the relation is not logically necessary, nor is a necessary connection between instances of events A and B something we observe in experience of A and B; we observe A *conjoined* with B, but we do not, as a feature of our experience of them, observe any necessary connection.

So (1) our *making the inference* from A to B, and (2) our *belief* that B will follow an observation of A, and (3) our belief that A and B are *necessarily connected* are not explained by our being rationally justified in the inference or the beliefs. Hume's conclusion is that these are not a matter of rational justification at all. It still remains to give an explanation of these matters.

The explanation Hume gives returns us to features of human nature, the principles of the association of ideas and how we react to certain experiences. The explanation in all the cases (1), (2) and (3) derives from habits or customs of the imagination: mental habituation. This tendency to mental habituation is a propensity of human nature. The basis of the explanation is that *repeated observation* of the constant conjunction of A with B as in C′′ sets up a habit of association in the mind of A and B, and it is this that leads us to (1) make the inference from *A* to *B* in cases we have not observed, (2) believe that *B* will occur having had a fresh impression of *A*, (3) believe that *A* and *B* are necessarily connected.

Hume gives an account in C′′ of the circumstances or conditions in which we *in fact* come to judge that *A* and *B* are causally connected, rather than where we are rationally justified in so doing. The explanation of our belief in causal connections then derives from the product of those circumstances and our natural reactions in those circumstances. Following the repeated observation of the conjunction of *A* and *B* in our experience in accordance with the conditions C′′ there is set up in our minds the habit or custom of associating *A* and *B*; and these are just the circumstances in which we say *A* and *B* are causally connected. Taking points (1), (2) and (3) above in turn, Hume gives the following accounts.

(1) *Making the inference from* A *to* B

It is just a *fact* about our fundamental psychological constitutions that in circumstances C′′, following the observed repetition of *A* and *B* in conjunction, we *do make* the inference from *A* to *B*. The repetition of *A* and *B* constantly conjoined in our experience sets up a habit or custom such that on the observation of *A* we compulsively move to the idea that *B*. Thus we infer the idea of *B* from the idea of *A* in cases we have not observed, but the move is not a rational move at all, since it is neither deductive nor justified by experience.

(2) *Believing that* B *will follow* A

To understand our expectation or belief that *B* will follow *A* on observing *A* in conditions C′′, we must understand what a belief is for Hume. He explains a belief as being just the degree of liveliness or force of an idea, and not a difference in, or addition to, the content of an idea; the difference between merely conceiving or thinking *X* and believing *X* is a matter of the force and liveliness with which the idea of *X* strikes us. In the case of believing *B* will follow *A*, Hume's explanation is that there is a transference of force by a kind of inertia from the fresh impression of *A* to the idea that *B*, which enlivens *B*, where the habit of associating *A* and *B* exists, and this turns the mere thought of *B* into a belief or expectation – a lively or vivid idea – that *B*. It should be pointed out that sometimes Hume presents a somewhat different theory of belief, whereby it is a difference of attitude towards an idea, or the manner in which an idea is conceived or entertained, which constitutes believing an idea, and which makes believing something feel different from an imagined fiction: it is an idea being more strongly or vividly conceived or entertained that constitutes a belief in an idea, rather than a difference in the vivacity of the idea itself. It is not clear if these two theories can be reconciled: in the first theory, belief is a matter of how an object of thought strikes us, in the second theory it is a matter of how we take hold of the object of thought.

(3) *Believing that* A *and* B *are necessarily connected*

The inference of B from A is not based on the necessary connection of A and B; rather, the idea of the necessary connection of A and B, essential to the belief in a causal relation C´, depends on our *in fact compulsively making* the move from the impression or idea of A to the idea of B following the repeated observation of the conjunction of A and B as in conditions C´´. We have no impression of a necessary connection between A and B derived from observing the conjunction of A and B themselves: we just see A happen, then see B happen. But if the idea of necessary connection, and hence our belief in causation between events, is not to be a delusion and meaningless, there must be some impression from which it derives. The idea of necessary connection derives from a new impression of *reflection*, which in this case is *the feeling of determination* resulting from the mental habit of our passing from the idea of A to the idea B, following previous *repeated* observation of the constant conjunction of A and B. The idea of necessary connection does not correspond to anything in the impressions of A and B themselves, nor does it arise from the perceived repetition of their conjunction *alone*, which would in itself produce no new impression; it corresponds to a new impression of reflection which is a generated feeling of determination, as we habitually pass in the mind, because of an associative propensity of human nature, from the idea of A to that of B, on having repeatedly had experience of the conjunction of A and B. The idea of necessary connection, and that of causality which depends on it, would not have arisen at all, because there would have been no corresponding impression from which it could arise, except for the propensity of human nature to produce a suitable new impression of reflection; no impressions of A and B would alone be sufficient to give rise to the idea of necessary connection. There is no circularity involved in this account: the idea of necessary connection derives from the *feeling* of determination, whether there is actually any determination or not, because we in fact move and have a propensity to move from A to B, which establishes a habit in our minds, following exposure to the repeated observation of constant conjunction of A and B. That the idea of necessary connection derives from an impression of reflection or feeling in this way has a very important consequence: that the necessary connection, and therefore causal connection, that we suppose to exist between events themselves and our ideas of those events is, in fact, *in the mind*, not an objective feature of the world; it is something we project onto the world owing to habit, not something observed in events in the world, and it is falsely regarded as an objective feature of the world or real relation connecting events we observe.

In sum, the belief in causal connections, which includes necessary connection, depends on our natural movement from one idea to another, not the other way around.

Hume gives an analogous account of the remaining fundamental beliefs (mentioned at the beginning of the Hume section): (b) the existence of the external world: bodies continue to exist independently of us in the external world and (c) the existence of a permanent self. The strategy is the same: we have no rational justification for these beliefs through reason or the senses, but nature through the imagination has ensured that we have these beliefs, and human nature gives an account of this non-rational mechanism. We believe that there are bodies existing continuously and independently of us, and that we are the same self over time.

Hume begins by saying that it is vain to ask if bodies (external material objects) exist or not, since we cannot help believing that they do; the question of interest, therefore, is what accounts for having that belief. The belief in the external world is constituted by a belief in objects that exist continuously (when not perceived, for example) and exist independently of perceivers. Reason cannot justify this belief: not only is it not the case that most people use rational arguments to come to this belief, but also it is not possible to give a demonstrative proof that the external world exists such that a denial would be a logical contradiction. The senses cannot justify the belief: all that we have, if we examine our sense-experiences or perceptions carefully, is impressions which are perishing (non-continuous or interrupted) and dependent (internal or mental) for their existence and nature on perceivers. All that we are aware of is perceptions which are perishing and dependent; we do not perceive any objects distinct from impressions. So what features of our perceptions lead us to believe, or produce the belief, that our impressions of sense are of external material objects which do exist continuously and independently of us? It is not the force or involuntariness of certain impressions that accounts for the belief, for these are features of impressions, such as pains, that we do not suppose exist independently in the external world. The features of our sense-experience from which the belief derives are the *constancy* and *coherence* of certain series of perceptions which lead the *imagination*, operating according to certain propensities of human nature, to overlook the fleeting and internal nature of impressions. The series of perceptions can be *constant* in that there are resembling collections of perceptions in a series even though there may be gaps between them, as when I look at the table in my room, go out and come back and look again. The series of perceptions can be *coherent* in that although the collections of perceptions in a series change, they do so in a predictable way, as when I come back to my room and find the fire has burnt down as expected. First, we resolve the conflict between the gaps in our perceptions and their constancy by regarding the gaps as only apparent, with the object of our perceptions really continuing to exist in the gaps. Second, we explain the coherence of our perceptions by the supposition that the objects perceived exist constantly and independently in the gaps when not perceived.

Our belief in continuous and independent objects is one in something that preserves identity through time; this would strictly involve perceptions which are invariable and uninterrupted. We have bundles of perceptions which, although perishable and interrupted, also exactly resemble each other and thus they exhibit constancy. Because these bundles exactly resemble each other the human mind overlooks the gaps and lazily treats them as if they were the same uninterrupted perception. Thus we come to form the belief in, or lively idea of, continuous and independently existing objects corresponding to these bundles of perceptions; the belief or lively idea which fills the gaps itself derives its liveliness from the resembling impressions either side of the gaps in our perceptions. In short, we naturally and habitually confuse a series of interrupted but resembling perceptions with the alike single continuous perception that would be invariable and uninterrupted, and thus believe that sensible objects exist as continuous and independent objects.

The belief in the self, or a personal identity that persists over time, receives similar treatment. Its existence is indemonstrable by reason. Through experience when we look into ourselves we do not perceive anything corresponding to the permanent self, or spiritual substance, in which perceptions inhere, but only particular fleeting perceptions themselves. The human mind is really a bundle of distinct perceptions between which we perceive no real or necessary connection. The explanation for the belief in the self which we nevertheless have arises from the natural association of ideas which is a product of the perceptions themselves with unavoidable wedding or associative propensities of human nature, giving rise to an impression of *reflection* which is a feeling that the ideas are connected; but this association of ideas and the consequent feeling of connectedness between the ideas depend on us and our nature, and the connection is not a real connection between the ideas themselves. It is from this *feeling* of connectedness, which is an impression of *reflection*, that the idea of the mind being unified in a single self, which is a continuous and unchanging thing, arises and is ascribed to what are really separate and variable perceptions; this leads us to mistake what is really a collection of logically distinct perceptions for something that is connected in a unity and has identity.

Generally we cannot know if the connections we feel exist between perceptions are real, for we never perceive necessary connections existing between them, but merely perceive one following another. In fact, we know perceptions to be distinct existences or atomic; they are able to exist independently of each other without logical contradiction. The idea of connection between them is just a copy of a parent impression of reflection – the sentiment or feeling of determination in the mind as we naturally associate ideas – but we can have no knowledge of whether the connection actually holds.

Nature has taken care that we hold our most fundamental beliefs. We irresistibly believe in causation and inductive inference, and believe in the existence of independent continuous external bodies and a persistent self, even though we have no rational justification for the beliefs from reason or experience. Thus nature ensures that the arguments of the sceptic find no purchase against processes that are not a matter of rational justification at all but are a matter of deep instincts in human nature.

CHAPTER SIX

Transcendental idealism: Kant

The German philosopher Immanuel Kant was born in 1724 into the midst of the European Enlightenment. The Enlightenment meant different things in different countries, but certain common features can be discerned. Kant referred to the Enlightenment as European man's coming of age; the assurance with which man had known his place in the universe was being destroyed for ever. This did not mean the replacement of one doctrine by another in which man could at least find a place, no matter how unpleasant it might be; man was cast adrift in a void, there to be dependent only on his own resources. The Enlightenment questioned the right of anyone at all to claim a monopoly of truth; this throws the decision as to what is the truth back on the individual. The abandonment of authority as the source of truth leads to a profound search as to the origins and justification of our beliefs. The eighteenth century is marked by many embarking on this search full of hope, confident that human reason has the capacity to provide answers and discover truths. It led many thinkers who were intelligent and honest in their deliberations to scepticism; an inability to see how claims to human knowledge can be justified.

Developments in astronomy, with the work of Copernicus in the sixteenth century, had already begun to undermine the medieval edifice which gave man his defined place in the universe. The Great Chain of Being, with God at its summit, stones at its base, and men and angels in between, was dismembered. The Sun, not the Earth, was the centre of our planetary system, situated in a universe of unthinkable immensity and man was denied his privileged place in it. Newton's synthesis of the astronomy of Copernicus and Kepler, and the terrestrial mechanics of Galileo, gave no one a privileged position; laws of nature are objectively and uniformly true in all places. There was also no need for a God to maintain the activity of the universe since it was relatively autonomous, like a clock, and perhaps only required someone to wind it up periodically; but this diminished God's influence to a point where He could be dispensed with, even if a highly religious man such as Newton did not wish to do so. The religious scientist must now serve God through the humble task of uncovering the wonderful order bestowed upon the universe by the Creator at its inception. However, a tension had now emerged in discoveries that appeared to reveal the magnificent workmanship of God's universe, but that at the same time made belief in God optional, since God's intervention in the universe, except perhaps at the very beginning, of which we knew nothing, was not required in explanation as it had been before.

Out of the Enlightenment we may evolve a criterion separating the religious from the non-religious, a criterion based on a more fundamental notion than the existence and authority of God. This can be based on whether it is thought that the universe has some special place or concern (negative or positive) for human beings. It is a universe unresponsive to all human values, one to which human values are simply not applicable, an amoral universe, that gives rise to the crisis begun for man in the Enlightenment. Some reject this aspect of the Enlightenment and continue in acceptance of God, although for many it can never be quite the same; others embrace the idea of an entirely amoral universe, and suffer the problems of discovering what, if anything, can then have value; still others act merely *as if* the universe still responds to human values; they live under the shadow cast by a figure that has already left the scene.

It would be wrong to think of all the most revolutionary intellectual figures before and during the Enlightenment as free-thinking atheists; some of the most important figures were Copernicus, Descartes, Locke, Spinoza, Newton, Leibniz, Berkeley, Kant, and all were religious men to varying degrees and in different ways, men often profoundly worried about where their thought seemed inexorably to be taking them; this sometimes forced them to take rearguard action against the consequences of their own thoughts. They all contributed to the complete change in man's world-view, whether they intended to or not.

Kant both benefited from, and went beyond, the Enlightenment (*die Aufklärung*). After an initial immersion in the rationalist philosophy of Leibniz, Kant could no longer accept it; under the influence of Hume, and the German Crusius, Kant says he was woken from his dogmatic slumbers. Another powerful influence on Kant was Newton. Before devoting himself to philosophy, Kant had been a scientist; he saw the effect that a Newtonian view of the universe was going to have on morality, God, and our freewill. For if Newtonian views were universally and rigorously applied, they left little place for God, and undermined morality in fundamental ways: a Newtonian universe was an amoral mechanical system in which objective values seemed to have no application; man himself was an entity subject to the universal remorseless laws of nature, whose actions were absolutely determined by events that had already occurred, and which were thereby always outside his control; whatever we may *feel* about the matter, we are not free to choose, and where there is no freedom there is no responsibility for action, and thus there can be no moral evaluations. A tree is not free to choose, despite being alive; so when it falls on someone, the event is neither moral nor immoral, it is amoral, just something that happens. Human actions were now in danger of becoming just things that happen.

Kant tried to respond to all these influences, and reconcile them in a new synthesis. The empiricism of Hume had, it seemed to many, led to scepticism about human knowledge, identity and freedom, and Kant could not accept this. The rationalist view argued that there were innate principles of the understanding or reason with which man could *a priori* comprehend the basic nature of the world, although not the world of appearances, but a real world that lies behind appearances which ultimately explains those appearances. Hume undermined this by showing that these principles either were analytic – restating what, in disguised form, had already been assumed – or went beyond being analytic and could not therefore be justified by reason alone; but Hume found they could not then be justified by experience either. There was no midway course for empiricism.

Kant set out to show that these views could be reconciled; he tried to show why the true nature of the relationship between experience and the world is such that we can know things about the world of appearances *a priori* – truths knowable independently of the evidence of experience – although we can have no *a priori* knowledge of a real world beyond appearances. Kant wants to show that we can know certain truths *a priori* which are not trivial logical truths known merely because of their formal structure. We can know the truth "If *p* then *q*, *p*, therefore *q*" *a priori* precisely because we can substitute uniformly any propositions we like for *p* and *q*; but for that same reason such logical deductions can, independently of experience, tell us nothing about the world. Our ability to know them *a priori* derives precisely from the fact that they commit us to nothing about the actual world. Kant thinks he can show how we can know universal necessary truths *a priori* about the world as it appears, although not the world as it is in itself.

Kant draws an analogy between his own revolution in philosophy and that of the Copernican revolution in astronomy, but only in the following respect: Copernicus had dared to suggest that some of the motions of the heavenly bodies were only apparent and were as a result of the motion of the observer. Similarly Kant suggests that some of the properties we ascribe to external objects are a result of constructive mental processes to which appearances have to conform. The philosophy propounded by Kant also attempts to be universally valid in covering all self-conscious rational beings. Kant proposes that our experience involves elements partly contributed by us, and partly by the world; this does not mean our conception of the world is merely subjective in being true only from a particular point of view, or that it is absolutely objective, since the conception of the world cannot be separated completely from ways that we experience the world.

Kant

Immanuel Kant (1724–1804) was born in the Prussian town of Königsberg, into a pietist Lutheran family; there he became Professor of Logic and Metaphysics in 1770, at the age of forty-six.

Kant is frequently seen as almost a caricature of the popular conception of a philosopher; outwardly his life was the very model of the fastidious, studious, self-contained philosophical speculator. There is no doubt that like many original people he was capable of great acts of self-discipline. Yet he was not an unsociable man, or an unentertaining lecturer; he was fond of female company, although he never married. He never ventured many miles from Königsberg. His life is therefore depicted as being, on the whole, dull and uneventful. This may well be true; we should temper this somewhat patronizing conclusion by reflecting that many of us do not have lives a great deal more exciting. Near the end of his life, when he had already been withdrawn from society for some time, Kant's intellectual powers crumbled; he failed to recognize friends, and he was virtually blind; yet those closest to him still had glimpses of his good nature and will power, and of the great philosopher behind the shell of the man that remained.

A discussion of Kant's epistemology and metaphysics naturally centres upon the *Critique of pure reason*, his most complete thinking on these subjects. An additional work on the same subjects is the *Prolegomena*. Kant published many other works on science, aesthetics, and on ethics.

Kant, to some extent, saw himself as solving the errors committed by Hume and Leibniz. Hume's philosophy has been interpreted by some as collapsing into scepticism; central claims for human knowledge, which are logically presupposed by natural science, are found to be unjustifiable on the basis of his empiricist philosophy whereby all such claims must be rationally justified either by pure reason *a priori* or by the evidence of experience *a posteriori*. Neither is found to provide such rational justification, although nature takes care that we nevertheless hold the required fundamental beliefs. Not only did our common-sense beliefs about the world become unsupportable, but the most powerful intellectual achievement of the day, Newtonian mechanics, was also undermined. Newtonian mechanics seemed to give a complete unifying explanation of the workings of the universe; it was revolutionary in regarding the universe not as operating under special laws for different regions, but as being unified throughout under one objective set of laws. Kant saw this as supremely worth defending against Hume's scepticism. Knowledge for Kant, as for Leibniz, had to be necessary and universally valid. Hume undermined this, leaving us with knowledge of the world, in so far as we could have any at all, which was subjective, particular and contingent. The most important basic beliefs about the world could not be justified by reason, but if we examined closely what we actually experienced – the information provided by experience – they could not be justified by experience either. The most important basic beliefs in question were: the belief that the world operates by necessary causal laws, so we can make inference beyond what we presently perceive to unobserved cases; the belief that there exist independent continuously existing objects; and the belief that there is a continuous self. In short, empiricism, with its adherence to the view that experience must be the sole source of evidence about the world, led to scepticism when it was found that experience in itself, if carefully examined, was not sufficient to justify some of our most basic beliefs about the world.

Kant was convinced both that, contrary to Leibniz, knowledge of the world had always to be concerned with the world of our experience, not a reality beyond appearances, and that, contrary to Hume, the senses were not alone as a means of justifying our knowledge of such a world. The way out of this is to deny that sensation and experience are one and the same. Kant's basic idea is a distinction between form and content; the form of our experience is knowable *a priori*, the content is given *a posteriori*, and only in combination can these provide knowledge of the world. We could not have knowledge of a world other than the experienced one; but sensation alone could not support our claims to knowledge. Sensation is always particular, changing and subjective, and our knowledge claims are general, universal, unchanging and objective. Leibniz was impressed by the power of mathematics; maintaining a distrust of the senses as a source of knowledge that led back to Plato, Leibniz sought a metaphysics that describes the fundamental or underlying nature of the world beyond appearances, which was independent of the evidence of experience, based on a few basic principles; the world of appearances is explained ultimately through the reality that lies behind it; it is this reality which is the metaphysical foundation for all other knowledge of the world. This is not to say Leibniz thought that humans could deduce all scientific laws from *a priori* metaphysical principles; such *a priori* principles are too general and the *a priori* principles and reason describe not appearances but the reality underlying those appearances. Metaphysics seeks to describe what the world must fundamentally be like if it is fully rationally explicable.

Kant thought Newtonian mechanics explained not a reality behind appearances, but those appearances themselves; the question was how this was possible in the light of Hume's attack on our ability to justify through examining our sensations the kind of necessary universal laws Newton proposed, and the application of such laws to experience. It could not be achieved through Leibniz's philosophy, for Hume had also shown that the machinations of pure reason alone could not generate any new knowledge concerning what is actual; a pure logical argument unpacks only items that are already contained in its premises. The finite ability of the human mind may give us the impression that something new is arising; but it is already there; for God there would be no point in doing mathematics, or logic, or playing chess; He would already know all the consequences.

There were other intellectual structures that Kant thought it necessary to defend: Euclidean geometry, absolute space, continuous infinite time, the applicability of mathematics in explaining the world. Underlying Newtonian mechanics especially are the concepts of causality and substance. Each area of human inquiry has its limits; one Newtonian limit consisted in not questioning the existence of matter, but instead concentrating on how all posited matter behaves. But without the establishment in reality of a general concept of an independent, self-subsisting stuff, Newtonian mechanics is left entirely hypothetical: *if* the world is a certain way *then* these are the laws of its behaviour. In addition the justification of general laws as such had to be attempted: universal causality, which allows us to go beyond seeing that this follows that to saying that this always causes that, and so make inferences to cases we have not observed. Hume thought that rational justification for our beliefs could lie only in either reason or experience; but neither reason nor experience could justify our belief in an external world of bodies, substance, causality, or the self of personal identity; we could only show how they in fact arise as natural beliefs in response to the experiences we have. It is just these general concepts or categories that Kant aims to show we are justified in applying necessarily and objectively to the world we experience, although that application could not be justified, or refuted, by experience.

It must be emphasized that Kant thought that in some areas of human inquiry some final answers had been generated. The world did obey Newton's laws, Aristotle's logic said all there was to say about logic; space was Euclidean and three-dimensional, time was classical and stretched like an infinite straight line towards the future and back into the past; causality did apply universally. All these things have been questioned by modern thinking; Einstein questioned Newtonian space, time, and motion; quantum mechanics questioned universal causality; modern logic generated a richer array of theorems, making Aristotelean logic a small fragment of it. Kant was not narrow-minded, but Newton's world-view in particular was so powerful and all-encompassing in its unified explanations of a vastly diverse range of phenomena that to be overwhelmed by its finality was understandable. Nor must we let Kant's adherence to these particular theories detract from his important and revolutionary views.

Kant's *Critique* is, roughly, divided into two parts: the Analytic and the Dialectic; the Analytic includes the Aesthetic. The word "aesthetic" derives from a Greek word *aesthesis* relating to perception by the senses. The special Kantian sense of "Aesthetic" concerns the *a priori* form or order necessarily imposed by our capacity to receive representations – our sensibility – on the material supplied by the senses. The form or order is *a priori* and necessary, and Kant discovers it by subtraction of both the material of sensation and the concepts contributed by the faculty of understanding. These pure forms of sensible intuition or of experiences turn out to be space and time. The Analytic is largely positive; in it are determined the *a priori* principles of the understanding; we are also shown the proper use of metaphysics in providing the basis for our objective knowledge. The Dialectic is largely negative. We are shown the misuse of metaphysics in using concepts to go beyond what we can possibly experience, to a world of illusion and contradiction; we are also shown why we are prone to be tempted to this kind of speculation. The Aesthetic and Analytic give us a metaphysics of experience; they display what must be the basic features of experience and reasoning. The Dialectic shows how we err when we attempt to extend our knowledge beyond that which it is possible for us to experience.

We now turn to examining some well-used terms in Kant's *Critique*. These divide into three pairs: *a priori/a posteriori*, analytic/synthetic, necessary/contingent. First we distinguish *a priori* statements, which once understood can logically be known to be true prior to, and independently of, the evidence of experience, from *a posteriori* statements, which once understood can logically be known to be true only by the evidence of experience. Analytic statements are true in virtue of the meanings of the terms in the statements and are known to be true merely by understanding the meanings of the terms contained in the statements; synthetic statements cannot be known just by examining the meaning of the terms in the statements. Generally speaking, although it is this that Kant will question, necessary statements (those that must always be true or must always be false) are *a priori* analytic, and contingent statements (those that may be true or may be false) are *a posteriori* synthetic. Thus, "All bachelors are unmarried" is *a priori* analytic; we can know it to be true without consulting our experience, nor could any experience refute it, for the meaning of "bachelor" includes "unmarried"; if someone was suggested to us as an example of a bachelor who was married, we would respond by explaining how we define "bachelor", not by seeking empirical evidence. Analytic truths are those truths whose denial is contradictory; the predicate "unmarried" is contained in the concept of the subject term "bachelor". However, "All bachelors admire Kant" may be true, or it may be false; the way we find out is by empirically investigating bachelors; it certainly is not part of the definition of the term "bachelor" that an admiration or otherwise for Kant should come into it, and so it cannot be known to be true *a priori*.

Hume thought that the only necessary propositions were analytic ones (mathematics, for example); but the price we pay for our only pieces of necessary truth is that they are quite empty; they tell us nothing about the world. They simply unravel linguistic definitions. Logical truths such as "not-(p and not-p)" are known to be true *a priori* precisely because they exhibit a universally valid form which is devoid and independent of content; any proposition could be substituted for p, therefore the whole expression can tell us nothing about the actual contingent world. Logic alone can tell us only what is necessary, impossible or possible, not what is actual and contingent: that which is, but might have been otherwise. Hume argues that all our knowledge of the world must come from the senses; but all we can generate from that source is contingent particular statements which cannot support general necessary statements, such as the reality of universal causation, the truth of universal laws, the real existence of an independent constant external world. If we observe A followed by B, we note that we perceive no necessary connection between A and B, which is an essential part of the belief that A causes B, that would justify saying B must always follow A; but this is the form of universal laws of nature and the basis of any inferences from the observed to the unobserved.

The disagreement between empiricists such as Hume and rationalists such as Leibniz centres on whence our knowledge of the world derives, on what knowledge of truths about the world logically depends, and on the emptiness of analytic propositions. In general, the issue is that of the informativeness of truths knowable independently of the evidence of experience: whether such truths can tell us anything about reality. The rationalists see analytic truths and deductive reasoning as an *a priori* source of knowledge, admittedly not of the ephemeral world just as we experience it, but of the reality behind those experiences. Leibniz has a problem maintaining any *a posteriori* synthetic truths at all, since he thinks all truths concerning underlying reality must ultimately be analyzable into the subject–

predicate form and be analytic. Unlike the rationalists, the empiricists see analytic truths as empty or trivial statements, which can tell us nothing about the actual contingent nature of the world.

Kant found himself agreeing and disagreeing with both parties. He agrees with the empiricists, and disagrees with the rationalists, that *a priori* analytic truths are empty, and that our knowledge must be of the world we can experience; but he also thinks that we can know necessary and universal *a priori* truths that tell us something about the real or actual world of experience. Kant agrees with the rationalists that not all *a priori* knowledge is empty, but disagrees that this knowledge can be of a world behind appearances. The answer for Kant is the existence of propositions that are synthetic *a priori* and in some way necessary; these truths, knowable prior to the evidence of experience, are irrefutable by any experience, and yet they go beyond the mere meaning of the terms used in expressing them and determine *a priori* certain truths concerning the world as experienced. The necessity and universality of the truth of synthetic *a priori* judgements cannot derive from their being analytic and their denial implying a logical contradiction; they must be necessary and universal truths for some other reason. Kant's positive project, his transcendental philosophy, is to show how it can be possible to know truths *a priori* which are necessarily true of the world as it appears, but which are not necessary by merely being analytic. Such a synthetic *a priori* truth is that every event has a cause.

The term "transcendental" does a lot of work in Kant's philosophy. Generally whatever is transcendental is not derived from, or justifiable or refutable by, experience, yet is applicable to, or is a condition for, all experience. Transcendental knowledge is knowledge not of objects, but knowledge of the necessary *a priori* conditions of our cognition of objects. Kant uses the term to denote the *a priori* factors in our knowledge.

Kant analyzes experience and understanding in order to justify objective knowledge. Intuitions consist of sensations which are necessarily subject to the forms of space and time; sensations are *a posteriori* and space and time are supplied *a priori* by our sensibility or capacity to receive representations; but sensation is not separable from those *a priori* conditions. Space is the form of outer sense, of objects in the external world, whereas time is the form of both outer and inner sense – our inner experience necessarily only involves succession in time. Space and time are the *a priori* forms of our sensibility as a whole. These pure forms of our intuitions are analogous to filters on a camera: the only images formed are ones that have passed through or been subject to the filters. The pure forms of intuition are not empirical: they are not derived *from* experience, rather they are the necessary form *of* all experience. Nor are space and time concepts, for there can be no object (like a table) corresponding to space and time in general. Kant further holds that the pure intuition of space is presupposed by geometry, and that of time is presupposed by arithmetic.

In addition to this, *knowledge,* as opposed to the mere having of experiences, involves the use of the basic concepts or categories of the faculty of the understanding. The knowledge that what we see is a table involves having and applying the concept of a table by a judgement of the understanding, not just seeing something in space and time. Furthermore our understanding *necessarily* operates with certain basic concepts or categories. Knowledge is possible through the conjunction of actual intuitions with the necessary categories of the faculty of understanding. The senses alone are literally thoughtless; the understanding alone is contentless.

A summary of the nature of intuitions, and the relation between them and concepts of the understanding producing knowledge, can be given in the following diagram.

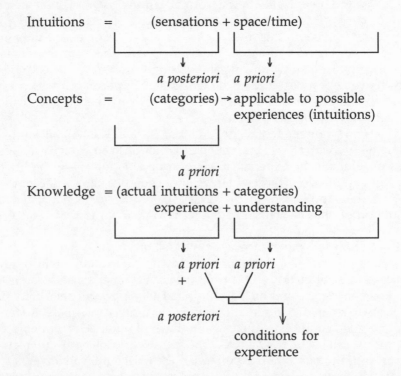

There is a sharp distinction between the intellectual and sensory elements in human knowledge. The mind is active in understanding nature, not a passive receptacle waiting to be filled by experiences. Transcendental philosophy does not give us particular scientific knowledge of the world we experience; but the transcendental deduction shows how we can know the necessary *a priori* elements *presupposed*

by such scientific knowledge of the world as experienced. For example, we cannot know *a priori* that *A* is the cause of *B* – that is a matter for scientific empirical investigation; but it can be known *a priori* that *B* has some cause – that much can be proved by transcendental philosophy.

Kant was well aware of the distinction, said to be confused in the work of some earlier philosophers, between the origin (*quid facti*) of something, and its justification (*quid juris*). The revealing of the origin or genesis of a truth or belief has to be distinguished from whether the truth or belief can be known *a priori* or *a posteriori*. The origin concerns facts about psychology; the question of whether a proposition is *a priori* or *a posteriori* concerns what logical type the proposition is. Propositions that can be shown to follow deductively from certain logically necessary premises can be known independently of the evidence of experience, since their denial would imply a logical contradiction; but some truths can be known only by consulting the evidence of experience, even if the belief in the truth happens to be psychologically innate. I may have been born with the belief, which is true, that "There are lions in Africa"; but the conditions for the belief being true depend on facts about Africa; knowledge of those facts, and hence knowledge of the truth of the proposition describing those facts, can be justified only by experience of Africa; it could not be proved *a priori* by deductive reasoning or *a priori* by merely understanding the meaning of the terms in the proposition that expresses the belief. To show that something is psychologically *a priori* does not show it to be *a priori* valid or true, still less that its truth is knowable *a priori*.

Kant was not engaged in speculative empirical psychology. If Kant can justify the necessity of the application of the forms of space and time, and the categories, to the world, he will have achieved a great deal. In the first case we have, for example, justified, and explained, applied mathematics; in the second we have justified concepts essential to science, for example, substance, causality, plurality, unity and the like.

Running through Kant's philosophy is a distinction between form and content. The form of experience is knowable *a priori*; the content or filling is given to us and is knowable *a posteriori*; but the two elements are not simply separable. The form of our intuitions is space and time, the forms of our understanding or thought are the categories. In actual intuitions, sensations and space and time are not separable; in actual knowledge, intuitions and categories are not separable. This idea is essential to understanding Kant's transcendental idealism: his notion of objectivity is designed to counter empirical idealism, which is the position that our knowledge is only subjectively valid concerning the content of our own minds.

The "schemata", which are kinds of restricting frameworks, are required to give rules for applying the categories, for the concepts of the understanding in their pure form are never met in intuitions; we must take the pure concepts and form schematisms by which particular intuitions can be identified as falling under pure concepts. If we take the example of the category of substance as that which is always a subject of predication and is never predicated of another subject, the schema of substance is that which is permanent in time while other things change. The schema of necessity is the existence of an object at all times. The schema of causality is the succession of real things according to a rule. Time is presupposed *a priori* in our experiencing things existing simultaneously or successively; and it is indeed temporal existence that is the primary condition to which schemata of the *a priori* imagination must conform. It is the schema which ensures that the categories are applied only to objects of possible experience; the understanding is effectively limited to experience (intuitions of our sensibility) by requiring that the application of the pure concepts is through schemata which involve the *a priori* pure form of inner intuition (time) and outer intuition (space); that is, the categories are limited to objects in time and space. Thus the categories become more than pure or formal logical truths, but come to have objects to which they apply; they come to tell us something *a priori* about the objects of possible experience, that is, possible intuitions. Through the methodological adoption of the mechanism of schemata, reason does not attempt to describe a world beyond or behind all possible experience; in this case it is not a world which is as a matter of fact out of reach of all experience from which we exclude ourselves, but rather a world which is necessarily out of reach of all possible experience. What is denied is "transcendent" knowledge: knowledge of things-in-themselves or, in Kant's terminology, noumena beyond the conditions for all experiences. For example, it can be said to be possible to experience atoms, although in fact they are too small to see (at least with the naked eye); whereas it is impossible that we should experience timelessness or eternity, since all experiences are in time as they involve succession; nor is it possible to conceive of a spaceless world.

We can see the categories as the highest point of a hierarchy of classificatory and ordering concepts. We use the concept "tree", which falls under the concept "plant", which is an "object", which is subsumed under "substance", something that is separable and can remain the same while undergoing certain sorts of changes. We can conceive of a world as experienced to which the lower and more particular concepts do not apply – a world without trees, in which the concept "tree" is not applied in our judgements – but we cannot conceive of a world to which the concepts of something that can endure through change, universal causality, plurality and unity do not apply. The same applies to the other twelve in the table of categories.

I
Quantity
Unity
Plurality
Totality

II   III
Quality   *Relation*
Reality   Substance and accident
Negation   Cause and effect
Limitation   Reciprocity

IV
Modality
Possibility and impossibility
Existence and non-existence
Necessity and contingency

These are the categories with which we must think if we think about the world at all, and they must therefore be presupposed in, apply to, any way the world can appear to us and be involved in all judgement and knowledge.

In the metaphysical deduction of categories, Kant tries to demonstrate how the categories arise from general logic – from different kinds of logical judgements. However, Kant's exposition is unusually terse. The judgement "Some S is P" ("Some cows are black') involves concepts; it involves the concept of *plurality*, since it involves two terms, it involves the concept of *reality*, since it states something is.

Perhaps of greater importance to the modern reader is the transcendental deduction, for here we have an argument that attempts to justify the application of categories as such; that there are concepts we necessarily have to apply to experience, whatever these concepts specifically turn out to be. The sense of "deduction" in the transcendental deduction is more akin to a defence in law than an argument in formal logic.

The transcendental deduction runs as follows. The aim of the transcendental deduction is to show not only that there are categories or concepts we necessarily apply to our experience, but also that that experience must be such that in applying the categories we can be said to be making objective judgements, or judgements about objects. The absolutely minimum condition for experiences which are *something to me* is that the experiences are subject to a synthesis such that they are all part of one consciousness. To say that experiences are thus united is equivalent to the condition of apperception, that is, the experiences are possible objects of self-consciousness; it must be possible for the "I think" to accompany all my representations. The "I" here is not empirical self-consciousness; sometimes I reflect, and sometimes I do not; it is the transcendental unity of apperception: the unity given by the mere possibility of my being self-conscious of whatever experiences I have. For this apperception to make sense it is necessary that I am aware of something which is not-self, objects which have a unity and independence of their own, distinct from my self; if they were not thus independent, I would not be engaged in an act of self-consciousness at all. The items on which I reflect in self-consciousness, that is, the items of my consciousness, are not-self and are therefore objects; they have objectivity. Now to reflect at all is to apply concepts; to say, for example, "x now", "there are more xs than ys", "x is different from y", "x again", "y has got bigger"; in reflection concepts must be applied, so what presents itself could not be a totally disordered stream of sensation, each item utterly unrelated to any other. In the final step, having shown we necessarily apply concepts, Kant, due to his faith in his metaphysical deduction, thinks he has shown that it must be just those concepts or categories deduced in the metaphysical deduction that we apply.

To sum up: consciousness is a uniting of intuitions, the condition for this is possible self-consciousness; the condition for self-consciousness is awareness of objects, or objective experiences (experiences under categories); the objects of conciousness on which we reflect in self-consciousness are therefore subject to concepts (are objects having order intrinsic to them); and if we must apply concepts, the categories revealed in the metaphysical deduction must be the concepts we apply.

Kant equivocates about the nature of objects, items of which we can claim to be able to make judgements independent of the particular state of the subject. Whether the objectivity granted by the categories as the necessary universally valid conditions for all experience is enough to give us everything we expect of an object, and an objective world, is open to dispute. But the transcendental deduction attempts to justify the application of the categories by all rational consciousnesses, not just the human mind. There cannot be forms of understanding quite different from our own. Kant does allow that there could be forms of sensible intuition other than our own human forms.

Hume correctly thought we could not derive an abiding self from the flux of perceptions open to introspection; but Kant argues that the ability to introspect at all assumes a self or subject which has the experience, for we say, "This is my experience"; it must be possible for the "I think" to accompany all my representations. But I can think only according to the categories; so there can be no experience such that it is not subject in my judgement to the categories, since then there would be experiences of mine which could not be accompanied by "I think", which is impossible. The awareness of self derives from the awareness of our power to unite representations in one consciousness.

This creates for Kant the possibility of objective knowledge of the world; knowledge must include experience, and we necessarily have to apply the categories which give the form of that experience.

Whereas Kant's argument may have justified the application of necessary conditions for experience – some set of categories or other – it is not clear that he has justified the application of all and only those categories he lists in particular; that would follow only if we accepted the metaphysical deduction.

This has led some to update the categories but maintain their necessity; it has led still others to update them but to abandon their necessity. The second of these positions seems to abandon the point of Kant's transcendental idealism, for then the categories are neither universal (for they apply only to human cognition) nor necessary (not transcendentally necessary but psychological facts). On the other hand, the first position has great difficulty generating categories which at once can be shown to apply necessarily to any comprehensible world, while at the same time avoiding the triviality of being entirely vacuous and non-specific.

Interpretations of Kant's transcendental idealism vary. One view asserts that we have obtained objective knowledge because the categories have been demonstrated to have universal intersubjectivity. Another view suggests that Kant has to show that there is a world of objects existing independent of us in some further sense than the world we experience and know, necessarily conforming to the categories which are not thereby merely arbitrary and subjective. But this destroys Kant's position by asking him to accomplish the impossible. We cannot possibly know that objects in themselves, distinct from how they are experienced or appear to us, are organized according to the categories, but we can know that objects as they appear or the world-as-experienced must be organized according to the categories, since the way objects appear partly depends on ourselves and we must apply the categories in thinking about what we experience. The world, or nature, just is the sum of possible experiences; the world of phenomena. Noumena, or things-in- themselves (*Dinge-an-sich*), are not objects of experience; they stand proxy for a world beyond appearances that is unknowable; this realm is nothing to do with the world as studied by science. Noumenon is not, it must be emphasized, the atomic world, or anything where our lack of actual experience of it is purely a matter of accidental contingent fact. The atomic world exists straightforwardly (or so it seemed in Kant's day) in space and time, even if the laws governing its behaviour are discovered indirectly by its effects; our inability to observe atoms directly is an empirical, not a transcendental, limit to our experience. The appearance/reality distinction is not between phenomena/ noumena, but between the variant/ invariant features of our experience. To suggest that we can still look around the edge of all our experiences, dropping our form of cognition, to a world untainted by that form, to see if the categories actually apply, is to attempt what Kant denies is possible, and to abandon precisely the ground from whence the objectivity of the categories arises. The categories which we bring to experience cannot be abandoned, for they are present whenever we have an intelligence capable of self-conscious thought.

Kant says his position supports empirical realism and refutes idealism. Whatever we may think of Kant's arguments, he cannot be defending empirical realism in the form of knowledge of objects devoid of our form of understanding; to think otherwise is to miss the point. If we tried to apply Kant's views to objects totally independent of our, and all intelligent, modes of understanding, Kant could never have hoped to justify the necessary application of categories; there would always be an unbridgeable gap between the way we think and what we think about; we would never be able to show the categories applied to reality in this sense, rather than merely indicating how we have to think about the world. If any conception of reality is inseparable from mind, then there is a possibility of explaining why our basic intellectual structures – causality, substance, plurality, and the like – must actually apply. The point is that as far as we are concerned, transcendental idealism delivers all that a bald empirical realism supposes to be the case; these two positions are in that sense equivalent and indistinguishable. A logically or transcendentally inescapable perspective is equivalent to an objective view. Universal objectively valid knowledge, invariant with, and not requiring qualifying reference to, the state of the subject, is squared with the argument that there cannot be a perspectiveless world-view of things-in-themselves through the establishment of the categories and forms of intuition as transcendentally necessary and objective for all possible appearances in being invariant with the experiencing subject. There is then no perspectiveless position from which the rational perspective itself can be checked; if the perspective is thereby universal it is also necessary and objective and independent of the individual subjective perspective.

This is not the only interpretation of Kant's position, and Kant himself was not entirely consistent or clear; he plainly felt uneasy about it. Kant sometimes speaks as if noumena are the unknowable causes of our experiences.

Kant attacks in the Dialectic the possibility of knowledge transcending experience and its *a priori* form or conditions to attempt to gain knowledge of unconditioned noumena, a perspectiveless view of things-in-themselves. Kant is setting the necessary presupposition of all human knowledge and so marking the bounds of legitimate inquiry. The Dialectic is the logic of illusion. That is not to say that we cannot think beyond the bounds of possible experience; we can form concepts – for example of substance – to think about that which exists beyond our possible intuitions, and so outside space and time; but knowledge is not possible.

Noumena are unknowable; we can speak of noumena only negatively: we can say what they are *not* as compared to phenomena that we can experience, since we can say that none of our concepts can be positively applied to characterize noumenon. It is indeed unclear if we can legitimately talk of either noumenon in the singular or noumena in the plural, since the first involves the category of unity and the second that of plurality. Whatever is the case, noumenon, or the thing-in-itself, is reality in the sense of being independent of all conceptual determinations which apply necessarily to the world as experienced; and, since all knowledge involves applying concepts, things-in-themselves are unknowable.

Illusory metaphysics which aims at knowledge has three main subjects: God, and proofs for the existence of God; freedom, which connects with cosmology; immortality, which connects with the soul. Metaphysical speculation which aims at knowledge of truths concerning these subjects has been endless, fruitless and contradictory. In contrast to physical science, disputes seem undecidable. As Kant says, it has involved "deluding the adventurous seafarer ever anew with empty hopes, and engaging him in enterprises which he can never abandon and yet is unable to carry to completion". Kant wants to show why this is so, and put an end to it. This is the overall aim of Kant's "critical philosophy".

Kant sets about this demonstration in the Antinomies. The strategy is, after taking some matter about which we illegitimately aim to know, to present a pair of equally logically compelling arguments from which are derived a thesis and antithesis which are mutually exclusive and collectively exhaustive alternatives. The conclusions cannot both be true, but we have no way of knowing which is true and which false. The proof of the thesis and antithesis is by *reductio ad absurdum*: showing that denying an assertion leads to an impossibility, thus demonstrating the truth of the assertion. Kant presents four Antinomies: first, the finitude or infinitude in space and time of the universe; secondly, the finite or infinite divisibility of substance; thirdly, whether there is freedom or no freedom; fourthly, whether there exists an absolutely necessary being or not. These matters are undecidable by human reason, since we are presented with equally convincing conclusions which are mutually contradictory. However, to agree that the Antinomies show this, we would have to accept the arguments for each thesis and antithesis in each Antinomy as equally valid; unfortunately their quality is variable.

Hegel (1770–1831) was to suggest that the opposing conclusions of Kant's Antinomies indicate not the limits of human reason, but the need for a synthesis which somehow encompasses the conflicting conclusions as to the nature of reality.

Arguments for the existence of God are classified in three ways: physico-theological, cosmological, ontological. The physico-theological is basically the argument from design, whereby, if an orderly clock needs a clockmaker, the world surely needs a worldmaker. Hume had attacked this argument on the grounds that if the clock/world analogy was weak, then the world might not need a maker; if the analogy was strong, then the worldmaker was no better than a clockmaker, and need not be a God at all. The cosmological argument harks back to the ancient unmoved-mover argument of a first cause required to start the universe off; this is already implicitly undermined in the Antinomies. The most significant attack is upon the ontological argument. Here God's existence is said to be deducible from the concept of God; God is perfection, it is more perfect to exist than not to exist, therefore the perfect being must exist. Kant's refutation of this proof rests on arguing that "existence" is not a descriptive predicate adding anything to the meaning or concept of a subject, so that to say something exists does not therefore attribute an additional property to a subject at all; rather it merely says that there is something to which the concept of the subject applies. We do not add an additional property, after we have listed all the attributes of Kant, by saying Kant exists; rather it is to say that all the properties of Kant – shortness, thin body, philosopher, etc. – actually have an instance.

Kant was concerned that he had, in a sense, done his job of providing necessary metaphysical foundations too well; especially with reference to the universally valid application of causality to phenomena, it seemed as if there was no place left for human freedom. Kant replies through an analysis of the self. Although the world of phenomena may be determined by the causal laws of physics and transcendental concepts, the noumenal world beyond experience is not. Kant's answer is to posit a noumenal-self, or transcendental-self, which is "outside" the phenomenal world; man viewed as noumenon can therefore act freely according to the moral law. The transcendental-self is the only transcendental object we have access to; here our perspective and a perspectiveless view become one and the same; the distinction between appearance and reality can be eliminated. This explanation of freedom leaves too many questions in obscurity to be satisfactory; moreover, because the moral law governs the operation of the noumenal-self, it fails to explain how we could ever act wrongly. If it is maintained that the operation of the noumenal-self originates totally spontaneously, then it amounts to nothing more than a reassertion of belief in freewill. In any event Kant's call upon the transcendental world should, on his own account, be illegitimate, as this world is unknowable, and its causal interaction with the phenomenal world impossible, since the concept of causality cannot apply to it.

Kant does leave some positive function to the ideas of unconditioned reason; they can be regulative of our inquiries, even if concrete knowledge of truths cannot directly be derived from them. If we treat the ideas of unconditioned reason as unobtainable aims, they may act as injunctions. For example, the idea of determining if the world has a beginning in time is not something we can settle by pure reason, nor could any empirical inquiry determine the answer; but the question of the universe's temporal origin requires us to keep searching for ever greater understanding of the universe's origin.

We can summarize the philosophy of Kant in the following way. Kant starts from the problem of justifying the objectivity and necessity of the form of intuitions and the concepts we apply to the world. Their necessity and objectivity seem unjustifiable by the raw sensations of experience alone or because their rejection would involve logical contradiction. The world for us can be nothing but the sum total of possible appearances, and the form given to those appearances – applied to the raw sensations – is the product of our minds; appearances, but not things-in-themselves, have to conform to the form given to them by our understanding; these forms are objective and necessary because they are that to which all appearances must conform if there are awareness and judgements concerning those appearances; these forms are universally valid for all rational beings. Thus they are objective because they apply to all worlds conceivable to us, and to rational beings in general, and so are independent of the subjective contributions of any individual minds. The world as noumenon is the world considered as other than how it can ever appear to us; such a world beyond all possible appearances is unknowable; it is a world in which the *a priori* form produced by our intellect is not valid, since it is the world as it is independent of all appearances, beyond possible experience. The function of philosophy is not to provide us with knowledge of the nature of reality as a whole or in itself – how the world might be beyond how it can possibly appear to us – but with knowledge of the *a priori* form or structure of those appearances themselves. Nor can philosophy lay down *a priori* the scientific laws of nature; but it can justify the presuppositions that the scientific empirical inquiry into the laws of nature involves. Philosophy studies the only thing it can: the necessary and universal *a priori* form of the world as it appears to us; the *a priori* forms are necessary and objective because they are how any rational minds must think; the forms are therefore applicable to any conceivable world, that is, to all that is a possible appearance to us.

CHAPTER SEVEN

Later German philosophy: Hegel, Nietzsche

The philosophers Hegel (1770–1831) and Nietzsche (1844–1900) in many ways could hardly be more different; they differ in style, method and conclusions. Hegel is methodical and technical where Nietzsche is deliberately unsystematic and literary; this renders them both obscure and difficult to understand, but in different ways. Yet there is a connecting intellectual element, although what each makes of this common element produces quite different philosophies.

The question arises as to what extent we can have a metaphysics of reality: to what extent we can be said to have knowledge of reality: how in a general way the world necessarily is in itself, as distinct from how it merely appears. A problem arises from the apparent separation of our view of how the world is and the world itself; once this separation takes place the problem is to determine to what extent our view of the world given in the concepts can be known to correspond to the world itself: reality. One way of looking at this problem of knowledge of reality is to try to determine which of our basic concepts with which we think about the world reflect actual objective and necessary features of the world, and which of our concepts reflect the contribution of what is merely subjective or contingent. In describing reality we aim to identify features that are true from any point of view, which is, so to speak, the point of view of things themselves.

A common connection between Hegel and Nietzsche is the German intellectual tradition derived from Kant. Kant's philosophy sets up the way in which the question of our knowledge of reality is asked. Kant suggests that there is no way that the basic concepts through which we have necessarily to think about the world can be shown to be valid for the world as a reality beyond experience and independent of all subjective conceptions. Such independence would entail a world to which we could never possibly know if our conceptions applied.

What Kant says is that our basic concepts do nevertheless have a kind of objectivity through being necessarily valid *a priori*, if not for things-in-themselves beyond experience, then in all cases for how things can appear to us and to any rational beings. We cannot justify the assertion of the objectivity and necessity of our conceptions of the world either from experience or logically by their denial being contradictory. Their necessity and objectivity are derived from the universal intersubjectivity of any rational mind necessarily using these concepts in all possible thought and knowledge; therefore anything that is experienced must be formed by these concepts. The function of philosophy is not then to give metaphysical knowledge of reality as a whole – thus including things-in-themselves beyond possible experience, and hence beyond being known as subject to our conceptions – but must be content to give us knowledge of the *a priori* structure of experiences, that is, the world as it appears. Kant also says that it is within experiences that the appearance/reality distinction must be made. The natural world as studied by science is the totality of possible experiences. The function of philosophy is to justify rationally the necessary application to appearances of the basic concepts which are presupposed by natural sciences. For example, philosophy alone cannot determine what causes what, but it can justify the necessity of the concept of causation that is logically presupposed by science: the concept of causation, that every event must have some cause, is shown to be necessarily true in so far as the concept is applied to all possible appearances but not to things-in-themselves.

Hegel and Nietzsche make something quite different of the philosophy of Kant. Hegel thinks he can show that our concepts of reason are necessarily and objectively valid for reality as a whole, which includes appearances and things-in-themselves but ultimately eliminates the distinction between them; thus knowledge of reality is possible; metaphysics is possible. Nietzsche concludes that our concepts can have no necessary and universal validity because no concept can; they are interpretations that must be seen as originating in certain features of the distinctively human condition; there can be no overall non-perspectival conceptual system, devoid of all and any points of view, which would give a complete description of reality.

Hegel sees the solution as lying in metaphysical or absolute idealism. In Kant's position, where the mind and the world are separate in some sense, the concepts used by the mind can be known to be *a priori* valid only to the extent that the world is regarded as subject to mind or basic mental categories; that is, they are *a priori* valid only for the world regarded as an appearance or phenomenon. This leaves a problematic residual noumenal world, or thing-in-itself, which is unknowable, beyond the phenomenon, because it is by definition that which is independent of all of our conceptual determinations. So long as features of the world are only partly a product of mind, our concepts are assured as objectively valid only for that part for which the mind is responsible. Thus with Kant we cannot know reality as a whole, including reality as it is in itself, but know it only as it appears: as it comes before the mind. The answer for Hegel is to show how the mind and the world really form an identity as one absolute spiritual entity which transcends the dualism of subject and object; the concepts of thought are thereby necessarily objectively valid for reality as a whole, not only for appearances, because to know those concepts is the same as to know the structure of reality itself; there is no world to which rational concepts could fail to apply because the world in its entirety is a developing product of the essence of absolute mind or reason. Our concepts no longer merely give the form of any possible appearance of things, objective merely for the world as experienced; rather, they are again absolutely or unconditionally objective for the world-in-itself because the world as determined by mental categories is one with the world itself. The world/concept dualism is collapsed, as is knowledge and the object of knowledge; thus the absolute objectivity of concepts is regained with respect to reality in its entirety because there is no residual thing-in-itself-world of which we have not taken account and for which our concepts can fail to hold. This is not to say the world is the product of finite individual minds as in subjective idealism; it is rather a manifestation of infinite mind or spirit, or mind as such. The understanding of the world is thus mind understanding the development of itself.

In Nietzsche we see the triumph of perspectivism: the concepts which constitute our notion of the world can have no unique objective validity and represent one partial possible set of concepts which give an interpretation which *is* the world to us; they give us, through a set of classificatory and ordering concepts, a usable picture of the world whose function and explanation are largely pragmatic. Our concepts, far from describing the world in an objective and necessary way – being valid from any point of view or universally – are constructed by humans for their own peculiarly human purposes, especially the purpose of survival. That is not to say that because there is no one necessary way of construing the world any way is as good as any other; but one view is not better than another in the traditional sense of corresponding better to reality at all; views are better because they enhance power and control to live one's life in certain specific ways and according to certain values. There can be no one conceptual framework that gives the complete truth about the world; all views are partial. Perspectives are a necessary condition of having a world at all. Our rational conception of the world seems objective and necessary because we seem not to be able to throw it off; but such conceptual ordering of the world as we experience it is a kind of simplifying fiction or falsification that serves to make the world amenably ordered and calculable for human beings.

Hegel

Georg Wilhelm Friedrich Hegel (1770–1831) was born in Stuttgart, the son of a minor civil servant with a Lutheran background. He was educated at the University of Tübingen, studying philosophy and theology. There he met the poet Hölderlin and the philosopher Schelling. The French Revolution, which occurred during his time at university, made a deep impression on Hegel; he thought it was momentous in its rigorous application of reason, but it was also a great failure because reason was applied in an abstract way that took no account of particular circumstances of the community. After university he held various private tutorial posts, and began working on his philosophy. Hegel taught philosophy at the University of Jena from 1801 to 1803. On leaving he began his first great philosophical work, *The phenomenology of spirit*. Jena was occupied by the French in 1807 following the defeat of the Prussians by Napoleon, and the university closed. After working as a newspaper editor, Hegel was from 1808 to 1816 the headmaster of a Gymnasium at Nuremberg. From 1816 to 1818 he was Professor of Philosophy at the University of Heidelberg where he wrote the *Encyclopedia of the philosophical sciences*. Hegel had by this time attained a significant reputation as a philosopher, and was offered in 1818 the prestigious post of Professor of Philosophy at the University of Berlin. In 1821 he published the *Philosophy of right*. The position in Berlin he held until his death from cholera at the age of sixty-one.

Seminal influences on Hegel's work derive from his study of Greek philosophy, particularly Plato and Aristotle, but also Heraclitus and Eleatics such as Parmenides. Of philosophers nearer to his time, Spinoza and Kant greatly affected Hegel's philosophical outlook. Among contemporary thinkers important to Hegel we have to look to Fichte (1762–1814) and Schelling (1775–1854).

The aim of philosophy, according to Hegel, should be to show how a complete understanding of reality as a totality is possible, and this entails that all reality has to be conceptually accessible; that there is nothing real which is not captured by the concepts of reason; there is also nothing which is a concept of reason which is not real. To reach this end Hegel claims to prove the necessity of absolute idealism.

Part of the key to the philosophy of Hegel is found in his rejection of Kant's limitation of rational philosophical knowledge to the basic *a priori* conceptual structure of appearances, which rendered things-in-themselves – things as not known in their appearances – unknowable.

Thus reality in its entirety is not knowable since things-in-themselves are beyond possible appearances and excluded. Kant's position gives an oddly bifurcated world: the world as experienced and the world as not experienced; and within this duality, if we are to talk meaningfully about "reality" at all, we must talk of some characteristics within appearances, and not ascribe it to things-in-themselves. Kant's "critical philosophy" aims to delineate the limits of philosophical knowledge and understanding; all knowledge and understanding are conceptual – bring things under concepts – or are expressed in concepts; and if the application of our concepts is limited, then so are knowledge and understanding. Hegel makes a distinction between understanding and reason; he thinks that proper philosophical reason can go beyond the limits set to our knowledge by Kant. For Kant the limits of knowledge of reality are reached when we meet antinomies or contradictory theses which are irredeemably opposed and between which we cannot rationally choose; for Hegel philosophical reason can find a way of transcending the contradiction in a new synthesis.

The question arises as to why Kant feels the need to posit an unknowable noumenon at all. Overall, the reason must derive from the realization that the sense of "reality" he is able to give within the realm of appearances is not fully satisfying. Kant suggests that the raw sensation of intuitions must have an external cause and the cause is the thing-in-itself; but the thing-in-itself cannot be the cause of anything, since the category of causality cannot apply to it. In any case, Kant's successors were quick to point out that noumenon is contradictory. Even if we avoid giving any function to noumenon, it is still said to exist; and this means the category of existence applies to it in flat contradiction of the assertion that no categories can apply to it; even if only one category is applicable to noumenon, it cannot be wholly unknowable, which contradicts the initial supposition that it is unknowable.

The collapse through contradiction of the conception of the thing-in-itself leads inexorably to absolute idealism, and to the complete knowability of everything. If noumenon is eliminated as the external source of the given element in knowledge, sensation, to which the mind introduces *a priori* form, then the distinction between form imposed by mind and given content derived from sensation is destroyed, and the universe must in its entirety be a product of mind. This attacks the vital Kantian distinction between form and content, between the *a priori* and *a posteriori*. What can be brought under concepts is knowable; but noumenon is contradictory if posited as that which cannot be brought under concepts, since it can at the very least be known to exist: it *is*. Therefore everything is necessarily knowable, since it is contradictory to posit that which cannot be brought under concepts. To posit an unknowable "something" is contradictory, since in positing it as something which *exists* we apply a concept, and to apply a concept is to know that thing to which the concept is applied. Indeed, Hegel suggests that the whole notion of being able to know the limits to our knowledge is impossible. We should also note that proving that all is knowable is by no means the same as saying that all is known and that there are not things of which we are ignorant. Everything must be knowable because a minimum condition for there being something unknown in the totality of the universe is that it is, but in that case it is something known, not unknown. If the thing-in-itself is said to be "nothing", we have applied a concept that makes it completely knowable. In short, if X is posited as unknowable, it is knowable, therefore it is knowable.

The result of this is that we must reject all talk which divides knowledge of reality from reality itself for we can have no conception of reality apart from knowledge, no place to stand where we could compare knowledge and reality. We always work from within existing knowledge to understand reality.

The argument that reality in its totality is knowable logically inclines one to monism: for the universe to be understandable as a whole everything must be explicable – which is not the same as everything being actually explained – and for it to be possible for everything to be explicable the universe must be posited as one self-explanatory, self-contained entity. This is the Absolute or reality as a whole revealing itself in the fully adequate conceptual description of the Absolute Idea or Notion where subject and object are one in a self-thinking thought. The Absolute is the universe or reality as a totality; in short, everything. Everything in the universe is understood through something else in the universe; but if the universe – reality as a whole – is to be understood or explained it must in total form a whole which is self-explanatory; otherwise a regress of explanation could not be ended. As Hegel puts it, "The truth is the whole", for to understand any part involves understanding the whole. If we try to understand the truth about a part in isolation we will find that a contradiction will arise in that we have to refer to some relation outside it; ultimately we can draw this process to a close only when we have a view of the whole and there is nothing outside left to refer to; we thereby transcend and include all relational thinking in describing reality.

Once the thing-in-itself that is inaccessible to our concepts is eliminated by being shown to be impossible, then all reality is accessible to concepts, for to posit that which is inaccessible to concepts is contradictory. Thus the real is the rational and the rational the real. What this means is that all that is real is the rational process of concept generation, and hence is knowable, and the rational process of concept generation is the real. The world in its totality is the necessary unfolding of the logic of concepts. There is no longer any question of our concepts failing to apply to reality in the sense of the totality of the universe, for just as Kant's categories were objective for all appearances, Hegel's concepts now apply to reality itself, for the world as it falls under concepts is all the world can be at any moment in its unfolding: it is the real.

The function of philosophy is to construct or understand the Absolute, to prove that the truth about reality as a whole is knowable. Since it is not possible to posit anything apart from what falls under mental concepts, to trace the development of concepts is to trace the development of reality itself. In the Absolute, mind (the subjective) and object (the objective) are collapsed into an ultimate subject that rises above the duality because its object is *itself*; that is, the totality thinks about what can be its only object, itself. The Absolute is the actualization of this self-thinking thought: reality as a whole fully understanding itself as a whole. Some writers have given the Absolute a theistic interpretation and have seen the description of the Absolute as a description of God; however, it cannot be a transcendent God, but God immanent in the world. Absolute knowledge is the point at which the infinite mind, through our finite mind, has a complete understanding of reality, and that is when the Absolute has a complete understanding of itself, including the process that led to that complete understanding. Absolute knowledge captured in the Absolute Idea gives a perfect conceptual description of the nature of reality including, of course, the charting of the logical progression of increasingly adequate concepts to that Absolute knowledge which is the realization that the true nature of reality is that of the totality which knows itself. Absolute knowledge is the realization in the Absolute Idea that reality is ultimately a self-thinking thought, that absolute idealism is necessarily true so that reality is ultimately one infinite self-thinking mind. Reality is like a sphere with a perfect mirror on its inner surface where every part is perfectly reflected in another – but in this metaphor we would have to realize that the sphere could not have an outer surface.

It is important to note that the mind referred to here – which produces through its concepts reality in its entirety and is thus identical with that reality, so that to understand reality is just the same as to understand those concepts of mind – is not finite individual mind, but one infinite or objective mind, whose essence is reason. Reality can be nothing but the conceptual construction of infinite mind (spirit or *Geist*), so knowledge of reality turns out to be mind's knowledge of itself. But the infinite mind understands itself through finite minds; and the conceptual development manifest in finite minds in various human activities, especially in philosophy, will reflect the conceptual development of reality itself. The development of the world, present reality as a whole, is towards the Absolute and is just the same as the development to that point at which reality has a fully adequate understanding of itself in the Absolute Idea under the category of a single self-thinking thought.

There is a strong teleological element in Hegel's account of reality; the universe moves towards the Absolute as the end or result. Reality is identical with, and includes, the process of infinite mind's conceptual development towards absolute knowledge, which is knowledge of reality, which is reality as self-knowing. Reality at any stage or "moment" in the development can be nothing other than the total system of concepts of reality, which are manifest through the conceptual development of finite minds. In the end state of this conceptual development, where the Absolute is a fully self-knowing thought, the subjective and objective, the concept of reality and reality itself, indeed all conceptual opposites, differences and relations, are an identity contained in a unity. A fully comprehensive knowledge of reality will involve the identity of all opposing concepts, for the Absolute includes in itself all concepts – all determinations. Otherwise the understanding will be inadequate, as it will not be complete; for what is rational is real, and what is rational is what can be brought under concepts, therefore if some concepts are not included, there cannot be an understanding of the Absolute, since such an understanding leaves something out. The Absolute cannot be either one thing or its opposite, but must be both in an identity. Where all conceptual opposites become one, or identities, it might be supposed that the Absolute is an indeterminate, undifferentiated and unknowable "something" where conceptual characterization is impossible because opposites have become identities. But Hegel does not think of the Absolute as the vanishing point at which all conceptual differentiation is destroyed; rather, it is where all opposing concepts are unified into one all-encompassing entity which preserves their real opposition: an identity-in-difference. The opposition of concepts is not merely apparent, but real, and their real difference is preserved in their identity. The Absolute, in knowing itself as a totality, recognizes the various phases that lead to that final state as real moments in its life. In the progress towards the Absolute nothing is lost. An analogy might be the way in which the colour white is produced by combining all colours.

If the rational is the real and the real the rational, this means that reality just is the process of infinite mind actualizing the end state: reality as the self-knowledge of the totality. This process of conceptual development, which is also necessarily the development of reality itself towards the Absolute, is dialectical. The dialectic development of reality towards the Absolute takes place under three headings:

(1) Logic
(2) Philosophy of Nature
(3) Philosophy of Mind.

We can trace the development of dialectical Logic working itself out towards the Absolute – towards the complete truth about the nature of reality, the whole, which is the Absolute's conception of itself – in any of the above. They must all amount to aspects of the same thing: the necessary march of reason towards the total truth about the universe, which is an infinite mind's understanding of itself.

In (1) Logic describes the inner essence of the Absolute in its pure form, including of course the necessary movements towards its actualization. It is the study of the development of the Absolute in the non-temporal dialectical Logic of conceptual development itself abstracted from its manifestations in human minds or the natural world. The manifestation of the process of the Absolute in (2) and (3) involves the discernment, among the mass of facts about nature and human world history, of the bare bones of reason's conceptual development in nature and through history given in (1). What is studied under (2) and (3) is the progress manifest in the temporal world of the Logic of the Absolute. In all cases this follows the same overall pattern: objectivity as thesis, subjectivity as antithesis, which form a unity in the Absolute Idea.

It is vital to understand that the terms of Hegel's Logic are not propositions but concepts and that, unlike traditional logic, it is concerned not with mere form but also with content. Traditional logic is concerned with valid argument-forms; the universal necessity of these forms derives precisely from their being valid regardless of content. We can see this in the following syllogism.

All X is Y.

f is an X.

Therefore f is a Y.

This argument is valid whatever we substitute for X, Y, or f; but for that very reason traditional logic on its own can tell us nothing about the actual world and is purely hypothetical, valid regardless of actual truth. It is important to understand that Hegel is concerned with a Logic of concepts which have content and which tell the truth about reality. Once the distinction between conceptual development and reality is ultimately eliminated as an untenable opposition, the dialectic Logic of conceptual development is the development of reality itself. The form/content distinction disappears, and thus the aim of Hegel's Logic is truth.

The dialectic of concepts is a structure whereby less adequate conceptions of reality are overcome but retained to form conceptions which are more adequate. We can envisage this as a series of expanding concentric circles, each of which is more adequate in its description of reality. At any level less than the whole, the concepts we employ to describe reality are found to be contradictory; what this contradiction amounts to is the idea that isolated description is contradictory in different ways in different cases, but always because it cannot be genuinely isolated. The attempt to describe a thing which is less than the Absolute or whole in isolation will be contradictory because it will necessarily involve relations to things outside it. Thus the concept A will be found to involve not-A. It is not that both are simultaneously true, thus breaking the law of non-contradiction, not-(A and not-A); it is that both separately are inadequate in expressing the truth, and to get nearer the truth they have to be raised up into a higher synthesis which contains the truth from both. The less adequate conceptions are not discarded but preserved in the more adequate conceptions. Ultimately it is found that the whole system of concepts is interdependent, and the whole system alone removes all contradictions and gives an adequate description of the truth about reality. Up to the point of absolute knowledge the impetus to improved conceptual mastery of reality comes from reason being driven by contradictions in its attempt to complete a conceptual description of a part of reality in isolation. The intellect cannot rest content with an incomplete and, in Hegel's sense, therefore an internally contradictory view of reality. The method involved in attaining the complete conceptual grasp of reality involves an essentially triadic structure: concept A ("thesis") is inadequate in capturing reality on its own and is found logically to involve its opposite B ("antithesis"); we cannot think the A without the B; A is thus "contradictory" in isolation from its relation to B; so both are found to be inadequate descriptions of reality, and thus form, preserving their opposition and identity, C ("synthesis"). But the C is also then a thesis and will also be found to be inadequate, and to involve its antithesis D, which will give rise to their resolution in E; and so on.

A (thesis)
        →   C (synthesis/thesis)
B (antithesis)   → E . . .
        D (antithesis)

The nature of reality is deduced from the first principle using the triadic dialectical method. The first principle turns out to be a category or concept, since concepts have the right kind of logical, rather than temporal, priority through their level of inclusiveness. The first concept with logical priority is Being or "isness". This is the fundamental category of reality: whatever is real *is*, it has the most abstract quality of "isness"; whatever the determinate character of any real thing in the world, it logically presupposes the category Being. But, just because it is the absence of all determination, Being is a vacuity and is found to be identical with Nothing; Being contains within it its opposite, Nothing. Reason cannot rest with this contradiction. From the process of Being passing into Nothing because the two are identical, we see that equally Nothing passes into Being; this leads to a concept in which the concepts of Being and Nothing are unified in an identity of opposites: Becoming. In the category of Becoming the concepts of Being and Nothing are preserved in their difference and also in their identity. They are "sublated" or "put aside" in a higher unity. The poorest, but still true definition or conception, of the Absolute is Being; this is the starting point of the logical derivation of all the concepts which give increasingly adequate definitions of the Absolute which is reality as a totality; the dialectical deduction of concepts produces increasingly adequate definitions or conceptions which include the earlier ones, ending in the most adequate definition of the Absolute, the Absolute is the Absolute Idea: self-thinking mind.

It should be noted that philosophy, in exhibiting the development of reason through our actual history, as in (3) above, is not disputing, or indeed discovering, historical facts; what it is doing is giving an interpretation describing their dialectical Logic. The mass of factual details is boiled off to leave the outline of the dialectical process.

In (3), which is the Absolute manifest as mind or spirit, we can trace the Logic of the conceptual development in consciousness towards attaining the complete truth about reality as necessarily being absolute idealism. The Absolute's knowledge of itself is not identical with the thoughts of any finite mind, but finite minds are carriers of the increase in conceptual mastery down through history. Thus we are tracing in the philosophy of spirit the conceptual development of mankind, which is the development of consciousness to ever higher levels of understanding, eventually participating in the Absolute's self-knowledge. The phenomenology of mind or spirit studies forms of consciousness as they acquire a better grasp of reality. We can trace the manifestation of the dialectic of spirit in its objective manifestations through the history of public institutions, societies and cultures, which is the development of the idea of freedom.

In the Philosophy of Mind we can follow the dialectical development in two connected ways: (a) "Subjective Mind", (b) "Objective Mind".

(a) *"Subjective Mind"*

This is the phenomenology of mind – mind's appearance to itself – the way that mind itself has developed with dialectical necessity to higher levels of consciousness so as to participate in absolute knowledge. Hegel traces consciousness from its lowest levels to the highest. This has three main phases.

(i) *Consciousness* This starts with "sense-certainty": the awareness of raw unclassified sensations. But it soon becomes clear that *knowledge*, through awareness of bare particulars, is contradictory because the awareness is ineffable: to articulate it without using the universal categories is impossible; even "this", "here", "now" take us beyond what is immediately given. Universal terms are required. This leads on to the next stage, "perception", in which we classify what we perceive under sensuous universals – "table", "star". But soon it is clear that non-sensuous universals are involved which are not encountered in experience – "many", "one" – and these are posited as existing as separate realities. These form the basis for scientific laws. The universals are studied as independent objects.

(ii) *Self-consciousness* This begins with the stage at which we realize that the conceptual structure of the world is a construct of mind; we become conscious of ourselves as active categorizers and law makers. Consciousness recognizes the object not as a not-self but simply as itself. This is the beginning of self-consciousness; we are turned back on ourselves. But the object still remains obstinately regarded as external to the self and at the same time really one with self. This gives rise to the next phase, "desire", in which the aim is *pure* self-consciousness where the only object truly is itself; so the self tries to destroy the external object by consuming it. But the very need to destroy the external object shows that the self is still dependent for its self-consciousness on the external. This solipsist phase gives way to one in which the existence of other selves are recognized in the world: other egos which are, of course, themselves self-conscious. If we cannot negate the object, it must negate itself; but only consciousness can negate itself; so the external object is recognized as an ego. The independence of the egos rival one another; this struggle is recognized in the master/slave relationship, in which one seeks to destroy the other. The independence of the other ego is negated by the master in regarding the slave as a thing without self-consciousness but as mere consciousness. Thus the object for the slave is not itself, but merely the external objects on which it labours for the master. But again contradiction arises because the master finds he is dependent on the slave through the fact that the extent of independence of his self-consciousness depends on negating the self-consciousness of the slave, which proves independence of the slave, but that means the slave must after all be self-conscious. The master finds he needs the slave for his recognition as the master. Also the slave becomes self-conscious in seeing himself in what he creates. Each now recognizes the other as self-conscious again. The mutual acceptance by all selves of each other ushers in the notion of "universal self-consciousness".

(iii) *Reason* The equal recognition of all egos means that another consciousness is for my self-consciousness another self-consciousness, and is therefore myself. Ego contemplates ego as its object. Thus the object of self- consciousness is in whatever it contemplates simply itself. Thus we reach pure self-thinking thought, where the only object of thought is itself, and the distinction between self and other is made within self, since there is nothing beyond infinite mind. Thus we have absolute idealism.

We can see how the triadic dialectic works here: objectivism and subjectivism are combined in absolute idealism where the distinction is transcended because the Absolute is the totality. The object for the totality identical with mind can only be itself.

      (i) Consciousness
         (the object is
         independent of
         self).

                       → (iii) Reason (subject/
                            object distinction
                            is collapsed).

      (ii) Self-consciousness
         (the object is
         identical with
         subject).

(b) *"Objective Mind"*

This constitutes the public manifestation of spirit, which is in turn the development of the dialectic. Hegel supports this belief with interpretations of actual historical periods. Roughly, this historical progression is "The Oriental World" (in which only one, the despot, is free), "The Greek World" (in which only some, non-slaves, are free), "The Germanic World" (in which, eventually, all are free). The overall direction of history is towards consciousness of freedom. Freedom is understood by Hegel not as absence of coercion and doing what one likes, but as acting from self-determination; and that means acting according to universally valid rational principles because in acting under the determinations of universal rational prescriptions one is most free from individual causal circumstances. Obedience to absolute moral laws and ethical individualism are synthesized in the "organic community" in which the individual is free because the rational moral principles he would, as an individual, obey in order to be free are also the specific rational laws of the community: they are in harmony. Moreover, since the community forms the individual, what he naturally desires or wills is no longer pitted against the attempt to obey abstract rational moral principles; rather, he naturally wills those rational principles which are also society's laws.

Hegel's philosophy of absolute idealism can itself be seen as a result of a triadic synthesis of Platonism and Kantianism in the search for knowledge of reality, which means the possession of necessary and universal truths about the actual world. Empiricism alone cannot through experience support such truths; such truths can only be known *a priori* as the conceptual truths of the intellect.

(I) Platonism is a form of objectivism: one in which the sensible world is found to be ontologically unsuitable for necessary and universal truths. So the concepts constituting these truths are said to be mind-independent and concerning an intelligible, world-transcendent realm of mind-independent things-in-themselves, but they are not properly applicable to the sensible world.

(II) Kantianism is a form of subjectivism: one in which the sensible world cannot rationally justify such necessary and universal truths. So the concepts constituting these truths are said to be mind-dependent and concerning a sensible realm of mind-dependent appearances, but they are not applicable to things-in-themselves.

(III) Hegelian absolute idealism. The concepts which are objective in Platonism (I), apart from mind and not applicable to the sensible world, and the concepts which are subjective in Kantianism (II), dependent on mind and applicable only to the sensible world, are synthesized in absolute idealism (III): they are found to constitute reality itself in its totality. The concepts constituting necessary and universal truths are subjective or mind-dependent *and* objective or mind-independent because rational essence of mind, infinite mind, is the only reality there can be; apart from reality constituted by the rational concepts of mind there can be no reality. Finite mind participates in infinite mind in so far as the infinite mind is in the finite, and that means in so far as finite minds accord with the dialectical rationality of infinite mind, which is to the extent that finite mind abides by reason which is what is universal and essential about mind. Thus objectivism and subjectivism, and the subject/object dichotomy, are synthesized and transcended in absolute idealism, where infinite mind and the whole of reality are one self-thinking entity: the Absolute.

We can conclude with a general remark on Hegel's philosophy. Absolute knowledge is reached when the Absolute fully understands itself in the Absolute Idea: for the totality to understand itself is to show how the completely adequate understanding of reality is possible. It is extraordinary to note that Hegel thinks that his philosophy *is* the culmination of the Absolute's self-knowledge, not just a description of it; Hegel's own philosophy is the manifestation in the world of the Absolute's full conceptual grasp of itself in the Absolute Idea in which the object and subject are one: the subject can have as its object only itself. The development of infinite mind has reached its culmination and is manifest through Hegel's finite mind: the philosophy of absolute idealism.

Nietzsche

Friedrich Nietzsche (1844–1900) was born in Röcken in Germany the son of a Lutheran pastor. His father died in 1849; his upbringing was dominated by his pious mother, also his sister and aunts. His rigorous early education, which included classics, took place at the famous boarding school at Pforta, near Naumburg. For most of his life Nietzsche laboured under the effects of poor health, including weak eyesight; for days on end he was struck down by crippling migraines. Nietzsche studied philology at the University of Bonn and then at Leipzig; while a student he encountered the greatest influences on his early thinking, the composer Richard Wagner (1813–83) and the philosopher Arthur Schopenhauer (1788–1860). Nietzsche's outstanding academic achievements are indicated by his appointment, when only twenty-five, as Professor of Classical Philology at the University of Basel. He resigned from Basel in 1878 because of ill-health. From 1878 to 1889 he led an immensely lonely life wandering from place to place in Europe, often in the high Swiss mountains. It was during this time that most of his major works were written. His romantic intentions were always hopelessly unfulfilled, and he remained unmarried. In 1889 Nietzsche rushed into a street in Turin and embraced a horse that was being flogged; he then suffered a massive mental collapse that plunged him into a vegetative insanity for the rest of his life; during the last ten years of his life all spark of intelligence left Nietzsche's mind; the decline may have been due to acquired or inherited syphilis. Until the end of his life he was looked after mostly by his mother but also by his sister Elisabeth, who propagated mythology and obscurity around Nietzsche's work.

It is impossible not to be controversial in giving an account of Nietzsche's philosophy; this is partly because of the scattered nature of his views on any one subject, and partly because of his manner of writing. In concentrating on that part of Nietzsche's philosophy concerned with the nature of philosophy, knowledge and metaphysics, one must be aware that a great deal of his interest lies in the realm of values and how one ought to live one's life; but the two areas are intimately connected in Nietzsche's thought. Nietzsche's grounds for rejecting the possibility of absolute knowledge in general include values in particular. Although Nietzsche deliberately does not produce a systematic exposition of his views, nevertheless all parts of his philosophy are interconnected. The overriding consideration in the account of Nietzsche given here is to take seriously his repeated pronouncement that he was doing something quite different from what had gone before in philosophy. With this in mind, one should avoid attempting to fit him conveniently into any philosophical school. It is all too easy to construe Nietzsche as presenting albeit novel answers to the same old philosophical problems. His aim, however, is to question the very concepts in which traditional philosophical problems are couched. Traditional philosophy has been concerned to present to philosophical problems answers which it aims to be universally and objectively true. But the presupposition that lies behind this advancement of a philosophical position as universally valid is that such universal and objective truths are possible – and it is exactly this that Nietzsche denies is the case. This denial is not the same as advocating scepticism with regard to knowledge, for scepticism too assumes that knowledge must involve necessity and certainty, but thinks it is something we cannot attain.

The key to Nietzsche's philosophy is his attack on absolutism of any sort, final universally binding answers to philosophical problems, which easily leads to dogmatism. There are, in fact, no eternal transcendental truths waiting to be discovered, independent of all thinkers whatsoever.

Nietzsche refers to all views or theories as false or as fictions. Everything is false, and what we regard as true are but convenient errors required for our lives. This applies to our common-sense or herd view of the world, which he regards as a convenient fiction, but on which our survival has come to depend: it is a world of independent things, of various kinds, that causally interact according to certain laws, and is observed by a relatively permanent self. This view has become so deeply entrenched that we no longer recognize it as a *view*, among other possible views, at all. In particular the *a priori* categories that Kant regards as universally valid, and hence objective, are regarded by Nietzsche as having no absolute necessity or universal validity, but as products of human interests and purposes; they are no more than psychologically *a priori*. All views of the world are attempts to schematize and organize experience for the sake of control and power over our environment. But there is no reason therefore to suppose that the way we view the world – our conception of reality – need be universally valid in terms of power and control for everyone. Nietzsche is opposing ideals which produce an ossified and idealized "fabricated world" which is then regarded as the only "real world". In *Twilight of the idols* Nietzsche says, "I mistrust all systematizers and avoid them. The will to a system is a lack of integrity."

We must come to see our truths, and our claims to knowledge, in all fields of activity for what they are: interpretations from certain perspectives. There is also no possibility of a complete view of anything or everything. Thus we find that he attacks metaphysics, knowledge, truth, moral values and values in general, in so far as definitive answers are proposed. Once we see that we have no more than different perspectives on the world, we are liberated from the tyranny of supposing that any view has ever to be accepted as a final universally valid view. It is not just a matter of being modest in our philosophical claims by saying that we are not sure if we have finally solved certain philosophical problems; it is a matter of actively denying that such final solutions are ever attainable.

Nietzsche objects to the pretence of philosophers that they have, or at least can have, a disinterested concern for the truth and knowledge, one that is unaffected by, and separable from, any considerations of conditions that would define in some way a point of view or perspective: the specific values, personal predilections, and attitudes to life that characterize what kind of people they are. It has been the habit of metaphysicians to juxtapose a superior absolute disinterested view of the world – which usually means positing another "real world" beyond or behind the apparent one – with the unthought-out vagaries of the common-sense view of the world whose chief aim has not been the disinterested pursuit of knowledge and truth. There is no such disinterested point of view which would fulfil the condition for describing reality; all views are inherently perspectival and thus not exhaustive; the view from nowhere is no view at all; it is not even an unattainable ideal.

Unlike the systems of metaphysics proposed by past philosophers, which give a view of reality, the indisputable value of the common-sense view of the world is that it at least has been of pragmatic use to us: it has promoted the survival of our species. Indeed, the common-sense view has prevailed and is regarded as "true" precisely because it aids survival; the views that did not aid survival have, of course, died out with their proponents or have been rejected as "errors". The entrenchment, the seeming necessity of our common-sense view, is determined not by its logically absolute or universal necessity or by its accurate reflection of reality, but by its huge value in promoting a particular kind of life and attitude to life: specific interests and values. The imposition of false simplifications or coarsenings by which we give order to our world is a precondition for survival; they arrange a world in which our existence is made possible. This applies to our belief in "things", natural laws and causality, the self, and even logic. In this sense Nietzsche's account of why we have the concepts we have, and which views we hold to be true, is naturalistic, rather like the position of Hume. Nietzsche says in the book *The will to power* that "Rational thought is interpretation according to a scheme that we cannot throw off." We become the prisoners of our "truths" and "knowledge": we forget they are fictions serving our survival, and instead of their serving our needs, we serve the "truths" and "knowledge" which we come to regard as more than instruments of survival. The "truths" and "knowledge" were designed to fit us and our needs; once we lose sight of this the relation is reversed, and we begin to fit the "truths" and "knowledge". For Nietzsche this relation is particularly important in the area of human values.

That a view promotes certain interests and values is not objectionable in itself because every view does this in different ways. What Nietzsche objects to is the dogmatism he sees as inherent in the various metaphysical systems of the past, which suppose they can rise above perspectival interests and values and present to us a disinterested, non-perspectival, complete, view of things truly, as they really are in themselves. The philosophers' metaphysical systems, however, are really doing the same kind of thing as common sense: they are producing organizing schemata that reflect specific deep values and interests. This would be fine provided we realized what we were doing, because we are not obliged to accept the systems unless we want to accept those specific values as well, values which point to a way of life and an attitude to life. The notion that metaphysics seeks a non-perspectival value-free view of reality contains latent dogmatism because if the view is transcendentally universal and necessary, as it is usually claimed to be, then it demands of everyone that they accept it regardless of their specific perspectival view and values. But Nietzsche's point is that there are *only* perspectives.

Nietzsche objects to the claim that the metaphysical systems of philosophers are superior to common sense in being more true in the sense of corresponding to the true nature of reality: all views are equally false or fictions in *that* sense. Nietzsche does not defend common sense against the metaphysicians because it gives the truer view of reality, but on the grounds that it has, at least in the past, proved beneficial to life. He does not attack common sense because it is false or a fiction – not presenting to us the truth about reality in the sense of corresponding accurately to reality – but because it has now become inimical to life and harmful to that which is strongest and best in us. Nietzsche wishes to *replace* the common view of the world, not on the grounds that his view is truer in the sense of more accurately describing reality in the way that traditional metaphysics advocates – the common view is not therefore claimed to be *refuted* – but because his view supports certain values, attitudes and a mode of life which he wishes to advocate for the future development of man. His attempt to replace common-sense or herd views of the world and values with new views does not involve utterly overthrowing existing values, but he admits it is dangerous because the herd view has undoubtedly had survival value; the ushering in of new views is difficult and opens up the possibility of our destruction through disorder or harmful views.

It is sometimes suggested that Nietzsche is rejecting the correspondence theory of truth, whereby we suppose we can accurately reflect an independent reality, and replacing it with a pragmatist theory of truth, whereby what is true is determined by the effects holding a conception has on the practical conduct of one's life and whether it thereby works. This, however, is most misleading if one thinks that Nietzsche's criterion for truth is the base utility of our views in the narrow sense of being practically useful. This would be greatly at variance with the whole spirit of Nietzsche's philosophical outlook. Nietzsche defends common sense because it has been shown to be motivated by serving specific values effectively – mainly practical values connected with survival – but that does not mean that a view has to serve *those* values, even if any view must serve some set of values or other. He is in fact arguing against the delusion that what promotes life guarantees truth in the sense of truths which must be agreed to by all.

It has been said that while Nietzsche ostensibly rejects the whole notion of views and theories of reality accurately mirroring, or failing to mirror, a world which is an independently ordered objective reality, he tacitly assumes a correspondence theory of truth in saying that common-sense views, and indeed all views, are in that corre-spondence sense false. Nietzsche is thus accused of inconsistency in that if all views are false in failing to correspond to reality, there must be some absolute standpoint which does correspond accurately to reality, compared to which all existing views are not true; so, in fact, not all views need be false. If, as Nietzsche says, error might well be a condition for life, and views that promote life are not thereby shown to be true, it suggests that there is some sense in which some theory might be true in reflecting reality more accurately. Be that as it may, Nietzsche wishes to undermine and replace the correspondence notion of truth with a notion of "truth" that is open about its being motivated by promoting some specific values or other, rather than claiming disinterestedly to pursue correspondence to an objective reality; and these values, and hence the associated "truths", need not be accepted by everyone. Nietzsche's claim is that we cannot rid ourselves of the values that motivate our "truths", which such "truths" in fact serve and which lead to our deciding what is "true". But it is arguable that because a view is shown to promote certain specific values, this is sufficient to show that the view cannot nevertheless just *be true* in the sense of reflecting reality.

Nietzsche does indeed present to us a theory in the "will-to-power" which is a view of the world; the world is the will-to-power, and nothing else besides. Partly he seems to do this in order to show that the world is such that no view of reality can ever be right if it claims the world has an objective order. But that seems to suppose some kind of correspondence notion of truth. However, he cannot consistently support his assertion that no view can accurately mirror reality by presenting an account of the world which gives just such an account of reality. The will-to-power must be advocated on grounds other than that it mirrors reality accurately, and this is what Nietzsche does.

Nietzsche's view is that the world is a never-ending flux or becoming with no intrinsic order. The world comprises power-quanta whose entire *being* consists in the drive or tendency to prevail over other power-quanta. Power-quanta differ from one another entirely quantitatively, not qualitatively, and they should not be thought of as things; their entire *being* consists of their *activity*, which is their attempt to overcome and incorporate in themselves other power-quanta. Each power-quantum is the sum of its effects; it *is* what it does. Thus the world is a constant flux of struggle, but it is not a struggle between "things", it merely involves a constant variation of power-quanta. We too are part of this flux. Human beings are nothing more than complex constellations of power-quanta.

In saying that the world is the will-to-power, Nietzsche sees the will-to-power as manifesting itself in multifarious ways. But the will-to-power as such in its general form is fundamental, and manifestations are modes of it. In all sorts of ways in personal and social life we see the will-to-power manifest: in the drive to control, organize and overcome. To control and make manageable does not mean necessarily physical domination, although this is one manifestation of the will-to-power. Any attempt to bring under control our environment is a mode of the will-to-power, and one of the prime examples of this is knowledge itself. Knowledge is a will-to-power because within what we know we have a framework in which what we deal with is manageable by being organized, so increasing our power. By organizing under concepts of things and kinds of things we have something that we call the world under which we transform nature into something that is, in the broadest sense, mastered, its disorder overcome and under control.

Nietzsche is advocating a view of reality in which his perspectivism and his belief in the value of that freedom resulting from the creative capacity to give various interpretations are supported, he is not claiming a disinterested motivation. These new interpretations are not easily achieved, nor can they be gratuitously adopted, since they involve the adoption of values which fundamentally guide our lives and characterize who we are.

Nietzsche's view of the world has an affinity to that of the Presocratic philosopher Heraclitus, whom he admired. In such a world of universal flux it is certainly extremely difficult to see how any theory of reality which identifies as real certain permanent "things" which behave in certain ways could be anything but false and a gross simplification of a flux so complex and ever-changing that it defies any theoretical description at all. It is a world without objective order, so there is nothing for putative objective truths concerning reality to be true of. Except in so far as it is trivially described as a world of constant change, it is a world in which no description can be objectively true at all. All views of reality which aim to be universally true presuppose some objective fixity, so any view which purports to be universally true of reality must be false if there is no such fixity. And it might be argued that a view like Nietzsche's, which merely asserts that there is no objective order, is no view of reality at all. Reality has no ultimate nature; that the world has a character is denied. Nietzsche is asserting that the world has no objective order; the denial that we can assert this without contradiction seems to amount to the assertion that it is a necessary truth that the world has an objective order – which surely cannot be right. There is nothing fixed for truths to correspond to. This leaves us free, although not frivolously so, to invent our own organizing systems, but not under the pretence that we are reflecting an already existing objective reality.

In rejecting the correspondence theory of truth, it must be emphasized that Nietzsche is not, I believe, giving a new *general* criterion of truth at all; that he is not arguing that one set of considerations is universally valid when deciding upon truth. That idea includes the rejection of both the correspondence theory and a generalized pragmatic theory which would impose one universally binding way of deciding on the truth. There is no universally valid criterion for truth, no single scale along which truth can be graded; but there are different views which serve or promote certain values and modes of life, yet all are "illusions" if they are required to be more than valid from a certain point of view. This is close to relativism, but not equivalent to the notion that one view is as good as any other. Some views are *better* than others from the standpoint of a certain set of values, interests, and attitudes to life, although they are not binding on all; it will certainly not be the case that one view will do as well as another for a specific standpoint; some "truths" will promote it, and some will be inimical to it. The view accepted is inseparably linked to the deepest values in life, the lives themselves, and who one is, and one cannot easily or flippantly swap one view or set of truths for another.

This, however, is not the only interpretation of Nietzsche's view of truth. Some commentators have argued that Nietzsche wishes to replace the correspondence theory of truth with a form of pragmatist theory; this is pragmatic value determined not by base usefulness but in terms of a more general criterion of power and control appropriate for those people of higher "rank-order", those capable of maximal power, control and creativity. Thus truth in the new sense can still be graded along a single scale, but this time not arranged in order of greater correspondence to "the facts" (which Nietzsche says do not exist apart from interpretations or views), but arranged in rank according to effectiveness of power and control.

Nietzsche famously proclaims that "God is dead", not so much because the belief that God exists is false – although Nietzsche thinks this is the case – but because God is a bastion for justifying objective values which must be valid for all. Nietzsche further wants to banish even the shadow of God from the world, that is, he wishes to banish the lingering effects of the belief in God from the world; for even non-believers still often act *as if* somehow there were a transcendent order of values outside the world, and as if this world were not the only world. He claims that it has not sunk deep into our conscious-nesses, and our way of living, that this world is the only world – there is no world beyond. If we accept this, it profoundly changes the evaluations we make in and of our lives. It is Nietzsche's aim to present to us a transvaluation of all existing values for the new life, and a suitable world-view, for truly free spirits, for the higher man's potentialities. Thus Nietzsche's views are not advocated because of their more accurate mirroring of reality – because no view does that – or because they are universally valid; but because of their efficacy with respect to certain values and ways of life which Nietzsche believes in and wants us to consider.

Another way of putting Nietzsche's perspectivism is that all truths and knowledge about the world are interpretations: a mode of organ-izing our experience under concepts which give us a world-view with the condition that no such view can possibly be complete because it is dependent on qualifying reference to a point of view. Nietzsche does not object to any view because it is an interpretation; he objects only to the view being seen as more than an interpretation, whilst there are values it probably deviously and dishonestly promotes under the false banner of being the objective truth. This applies to the various systems of metaphysics, Kantian *a priori* categories, natural science, common sense, and even logic. What Nietzsche objects to is what are in fact interpretations down to their most basic constituents being viewed as other than interpretations and as absolute transcen-dental objective truths.

What underlies Nietzsche's position is a general attack on the whole notion of separating our theories about the world from the world itself. There are no facts but only interpretations, and no world left over once all interpretations are subtracted. Our theories, when considered in their entirety, cannot be compared with reality because there is no reality outside our interpretation which is not itself part of an interpretation. There is no neutral ground on which to stand whereby our interpretation can be compared with reality because to have a conception of reality with which an interpretation could be compared is itself to articulate an interpretation. So Nietzsche is not saying we always have *mere* interpretations, because the use of the word "mere" here suggests a comparison with something we actually have that is not a mere interpretation, compared with which mere interpretations are shown to be "mere". Nietzsche denies that there is a view which is not an interpretation; he denies the existence of a non-perspectival, non-interpretative view that would alone make any sense, by contrast, of any view being *merely* or *only* an interpretation.

It might be suggested that there obviously is an interpretation-independent reality. But the response to this is that this view of the world is itself an interpretation. The obviousness of the view that there is an interpretation-independent reality made up of objective "things" of various kinds that behave in certain ways, and our inability to see it as an interpretation, both derive from the way that the view is deeply entrenched in our form of thinking and way of life; and this entrenchment manifests itself chiefly in the structure of our language. Our world-view is inherited in our language, and for this reason we have to use language self-consciously and critically. Deeply embedded in language is the notion of a "subject" to which "predicates" are applied, and we take this to reflect a metaphysical as well as a linguistic distinction. The structure of the language we use to speak about the world implicitly involves a metaphysics: it immediately leads us to talk of the world as containing relatively autonomous "things", which "causally" interact, which are observed by relatively permanent "selves". Indeed, the notion of "things" results from the projection onto the world of the fiction of the "self" (the "I" or "ego"); and the "self" derives from our linguistically requiring an "agent" whenever we speak of actions. We do not just say "think", but grammatically normally require a subject who does the thinking.

Rather like Hume, Nietzsche explains our belief in causally necessary connections through our acquiring it in a way that is rationally unjustifiable; the belief is rather a result of non-rational processes whereby through the observation of constantly conjoined events we acquire habits of association; there are no objective causal connections. The division of the world into recognizable repeatable events and things is the imposition of a fiction by us. No two things are ever really identical, and no two events the same; but we ignore differences in order to establish an order; and we are not refining our experience by this process, but rather coarsening it by making similar what is different. More sensitive creatures who refused to categorize under universal terms would have perished, for a simplified world is required for survival. We treat the world *as if* what is referred to in our concepts is real. But these organizing concepts are only psychologically *a priori*, not transcendentally *a priori* as Kant suggests.

Such concepts are rightly said to be irrefutable by experience; experience already presupposes them and is organized in accordance with them. But that does not mean, particularly with respect to our values, which we have inherited – our whole notion of a single scale for "good" and "evil" – that our entrenched beliefs cannot be *overcome*:

they may not be refutable, but they can, perhaps with difficulty, be *replaced* by something new. Philosophy has spent much of its energy finding a rational justification of existing values without first questioning the value of those values themselves.

We find it difficult to articulate any other interpretation of reality than our usual one because a metaphysics is embedded in the very language in which any other view is to be expressed. The same applies to values. It is not that Nietzsche thinks there is some ideal language which would free us from the common-sense or herd interpretation or metaphysics and give us a true picture of the world: a correct or true metaphysics. Rather we are to be freed from the tyranny of seeing *any views* as true in the sense of mirroring reality in order to release our powers to create new independent interpretations that are fashioned to suit what we value most in life; but we can do this only once we are released from pursuing the chimera of the absolutely true complete view of reality and universally correct system of values.

Another way of putting the point about all views being interpretations is that the old philosophical dichotomy of the appearance /reality distinction is eliminated; the "real world" goes because there is no single universal complete description possible; it cannot be formed from piecing together or summing various different views either. That does not mean we are left with the *merely* apparent world; "appearance" and "reality" are mutually dependent contrasting concepts, and once the "real world" goes, there remains no sense to the supposedly contrasted "apparent world", so that goes too. The apparent world *is* the world; the world as construed under an interpretation *is* the world. To suppose otherwise is merely tacitly to suggest that there is another view which is not an interpretation characterizing "the world" with which our supposedly mere interpretation could be compared; but there is no view that is not an interpretation; any other view would always be an interpretation too.

Nietzsche found it difficult to express his perspectivism because of the way that a certain view is already inherent in the language which we have to use to express ourselves. It seems as though in asserting perspectivism – that there are only interpretations of the world – that we admit that there is a real world which could be described in some way that was not an interpretation. This, it can be argued, is merely a grammatical point: only trivially are our interpretations different perspectives on "the world", because this notion of "the world" is utterly empty until an interpretation is submitted to fill it in; so there is no "world" to compare with all interpretations; take the perspectival interpretations away and "the world" vanishes. Truth and knowledge necessarily involve having a view; without a view involving certain basic concepts there is nothing for propositions to be true of, no world for us to know; but there are no concepts we have to regard as necessary and universally binding.

It is sometimes said that Nietzsche's perspectivist position is plainly self-refuting. For if all views are perspectives – that is, interpretations – then perspectivism must apply to itself, so perspectivism may be false. There are a number of complex discussions of this matter. Some critics are unable to see how self-refutation can be avoided. Others argue that perspectivism does not apply to all views, but only to "first order" views about the world, and it does not therefore apply to itself, which is a "second order" view about views. Still others argue that perspectivism is not self-refuting: perspectivism must admit that it is possibly false, but that is not the same as admitting that it is false; that it is false could be shown only by actually producing a view that was not an interpretation – one that is free from being motivated by, and independent of, specific values – and not merely by suggesting that a view which is not an interpretation is possible. Perspectivism, on this account, cannot claim that it is necessarily true, and that means it cannot claim that views which are not interpretations – which are objectively true – are impossible.

Nietzsche's perspectivism is not equivalent to relativism if relativism is construed as saying the world has more than one character and there is no way of choosing between various complete views of that world; perspectivism denies that the world has any character independent of interpretations, and that any view could possibly be complete or exhaustive. Perspectivism also holds that some views are better than others on the grounds that they are more fitted for certain purposes, promoting the way one wishes to live one's life and the values one holds most deeply about life, but these values are not universally applicable to all individuals of different sorts at all times and places; they are not "better" from all points of view. Nietzsche rejects the positions which suggest that there are views of the world and systems of values that are binding on everyone equally. He also rejects the notion and pretence that truth can be pursued in a disinterested fashion. The view that there is one truth, and one system of values, is itself a view which is intended to promote – although it may do so covertly and even deviously – certain values which involve holding back more creative and courageous spirits who want to counter the idea of universal truths and values themselves. Thus the advocation of universal truths and values binding on all is itself one manifestation of the will-to-power, to control; but it is also a sign of weakness; for the belief in universal objective views and values binding on all itself manifests the lack of power or strength and creativity – unlike the "highest type" or "free spirits" – to transfigure the world with new views and interpretations of one's own and sustain those views and interpretations without the support of a belief in their being universal and absolutely objective.

It can clearly be argued that, far from leading to an advocation of domination and tyranny, Nietzsche's position that there cannot be objectively true or false values suggests that each person must now go away and find his own way, do his own work – as Zarathustra suggests at one point – and Zarathustra tells of one way which gives new meaning to the world. As Nietzsche writes in *Thus spoke Zarathustra*, at the end of Part I:

> I now go away alone, my disciples! You too now go away and be alone! [. . .] Truly, I advise you: go away from me and guard yourself against Zarathustra! [. . .] Perhaps he has deceived you [. . .] One repays a teacher badly if one remains only a pupil [. . .] You are my believers: but of what importance are all believers? You had not yet sought yourselves when you found me. Thus do all believers; therefore all belief is of so little account. Now I bid you lose me and find yourselves; and only when you have all denied me will I return to you.

In *Ecce homo*, before quoting from the above passage of Zarathustra, Nietzsche points out that these words are "Precisely the opposite of that which any sort of 'sage', 'saint', 'world-redeemer' and other *décadent* would say in such a case . . . He does not only speak differently, he *is* different."

However, there is the possibility that pursuing my own way, such as that involved in the way of the *Übermensch* (Superman) depicted by Zarathustra, could involve the subservience of others, in particular that of the "herd", who have a slave mentality in that they need masters to lead them, and who lack the creative power to generate and sustain their own new views. Nietzsche indeed seems to suggest that such subservience is required.

There are two central notions in Nietzsche's world-view: the will-to-power and eternal recurrence.

The doctrine of "eternal recurrence" has its origin in the idea that the world is infinite in time, but finite in space or energy, and therefore states are bound, given sufficient time, to repeat themselves. Thus *this* world is our eternity. Although Nietzsche does seem to have believed in "eternal recurrence" as a scientific cosmological theory, the importance and main grounds of the view lie not there but, rather, in its power as a myth whereby our decisions are concentrated on this world; we had better be authentic and true to ourselves, and not wasteful of our lives, for this is the only life we have and we are destined to repeat what we choose for eternity. We must free ourselves of the attitude carried by the belief that this life is a "waiting room" for something else. There is nothing beyond, no life beyond, which would compensate for, or relieve us of, the weight placed on our choices in this life. To carry this burden is to support the values of strength and independence, and not to view this world as inferior: this is *amor fati*, a yea-saying to life.

These views are *better* because of their fecundity in promoting a certain way of life. But this notion of better does not apply with absolute universality. The life is that of the "Superman" or *Übermensch*, as foretold by Zarathustra. This is the life of the "Beyond-Man" or "Overman" who sees all views as interpretations, and is released as a free spirit to transfigure the world according to newly created "truths" and values which are his own, and he has the strength or power to do so. The notion of the *Übermensch* as creator involves the idea of creating one's own self. Now we are, of course, free to accept this view or not. If we wish to embrace the values of strength and enhance our feeling of power and control as free spirits, then Nietzsche commends to us the will-to-power and eternal recurrence as "truths" to live by. Previous interpretations have outlived their usefulness and have become constraining and inimical to the exploration of new interpretations that would transform or transfigure our world-view. Once we see common sense, and indeed any view which seems more than an interpretation, *as* an interpretation, we are liberated to explore, and will feel we should explore, other ways of viewing the world. Nothing could be more stultifying to pursuing other ways of viewing the world than the belief that one has found the final correct, complete, view; the pursuit of other views will in such circumstances, as with much metaphysics, carry no conviction and will be seen as a mere game played away from the only correct view. But once the notion of an absolutely correct view, and even its pursuit, is abandoned, the exploration of alternative modes of interpreting the world cannot in this way be deleteriously compared. This mode of viewing the world – that all views are interpretations from a perspective – commends itself to those who have the strength to break with habit, custom, the belief in absolute standards, and to produce their own views, suited to their own values and purposes, which in turn will fundamentally characterize who they are. One cannot separate the basic beliefs and values one holds, and what one does, from who one is, but thereby who one is can be changed; and Nietzsche praises those who have the strength to give themselves laws and so create themselves.

The will-to-power, both as a view of the world as one of ontological flux with no objective order, and as an account of the drive behind knowledge itself, undermines the idea that knowledge can be a disinterested activity separable from specific values; knowledge is rather a means to support specific values. The doctrine of eternal recurrence emphasizes the weight of the choices we make in our new-found freedom as free spirits who have the strength creatively to transfigure our world with new truths and values in a way that has no end.

CHAPTER EIGHT

Analytical philosophy: Russell, Wittgenstein

Analytical philosophy refers as much to a method as to a body of philosophical doctrine. It is extremely difficult to give a unifying characterization of analytical philosophy that picks out what is common to all its instances. It was regarded as revolutionary; but it is questionable whether the new philosophy really marks such a discontinuity from what came before.

Analysis is a process which aims to elucidate complexes by reducing them to their simpler elements and the relations between those elements. This can apply to complex concepts, entities, or philosophical problems. In analytical philosophy, the analysis is characteristically linguistic. It is done through analyzing the language in which a complex philosophical problem, say, is expressed; perplexing complex philosophical concepts are dealt with by resolving the complexes into what are logically equivalent related simple constituents, which can be better understood.

The origins of analytical philosophy lie in work done in the latter half of the nineteenth century and the beginning of the twentieth century on logic and the foundations of mathematics. This work involved the construction of a new and powerfully expressive formal logical symbolism. Much of this work was carried out independently by the German logician Gottlob Frege (1848–1925). The culmination of the work in England was *Principia mathematica* (1910–13), written jointly by Bertrand Russell and Alfred North Whitehead (1861–1947). The motivation for this work was the rejection of psychologism, and indeed all forms of naturalism, as providing a foundation of mathematical truth; the new view embraced objective logicism concerning mathematical truths. What this amounted to was the attempt to show that mathematics was reducible in principle to the propositions of logic. The philosophical significance of this is that mathematical truths were shown to be independent of human thought, such as structural features of our way of thinking, and were absolutely necessary objective truths. This meant that mathematical truths were, contrary to Kant's view, independent of whether they expressed even essential features of human thought. Nor did such mathematical truths express extremely general empirical facts as John Stuart Mill (1806-73) suggested. Mathematical truths were shown to be necessary and objective because they depend only on certain basic rules of logic which hold independently of mind or the empirical world. The new logical language is formal in that the rules governing its terms are known exactly; it is powerful in that, unlike traditional Aristotelian logic, it is able to express an enormously richer range of meanings. Aristotelian logic, which dealt with the relations between classes, is shown to be only a tiny fragment of the new logic, which could deal with whole propositions and the internal structure of propositions.

Analytical philosophers saw in the new symbolism a way of tackling old philosophical problems. The new logic delivered an ideal or perfect language which was at the same time powerful enough for the formulation of propositions and arguments previously only expressible in ordinary everyday language. Ordinary language developed for purposes which mean it is ill-suited for the expression of philosophical concepts and problems. The precision, clarity and unambiguity that were possible in the new logic promised to give a way of reformulating philosophical problems so that their solution would become apparent, or the original problem would simply disappear as a pseudo-problem – this perhaps describes the essence and promise of analytical philosophy. Even those philosophers who did not actually reformulate the propositions of philosophy, and the propositions of science and common sense, into formal symbolism saw that the ordinary language in which the propositions were expressed could be systematically misleading, and that we must logically analyze the propositions into their underlying logically related constituent parts to understand what they really mean, if they are meaningful at all, so better to assess how their truth or falsity might be discovered. This process of analysis chiefly involves revealing the underlying structure, or logical form, of propositions in everyday language so as not to be philosophically misled by the apparent grammatical structure. The apparent linguistic structure can be misleading because it can be taken as mirroring structures in the world; but there is no reason why this is necessarily the case. The *logical form* expresses only what are the essential or common features of apparently different linguistic expressions, thus characterizing all expressions of the same given sort. A simple example is "The flower is red" or "The book is red", which can be expressed as "a is F" and "b is F"; the common logical form is "x is F", or more concisely "Fx".

For example, if we take the proposition "I see nobody coming down the road", we might be tempted to think "nobody" functions grammatically as a proper name and names someone, in the same way that in "I see Alan coming down the road", "Alan" functions as a proper name and names someone. If we take the example of the proposition "Numbers can be both odd and even", we might think that "numbers" functions in the proposition in just the same way as "tables" does in "Tables can be both large and small", and so assume that there must exist things called "numbers" in the same way that there exist things called "tables". Philosophical problems might then arise in deciding in what peculiar sense numbers exist.

Often it is the case that the surface grammatical form is not the same as the underlying logical form. In everyday use this rarely matters; but if we are asking philosophical questions, we can be misled not only by ambiguities of sense but also by what the grammatical form apparently implies; we thus misunderstand the philosophical implications or philosophical meaning of the proposition. This misunderstanding can be brought out by revealing the logical form of the propositions, which is to say that all that is ambiguous and grammatically misleading is removed. We then understand what kind of philosophical problem, if any, we are still really confronted with.

Analytical philosophy is characterized by an awareness of the need for self-consciousness in the use of language as the vehicle of human thought about the world. In its less ambitious moods, analytical philosophy has sought to clarify through pre-emptory analysis philosophical problems, and to show that some were only problems at all because we were misled by language, but some philosophical problems remain genuine. In its more ambitious moods, analytical philosophy has sought to show that all philosophical problems are illusory pseudo-problems which originate in our being misled by the language in which they are expressed, resulting in misunderstanding. The former position is more characteristic of Russell and the latter of Wittgenstein. Russell saw the new logic as an ideal language which in philosophy could sometimes replace the vagaries of ordinary language. Wittgenstein saw the new logic as revealing the essential structure of ordinary language itself; ordinary language was in logical order, but this needed to be shown through logical analysis.

The account so far presents mostly the negative or destructive side of analytical philosophy. For philosophers who think that logical analysis reveals all philosophical problems as pseudo-problems, the negative side is all there is. For others there is also a positive or constructive side. If ordinary language is misleading in philosophy, then it has led, among other things, to bad metaphysics. For example, the subject-predicate structure of ordinary sentences has led to our positing the existence of all kinds of puzzling entities apparently denoted by the subject-terms of propositions. In this way we misconstrue the true nature of reality by supposing certain things must exist which need not. The positive side of analytical philosophy is that if we display the true logical form of propositions through a full analysis, rather than disposing of metaphysics, we also produce a true metaphysics: in our new language we *do* reveal the true essential nature of reality, that to which we are ontologically committed whatever else we might suppose is real. The displaying of logical form involves making explicit, behind the apparent structure, what is the implicit but true structure.

Ordinary language contains, chiefly inherent in its structure, implicit metaphysical assumptions. We can either clear these assumptions away and conclude that there are no metaphysical problems left, or we can clear the assumptions away to reveal a true metaphysics: a description of the essential structural features of reality. In Russell and Wittgenstein, in rather different forms, this metaphysics is that of logical atomism. It can be supposed that analysis must come to an end somewhere: if complexes depend, in a general sense, upon related simpler elements, we must, if we are not to embark on an infinite regress, reach ultimate elements which cannot and need not be further analyzed.

Generally speaking, Russell's interest in analysis is epistemological: complexes are better understood and our knowledge of them secured by their analysis into better understood elements with which we are most directly acquainted. Sentences with complex meanings, if they are to be understood, must be composed wholly of constituent atomic meanings which are understood through their reference to atomic entities with which we are directly acquainted. The tendency of Wittgenstein's thinking is metaphysical: he thinks that there simply must be such atomic elements in order to make the understanding of everyday language possible, but not that we need to be directly acquainted with such elements.

We can bring to the surface what is implicit under the grammatical structure of ordinary language: by complete analysis we can reach the ultimate logical form or true structure. Complete logical analysis reveals the logical form, not of any particular proposition expressed in ordinary language, but of the essential structure, or the minimal conditions, for any language capable of representing or describing the world at all. Full logical analysis reveals what must be common to any possible language capable of representing reality; in that way the logical analysis also reveals what must be common to any possible world; it displays the essential nature of reality. Logical analysis is required because we cannot assume that the structure of everyday language reveals the essential nature and ultimate constituents of reality as a whole; for that we must look to the essence of language and leave out what is accidental and inessential. The absolutely minimal structure for any language capable of describing the world or reality at all must also reveal the essential structure of the world or reality itself. It does not reveal contingent features of the world – those are to be discovered by science – but it reveals the logically necessary minimal features of any reality or any world by revealing the necessary minimal features of any language capable of representing any reality or world. Philosophy cannot reveal, for example, what are the facts, but it might reveal that the world is ultimately constituted of independent facts. Language has a structure; the world has a structure; the essential structure of language which is the condition for its being capable of mirroring reality at all must be the same as the essential structure of reality, because without this similarity of structure language could not mirror the world at all. What kind of minimal entities a fully analyzed language requires to function meaningfully are the ultimate entities of the universe. What can be represented or described in language pared down to the logical minimum of descriptive power, beyond which it is logically impossible to go, is what must be part of reality; much else may be a reality, but need not be. If language derives its meaning from its relation to the world, then what must be the case about reality, if language descriptive of reality is possible at all, is what is essential or common to all possible real worlds, however else they may differ. But this conclusion can be interpreted variously: it is unclear whether we have revealed the structure of any possible reality or only any reality that is describable.

Russell

Bertrand Russell (1872–1970) was born into an aristocratic family; his father was the son of the first Earl Russell. His life was eventful and often controversial, and he is notable among philosophers, mainly because of his public activities and his social and ethical views, in being extremely well known even outside philosophical circles. He was noted for the analytic sharpness of his intellect and wit. He was a passionate advocate of reason and debunker of superstition; we should seek out evidence for beliefs no matter how much this might mean abandoning beliefs we may wish to be true. He came to recognize the limits of human certainty and the limits on attaining timeless impartial objective knowledge of the world. After his early years Russell was an atheist, and regarded the existence of God and personal immortality as at best mere logical possibility, and belief in God as generally harmful as well as false. The evidence for a belief in the existence of God was totally insufficient and must therefore be regarded as false. As a boy he was educated privately at home. He took an early interest in mathematics, and in 1890 he went up to Trinity College, Cambridge, to study mathematics. He soon became interested in philosophical matters through dissatisfaction with the foundations of mathematics. He became a Fellow of Trinity College in 1895.

In 1912 Wittgenstein came to Cambridge from the University of Manchester to study with Russell the foundations of mathematics. Russell was impressed by Wittgenstein, and was greatly influenced by his early work. Russell was briefly imprisoned for his pacifist activities during the First World War. In 1931 Russell became Lord Russell when he succeeded to the peerage. In 1938 he moved to America, teaching at the University of Chicago and the University of California in Los Angeles. In 1944 he returned to be re-elected Fellow of Trinity College, Cambridge. In 1950 he was awarded the Nobel Prize for Literature. His last substantial philosophical work, *Human knowledge: its scope and limits*, appeared in 1948; but he was disappointed by the poor attention it received; this he put down to the rise of ordinary language philosophy and to Wittgenstein's later approach to philosophy, which differed sharply from Russell's; he regarded both as largely misconceived. In the last part of his life Russell had an increasingly high public profile by becoming embroiled in social and political issues. His outspoken opinions on private and public morality caused considerable opprobrium to be heaped on him. Russell died at the great age of ninety-eight.

In his early thought Russell swiftly moved through two diametrically opposed philosophical positions: Hegelian absolute or monistic idealism and extravagant pluralistic realism. He then moved to a third view that was supported by a belief in analysis and the process of logical construction: parsimonious pluralistic realism – this he held in various forms from then on.

Russell started with Hegelian monistic idealism, which holds that the world is essentially mental and apparently independent facts are really imposed abstractions which cannot really be characterized or understood in isolation, but can be properly understood only in relation to the whole of reality. Initially Russell was a convinced advocate of Hegelianism. But the Hegelian denial of external relations made mathematics impossible, since the terms of mathematics could not then be characterized in isolation. The denial of external relations, and the consequent doctrine of internal relations, amount to a rejection of ultimately independent facts and entities in the universe; any relation between facts is reducible to properties of each fact concerned and ultimately the whole which they form; in this way no fact can be fully conceptually characterized in isolation and the characterization must eventually expand to the only independent and therefore fully real entity: the universe as a whole. It followed from this doctrine that no proposition concerning less than the whole universe could ever be wholly true. Russell rejected monistic idealism, not only because it undermined mathematics, but also because he thought it was plain that propositions were true because they corresponded to individual facts alone by expressing the structure of the relation of the constituent elements of the facts. Monistic idealism also makes any philosophical analysis into intelligible simple or atomic entities impossible, because one cannot understand the constituent elements in isolation but only after one sees how they fit into the whole.

The rejection of monistic idealism moved Russell to a form of extravagant realism where all the apparent references of propositions have being in some extralinguistic way. It involved adopting a form of Platonic realism. This applied to mathematical truths and concepts: the necessary truth of mathematical propositions derived from their describing the timeless relations between immutable entities which do not exist in physical space. But that such things as numbers existed in some Platonic heaven eventually offended Russell's intuitive sense of reality.

This leads to the final position which in various forms Russell held for the rest of his life: parsimonious pluralistic realism. It amounts to the view that the world consists of a plurality of independent elements, but that many apparent entities are "logical fictions" that are really constructs of other simpler elements. Through the notion of logical construction, entities whose existence is doubtful or problematic can be replaced by entities whose existence is more certainly known and better understood. The view applies a version of Ockham's razor: "Whenever possible, substitute constructions out of known entities for inferences to unknown entities." The three important areas to which Russell applies this principle are mathematics, physical objects, and mind. The purpose of this is in part metaphysical and in part epistemological, and it is sometimes difficult to disentangle the two; the former concerns what there is, the latter our knowledge of what there is – and these matters are, however, distinct.

As far as knowledge of entities, as opposed to knowledge of truths, is concerned, Russell holds that we can know with greatest certainty the nature and existence of those entities with which we are most directly acquainted; knowledge of the nature and existence of all other entities, where a reduction to entities with which we are directly acquainted is not possible, will involve some kind of inference from those entities with which we are directly acquainted. This inference will involve various degrees of certainty, and our aim should be to see how certain this inference is in various cases. The way of making the belief in certain entities most secure is logically to reduce everything we wish to say about the doubtful entities to propositions concerning entities about which we have less or no doubt. On the one hand this has the epistemological purpose of revealing what justification, if any, we have for asserting the existence of entities with which we are not directly acquainted; on the other hand it might have the metaphysical purpose of suggesting that if statements about entities with which we are not directly acquainted can be reduced without loss of meaning to propositions about entities with which we are directly acquainted, it is the entities with which we are directly acquainted which are the basic elements of the universe. Thus among knowledge of things we must distinguish between "knowledge by acquaintance", where we have knowledge of things by direct awareness of the things concerned, without any intermediary inference or knowledge of truths being involved, and "knowledge by description", where we have no direct awareness of the things concerned, but have knowledge only by inference from direct awareness of intermediary things and knowledge of truths. There is no state of mind in which we are directly aware of the things known by description; all knowledge of such things is really knowledge of truths concerning those things; we never know the actual things themselves. Russell's considered position is that what we can justifiably claim to know about posited entities irreducible to objects of immediate acquaintance is inferred from entities with which we are immediately, non-inferentially, acquainted. Thus we have knowledge by description of such physical objects as tables, which it is possible to doubt exist, through our direct acquaintance with sense-perceptions, which it is not possible to doubt exist. The logical reduction to objects of direct acquaintance does not show necessarily that such reduced entities do not exist; it shows merely that we are not committed to their existence; we can say everything we want to say without mentioning them. If we honestly examine our experience, the objects with which we are directly acquainted are not continuous invariable physical objects but the discontinuous variable immediate data of sense-perceptions and introspection. At one time Russell included ourselves and universals as objects of direct acquaintance. With universals included as objects of acquaintance it is easy to see how propositions could be made up of elements with which we are acquainted. The key general point is that understanding and knowledge of propositions describing entities or states of affairs with which we are not directly acquainted must be composed wholly of elements with which we are directly acquainted.

The following general characterization can be given of Russell's mature philosophy. There are two kinds of truths: logical and mathematical truths, and factual truths. Logical truths are necessary and can be known to be true *a priori*, since the truth of such propositions is independent of any facts about the world; such truths are tautologies; tautologies are true because of their intrinsic logical form and regardless of content. A proposition is a tautology if it always comes out true regardless of the truth or falsity of its constituent parts; because of this it can tell us nothing about the world; it is devoid of factual content, since it remains true regardless of the truth or falsity of any propositions stating facts about the world; such a proposition is "*p* or not-*p*". There is no *a priori* way of proving the existence of anything. The world consists of a plurality of logically independent facts. Factual truths are contingent and can be known to be true only *a posteriori*, through experience, since the truth of such propositions depends on their corresponding to non-necessary facts about the world; such a proposition is "*p* or *q*". If facts are complex, then sentences are true if they express the relation of the constituent parts of the complex facts. All non-logical truths are true in virtue of their accurate correspondence with some independent extralinguistic fact about the world, and are false otherwise; and such facts can logically stand in complete isolation from any other facts and the universe as a whole. Some facts about the world we know directly, without inference, and some only by inference from facts we do directly know. Our knowledge of facts that we do not know directly, if they cannot be logically reduced without loss of meaning to facts that we do know directly, depends on inferences from facts that we do know directly by principles of inference that are non-demonstrative. No deductive or demonstrative relation exists between ultimate matters of fact, since it is logically possible – it implies no contradiction – that an isolated fact could be the case although the rest of the universe has been extinguished. If deductive relations existed between matters of fact they would be necessarily connected; but, properly analyzed, facts are never necessarily connected. That facts can appear to be logically dependent arises from our putting together two facts as if they were one fact. From "*A* and *B* are men" it logically follows that *B* is a man; but from the truth "*A* is a man" alone we cannot deduce anything whatever about *B*. Russell sharply differentiates between truth and knowledge: between a truth and verification or proof of that truth. Primarily, beliefs, and derivatively propositions, are true in virtue of objectively and correctly corresponding to the facts. A belief or proposition just *is* true if it corresponds to the facts, regardless of whether anyone knows or could know it to be true by its actual verification, and regardless of any other beliefs or propositions thought to be true. The fact in virtue of which a belief or sentence is true is called its verifier. Russell is adamant that there are many true beliefs that no one will ever know to be true; what is true is not limited by our capacity for knowledge of truths and powers of verification. Increasingly he was forced to admit the perspectival nature of our knowledge, and our inability to attain complete certainty, impartiality, and objectivity divorced from our point of view; nevertheless, such an objective point of view should be our aim so we can mirror the world with as little distortion as possible.

Russell clearly rejects both the pragmatist theory of truth, where a proposition is held to be true in virtue of the satisfactory practical consequences in relation to our experiences of its being accepted, and the coherence theory of truth, where the truth of a proposition is dependent on its consistency with other propositions which form a complex system. Truth, apart from in logic and mathematics, consists of a relation to non-linguistic facts that are in general non-human.

In the philosophy of logical atomism Russell argues for a metaphysics in which the world consists ultimately of logically atomic objects or particulars qualified by properties or standing in relation; these are atomic facts; logical relations between atomic facts form complex facts. Particulars are logically independent; there is no logical impossibility involved in saying the universe might consist in one particular. Thus the truth of any complex proposition concerning a complex fact depends on whether it correctly describes the relation of the elements of the complex fact. Complex propositions are compounds which depend for their truth or falsity on the truth or falsity of their constituent parts: they are truth-functional compounds of atomic propositions. So there must be ultimately simple objects whereby analysis comes to an end. The ideal logical language would clearly show what was simple and what complex. The simplest objects are those that can only be denoted by logically proper names; that is, names that have no hidden descriptive content which would imply the objects named have parts. The meaning of a proper name is fully given by an acquaintance with the particular named. Either a logically proper name names a particular or it has no meaning. The simplest of atomic facts would be stated as "Fa", where "a" is a logically proper name qualified by a predicate "F", or "aRb", which expresses the relation between atomic objects a and b which have the logically proper names "a" and "b". This gives a logical definition of what particulars would be; whether there are any is another matter.

The only logically proper names which are guaranteed meaning, because they cannot fail to have a reference, seem to be the demonstratives "this" and "that", which refer to the smallest perceptibly distinguishable part of a sense-datum (a minimum sensible); that is, they must refer to an absolutely simple part of the immediate present content of our sense-experience; thus we might have the atomic fact "This is white" if this means the minimal sensible sense-datum of my immediate sense-experience. But a consequence of this would be a vocabulary private to the speaker and shifting in meaning, for "this" and "that" would mean different things for different speakers, and different things for the same speaker at different times, since "this" and "that" refer only to the minimal content of experience at a moment. A molecular proposition is a truth-functional compound of atomic propositions, such as "Fa and Gb". Such qualified proper names as "a" and "b" either name an object or are not meaningful at all. Logically proper names do not name physical objects, since they are complex. The names of physical objects might cease to be meaningful if the complex physical object named ceased to exist through its disintegrating; such names can be replaced ultimately by descriptions of atomic facts that describe sense-experience.

Later Russell came to see problems with logical atomism and to think that whether there are atomic facts and objects which are unanalyzable was a question which did not need answering, and the lack of an answer did not detract from the value of analyzing complexes into constituent parts.

Russell maintained a deep respect for the findings of science; whatever doubt we may have about the details of the discoveries of science, he thought that the scientific view of the universe, particularly as derived from the most basic science of physics, was essentially true. The existence and nature of the world or reality are almost entirely non-human, and are quite independent of mind, modes of cognition, or capacity for knowledge. Fundamental features of the world are not in any way dependent on concepts contributed by mind. Most of the universe is governed by laws in which the mind plays no part, and in which mind – in particular the human mind – occupies only a tiny fragment of space and time. How we know is itself only a small part of what we know; otherwise, Russell says, we would be inclined to think that the mind in some way determined the nature of the world. Russell accepts that there might be things we cannot know. These views fit with Russell's rejection of idealism, including the philosophy of Kant, and also of some tendencies of empiricism.

This connects with Russell's attitude to extreme scepticism, as practised by Descartes. Russell, although initially sympathetic to scepticism because he saw it as a way of discovering certainty, came to think no progress can be made from the starting point of extreme scepticism. He is not an insincere sceptic who would reject beliefs that no one acquainted with the current state of knowledge could seriously doubt; we should accept the best current knowledge of the time unless we have specific reasons for rejecting it. Scepticism can, however, be useful as a methodological device to see how many assumptions can be eliminated as unnecessary, so making our knowledge more secure by eliminating the number of assumptions required to be accepted. This attitude to scepticism amounts to an admission that extreme scepticism cannot ultimately be refuted; but Russell also denies there are any grounds for thinking it true. It is logically possible that the whole universe came into existence five minutes ago with our having false memories apparently of a time before that; everything now is as it would be if the universe had existed before that time – there is no way of showing such a hypothesis to be impossible. There would be no way of proving that it did not exist earlier; indeed all the evidence would point the other way. That scepticism cannot be ultimately refuted does not mean that its grounds cannot be minimized; it is just that it is logically possible that it is true. The only way of giving an absolute refutation of any position, including extreme scepticism, is by showing that it involves a logical contradiction and is hence logically impossible; this often cannot be done. But that does not mean any view that cannot be shown to be logically contradictory must be equally believed to be true. Intellectual honesty demands that reasons or evidence for and against should be the overriding consideration in deciding what we do and do not believe. Russell reduces, in his later work, his expectations as to how much certainty is possible. Essentially his view is that absolute certainty of the sort that would satisfy exaggerated scepticism exists only with respect to logical truths (and only then because they are contentless tautologies) and with respect to our awareness of the immediate content of our minds; elsewhere absolute certainty is impossible and doubt logically possible.

Russell was convinced that much bad philosophy was a product of a naive acceptance of the structure or syntax of ordinary language as reflecting the structure of the world. The ambiguity of the vocabulary of ordinary language produces additional but less profound difficulties. Language could display the metaphysical structure of reality – the logically basic, or essential, features of the world – but only if the language in question were purified of the accidental accretions which lead to unwarranted metaphysical commitments. The purification of ordinary language is carried out by displaying the logical form buried in the grammatical form of ordinary language. Otherwise we find ourselves ontologically committed to some entities having some kind of being which both is problematic and which leads to paradox. The purpose of constructing such an ideal language is to eliminate unnecessary assumptions as to the existence of certain entities by paraphrasing expressions which denote those kinds of entities and seem to presuppose their existence in expressions which do not contain such a presupposition. The question of whether such entities actually exist is not a matter that can be settled by logic alone; but we are not committed by our language to supposing that such entities must exist.

An application of this idea, and of logical analysis, can be seen in Russell's theory of descriptions. Russell assumes that the meaning of a name is to be identified with the object that it denotes; he also assumes that if we have a meaningful declarative sentence, it must be either true or false. Take the proposition "The present King of France is bald", when there is no King of France. This obviously seems to be a meaningful declarative sentence. By a denoting phrase Russell means an expression of the form of "the so-and-so". If a denoting phrase such as "The King of France" functions as a name, and expressions in which the phrase occurs are to be meaningful, we seem to be committed to the existence, in some sense, of an object named by the denoting phrase. Moreover, any proposition in which a predicate is ascribed to a subject would seem to involve the implication that there is an object which the subject term denotes. Indeed decidedly paradoxical results arise where we wish to deny the existence of objects; if "X does not exist" is to be meaningful, "X" must denote an object, so we seem to have to suppose that X after all has being in some way. The way Russell deals with this problem is with his theory of descriptions. He denies that definite descriptions function as names; so for them to contribute to the meanings of propositions in which they occur there need not be objects that they denote. The temptation to assume that there must be an object which a definite description denotes is removed by making explicit the implicit assumption and paraphrasing the propositions so that the definite description does not occur.

Thus the full and correct analysis of "The present King of France is bald" is a conjunction of three propositions:

(a) There is a King of France

&

(b) There is not more than one King of France

&

(c) There is nothing which is both King of France and is not bald.

More formally this can be stated as follows:

There is an x such that

(a') x is now King of France

&

(b') For all y, if y is now King of France, y is identical with x

&

(c') x is bald.

This shows that although the whole original proposition, "The present King of France is bald", is meaningful, there is thereby no need to find oneself committed to assuming the existence of any object denoted by the subject term of the proposition. The analysis enables us to affirm or deny what was merely assumed, that there exists an object denoted by the subject term of the original proposition. It also maintains the principle that all meaningful declarative sentences must be determinately true or false, because the whole original proposition is false. The whole original proposition is false because (a) is false, that is, (a') is false for every value of x, and if one of a set of conjuncts is false, then the whole set is false. If the King of France did exist but was not bald, then the whole original proposition would be false because (c) is false, that is, the conjunction (a') & (b') & (c') would be false for every value of x, while (a') & (b') was true for some x.

Russell's logical constructionism involves the construction wherever possible of the world from those items with which we are directly acquainted, unless we are forced to do otherwise. This means that entities X can be constructed out of entities Y. The principle of this *logical* construction proceeds through showing that all sentences about Xs can be translated without loss of meaning to sentences about Ys; the direction of the construction always involves the construction of those entities of whose existence and nature we are most doubtful out of those entities about which our knowledge is least doubtful and most secure. This attempts to give greater security against doubt to beliefs concerning the nature and existence of entities.

Russell applies this idea to mathematical truths; here the aim is to minimize the number of truths that have to be accepted without proof, and the number of entities that need to be postulated. The aim is to show that all mathematical truths can, in principle, be stated in terms derived from logic alone. Mathematics seems to refer to various problematic entities – for example, numbers; but numbers are not empirical entities and do not seem to be in space or time at all. It is extremely unclear, in that case, what sort of being such entities can have. The strategy here is to define numbers in terms of classes: the number one is the class of all classes in which any member is identical with any other member; the number two is the class of all classes of couples, and so on. We must note that the number of members a class has is defined in a non-circular manner using the notion of "similarity" of classes where there is a one-to-one relation which correlates the members of the one class each with one member of the other class. Thus the need to posit problematic entities outside space and time is avoided, and we can think of numbers as classes of classes of unproblematic entities. In the end Russell came to accept reluctantly Wittgenstein's view that mathematics consisted of tautologies; he was reluctant to do this because it destroyed the idea that mathematics was a system of certain discoverable eternal truths about a non-human world beyond the uncertainty concerning the world revealed by the senses. The conclusion is that the interest of mathematics for us derives entirely from our limited intellectual power, and its truths would to a mind of sufficient power be as trivial as $2+2=4$.

The same logical constructionism is applied to our knowledge of physical objects and mind. Russell's convictions with respect to our knowledge of the world are basically empiricist, but he accepts certain limitations to empiricism; experience alone is not sufficient to justify many of our non-logical knowledge claims. He accepts that our knowledge of the world must be through experience, while at the same time he holds that certain of the suppositions required for such knowledge, given the range of what we wish to claim to know, cannot be justified by experience. If strict empiricism were followed, we would seriously have to limit our claims to know by being unable justifiably to go beyond the information we strictly immediately experience. Either what we normally claim to know we do not really know, or we must accept certain principles not justifiable by experience in order to claim such knowledge.

Russell accepts the traditional view that we do not directly experience physical objects; rather, we directly and indubitably experience private objects, actual sense-data and possible sense-data – sensibilia – which are not thereby necessarily something mental, and it is from these that physical objects are to be either constructed or inferred. This is because when we say we are perceiving a table, we and other people perceive different things depending on things about us (our position, for example); since there is no reason to show favouritism and say that any one of the perceptions *is* the "real" table (its real shape or colour, for example), what we actually perceive cannot be the real table itself, but must be something else.

Initially Russell adopted a dualism of mind and matter and a triadic structure for our sense-perception. In any act of sense-perception there are said to be three elements: act, content, object. By "act" is meant the subject's act of awareness; by "content" is meant the private sense-data of which the subject is aware; by "object" is meant whatever is the cause of the sense-data. The problem that immediately arises is how one is to justify the belief in the existence of public physical objects if one is never directly aware of them. This problem, along with the fact that the supposed act of awareness, as distinct from what one is aware of, is also never a datum of experience, led Russell to adopt a form of neutral monism. This view accorded, Russell believed, more exactly with modern science. According to this view, neither matter nor mind constitutes the ultimate stuff of the universe (neither are substances); both are logical constructs out of something more fundamental: events. Events are analyzable into qualities in some space-time region, space and time being constructs out of relations between qualities. These events, in so far as knowledge rather than truth is concerned, are identified by Russell with "percepts", which are the immediate data of our experience, but which as possible objects of experience can exist unperceived. In this way both matter (physical objects) and mind can be logically constructed out of percepts, and the only difference between matter and mind consists in the way in which they are collected into related bundles. Objects are constructed out of the class of all actual and possible appearances or aspects; subjects are the class of percepts which constitute a perspective bound together by memory. Roughly we can think of this as "act" and "object" being collapsed into "content".

What I am immediately aware of is a percept in my private perceptual space, which is an event in my brain; but my brain, for me, does not form part of my private perceptual space, although my brain is an object in public neutral space. In saying "I see X" I am directly aware of percepts in private perceptual space, the necessary and sufficient conditions for which are brain events in public neutral space, and such events are causally linked in some way to events constituting X in public space. Particular percepts which I experience are associated with two places: the place associated with the group of particulars, which is my biography, and the place associated with the group of particulars, which is the "thing" X; these are two ways of grouping the same percepts.

With respect to knowledge of the world we are acquainted indubitably without inference only with present private experiences; the problem then arises as to the principles by which we are justified in claiming knowledge beyond the evidence of our immediate experience. We claim to know truths about the past, and the future, and universally valid laws of science. Russell holds that whatever the required principles might be, they cannot be deductive, because no deductive connections hold between matters of fact. The inference from matters of fact with which we are immediately acquainted, if they cannot be reduced without loss of meaning to propositions about immediate experience, must depend on a non-demonstrative principle of inference. Russell is asking what logical justification there can be for beliefs beyond what we immediately experience; he is not asking in what circumstances we are in fact caused to make such inferences and have such beliefs.

We can ask, for example, what is the justification for the belief in material objects that continue to exist unperceived? There is also the problem that inference from "Some As are Bs" to "All As are Bs" is never deductively valid, for there is no logical contradiction in supposing that the next observed A will not be a B. The principle we are seeking to justify such an inference is one that somehow validates the move from things that we have observed to things that we have not observed. Russell ultimately rejects the view that this principle is one of simple enumerative inductive inference: that the more observed As have been Bs, the more probable it is that the next A will be a B. He rejects it because it is more likely, if unlimited by common sense, to lead to false beliefs than to true beliefs. Given any finite set of facts, there is, logically speaking, an infinite number of possible theories which will fit the facts, all of which are equally probable. If, however, we start with certain assumptions about the world antecedent to our empirical investigation, then some outcomes, following the empirical gathering of facts, will be more probable than others. These Russell outlines as five "postulates" in *Human knowledge*. These postulates are indemonstrable; if they were logical *a priori* principles, then they would, through being tautologies devoid of content, be unable to fulfil their function of factually describing the world by ruling out certain factual possibilities, going beyond mere logical non-contradiction. On the other hand, such postulates cannot be verified by experience, for they are being presupposed in all empirical reasoning. Although the postulates cannot be proved, Russell's valuing of them is justified by his claim that they distil from obvious cases of scientific practice the details of what is actually assumed in such empirical inquiry. This fits with Russell's general notion of philosophical analysis: the aim is not to speak obscurely about science, and empirical inferences, being a valid practice; the aim is to make clear by analysis exactly what that practice logically assumes. Although the ensuing postulates cannot be proved, we at least know where we stand, and what exactly is being assumed. These postulates in turn mark the limits of empiricism, but limits which Russell in one sense does not overstep because he does not think that the postulates could have other than an empirical justification; the limitation arises from the fact that no empirical justification is possible. He does not suggest that they can be known to be objectively valid by being Kantian *a priori* principles because he does not think the mind can legislate for facts about the world; mind cannot dictate facts to the world.

The problem with empiricism as a theory of knowledge is its inability to justify our knowledge of things which we clearly wish to claim to know; it is unable to do this because it would require, but cannot justify empirically, principles of inference which take us beyond what is justified by private present immediate experiences. Empiricism as a theory of knowledge must have limits, since it will involve some general proposition about the dependence of knowledge on experience, such as "All knowledge is based on experience", which is not itself knowable by experience; so, if true, empiricism cannot be known to be so.

Wittgenstein

Ludwig Wittgenstein (1889–1951) was born in Vienna into a wealthy merchant family; he was the youngest of eight children. Wittgenstein's paternal grandfather had been a wealthy Jewish merchant who had converted to Protestantism. Wittgenstein's mother was a Roman Catholic, and he was brought up in that faith. The house was one of great cultural sophistication, particularly with regard to music, Brahms and Mahler being regular visitors. The attempt was made to tutor the children at home; but this proved a failure academically. At an early age, Wittgenstein showed great aptitude for practical engineering, and constructed a small sewing machine. His poor academic performance meant that he failed to enter Vienna University, and instead went to a technical college in Berlin. He left the college in 1908 and went to the University of Manchester as a student of aeronautical engineering. Naturally his work involved the application of mathematics; this led him to be interested in the foundations of mathematics itself. He asked who had done work in this area and was directed to Bertrand

Russell's *Principles of mathematics*. This proved a revelation to Wittgenstein, and he was advised by Frege to study with Russell in Cambridge, which he did in 1912. Although the personalities of Russell and Wittgenstein were frequently at odds, Russell soon developed a deep respect for Wittgenstein's early philosophical and mathematical ideas.

Wittgenstein went to Norway in 1913 and built himself a hut in a remote location in which to continue his work on logic. When the First World War broke out, Wittgenstein enlisted in the Austrian army. He survived the war and was taken prisoner by the Italians. One result of the war was that a new austerity or asceticism characterized his life. Throughout his time in the army he had been completing his first great book, the *Tractatus logico-philosophicus*; this was eventually published in 1921. Since he thought that the *Tractatus* disposed of all the problems of philosophy, he quite consistently gave up the subject. From 1920 to 1926 he was a primary school teacher in rural Austria. Under the influence of discussions with other philosophers, and through dissatisfaction with the *Tractatus*, Wittgenstein resumed his philosophical activity. In 1929 he returned to Cambridge and received a PhD for his *Tractatus*. Around this time Wittgenstein began the transition from his early philosophy to his later ideas.

After returning to Cambridge Wittgenstein was, with Russell's recommendation, awarded a Fellowship at Trinity College. During this time the second, and in many ways quite different, phase of his philosophy in the *Philosophical investigations* developed, although there are connections with his earlier thought. After another year in the hut in Norway Wittgenstein was in 1939 made Professor of Philosophy at Cambridge. As he had always done, he continued to travel restlessly. In 1949 he discovered he had cancer, and he lived with friends in Oxford and Cambridge until his death at the age of sixty-two.

Wittgenstein was in many ways an extraordinary person. He was a man of lacerating self-criticism, troubled about his own life. He could be extremely difficult, but he elicited great loyalty from his friends. Although cultured, he was relatively unread in the philosophical classics. It is difficult to identify philosophical influences on Wittgenstein; some known influences are Spinoza, Schopenhauer, Kierkegaard (1813–55), William James (1842–1910) and also Frege and Russell. He also admired writers such as Dostoyevsky and Tolstoy. He was driven by his character to think about philosophical problems; good philosophy was not seen by him as something that could be compartmentalized as a professional job distinct from the rest of one's life and the deepest considerations as to how we ought to live; philosophy and wisdom were, or ought to be, interlinked. His thought was profound, and yet he had doubts about the nature, function and value of philosophical thought. He had a deep desire to solve philosophical problems, and not use them as a field for mental exercise.

In order to understand the *Tractatus* it is necessary to give an account of its overall aim, motivation and method. The aim of the book is to draw the limits of the thinkable; and this is the same as drawing the limits of language; beyond those limits the attempt to say things can only produce nonsense. This brings us to the motivation for the book; this can be seen as ethical, or perhaps aesthetic. In the face of that which is "higher", matters concerning ethics, religion, aesthetics and profound questions about the meaning of life, we should stand in silence; the attempt to say things about such subjects offends not only against the logic of what language is capable of saying, but also against a cultured sensibility which refuses to babble futilely in the presence of what is awesome and mystical. The attempt to say things about what cannot be said is worse than silence, not only because it is a waste of time, but also because it leads us to corrupt and destroy the true nature of that of which we speak. This idea accords with the intuition of many that words are somehow inadequate in the face of the things that really matter most – the most profound aspects of the human condition – and that silence is the only proper response; the attempt to speak only sounds gauche, shallow and tactless.

Much of philosophy has been concerned to tackle philosophical problems head-on by trying to develop answers to the problems as stated. The notion that there are limits to thought and language can be applied to the problems and questions of philosophy itself. Wittgenstein rigorously develops the critical tradition in philosophy. There is some similarity with Kant's assault on transcendent metaphysics. To give a philosophical critique is to describe the logical limits of something, such as knowledge, thought or language. In the *Tractatus* the aim of the critique is to show that the problems of philosophy do not need to be addressed because they are pseudo-problems which arise from illegitimately going beyond logical limits. Thus we should try not to tackle philosophical problems head-on but rather to show that they are not genuine problems; they are necessarily nonsense, and no more require to be answered than "How many goals have been scored in this cricket match?" requires an answer in terms of the number of goals. Philosophical problems are not solved but dissolved.

In Wittgenstein the method used to carry through this critique is deceptively simple: how every and any language acquires its meaning determines the limits of what is meaningful in language. These limits are determined by discovering the essence of language: what all meaningful language must have in common, that without which it would not be meaningful language. Wittgenstein regards the limits of language as the limits of thought; beyond those limits we not only lack any possibility of knowledge, we also reach what is unthinkable. It is vital to realize that Wittgenstein assumes that language at bottom has an essence, a single or unified logic; there is a single universal form of language. There are features common to all and only languages that make them language. Anything that has these features is a language, and anything that is a language has these features. In short, it is possible to define language by a set of features that are together necessary and sufficient for anything to count as language.

Language is considered as the totality of propositions. Propositions are linguistic expressions that can be determinately true or false. What we have to show is the way that words and propositions, the basic units of our language, acquire their meaning. We analyze the essential way that propositions – such as "The cat is black" – acquire their meaning or sense; all that can be meaningfully said can be expressed in propositions; it follows that we cannot speak, or can speak only nonsense, if we try to use propositions to talk about subjects in which they cannot have a meaning. In short, we must study the way language essentially acquires its meaning in order to show that there are limits to what can be meaningfully expressed in language. That is, the discovery of the necessary and sufficient conditions – the essential features – in virtue of which any linguistic expression is meaningful entails that anything that fails to satisfy those conditions must be meaningless. The limits of the meaningful mark the limits of genuine propositions, and thus of language.

It must be pointed out that, generally speaking, the propositions in which philosophical problems are stated appear meaningful. But this appearance is an illusion; once we understand the logic of our language, that is, how ultimately and necessarily language becomes meaningful, we will see that such propositions do not accord with what can be meaningful. Russell in the theory of descriptions had shown that certain philosophical problems disappear once we see the underlying logical form beneath the apparent surface grammar. Such insight into the nonsense of the apparent propositions of philosophy reveals itself not immediately, but only after analysis. According to Wittgenstein, it is unnecessary to do this analysis piecemeal; one can show the limits of meaningful language, and that philosophy lies outside those limits, all at once. The aim is to indicate what cannot be said by clearly presenting what can be said; we thus indicate what cannot be said from inside the boundary of what can be said.

Wittgenstein's inquiry is not an empirical one; it is a matter of pure logic; it is a matter of showing how any propositions of any language acquire their meaning by showing in what that meaning essentially consists or must consist when all superficial differences are removed. There is just *one* way all language is meaningful. This involves showing what *must* be the case in the deep structure of language and the nature of the world if meaningful language is to be possible – as it obviously is – at all. The key to this is to understand that ultimately language gets its meaning from its having a certain relation to the world; apparently meaningful expressions which cannot have that relation are not really meaningful.

If we are able to determine the essential conditions required for meaningful descriptive language, and these derive from something about the world, we have also displayed the essential nature of reality; that is, how any possible world logically must be if any world exists at all. There will of course be all sorts of contingent features about the world which we cannot determine by logic alone; but there must be some essential features that are common to all possible worlds regardless of their contingent differences. The minimal conditions for having a meaningful descriptive language at all reveal the minimal nature of any possible world – the substance of the world. Basically this will come down to what is common between the essential structure of meaningful language and the essential structure of the world.

In giving an account of how language gets its meaning, it must be understood that we are looking below the surface structure of language to the hidden deep structure on which its meaningfulness depends. Wittgenstein is saying: if language has meaning, then, as a matter of logical necessity, this, at its deepest level, is how language must be.

Language gets its meaning in virtue of a relation between it and the world. So language that cannot have this relation is meaningless. The starting-point of Wittgenstein's view of language is roughly outlined as follows. The meaning of a word is the object for which it stands; the meaning of a word is the object to which the word refers. Words are basically names. The world is made up of objects, and the relations between objects form facts. Propositions describe the facts by describing how the objects stand in relation to each other. If the relation of the objects expressed in the proposition is the same as the relation of the objects themselves, then the proposition is true, otherwise it is false. What the facts are is quite independent of language or thought; we do not make the facts.

As an account of ordinary language the above seems obviously inadequate. If the meaning of names is their objects, then names referring to objects that cease to exist, or never did exist (such as "Excalibur"), become, or are, meaningless. This means that any proposition containing such names will also be meaningless. Also there are various components of ordinary language that do not seem to be names at all – such as "is", "or", "must" – so their meaningfulness is unexplained. The answer to this is that ordinary language hides a complexity that can be revealed by analysis.

Suppose we have a proposition "p" asserting "x is F", but x does not exist. If "x is F" is false just because x does not exist, then "x is not-F" is also false; but it is a principle of logic that propositions "p" and "not-p" cannot both be false or both true. So what the proposition "*p*" really asserts is that some related complex combination of objects constituting *x* in fact obtains. But although the elements of the complex exist, the described relation between them concealed in the name "*x*" does not hold; "*x*" covertly describes a fact rather than names an object. So "*x* is *F*" is false because part of what it describes, under the guise of the term "*x*", is false; the complex combination of objects constituting *x* does not obtain, although the constituent objects exist.

We might say "*x* is *F*" is not false but meaningless if *x* does not exist. On Wittgenstein's view of language, if we find a complex expression that contains a name referring to an object that does not exist, then it would seem that the whole expression must be meaningless. If the expression is to be meaningful, then the terms referring to the object that does not exist must really be a description using terms referring to more fundamental objects that do exist and to the relation between them. Then the original whole expression is not meaningless, but simply false, because one of its constituent parts describes a relation between fundamental objects that does not hold, although those objects themselves exist. Because those objects exist, the whole expression referring to them is meaningful, although the relation it describes as holding between them is incorrect.

The implication of this is that proper or *real* names ("simple signs") should refer to simples – atomic objects that are logically without parts and so cannot break up – if expressions which include names are not to run the risk of being meaningless or nonsense when the object named does not, or ceases to, exist. "Excalibur has a sharp blade" is meaningful whether Excalibur exists or not; so the word "Excalibur" is really a description which must by analysis be eliminated and replaced by names of simple parts, which, if they are not combined in a certain way, means that Excalibur does not exist, but to which the names cannot fail to refer and so have meaning.

If we are not to embark on a regress in which we are unable to guarantee that propositions have a determinate sense, we must reach real names that cannot fail to refer to objects; that is, absolutely simple objects that cannot be described. If the terms of propositions did not ultimately name objects that are not complexes, then any proposition could always fail to have meaning, since it might be constituted of terms that had no reference, and hence no meaning. The only way to guarantee that terms have meaning is that they are ultimately constituted of terms that cannot fail to refer to objects that exist if the world exists at all. This means the objects cannot be complexes, but must be without parts. If they are without parts, they cannot be described but can only be named, for a description is an analysis into constituent parts. This is the only way of guaranteeing that propositions have meaning; otherwise any proposition could fail to have a meaning by containing terms that are ultimately words referring to non-existent entities. Wittgenstein calls these ultimate terms simple or atomic names and their references simple or atomic objects. Thus Wittgenstein gives an account of what must be the case if language is to be guaranteed as meaningful.

This emphasizes the requirement that sense be determinate; propositions must have a definite sense, for a proposition without definite sense could not be said to have a sense at all, and could not be determinately true or false.

Wittgenstein's aim is to produce a theory of language whereby propositions have meaning even when they appear to refer to non-existent objects. If the meaning of words consists in the objects for which they stand, and propositions are made up of words, then, for it to be the case that propositions are guaranteed a sense even when they apparently name non-existent objects, at a deep level it must be the case that language as the totality of propositions consists of names that cannot fail to have meaning by having objects for which the names cannot fail to stand. At the deepest level language, as the totality of propositions, must consist of names of logically simple indestructible objects.

When completely analyzed, the structure of language mirrors the structure of the world. The most basic constituents of language are atomic names which mean their atomic objects; the meaning (*Bedeutung*) of a name is the object to which it refers. Atomic names and objects are, respectively, the simplest constituents of language and of the world. Atomic objects are the substance or form of the world in that they are common to any possible world. These objects are logically atomic: they can only be named and not described, for if they could be described they would consist of a complex combination of elements which would mean they were not simple; but atomic objects are indestructible, permanent and unchanging. Atomic objects are the constant elements of all change and enter into combination with other atomic objects to form a state of affairs or atomic fact (*Sachverhalt*). The possible ways in which atomic objects can enter into combination with other objects fix the form of such objects, the sum of which ways is the possible states of affairs in which such an object can be an element. This form is the timeless order determining all the possible states of affairs into which it can enter. When we know (*kennen*) an atomic object, it is "given"; we then know all the possible states of affairs into which it can enter; in that sense we then know all other objects and all possibilities. Possible and actual states of affairs, which are arrangements of atomic objects, are depicted by elementary propositions, which are concatenations of atomic names. In elementary propositions atomic names substitute for, or stand proxy for, objects. The totality of existent and non-existent states of affairs is the totality of possible arrangements of atomic objects. Understanding the essence of a proposition means understanding its constituent atomic names which means knowing their atomic objects, and that is to know all possible combinations of those objects: all possible states of affairs or the whole of logical space. An elementary proposition is meaningful or has sense (*Sinn*) in virtue of its describing a possible state of affairs in logical space; it is true if it describes an actual state of affairs and false otherwise. Thus an elementary proposition will be meaningful even when it is false in virtue of its being wholly a concatenation of names which cannot fail to have meaning because they cannot fail to stand for their atomic objects.

The meaning of a name is its reference; but a name does not have a *sense*; a name does not say anything about the world; it does not describe the world, but stands for objects in it; names cannot be true or false. Propositions are true or false; they describe how things stand in the world. Propositions have a sense in that they each describe possible facts in the world; the sense of a proposition is what would be the case if it were true.

The world is the totality of facts. When complex facts (*Tatsachen*) are broken down this ultimately means the totality of states of affairs as described by elementary propositions. The facts are always constituted by rearrangements of the same constant atomic objects. Every proposition which is not an elementary proposition can be analyzed into one, and only one, compound of elementary propositions.

Such elementary propositions consist entirely of concatenations of names. An atomic fact might be that object *a* is to the left of *b*; we might write this as "*aRb*" where "*R*" stands for the relation between *a* and *b*. But ultimately "*R*", if it is not a name standing for an object, must be eliminated so we have only atomic names. Indeed, "*ab*" does show the relation of the named objects *a* and *b*. The arrangement of names within the proposition, if it is true, directly *shows* how things are in the world. This is the picture theory of language, whereby the way that language depicts facts in the world ultimately derives from a common logical form: a structural isomorphism between language and the world. Language models or maps the world. How this picturing takes place in propositions is unclear. Even allowing for the spatial *ab* relation, there are more kinds of relations than spatial relation to be depicted. Nevertheless, it can be pointed out that a variety of relations is depicted in other areas, such as that which occurs between a musical score and the music itself. This picturing relation is not apparent for the sentences of ordinary language but holds at a deep level. The idea is that to represent something there must be a one-to-one correlation between elements in the picture and elements in the state of affairs represented; some kind of arrangement or ordering of the elements in the picture shows how the corresponding elements in the world stand to each other. The nature of the ordering of the elements depicted and the nature of the ordering in that which depicts may be different, but the ordering itself is in both as their common *logical form*: the minimum required for picturing to occur at all. It is in virtue of their logical form that propositions are able to depict facts. This minimum universal logical form cannot itself be depicted, since it is what is common to all pictures; to picture logical form alone one would need to stand outside all ways of picturing; but then one could not picture at all.

This picturing theory applies to thoughts; a thought is a proposition; for a thought to be of a possible fact in the world it must, like the proposition, be constituted from an arrangement of psychical elements that correspond to the elements making up the fact in the world. What cannot be stated in a proposition cannot be thought. That which does the representing of a fact is itself a fact, not something other than a fact.

Wittgenstein makes an important distinction between *showing* and *saying*. The thinking here is that ultimately we must reach propositions that simply *show* their sense; their sense is manifest. Proposition *"p" says* that things are so-and-so. We might attempt to explain the sense of proposition *"p"* by proposition *"q"*; but if *"p"* is to have a sense, we must ultimately reach elementary propositions whose sense simply *shows* itself. In a sense one cannot say what the meaning of a proposition is. If *"q"* does its job of explaining the sense of *"p"* properly, then we have got no further, but have merely re-expressed the same sense. The sense must show itself, and what can be shown cannot be said. Wittgenstein is convinced that the cardinal problem of philosophy has been the attempt to *say* what can only be *shown*; that is, the attempt to explain by saying things which can only be shown; and that can only produce nonsense.

Propositions compounded of elementary propositions are called molecular propositions. Molecular propositions are truth-functions of their elementary propositions: that is, the truth or falsity of whole molecular propositions depends entirely on the truth or falsity of their constituent elementary propositions. Molecular propositions have logical structures which are compounded from elementary propositions by truth-functional logical constants. These truth-functional constants are defined by the way in which they determine the truth or falsity of complex propositions in which they occur. These truth-functional constants, "or" (v), "and" (&), "not" (-), "if . . . then . . . " (→), " . . . if and only if . . . " (≡), are now a standard part of propositional logic. In addition there is the apparatus of predicate logic, which includes within it propositional logic, and which takes us "inside" propositions, which involves as logical constants the universal quantifier "all" (∀) and the existential quantifier "some" (∃). A particular proposition *"p"*, "The chair is red", might be expanded and symbolized as *"a is F"* or *"Fa"*, where *"a"* names an individual thing (the chair), and *"F"* is a predicate term (is red). The common structure or general logical form of all propositions like *"p"* can be symbolized as "Fx", where "x" is an individual variable (for which constant terms denoting individual things can be substituted) and "F" a predicate term. The logical form of the conclusion we can draw, given any one proposition such as "p", that is "Fa", is expressed in the propositional function "There is some (at least one) x such that x is F" which is symbolized as "$(\exists x)(Fx)$".

Take "and" (&) as an example of a truth-functional constant: it is clear that a molecular proposition "p & q" is true just in that case where both "p" is true and "q" is true, and is false otherwise. With "not" ($-$) or negation, for example, we can see that if "p" is true, then "$-p$" must be false, and vice versa. The way that truth-functional connectives operate is displayed in truth-tables. For example:

p	$-p$
T	F
F	T

p	q	p & q
T	T	T
T	F	F
F	T	F
F	F	F

The most important point is that all molecular propositions can be analyzed into elementary propositions by truth-functional analysis and that the truth or falsity of the whole original molecular proposition is a function of the truth or falsity of its constituent atomic propositions related by truth-functional connectives.

The essential structure of language, at its various levels of simplicity and complexity derived from analysis and synthesis, mirrors the world. This can be displayed in the diagram opposite, in which the arrows show the direction of analysis. That a proposition describes a possible fact gives the proposition its sense; it describes an arrangement of objects in the world; that the fact is actual or not actual determines the truth or falsity of the proposition. Propositions have a sense even when they are false because they are ultimately a concatenation of atomic names that cannot fail to have meaning because they cannot fail to stand for atomic objects.

The truth of all elementary propositions is logically independent: it is impossible from one elementary proposition to deduce the truth or falsity of any other and impossible for any elementary proposition to contradict another. From the existence of one state of affairs it is impossible to deduce any other state of affairs. If one proposition can be deduced from another, then the proposition from which it is deduced cannot be elementary, but must be a truth-functional compound. One proposition can be deduced from another only if the deduced proposition is contained in the original proposition. For example, "p" is deducible from "p and q", because "p" is already con-

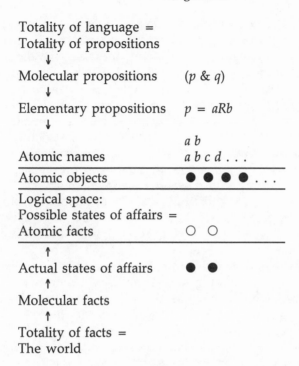

Totality of language =
Totality of propositions
↓

Molecular propositions $(p \ \& \ q)$
↓

Elementary propositions $p = aRb$
↓

                           $a \ b$
Atomic names $a \ b \ c \ d \ . \ . \ .$

Atomic objects   ● ● ● ● . . .

Logical space:
Possible states of affairs =
Atomic facts   ○ ○

↑
Actual states of affairs   ● ●
↑
Molecular facts
↑
Totality of facts =
The world

tained in the complex proposition "*p* and *q*". A deducible proposition is contained in the proposition from which it is deduced by being a truth-functional component of the complex proposition from which it is deduced. If the individual propositions "*p*" and "*q*" are really elementary propositions, and are not compounds of simpler propositions, then there is no complex for any other proposition to be contained in. This logical independence should show itself clearly in the ideal notation; we can see that if "*p*" and "*q*" are elementary propositions, "*q*" cannot be deduced from "*p*", and vice versa; "*p* and not-*q*" is never a contradiction and "not-(*p* and not-*q*)" is never a tautology.

This brings us to logically necessary truths, and contradictions. No elementary proposition can be necessarily true or necessarily false; such propositions are essentially bipolar: true-false, that is, contingent. The only necessarily true propositions are logically necessary truths or tautologies; the only necessary false propositions are contradictions. Necessary truths are necessary because they are truth-functional compounds formed of simpler propositions in such a way that, whatever the truth or falsity of their component parts, the whole proposition is always true. Necessary falsehoods or contradictions are truth-functional compounds formed of simpler propositions in such a way that whatever the truth or falsity of their component parts, the whole proposition is always false. Tautologies say nothing about the world precisely because they are true independently of whatever the facts are about the world which give a truth-value (true or false) to the components of the tautology. Contradictions are false regardless of any facts about the world. Wittgenstein suggests that both tautologies and contradictions are in fact called true or false "propositions" only by courtesy of genuine propositions which are contingently true or false. Tautologies and contradictions are thus senseless (*sinnlos*), but not nonsense (*Unsinn*). Although tautologies and contradictions say nothing factual about the world, they show the logical structure of the world and language, and show the boundaries within which all propositions which can say anything about the world must fall. They mark the boundaries of factual discourse, and only factual discourse has sense; language gets its meaning from the world, the totality of facts, it cannot therefore say anything about matters outside the world; ethics, values, religion, the meaning of life lie outside the world of facts; they make themselves manifest to us; they show themselves, but we cannot say anything about them. Genuine propositions state possible facts, and can have sense only by doing so, or are tautologies or contradictions. Beyond those boundaries there is only nonsense which does not say anything, but merely shows itself to be nonsense. In short, language gets its entire meaning *from* the world – ultimately from names of objects – and so language is meaningful only when it states facts *about* the world. The following diagram summarizes this view.

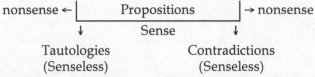

Tautologies   Contradictions
(Senseless)   (Senseless)

Many problems arise from the *Tractatus*, some of which led to Wittgenstein's later thought. One is the absence of any examples of atomic objects and atomic names. An atomic object must be such that it cannot be described, but only named, and the name is guaranteed to have a reference, and hence a meaning. Russell suggested such real or proper names might refer to the present content of our sense-experience (sense-data): that is, demonstratives such as "this" and "that" are the only logically proper names, which cannot fail to point to the present content of our sense-experience and hence to their reference. But the fleeting nature of such objects of experience means they are not what Wittgenstein wants. A real name should not only have a guaranteed reference, but must also refer to the *same* enduring and unchanging object if its meaning is to be fixed and determinate. But "this" and "that" will mean different things depending on the present content of experience which will vary within the same person and between different people. So Wittgenstein could not share Russell's view. Indeed it seems inevitable that atomic objects are ineffable in that we cannot say anything about them because to say anything about them would be to describe them, and in that case they could not be simple. Wittgenstein's view seems to be that as a logician it is not his job to decide what are atomic objects, atomic names, and the ultimate psychical constituents of thoughts; but it is a matter of logic that there *must be* such things if the propositions of language are to have a sense. We cannot even say of a simple object *a*, that "*a* exists", for the assertion is either meaningless in the case where *a* does not exist, or trivially redundant.

An important problem is the status of the propositions of the *Tractatus* itself. It is not uncommon in philosophy for a philosophical theory or system to cut off the branch on which it is sitting. The attempt to assert and show that some ways are the only ways of being intelligible or knowing things turns out to go beyond those ways and involve just those ways which are said to be unintelligible or unknowable. The point of the *Tractatus* is to put an end to philosophy, or at least all metaphysics, by revealing its propositions to be nonsensical (*unsinnig*). More generally it reveals what can and what cannot be said; what can be said are the propositions of natural science which are factual: they state facts about the world. This means that about important matters, such as ethics, religion and the meaning of life, nothing can be said, since they are not concerned with facts about the world. It is not that ethics, religion, and the meaning of life are nonsense; what produces nonsense is the attempt to say things about them. But in attempting to make its point it would seem that by its own criteria the propositions of the *Tractatus* itself are just such nonsense. They do not state facts about the world, but say things about the necessary structure of all fact-stating and the necessary structure of the world, which are not themselves further facts about the world. Wittgenstein is aware of this, and declares that one must transcend the propositions of the *Tractatus*: one uses it like a ladder up which one climbs, and which, once used to make clear that metaphysics and the propositions of the *Tractatus* are nonsense, can be thrown away.

CHAPTER NINE

Phenomenology
and existentialism:
Husserl, Sartre

Historically and intellectually there are complex connections between phenomenology and the later manifestations of existentialism. The phenomenology of Husserl was one of the major influences on Sartre, although Sartre came to reject some of Husserl's most distinctive doctrines. Some of the connecting and discussed doctrines are: that the defining feature of consciousness is intentionality so that every and only acts of consciousness are directed to a meant or intended object; the nature of the ego or I; the question of which is logically prior, essence or existence; and the possibility and adequacy of a disinterested or pure transcendental conceptualization of reality or being.

Husserl

Edmund Husserl (1859–1938) was born in Prossnitz, a village in Czechoslovakian Moravia, at that time part of the Austrian Empire. His early university studies at Leipzig and Berlin were in mathematics, and he received his PhD in mathematics in 1881. He also attended the philosophy lectures of Wilhelm Wundt at the University of Leipzig. Husserl decided to devote himself entirely to philosophy and he moved to Vienna, where he attended philosophy lectures by Franz Brentano (1838–1917), at which students were acquainted with the philosophy of David Hume and John Stuart Mill. Husserl taught at the universities of Halle and Göttingen, and from 1916 to 1929 at Freiburg, where he spent the rest of his life. Husserl was an important influence on Martin Heidegger (1889–1976), who became Rector of Freiburg University in 1933. Husserl had a dedicated attitude to philosophy and saw it as a calling rather than merely a job. During the thirties, following the rise of Nazism, life became increasingly difficult for Husserl because of his Jewishness. If he had not died in 1938, he might well have gone the way of multitudes of other European Jews. At his death his unpublished manuscripts were under threat of being lost. High drama accompanied their removal to safety; following some failed attempts to transport the manuscripts over the Swiss border, they were eventually taken in the diplomatic baggage of the Belgian Embassy to Louvain, where the Husserl Archives were established.

The chief concern of the philosophy of Husserl is that philosophy should develop as a truly universal "rigorous science". Philosophy must be a science that begins right at the beginning, taking nothing for granted; that is to say, it must be a presuppositionless science of sciences. All deductive or inductive reasoning depends for its validity on the immediate, intuitive apprehension of truths for which further justification neither can be given nor is required; such apodictic (necessary) evident truths require no further foundation. If there is not to be an infinite regress of justification, so that nothing is in fact ever categorically justifiable, there must be such apodictic truths; not everything can be justified. In this sense Husserl's project of establishing a unified certain foundation for all knowledge is close to that of Descartes.

Husserl's first major work in philosophy was closely connected with mathematics. In the *Philosophy of arithmetic* he sought an epistemological account of the origin of our ideas, understanding and knowledge of the central concepts of arithmetic: numbers, functions, arithmetical truths and the like. For example, the foundation of the possession of the concept of number derives from intuitions of aggregates as such. This was construed by the mathematician and logician Gottlob Frege (1824–1925) as an attempt to set out a naturalistic, and specifically a psychologistic or subjective, account of arithmetical objects and truths themselves, and Husserl consequently encountered Frege's fierce criticism. The conventional opinion is that, partly as a result of Frege's criticism, Husserl did a complete intellectual turnabout in his early philosophical studies from a view supporting psychologism to a view rejecting it which resulted in the philosophy of phenomenology. However, it can be argued that Frege's view of the *Philosophy of arithmetic* has spawned misinterpretation, and that Husserl was concerned to study the nature and origin of our ideas of arithmetical concepts and truths, and that that inquiry is neutral with regard to the objectivity or otherwise of those concepts and truths themselves. Indeed, it seems clear that Husserl was fully aware of the need to distinguish our ideas of numbers from numbers themselves.

Whatever is the truth of the matter, Husserl's later work does involve an attack on psychologism. The psychologistic account of deductive reasoning suggests that the justification of deductive reasoning and of logical or mathematical truths such as $2+2=4$ rests upon their displaying certain very fundamental facts about the way we think, even if such logical truths are not dependent on facts about the physical world. This position, however, rests on a confusion; such a view both removes the absolute necessity of logical truths and is also question-begging. If logical truths did rest on any kind of facts – even universally true facts about the way human beings think – then they would rest upon facts that might have been otherwise since such facts are always contingent. If we take the deductive inference involving any two propositions "p" and "q", "If p then q, p, therefore q", it is tempting to regard this as receiving its justification as a valid inference from its describing a psychological fact about the way people must think: if someone thinks "If p then q," and thinks "p", then they must think "q", or must see that "q" follows. This, however, confuses a factual causal psychological compulsion, which is contingent even if universal, with a logical inference which is necessary regardless of whether anyone in fact makes the inference or not. Now the inference may describe the way all people think – although that is extremely doubtful – but that is not what the validity of the inference rests on. The validity of the deduction does not depend on any general facts about psychological processes; and, indeed, a rejection of all forms of naturalism holds that logical truths do not depend on any facts at all. Logic is prescriptive, not descriptive. Moreover, any such naturalistic attempt to give logic a psychological justification would be viciously circular, since all reasoning, including that required to do psychology and produce arguments in psychology, already assumes the validity of logical rules of inference. In short, the natural sciences presuppose the validity of the rules of logic and so arguments using the propositions of natural science cannot be used to justify the rules of logic. Such naturalism would encourage various forms of relativism: if logical rules describe psychological laws of thought, then these laws might for us, or other beings, in another time or place, be different. The connections in logic between premises and conclusions, between evidence and conclusions – reasons and their logical consequences generally – are not mechanical or causal but are conceptual and concern meanings. Husserl rejects, in the *Logical investigations*, psychologism and the universalization of naturalism, and the misplacing of naturalistic explanation.

One of the initial motivations of Husserl's philosophy can, then, be seen as a reaction against scientism: the belief that everything is explicable in naturalistic scientific terms. Husserl is not hostile to science, he merely wants to point to its limitations: it makes presuppositions about the nature and existence of reality which it does not question, and so cannot give fundamental explanations in the required sense of an ultimate starting-point for a rational explanation of the world. Naturalism has its place: in natural science. Natural science is too underpinned by unquestioned presuppositions, which cannot be questioned within naturalism, to be a certain foundation for all knowledge. For philosophy to be a rigorous science it must return to what is *given* in experience in its generality prior to all theorizing and interpretation, and approach what is given with an attitude shorn of preconceptions or assumptions both apparent and hidden. Philosophy must aim to reach apodictic certain truths: absolutely necessary and certain truths which are devoid of the presuppositions that would undermine their absoluteness. Philosophy seeks what remains and self-evidently must be the case once all that need not be the case – the contingent – is set aside: we are left with that which must be presupposed in every form of rational inquiry.

Husserl speaks of the "crisis of European man", by which he means that the inability to establish rationalism on firm foundations has led to irrationalism and barbarism; however, it is not the essence of rationalism that is at fault, but the misconception that rationalism and scientific naturalism are one, and that scientific naturalism can provide ultimate rational explanations. When this is seen to fail, rationalism itself is in danger of abandonment, whereas it is the false identification of rationalism with naturalism that should be rejected. That naturalistic science fails to deliver ultimate certain truths about the universe should not be seen as a failure of that rationalist project itself.

The historical starting-point of Husserl's phenomenology is Brentano. Brentano believed he had discovered the essence of the mental or consciousness: that which is common to all and only the mental. This common defining feature is *intentionality*: what the mental *is* – what its existence consists in – is uniquely characterized by its being intentional. Each mental act (or mental attitude) is directed towards an object, an *intentional object*. Consciousness in its various modes (thinking, believing, desiring, loving, hating, remembering etc.) always has an object or content. In the different mental acts, intentional objects will be related to consciousness in different ways. But in all cases consciousness is consciousness *of* something: it always has an object, and it is moreover directed upon or towards – it "intends" – some object. The intentional object is the object of one's attention in a mental act. The notion of intentionality developed when it was realized that consciousness is distinguished by its directedness towards an intended object regardless of whether that object actually exists in the world or not. The objects of mental acts may be "intentionally inexistent" in being neither physical nor mind-dependent. Thus if I am scared of the spider in the room, the intentional object is the spider of which I am scared; the intentional object is the content of that mental act of being afraid, regardless of whether there is actually a spider or not. I might believe I see a man walking towards me in the fog: the intentional object of what I believe I see is the man I believe I see, although the extensional object in the world may turn out to be a tree. It is always indisputably true that my mental act has such-and-such an object; my consciousness, and its acts (recognizing, believing, remembering, etc.) are not accidently associated with their intentional objects which are a necessary part of the mental act whether the object turns out to exist or not: the intentional object is *immanent* in the act. By contrast, any physical (non-mental) act always requires an existent object on which to perform the act: kicking a chair requires a chair that exists which is kicked, but thinking of a chair does not require any chair to exist.

The view that intentionality is the essence of the mental seems to work well as a defining feature of some mental acts, such as believing, judging, and remembering, but it seems less applicable to other mental occurrences, such as general moods like anxiety or well being, which appear to be objectless. Brentano's answer to this, which maintains intentionality as the essence of the mental, is that in the cases of occurrences such as moods the mood itself is its own object. The notion that the mental is essentially intentional undermines the dualism of Descartes' view of mind as an autonomous mental substance which might exist independently of all objects of consciousness; for, according to the thesis of intentionality, thought (the *cogito*) and the object of thought (the *cogitatum*) are inextricably linked: there is no consciousness without consciousness of objects – there is no such thing as bare consciousness devoid of an object – there can be no objects with meanings without consciousness.

Husserl's acceptance of the role played by intentionality in defining consciousness further expresses the limitations of causal naturalism; the realm of conscious acts and of their meant or intended objects gives a field where the connections are understood only through the notion of a connection of meanings and rational justification, which is irreducible to merely causal or associationist psychological explanations. The intelligibility of the sequences of mental acts and their objects as meanings (believing x because of believing y) is one where the connections require an account in terms of concepts, reasons and purposes, not in terms of the causal or mechanical association of mental events. "What justifies your certain belief that $1,574 \times 6,266 = 9,862,684$?" or "Why do you hate the man who sold you the cat?" require not causal answers or explanations, but reasons or evidence: rational or logical justification. There are, on the one hand, situations where someone as a matter of causal psychological fact holds a belief or draws a certain conclusion, even though it does not rationally or logically follow; and, on the other hand, there are cases where a belief or conclusion does rationally or logically follow, but as a matter of causal psychological fact people do not hold that belief or draw that conclusion. So the question of the causal circumstances in which someone as a matter of psychological fact *does* hold a certain belief or draw a certain conclusion is distinct from the question of whether he is rationally or logically *justified* in doing so.

Husserl is not really so concerned to argue for the conclusion that intentionality is the distinguishing feature of the mental; what is important for Husserl is that the realm of intentional objects or meanings gives philosophy an autonomous guaranteed subject for study independent of, and irreducible to, any wider naturalistic causal assumptions concerning the nature or existence of those objects: we have in any case objects as meanings of which we are conscious if we are conscious at all. Whatever assumptions we make about the nature of reality, it is nevertheless the case that our mental acts will be possessed of certain contents or *meant* objects in virtue of their intentionality: things appear to us a certain way. The mental always involves reference to an object or content which in any sense other than as the object intended in our mental act need not exist. The subject matter of phenomenology is the essential nature of these contents taken or viewed purely as the intentional objects of mental acts. It is important to note that "object of consciousness" does not just denote the sensuous objects of empirical experience. Anything that can be an object of consciousness – colours, physical objects, mathematical equations, love, time, comradeship, etc. – is a potential subject for phenomenological study: it can be studied as it is as a phenomenon. What underpins phenomenology is the idea that in coming to view objects (in the most general sense) just as appearances to consciousness we can see certain and necessary truths concerning the essential features of those objects, for we can then see those features of things which cannot, without self-contradiction as to what they are, be thought away; we thereby understand objects as they are in themselves stripped of all presuppositions and added-on interpreta-tion of any sort. The essential – necessary and sufficient – invariable features of objects, of which we can be certain, are those features which, if they appear to us at all, cannot be thought away if those objects are to appear to us as objects of such-and-such a sort. The way objects *must be* if they are to appear to us at all *as those* objects constitutes their essence.

The word "phenomenology" derives from the Greek *phainomenon* meaning an appearance, and *logos* meaning a reason or law. The ultimate objects of presuppositionless science are phenomena: the word "phenomenon" designates that which *is* what it appears to be, which is therefore something seen as it is in itself. Phenomenology is in fact the science of the intentional objects of consciousness; it consists of laws based on meanings which describe the necessary structural or formal features of appearances of various sorts. In the case of phenomenal objects there can be no appearance/reality distinction: what they are is what they appear to be, for we are concerned with them only as they appear. One cannot be mistaken that things *appear* in a certain way: and as long as one does not go beyond (transcend) things as appearances, one has a realm of objects about which one can form necessary and certain descriptive truths. Appearances themselves cannot present themselves in varying perspectives, although we can have various different appearances. The force of the slogan of phenomenology "To the things themselves" (*Zu den Sachen selbst*) is that we must confront things *just as experienced by consciousness*, independently of any theoretical or metaphysical presuppositions, rather than as objects in any other sense – as physical objects for example. We must return to experiences themselves, to "transcendental experience": a realm of "pure consciousness" or "pure subjectivity". That there is subjectivity or consciousness as such Husserl called "the wonder of all wonders". The wonder resides not in being or existence itself but in that there is a being that is aware of being.

Beneath the various natural sciences and the common-sense view of the world there is a network of presuppositions as to the nature of reality which are trans-phenomenal or "transcendent": we make assumptions about objects which go beyond what the objects are when considered as pure phenomena. These assumptions go beyond what is essential to those objects as phenomena. The pre-philosophical view of the world Husserl calls the "natural attitude". Even logic and mathematics do not have the required presuppositionlessness, for they do not within their subject question all the grounds of their basic concepts and rules of inference. Indeed, it became apparent by the end of the nineteenth century that it was possible to set up a variety of equally consistent but mutually contradictory formal systems. There are for example several different geometries.

The means of achieving the lowest level of presuppositionless awareness which is required for a truly philosophical attitude is through what Husserl calls the phenomenological reduction, "bracketing", or "*epoché*" (from the Greek word "*epoché*" referring to a "suspension", in this case of belief or judgement). The phenomenological *epoché* is the heart of the phenomenological method. What we are left with when all presuppositions concerning objects are set aside is only what is certain and necessary about those objects. In fact the phenomenological reduction has two stages:

(I) That in which we suspend judgement as to the existence or non-existence of the objects of consciousness so we can concentrate on them as pure phenomena: that is, as they are as appearances.

(II) That in which we view the objects reduced to pure phenomena not in their particularity, but in their generality and essence: we are to concern ourselves with phenomena only as samples or examples of types or sorts of phenomena, not with what makes them particular "thises"; we thus bracket off the particularities of phenomena. This is termed the "eidetic reduction" because it reduces phenomena to the residue of whatever makes them the type or sort of phenomena they are, without which they could not appear at all. "Eidetic" derives from the Greek "*eidos*" for "form", which alludes to Platonic Forms which are essences.

In order to concentrate on objects merely as they are given to consciousness as such, we bracket off all our normal everyday and scientific theories and presuppositions as to the nature and existence of those objects. In this way we set aside the presuppositions which are unquestioned in both the common-sense and the natural scientific views of the world in order to study the contents of pure "reduced" consciousness as such. Whatever assumptions we previously made about the contents of consciousness – concerning their cause, their existence, their nature, their representing or not representing objects in the external world – are suspended. Independently of all these assumptions, everything that can come before the mind can be studied as purely phenomenal objects: as they appear to consciousness. This *epoché* involves neither denying nor affirming the existence or being of the external world; the reality of the external world is not eliminated but simply set aside from consideration, as are judgements concerning the truth or falsity of the claim. In this way one attains the proper philosophical attitude.

Philosophy, once it has attained the required phenomenological attitude to the "reduced" objects of consciousness, is not concerned with them as the contents of particular mental events, rather it is concerned with them in their significance or meaning. The *epoché* detaches the pure phenomenal objects of consciousness from both their existence or non-existence and all that is inessential for them to be what they are: we then see them as they are in themselves: as they *must* be from any point of view in order for them to be whatever kind of phenomenal object they are. Phenomenology is concerned with phenomenal objects in themselves and as *essences*: the "whatness" whereby the phenomenal object is an object of the kind it is. Husserl uses "*eidos*" to mean "essence" or "pure essence". We are concerned with objects as appearances to consciousness in their universal or essential aspects, whereby all and only objects of that sort must possess such-and-such a set of characteristics if they are to be that kind of object at all. Phenomenology, and indeed true philosophy, aims in Husserl's view to be nothing less than a "science of essences" or "eidetic science".

These essences are independent of any individual consciousness, and are absolutely objective and universally valid, for they reveal to us what, if a certain object or content is present to consciousness at all, must be part of the consciousness of that object. Indeed, knowledge of essences is independent of all questions or knowledge of existence or fact: the "whatness" of an object is totally independent of whether any instances of that object actually exist.

Husserl is further convinced that such essences are *intuited*: there is an immediate intellectual vision or grasping of essences (*Wesensschau*). In a sense we confusedly apprehend essence all the time. When a certain object is present to consciousness, it is always present *as* such-and-such an appearance, not as mere appearance: that is, it has a significance or meaning. That significance or meaning is captured by its essence. Without these essences or significances, objects would be nothing to us at all. But objects have a significance, and whatever the accidental circumstances or features of their presentation, their essential features deliver the significance or meaning of that experience. Essences – giving significances *as* . . . – are the ultimate phenomena of consciousness. In the Cartesian manner Husserl argues that the essences of a thing are those features which it has beyond doubt, for without them it would not be presented *as that sort* of thing at all. It is this common meaning that is invariant in all our varying perspectival presentations of a thing (for example as we move round an object), that unites those varying presentations in referring to the same object. Thus the consciousness-of-house means house only in virtue of its including the essence of house: in this way the various acts of consciousness are related and directed towards a *house*, rather than something else.

This is related to an idea in Frege. Expressions can have meaning or sense (*Sinn*) even though no object or reference (*Bedeutung*) exists that satisfies that sense: the sense has a reference only if something satisfies the sense, otherwise it has no existing meant object or reference. Thus sense is independent of whether anything satisfies that sense, that is, whether the meant or intended object exists or not. In addition different singular naming expressions or signs and definite descriptions can designate the same object either through their having the same sense or through their different senses being different senses for – modes of presenting – one and the same object: as with "the Morning Star" and "the Evening Star" picking out Venus, or "1+1" and "5–3" designating the number 2. If the meaning of an expression were identified with its reference, then if I understood two expressions I would as a consequence know whether they referred to the same object or to different objects. If understanding the meaning of an expression is knowing its reference, it is impossible, if I understand what is meant by "the Morning Star" and "the Evening Star", not to realize that the two expressions refer to the same object: Venus. For to understand the meaning of the expressions would involve in each case being acquainted with their common reference. Such a consequence is clearly false. It is obviously the case that the statement "the Morning Star = the Evening Star" is an informative discovery of astronomy and is not equivalent to the trivial logical statement "$a=a$". The upshot of this is to make it clear that there can be meaningful expressions which may or may not have references; so the meanings are not to be identified with their references and are independent of them. There is no need to postulate the mysterious "subsistence" of Pegasus in order for the expression "Pegasus" to have a sense and hence be meaningful.

Husserl accepts that we will need to experience individual cases of white in order to grasp the essence "whiteness"; but one then immediately grasps the essence of whiteness, since one sees the object *as* white. Seeing an object *as* white implies that one already understands what whiteness is. Objects are perceived *with* a certain significance. It is a mistake to think that our grasp of the essence or concept "whiteness" derives from inductively abstracting from a series of particular white objects some feature they all and only they have in common, for this process already involves the ability to pick out white objects; we are already picking out some objects, and rejecting other objects, as white objects. It is rather that in seeing something as white we do, in that very mental act of seeing *as*, intuitively "see" the essence of white. We already have the *ability* to pick out white objects: phenomenology articulates the awareness of the essence implicit in that ability. An analogy might be the way in which we could recognize the man who robbed the bank ("I would know him if I saw him" – which gives the point to identity parades) although we are quite incapable of giving any defining description of the man. Phenomenology aims to produce a state of mind where such an intuitive descriptive articulation of essence is possible by setting aside all that is neither necessary nor sufficient for a phenomenal object to be the phenomenal object it is; we are left with an essential residue of necessary and sufficient features which will give us certain and necessary truths.

Particular objects of consciousness may be used as examples in order to identify essences, rather in the way that a particular geometric drawing of a triangle may be used to illustrate some theorem of geometry such as Pythagoras' theorem; but the truth concerning the nature of the essence in no way depends upon the existence of the particular item used as an example or on any other item existing. In using examples, we describe what Husserl terms the "horizon" of a thing; by the free play of the imagination – "free variation" – we determine the limits within which a thing can vary while still remaining the kind of thing it is. Thus we transform our experience of an individual entity into experience of essence: we have then a non-sensuous *eidetic intuition*.

Another way of looking at this is to say that in intuiting essences, we are aware of pure possibilities independent of actual being: that which is essential to any actualization of that sort of object. Without its essence no concrete actualization of the object whose essence it is could occur, whatever else may be true of the object. It must therefore be present in any possible experience of that object. For example, the essence of any physical object, or a man, or a colour, is not identical with any individual physical object, man or colour; the essence is what is common to all and only things of those kinds, which describes what is required for them to be things of those kinds, and without which they would not be those things at all.

Through intuitions we describe the essential structure of our experiences viewed as pure phenomena. The phenomena include reflexively mental acts and the phenomenal objects of those acts: the thought and the object of thought. Phenomenology, and hence philosophy, is the foundation of any science whatsoever because any intelligible awareness of the world at all must begin with this fundamental grasping of essences: without these essences the world would have no significance for us at all. In this sense Husserl regards phenomenology as *a priori*: the apprehension of fundamental essential meanings, significances, and "whatnesses" is logically prior to all theorizing and independent of all contingent facts; phenomenology is concerned with the characteristics known to be necessarily connected with kinds of phenomena. Phenomenology aims to produce absolutely certain objective necessary truths that are pure in having no relativity to cognitive, spatial or temporal perspective. Such truths are in this sense absolutely categorical: they are directly intuited from experience and do not depend for their acceptance on the acceptance of any other truths. Thus such truths cannot be argued for, inferred, or derived, for then their truth would not be guaranteed as absolute because we would not have to accept them until we had accepted other truths. Such basic truths concerning the structure of phenomenal objects must be seen immediately or not seen at all. They cannot be argued for because any argument would presuppose the most basic level at which intelligibility or significance arises. Such intuitions of essences are self-given because there is nothing else from which the essence could be inferred which does not itself assume an intuitive grasp of categories of meaning or concepts. So, unlike in Kant, the preconditions for any significant experience are not deduced, but intuited directly. Any attempt at deduction, since the deduction itself is also a phenomenon with significance *as a deduction*, already assumes the lowest level of classificatory categories of consciousness without which no experience would have any significance at all, and an experience without any significance at all – not of an object of a certain sort – would be no experience at all. To construct any argument presupposes that we can understand what an argument is; so understanding what an argument is cannot itself be derived from an argument. We cannot in any way derive the essences of phenomena from anything more fundamental. We may need through experience to acquaint ourselves with the various kinds of intentional objects and mental acts there are: but the essence, in virtue of which any mental act is aware *of* a certain kind of object, is utterly independent of whether there is such an object or anyone in particular experiencing that object as a content of consciousness. If phenomena were utterly neutral with no significance or meaning at all, there would be no hope of getting any science off the ground; the absence of the basic meanings or significances of the objects of consciousness would destroy any possibility of a science connecting items in our experience into any intelligible repeatable patterns whatsoever. The aim of phenomenology is to return to the ultimate original or primordial significances of experiences shorn of the baggage of accumulated significances embodied in the theories of science and everyday assumptions. We then view the world with new wonder and freshness.

The philosophy of Husserl involves a further radical application of the *epoché*. The phenomenological reduction brackets the natural external world, and all of the assumptions associated with belief in such a world. But something still remains to be subject to *epoché*: the individual ego or consciousness. Any act of consciousness presupposes an ego: but the particularity of the ego is unimportant; what is important is what is essential to the ego. The individual ego too must be bracketed in order to intuit the essence of the thinking individual itself. As with other essences, the existence of any particular ego is irrelevant to the identification of the universal "whatness" of ego in general which is pure intentionality. That which is engaged in the process of bracketing the natural world, including the empirical ego itself, must be something, and Husserl calls it the *transcendental ego*, which stands outside the world. The essence of this transcendental ego is that it stands as a precondition of any mental act or experience whatsoever, including all acts of phenomenological reduction. We now have a triadic structure for consciousness, ego-*cogito-cogitatum*; these are the three logically linked elements of: pure ego (the "I", what it is that thinks), mental act (thought), and content (the object of thought). This gives us full transcendental phenomenology, the ultimate objects of which are a vast variety of sorts of meaning or significance (*noema*, adjective *noematic*) which are correlated with meaningful acts (*noesis*, adjective *noetic*) of the transcendental ego. The ultimate phenomenological *noetic-noematic* relation is not between psychic elements and empirical objects, but between their essential meanings. The transcendental ego is, ultimately, the only absolute, for it remains after all bracketing: it is presupposed in every act of consciousness or experience whatsoever, even the activity of bracketing itself. The transcendental ego is the precondition of all meaning: it alone cannot be thought away because it is presupposed in all thinking.

The later philosophy of Husserl led him to give an active role to the transcendental ego; the conclusion is that not the individual ego, but the transcendental ego, actively constitutes or constructs the significance or meaning of the objects of consciousness. Pure ego gives objects their meaning or significance which makes them objects for consciousness. This does not necessarily lead to idealism – that reality is existentially dependent on consciousness – because it might be the case that the transcendental ego simply places an existentially independent reality under intelligible categories or concepts and so makes that reality an object for consciousness. If, however, the only reality an object can be said to have is that significance actively given to it by the transcendental ego, then reality or the world is existentially dependent on the transcendental ego, and that is idealism. If a world without significance for consciousness is existentially impossible, and all significance is a product of the transcendental ego, it follows that the world is existentially dependent on the transcendental ego. This suggests that the transcendental ego is the only absolute because everything is existentially dependent on it, and it is not existentially dependent on anything else.

Husserl's view points towards a form of subjective idealism – reality is existentially dependent on the subject – where existence is exhausted by and tied to the meaning given to objects by the transcendental subject or the subject as such. It might still be argued that such significances in the form of essences are objective by being independent of the existence of any particular consciousness and are common to all consciousness as such: that objects present themselves with the meanings or essences that they do is not an accidental feature of any empirical ego but a product of consciousness as such. Husserl's later views tend towards idealism because he holds that to speak of the world really existing, independently of the categories of significance which are dependent on pure consciousness, is senseless and absurd. Still, it might be said that the world would continue to exist independently of pure consciousness. If this were granted, then it can be replied that the world so characterized would be without significance in the same way that a written sentence would be without significance if there were no minds to grasp its sense; it would be a "world" that is literally inconceivable. Husserl moves from the view that nothing can be conceived except as an object for consciousness to the view that nothing can exist except as an object of consciousness. His answer to scepticism about the nature and existence of the external world is to say that the world that appears with meaning just *is* the real world and the positing of some other world which might exist or fail to exist is senseless.

Husserl also became concerned with a phenomenological analysis of time: the experience of duration itself as it appears to consciousness. Time is particularly fundamental to the constitution of experiences. The phenomenological analysis of time concerns the essence of time as it appears: that is, what is necessarily and invariably involved in an appearance which is temporal. He says that every real experience is one that endures, and this duration takes place within the stream of an endless filled continuum of durations which forms an infinite unity; every present moment of experience – every now – is fringed by a before and after as limits.

In the last part of Husserl's life he introduced the concept of *Lebenswelt*: the "lived-world". Before any theorizing, including philosophizing, one is confronted with the world as it appears in life. The *Lebenswelt* is in some sense primary: the theoretical sciences are derivative of, or parasitic on, its meanings. Objects already appear to us loaded with a significance that points beyond themselves: their meaning points to their own horizon, which is not currently present in the experience, and defines them as the objects they are and indicates the context in which the objects occur. The meaning of experiencing the front of a house includes, among many other things, the presently unseen back of the house. Husserl also became concerned with avoiding solipsism by discussing the dependence of intentional objects on the intersubjectivity of a community of individual egos. The essence or meaning of objects as experienced often points beyond my subjective awareness and depends on the awareness of others. This is obvious if we think of the meaning to us of a great work of art. On the face of it this seems like a rejection of eidetic phenomenology. Some commentators have taken it that way, but Husserl seems to have seen no discontinuity between his earlier and later work. Others have viewed the later *Lebenswelt* as an indication that the eidetic intuitions – the essences – we seek are to be found in the objects of the world as lived.

Sartre

Jean-Paul Sartre (1905–80) was born in Paris. In 1924 he went to the École Normale Supérieure where he studied philosophy, and in 1929 he began teaching philosophy. From 1933 to 1935 he studied in Berlin and Freiburg. While still a student Sartre met Simone de Beauvoir with whom he had lifelong connections. In 1939 he joined the French Army; because of his poor eyesight his duties were non-combatant; in 1940 he was taken prisoner by the Germans. His experience of captivity was to hone his views on the true nature of human freedom. The war also aroused his interest in politics. In 1941 he was repatriated; he returned to Paris where he taught philosophy and took an active part in the Resistance.

There is a strong German influence on Sartre's philosophy, which started with his Protestant Calvinist upbringing. Many of the philosophers most influential on Sartre are from the German intellectual tradition, such as Kant, Hegel, Husserl, and Heidegger (1889–1976). But an ever present influence for a French thinker such as Sartre is Descartes. Talk of influence does not necessarily entail agreement, of course. At one time Sartre was also in close contact with philosopher and contemporary Maurice Merleau-Ponty (1908–61). After the war Sartre became one of the founders of the literary and political journal *Les temps modernes*. He was increasingly involved in contemporary political and ideological controversy; he was part of an unsuccessful attempt to found a socialist, but non-communist, political party. His later political writing espouses a form of Marxism which he attempts to reconcile with his underlying philosophy of existentialism.

It is difficult to give any general characterization of existentialism. Existentialism has been characterized as a form of anti-intellectualism, or irrationalism or subjectivism; but the view of existentialism put forward here accepts none of these accounts. The view advocated here is that existentialism is a philosophy concerned to go back to what it regards as the logically prior description of what it is like to be a human being in the world before the accretion of a world-view based on supposedly detached or disinterested theorizing. The philosophical significance of this is the existentialist's view that the-world-as-it-is-for-human-beings, the human-world, the humanness of the world, before metaphysical and scientific speculation, is logically presupposed by any such speculation. The reason for this is that our possessing any concepts and categories, some of which must be involved in all possible talk about the world, logically depends on our practices and interests as human beings without which concepts and categories – more generally meanings and significances – would not arise at all. The significance of the world and its objects arising from practice and action is presupposed by the distilled categories of a disinterested intellectual observer or spectator. Being a detached spectator is not the logically primary way of our being-in-the-world. That there is "a world", objects with various significances and meanings, depends upon and cannot be separated from the significances and meanings that they have for human beings as a result of human interests and agency.

The existentialist position requires us to shake off the grip of various ingrained metaphysical assumptions about the world and ourselves. One of the most profound of these is the view that we could, logically speaking, exist as pure autonomous consciousness or thought regardless of whether any external world existed at all. Another metaphysical speculation is that reality can be reduced to either mental or material substance. The existentialist's contention is that we must be reminded that such metaphysical speculations use concepts whose meanings are parasitic on our concrete engagement as human beings through practices, actions and interests; metaphysical speculations logically depend for their possible intelligible articulation on terms whose meanings only arise at all out of our *not* having a disinterested or detached point of view. There are useful comparisons to be made here between existentialism and the philosophy of the later Wittgenstein in which he says the "form of life" is what is given. The meanings and significances of objects as such-and-such, which are logically necessary for any "view" of the world – any intelligible description and theorizing about the world – would not arise as they do but for specifically human partisan characteristics, concerns, and activities or for being sufficiently like human beings; and objects with meanings and significances would not arise at all but for some form of active engagement with the world.

The general aim of Western thought in metaphysics and science has been quite other than that of existentialism. The aim of science, for example, is to evolve what is regarded as a superior "objective" description of the world abstracted from specific perspectives: to generate a body of truths about the world whose validity holds across the contingencies of spatial, temporal or cognitive perspectives and which mirror the world independently of the practical or instrumental uses of objects in the world. The most obvious examples of such non-perspectival truths are those of mathematics and logic such as $2+2=4$, which is true however you look at it, so to speak; such a truth is a necessary truth. Literally perspectival truths such as "The tower is very small" (from the hill overlooking it) or "The bath water is hot" (to my cold right hand) are true only relative to a perspective and would be false if the conditions determining the perspective changed – if I came down the hill, or inserted in the water my warm left hand. What existentialism argues is that the concepts used to describe a world as such-and-such a sort, a world said to contain certain kinds of objects, would not arise at all except for some practical mode of relating to the world, which in our case arises from our humanness. True or false descriptions of the world depend for their articulation on meanings which arise only because of practical human projects. The concept of a "desk" and a world containing desks would not arise if no one ever wrote anything and did the usual things which lead us to call a certain object a "desk"; without a certain sort of behaviour the concept "desk" would never emerge. Existentialism undermines the aspiration of there being, and our possessing, the one true systematic description of everything, for existentialism denies that any kind of description would arise at all if in the cause of a universally valid account, the attempt were made to describe the world from an utterly detached spectatorial standpoint. Such a standpoint would be a "view from nowhere", a phrase which perhaps only thinly disguises the fact that it would be no view at all.

All this does not mean that science and abstraction are wrong in some way, rather it is to argue that our ordinary view of the world, in which objects, events, and ourselves have various meanings or significances, cannot be thought away as quirks of the merely contingent way we happen to encounter the world in favour of, and possibly to be replaced by, a supposedly superior system of descriptive categories that are more universally valid through being detached from the contingency of our situation as human beings concretely dealing with the world. For meanings and significances, and hence the possibility of description whether true or false, would not arise in the world without our engaged perspectival interests, practices, projects, and actions. Objects – for example hammers – have the meanings they have for us because of their function as obstacles to, or instruments in, human projects. Existentialism regards it as a mistake to propound either a subjectivist or an objectivist philosophy: both positions are based on the misconception that reality can be completely separated from all conceptions; that somehow we can have direct access to reality apart from all descriptions.

Many of these points are brought out by examining the reaction of Sartre to the phenomenology of Husserl. In *Being and nothingness* Sartre requires a phenomenology that is existential. It is important to note in this matter the significant influence on Sartre of Heidegger's monumental work *Being and time* (1927). The seeds of Sartre's existential phenomenology are found in his short work *The transcendence of the ego*. Husserl's philosophy of pure phenomenology derives much of its inspiration from Descartes. Husserl contends that consciousness is essentially intentional; that is, consciousness is defined and uniquely distinguished by its "aboutness"; if we are conscious at all we are always conscious *of* something with such-and-such a significance or meaning. With this point Sartre agrees completely. But the meanings to which Husserl's phenomenology aspires are the pure, essential, or defining features of the objects of which we are aware. In Husserl's account, to get at the pure essences of objects of consciousness it is necessary first to think away all those characteristics which are unnecessary for the thing of which we are aware to be just what it is. The immediate result of this "bracketing" is the suspension of judgement concerning the existence or non-existence of that of which we are conscious. The aim is to seek the features something must have from any "point of view" if it is to remain that kind of thing. The thought here is again the Cartesian one that what is true of an object from any point of view whatsoever – and so is non-perspectivally true and not true merely from a certain perspective – describes how things really are in themselves with the contingencies of what is added by our point of view, in its most general sense, subtracted. This gives the possibility of a transcendental perspective on the world and a science of essences. Husserl supposes that the bracketing process suspends judgement not only on the existence of the physical world but also on the contingent individual empirical ego; what remains is what Husserl calls the transcendental ego, which is the common essence of consciousness or consciousness as such. The picture that remains is one of a transcendental or pure spectatorial ego which intuits pure essences or meanings that are present or immanent in consciousness and experience, which are devoid of any contingent assumptions about the existence of the world or individual selves or the practical use we make of objects in specifically human projects.

The two notions of the transcendental perspective and the transcendental ego are interrelated and fall together as the chief targets of Sartre's attack on Husserl. Sartre's position is that there is no such transcendental pure disinterested perspective and no transcendental ego. The transcendental ego betrays the doctrine of the essential intentionality of consciousness for it posits a pure consciousness of objects which are themselves modes of consciousness, disengaged from concrete acts of awareness of particular intentional objects *in the world*. Sartre rejects the subjectivization of the doctrine of intentionality. His view is that there is no transcendental perspective and no pure or transcendental consciousness detached from the world, for consciousness makes sense only in relation to an awareness of objects in the world which are not modes of consciousness. A disinterested, passive and pure view of the world is impossible, in Sartre's view, because without particular intentional acts arising from our existence as beings-in-the-world engaged with what concretely concerns human beings, consciousness would not arise at all, since the being of consciousness is defined by its "aboutness" of something other than consciousness itself: something that is not-consciousness. Consciousness is not a *thing* at all, not even a transcendental thing "outside" the world. If all actual intentional acts, directed to something other than consciousness – in sum, all awarenesses *of* – are removed, then consciousness simply evaporates; so there can be no disinterested transcendental ego "outside" the world.

Phenomenology becomes existential when it is realized that consciousness and the world are logically interlinked: that is, no sense can be given to consciousness in the form of a transcendental ego if it is separated from its intentional awareness of objects which are not themselves modes of consciousness. The converse is also true: that no sense can be given to "the world" if separated from the sense of what the world is that arises from an actual engagement of human beings with the world in pursuit of their human concerns. One of the consequences of this view is the collapse of the mind–body dualism which supposes we could still make sense of consciousness if all the world was destroyed, and still make sense of "the world" devoid of the sense that arises from consciousness engaged in the embodied pursuit of human interests, purposes and aims. The world for us is a world of significances and meanings which it would not have without us. There are no pure meanings or essences of things waiting to be discovered by a disinterested pure consciousness; that there are recognizable separate things with certain significances only arises from our practical contact with the world in pursuit of various human purposes and interests. No sense can be given to what a hammer is – what is meant by a "hammer" – independently of a network of other objects and what embodied humans *do*. The significance of an object such as a hammer would not arise as it does if no one ever made anything; a *hammer* emerges as an object of the kind it is because of the sorts of things human beings do. In the case of a being which was merely spectatorial or contemplative, totally detached from the world, the meanings and significances of objects, whereby a particular object is a such-and-such, would not arise at all. Consciousness consists strictly of intentional acts – we are conscious as an awareness *of* objects *as* such-and-such a sort – but such intentional or meant objects would not arise if we were purely passive spectators. Human beings exist as active beings-in-the-world, not as pure egos; we are consciousnesses "thrown" into the world, and have to cope with it, and it is only as coping agents that the vast and intricate network of meanings and significances of objects we encounter arises. Any abstract theorizing about the world is logically dependent on our initial natural active engagement with the world. Phenomenology becomes existential in not dealing with the structure of a supposed realm of abstract pure essences which remain after we put ourselves in the transcendental position separated from practical involvement with the world: instead existential phenomenology examines the structure of the meanings and significances the world has as it appears to us everyday in life as a lived-world. We are embedded *in* the world: the-world-as-it-is-for-human-beings.

The world does not cease to exist with our ceasing to exist; but in so far as the world is a system of meanings and significances it is a human world because significances and meanings are a product of our human activities and interests. In this sense when a man dies a world dies with him.

We find the same existentialist points in Heidegger's *Being and time*. Again there is the emphasis on our "thrownness" into the world of significances-for-human-beings. The significance the world has as an instrument, through our active concrete engagement with the world in pursuit of human purposes and interests, is the world as "ready-to-hand" (*zuhanden*), which is logically presupposed by the passive detached description of the world "present-at-hand" (*vorhanden*) which is found in natural science.

In this way existentialism undermines the picture of man alienated or estranged from the world. The world is not primarily a place from which we stand apart, which is not amenable to human values and significances. The world is first a place which has human significance – it is our world – and there is no reason to denigrate the world as a network of significant objects for human beings in order to replace it by a detached view of the world "as it really is" rendered alien and devoid of human significance. Human reality is a *Dasein* (being-there): that is, we always exist as beings-*in*-the-world, not detached from it. As Heidegger points out, we are "cast" or "thrown" (*geworfen*) into the world to which the primary relation of our *Dasein* is one of "concern" or "care" (*Sorge*) where some objects are more important than others; the world is not neutral or flat with all significances being on the same level. The significance that things have is inextricably linked to the kind of being we are; we do not relate to the world as disembodied disinterested consciousnesses but as embodied agents.

In Sartre's novel *Nausea* we find him beginning to deal with the issues outlined above. In *Nausea* Sartre's protagonist Roquentin is a disappointed rationalist. We can begin by distinguishing between the notions of existence and essence: the existence of a thing refers to the fact *that* it is, the essence of a thing refers to *what* it is. Particular, actually existing, things like trees are always inadequately captured or explained in rational systems of concepts designed to render the world ordered and intelligible. Sartre seems to have in mind here a stringent notion of explanation which involves relations of deduction or entailment between concepts. We find such relationships in a field such as geometry: all the properties of a triangle follow necessarily from its initial definition, that is, from its essence or "whatness"; nothing about a triangle as such is "superfluous"; everything about it is explained as a necessity that follows from what it is; there is nothing about a triangle that is left over from what is entailed by its essence. In other words, all the properties of a triangle follow from its essence, so nothing is left unexplained. However, neither the existence of objects in the world, nor the nature of their existence in their full particularity can be explained by any conceptual system of essences. The "thatness" of an object – *that* it exists – and the features in virtue of which it exists as that particular object are not explained by being deducible from any system of universal concepts. Only in the realm of essences which do not exist do we have full explanations for why things are as they are, for in the realm of essences the properties a thing has are all and only those logically entailed by its essence: its "whatness".

The relations between different essences also produce necessary connections. But there are no such necessary connections between objects in the world, for the objects in both their individual existence and nature transcend and are not exhausted by universal concepts purporting to reveal their essence. In so far as objects in the world are brought under universal concepts, necessary relations can exist between them; but no existing particular object can, just in virtue of its existence and particularity, ever be fully explained or described by universal concepts; so the causal relations we aim to describe as existing between existing particular objects are contingent and have no logical necessity. Essences are necessarily inadequate in fully describing all that can be said about particular objects in the world, for they cannot capture their particularity and their "thatness". There is a logically necessary connection between X being what it is, a triangle, and X having internal angles equal to 180 degrees; but no such necessary, deductive connection exists between events in the world. There is no logical entailment between putting the kettle on the heat and the kettle boiling, no matter how often we have observed the conjunction of those events in the past; the one event cannot be deduced from the other. In this sense Sartre expresses a position in *Nausea* that is very close to that of Hume. By its very universality a concept considers and explains an object – gives a reason for why an object is as it is – only in so far as it falls into some general class not in its concrete particularity. We may consider an object, for example, in so far as it falls into the class of trees; but that does not explain the existence of, or all the features of, *that* thing over there we have called a "tree". Its existence – its "thatness" – does not follow from its description as a tree, nor do most of its features peculiar to *that individual* tree – its roughness, its colour, its hardness – these are all left out of the concept of "treeness". They are contingent, unexplained, excessive, accidental; they are "absurd" in being without sufficient explanation or reason; there is no sufficient reason as to why they are one way rather than another.

In *Nausea* Sartre mentions other things besides geometry that have the characteristic of complete intelligibility, such as music and stories; there is a sufficient reason for their being one way rather than another, for these have a complete internal logic that can be distinguished from any manifest individual existence. One can smash or damage a record of Beethoven's Fifth Symphony, but not smash or damage the Fifth Symphony itself, for it consists, as a symphony, of abstract relations between idealized non-actual musical events. Nothing is superfluous about a work of art: it is *what* it is.

One way of looking at *Nausea* is to think of it as the realization of the Humean nightmare or the collapse of all the supposedly necessary Kantian concepts: we are reminded in the book of the brute contingency of relations between objects and events in the world by the depiction of a world in which the causal order we take for granted does actually break down. In the extreme case our ability to bring objects under any intelligible categories also breaks down. *That* particular root over there has features not exhausted by its description as a kind of pump. There is a central scene in *Nausea* in a park when the root of a tree manifests itself as a bare individual unclassified "thatness" – its pure existence is manifest devoid of its identification as a neatly pigeon-holed sort of thing. The world is experienced as failing to behave according to our ordering conceptualization of it, in virtue of which we render what happens intelligible and explicable; that and the rationally inexplicable excess both of the particular features of things and existence itself generally induces the disorientating "nausea" of which Sartre speaks. The picture we have of the world is that this object, because it is of a specific kind, will do such-and-such; but in *Nausea* Sartre depicts a world in which individual objects cease to act according to their kind, because as individual objects they are not exhausted by essences.

There is something else of importance that emerges in *Nausea*: that we are free. We are free, and in Sartre's sense "absurd", in that, even more than physical objects such as trees, we are not determined by an essence; indeed we have no essence. Our existence ("thatness") precedes our essence ("whatness"): we first *are*, and it is then through what we *do* that we give ourselves any "whatness" or defining identity. We do not have a predetermined essence or nature that assigns to us a place in the world and a given character: we are forced to be free and make ourselves through our actions. We cannot pass the responsibility for what we are to any objective standards that lie outside ourselves: we must take responsibility for our choices, which determine what we are. Awareness of the responsibility arising out of the truth that there is no pre-existing self which is the "real I", and that the self is identifiable only through what we do following an initial, ultimately groundless, choice, gives rise to *Angst*. The passing of responsibility for what we do to something other than ourselves is what Sartre calls "inauthentic" or living in "bad faith" (*mauvaise foi*); the abdication of our responsibility for what we are and do Sartre sees as a kind of self-deception; it is as if really we know we are responsible for what we are through what we choose to do, but we often fail to face that uncomfortable truth. Freedom is not something we can avoid, but is an inseparable part of being human. For example, by not killing ourselves we choose to live. We cannot, of course, divorce ourselves from the situations in which choices are made, but there is always some room for free choice – even if it only consists of dissent and saying "no". Living with consciousness of the truth of my freedom is to live with "authenticity".

A person is never simply identifiable with any label applied to him which aims to define his essence. Thus a waiter is a waiter in the predicative sense of "is", but that is not what he is in the identity sense of "is"; being a waiter is not his essence – "person X = waiter" is false – so what a person does is not logically determined by an essence. Indeed, there is nothing that I am in the identity sense of "is". What I *am* is constantly remade through my actions: only in death is there the possibility of final judgements being passed upon what kind of man I am which I can no longer confute. The most blatantly "inauthentic" life would be one in which I negate my own freedom altogether by regarding my self as being as fixed as an object; this may be because that is how others regard me. An act of "bad faith" involves my simply giving up any attempt to determine and take reponsibility for my future because I regard a label I have given myself as binding on, and sufficient to determine, what I will do; but such facts about me are never sufficient to determine my actions, for I can always try to revolt against the facts of my situation.

Nothing about the existentialist belief that we are free implies that we should act wildly or capriciously, as is sometimes suggested, for to choose to act wildly or capriciously is only one of the choices we can make. What is important is that whatever choice we make is accepted as *our* choice; we must take responsibility for it and its consequences. It is in this way that our lives are said by the existentialist to be "authentic". Existentialism does not argue, as is again sometimes suggested, that the aim should be to return to some inner "real self", for there is no sense to self other than the sum of what one does; rather than there being a persistent self existing over time independently of what one does, the self is constantly remade through action. The notion of a self independent of actions would indeed be another route to "bad faith", for it suggests that I can do one thing but be another in some inner sanctum of the "real self". I cannot betray my friend, but refuse to accept the kind of person that makes me, by saying that in my "inner self" I was loyal to him, for the self – what I am – is constructed out of the choices I make.

The attempt fully to rationalize the existing world of particular concrete things in a system of abstract universal concepts or "what-nesses" fails. Although any language which can function descriptively cannot do without some degree of abstraction, we can maximize the concrete and particular and not regard it as an inferior view of the world to be "reduced" to something more universalizable. The attempt to impose such a universally valid intelligible structure in fact falsifies the world: it falsifies the uniqueness and particularity of our experiences of, and our encounters with, the world. Even if we merely say x and y are both red, we ignore the differences – perhaps the shade of red – that make x and y distinct concrete particulars, and so distort reality in the attempt to fit x and y into a scheme of descriptive categories. The uniqueness and particularity of our experiences are not to be rejected as worthless in favour of considering the experiences as merely examples of certain general classes or types.

The connected but distinct nature of consciousness and the world is reflected in the ontology described in Sartre's *Being and nothingness*. The fundamental kinds of being there are underpin the notion that consciousness cannot be an autonomous, isolated, "inner" realm unrelated to the awareness *of* an existent objective world that is not a part of consciousness, and the world has significance primarily as it figures in human projects and actions. Sartre identifies two basic categories or sorts of being.

(a) *être-en-soi*: being-in-itself. Things or non-human being.

(b) *être-pour-soi*: being-for-itself. Conscious or self-aware being.

However, he identifies an additional important category of being:

(c) *être-pour-autrui*: being-for-others. Being, especially of persons, which arises from relations to others.

Together these are Sartre's complete irreducible, uneliminable list of sorts of being or ontological categories; these are what we are committed to saying there must be, whatever else there may be, given the nature or structure of consciousness.

Being-in-itself is the kind of being that inanimate, inert, non-human objects have. In contrast being-for-itself is the kind of being that consciousness has. The two are brought together as being-in- the-world. Consciousness, the for-itself, arises only through its intentional awareness of something other than itself; that is, it is awareness of the in-itself, of not-consciousness, and that it is not the in-itself of which it is aware. Sartre is anxious to maintain that consciousness is not any kind of thing; consciousness is a negativity, a lack, or a no-thing-ness. Consciousness is not-a-thing which arises as a negation of objects of awareness. The primary nature of consciousness is its intentionality: it depends for its existence on things other than itself of which it is aware. Consciousness comes into being as an awareness of not being – as a separateness from – the objects of which it is conscious. We are conscious *of* an object *X*, and the being of consciousness is a negation through a simultaneous awareness of not-being-*X*. Consciousness is not an absolute nothingness, but is the awareness of itself as not being – as not being absorbed into – whatever objects are objects of consciousness. If I am aware of a table, the being of consciousness consists in my self-awareness of not- being-a-table. In our awareness of objects of consciousness we are at the same time pre-reflectively aware of our being aware. Awareness of our own awareness or consciousness cannot be a relation of subject and object or we would embark on an infinite regress of awarenesses, and awareness of ourselves as aware would never arise at all. To be conscious of *X* at all is to be conscious that we are not-*X*, because the *being* of consciousness in our consciousness of *X* is the consciousness of not-being-*X*. The logical dependence of the existence of consciousness on something other than itself ensures that it does not exist as an in-itself. Consciousness is not some thing that can be separated from the world as a pure ego; rather, consciousness and ego arise only in *acts* of awareness of objects and awareness of the separateness from those objects. Consciousness arises as a self-awareness of being not-the-objects-of-awareness; in this way consciousness is a kind of nothingness or negation. Consciousness is not what it is and is what it is not, since it has yet unfulfilled potential as to what it can be.

Sartre's concept of the nature of consciousness ties in with his concept of freedom. It is the nature of consciousness, the for-itself, that it is not an object or thing. That our being is as not-a-thing frees us from the causal nexus that determines the realm of the in-itself. There is no fixed ego or self in the Cartesian sense and consciousness is not to be identified with ego. The ego or self is our view of the sum of free intentional choices consciousness has made in the past, so that what the ego is can change in the future through its as yet unfulfilled or potential free choices. We create our own essence – what we are – through our choices and are therefore totally responsible for what we are. We are our freedom; our "whatness" is our choice. "Bad faith" arises when we treat the predicative "is" as to what we are – we are a waiter, a soldier, a coward, a liar, a Frenchman – as if it were the "is" of identity defining an essence, and abdicate our responsibility as to what we do by virtue of an explanation following from our supposedly fixed essential nature which, we might argue, is imposed upon us. The overarching exemplification of "bad faith" is thus to see ourselves as an object, as fixed: as a being-in-itself. Similarly it is "bad faith" to live as though values and attitudes were derived from the world and not derived from us. To overcome the *Angst* involved in our awareness of our freedom we tend to retreat to the pretence that we have no choice by adopting roles, characters, values and attitudes, as if they were imposed upon us. I do not choose the condition or situation that is forced on me from the outside, which is my "facticity", but I am always free in what I make of it. We try to fill our nothingness with actions to define what we are, but what we are is always, unto death, incomplete, since future choices characterizing the kind of persons we are always remain open to us. Our incompleteness as a for-itself means we can be free because we have the power, unlike the in-itself which is just what it is, to be not what we are and to be what we are not.

With respect to being-for-others, Sartre first rejects the dualistic presuppositions of the "problem of other minds". The problem is said to arise from the problematic inference from the bodily behaviour of others to the hypothesis that they are conscious like ourselves. Sartre's dissolution of the problem denies that the bifurcation of other people into body and mind in our experience is possible in the first place. We immediately recognize important modes of our being – such as shame and guilt – which are a result of existing in relation to other people and depend on there being other people aware of us. In perceiving others we immediately perceive them as *persons*, and this is a primitive feature of our experience. There is no inference to "other minds" to justify because such an inference does not occur at all.

Many of the most fundamental meanings of the human world, the world-as-it-is-for-us, involve an intersubjectivity that depends on the existence of other persons. The meanings that the world has for us depend on the recognition of there being others. My experience of the world as a public world, and of myself, in various important ways depends on my acceptance of the existence of others. To deny the existence of others would, among other things, be to abandon some of the most fundamental ways in which the world and myself have significance for me.

One of the basic ways in which I relate to others is through my consciousness of being looked at by another person, which Sartre calls "The Look" (*Le Regard*). My relation with others is a struggle not to be fixed by The Look as an *object* for the other. The struggle is to maintain my freedom when The Look of others fixes me as an identifiable object. To preserve my freedom I may attempt to turn others into objects for me and so attempt to destroy others as a source of The Look. Thus each person is apparently a threat to the other's freedom. At the same time, however, my reflective (as opposed to pre-reflective) self-consciousness arises only from my awareness of how others see me. That I am ashamed of myself, for example, is necessarily connected to my seeing myself as being seen by others doing disreputable things. My self-consciousness derives from my taking another's view of my behaviour.

The mutual recognition of freedom is constantly compromised as people fix others as objects. To fix another as someone who loves me, for example, involves the paradox that, on the one hand, we wish the love of the other to be unconditionally given, while on the other hand, if it is to have its value as the love of another, it must be given freely.

The ethical implications of Sartre's philosophy are complex, but central is existential freedom. Existentialism does not imply that one should simply do what one likes and there are no moral considerations guiding us; rather, it implies that what moral considerations we choose to guide us are our responsibility. But that does not mean that what is morally good or bad is itself dependent on mere individual subjective appraisal or whim. Existentialism does not entail accepting that there are no reasons or justifications for actions independently of subjective predilections. If this were the case, then no moral dilemmas would ever arise in my free choices; that such dilemmas do arise is clearly something existentialism accepts and through which freedom to choose is given its importance.

Since the notion of freedom and living an "authentic" life in the awareness of that freedom are central to existentialist philosophy in general, and values in particular, it is important to see whether any fairly specific moral "directives" emerge from the notion of "authenticity". One point that emerges is that the notion of an "authentic" life – one lived in awareness of freedom – is increased in proportion as we are not aware of ourselves fixed as objects by others. But the strategy of evading the fixity ensuing from The Look of others by in turn objectifying others is in the end self-defeating. For as I regard others as objects, so I come to regard myself as an object like them, which is the paradigm of "bad faith" or "inauthenticity". This seems to imply a moral directive on action concerning the treatment of others whereby both we ourselves and others can collaborate in maximizing the awareness of the freedom of our lives – their "authenticity" – by increasing the extent to which we refuse to fix each other as objects. We thereby move in the opposite direction from the downward spiral of mutual objectification by trying not to start the fixing of each other as objects in the first place. Whether actual human relations with others can allow, or easily allow, such reciprocal support of freedom, and if so what such relations would be like, are further problems.

CHAPTER TEN

Logical positivism and falsificationism: Ayer, Popper

It is perhaps unnecessary to make any connection between A. J. Ayer and Karl R. Popper other than to point out that they both had great influence on Western philosophy during the middle part of this century, an influence that has continued to this day. However, a common historical and intellectual connection is the Vienna Circle; this was a group that met in Vienna during the 1920s and 1930s and developed the philosophy of logical positivism, which was intent on setting philosophy on a sure footing so that the scope of its tasks was clear. Logical positivism, by way of a theory of meaning, involves the elimination of much of traditional philosophy, in particular metaphysics and also theology, as literally meaningless. What this amounted to was the view that the investigation of any substantial facts about the world was the province of science alone, not philosophy, which could be concerned only with conceptual elucidation and the linguistic task of precise definition. Both Ayer and Popper attended the meetings of the Vienna Circle, but whereas Ayer initially became a powerful advocate of its views, Popper, although deeply interested, like the Vienna Circle, in the philosophy and methodology of science, was critical of logical positivism. Popper aims to demarcate science from non-science so as to understand better the nature of scientific knowledge. Non-science includes pseudo-science: areas which are not scientific but claim to be so. It does not follow from this that what is non-science, including pseudo-science, is thereby literally meaningless, as logical positivism supposed, or even that it is untrue. Ayer has always had a great interest in the problem of meaning, which Popper regards as a largely fruitless field of philosophical investigation if regarded as an end in itself. What perhaps unites Ayer and

259

Popper, although they are by no means alone in this, is their view that the heart of philosophy is epistemology, and in particular the nature of empirical knowledge.

Ayer

Alfred Jules Ayer (1910–89) was educated at Eton and Christ Church, Oxford; his tutor in philosophy at Oxford was Gilbert Ryle (1900–76). After graduating, he thought of going to Cambridge to study with Wittgenstein; instead he went to study in Vienna in 1932 in order to find out more about the logical positivist philosophy of the Vienna Circle. After a short period in Vienna he returned to Oxford and became a lecturer in philosophy at Christ Church. In 1936 he published *Language, truth and logic*. While we must allow for differences within the logical positivist movement, *Language, truth and logic* states clearly what is essential to the doctrine of logical positivism. In 1940 he joined the Welsh Guards and worked for most of the war in military intelligence. He returned to Oxford in 1945 to become Dean of Wadham College. From 1946 to 1959 he was Grote Professor of the Philosophy of Mind and Logic at University College London. From 1959 until his retirement in 1978 he was Wykeham Professor of Logic in the University of Oxford. In 1970 he was knighted. Although he came to reject the most radical proposals of logical positivism, Ayer remained a close follower of the British tradition of empiricism and logical analysis. It was Wittgenstein's *Tractatus* that set Ayer on the course which led to *Language, truth and logic*. However, the greatest influences on Ayer were Russell and Hume. He continued to admire Bertrand Russell, regarding him as probably the greatest philosopher of the twentieth century; and, like Russell, he was an enthusiastic atheist. Ayer also became interested in the American pragmatists, such as William James (1842–1910). Again, like Russell, Ayer was a passionate advocate of reason, and thought that intellectual honesty demanded that we seek sufficient evidence for any beliefs that might be proposed for acceptance.

The motivation for logical positivism stems from two connected lines of thought: (I) the unity of science, and (II) the elimination of metaphysics. In short, this amounts to the view that really all science forms a single system; it alone is able to give true characterizations of the nature of the world which can in the end be exhaustive. The unity of science means that all branches of scientific inquiry have a common epistemological basis: it is that determining the truth or falsity of scientific theories about the nature of the world depends entirely on an appeal to the evidence of experience and observation. The elimination of metaphysics complements this, because metaphysics commonly supposes there is some way of determining the nature of the world – perhaps its real or essential nature beyond appearances – other than by an appeal to experience and observation. The apparent assertions by metaphysics about the nature of the world are, according to logical positivism, not true or false, but nonsense – literally meaningless. With the elimination of metaphysics as a source of knowledge about the world, science is unified as a system of factual propositions, that is, statements whose truth or falsity and, indeed, meaning depend on their being open to the test of the facts of experience.

Propositions are what is determinately true or false: that is, they are *literally meaningful*. Propositions are what literally meaningful indicative sentences (sentences which grammatically appear to state things) of any particular language express; this is important because sentences of different languages can express the same proposition, as in *it is raining* and *il pleut*. The criterion for a sentence is that it is grammatically well formed, that is a necessary condition for it to be meaningful, otherwise it is mere gibberish, such as "foot a fight will". The logical positivists argue that many grammatically well formed sentences do not express genuine propositions, although being grammatically well formed sentences they may appear to do so. Sentences that appear to express a proposition, whether they do so or not, Ayer calls putative propositions or statements. The logical positivists argue that all genuine propositions are either analytic/tautologies or verifiable by experience; statements – that is, indicative sentences which appear to express propositions – which are neither analytic nor verifiable by experience are literally meaningless or nonsense. Sentences and statements that do not express genuine propositions may be meaningful in some other way – they may have poetic or emotive significance – but they are not *literally* meaningful. If a statement is literally meaningless, then the question of its truth or falsity cannot arise.

It has to be the case that a distinction is made between sentences being meaningful in some broader sense than *literally* meaningful because otherwise the criterion of literal meaningfulness would have no possible application; in order to discover if a statement is analytic or empirically verifiable, we already have to understand what it means.

A sentence expresses an *analytic proposition* if, and only if, its truth or falsity follows solely from the definition of the terms it contains. Thus "All bachelors are unmarried" is analytic, since the predicate "unmarried" is part of the definition of "bachelor"; establishing the truth or falsity of the proposition consists in merely unpacking the definition of its terms. The truth or falsity of analytic propositions depends entirely on the meaning of the symbols in the sentence the proposition expresses. Analytic propositions are true or false, and can be known to be so, *a priori*, that is, independently of the evidence of experience; they are also devoid of factual content as they make no claim about the world; their truth or falsity is compatible with any evidence of experience whatsoever. That which is necessary is that which must be and cannot be otherwise. If an analytic proposition is true, it is *necessarily* true – it must be true and cannot be false. If an analytic proposition is false, it is *necessarily* false – it must be false and cannot be true. The denial of a true analytic proposition implies a logical contradiction.

A sentence expresses an *empirically verifiable proposition* if, and only if, some possible experience is relevant to determining its truth or falsity. The truth or falsity of such empirically verifiable or factually significant propositions cannot be determined merely by examination of the definition or meaning of the symbols in the sentence the proposition expresses. Thus "The cat is on the mat" is a factually significant proposition; its truth or falsity does not follow from the meaning of the terms it contains – it is not an analytic but a synthetic proposition; its truth or falsity can only be determined *a posteriori* by consulting experience. That which is contingent is that which may or may not be: that which could be otherwise. If an empirically verifiable proposition is true, then it is *contingently* true – it is true, but could have been false. If an empirically verifiable proposition is *contingently* false, it is false, but could have been true. The denial of an empirically verifiable proposition never implies a logical contradiction.

The two classes of analytic and empirically verifiable statements are mutually exclusive and collectively exhaustive of all literally meaningful statements: they are the totality of genuine propositions. That is, it is a necessary and sufficient condition for a statement to be literally meaningful, and so capable of being true or false – a proposition – that it be either analytic or empirically verifiable. Put another way, a statement is a genuine proposition if and only if it is either analytic or empirically verifiable, otherwise it is nonsense.

Metaphysics generally attempts to describe the essential structure of reality: what the real world *must* ultimately be like according to intellectual argument, although it may appear otherwise. Plato speaks of fixed "Forms" beyond the flux of experience and space and time, but accessible to the intellect, defining the "whatness" of things; Leibniz speaks of non-spatial "monads" as the indivisible, indestructible substance of the world which remain the same through all natural change; Hegel speaks of the fully real as "The Absolute", the universe as ultimately a self-thinking totality. There are also theological statements asserting the existence and nature of an eternal transcendent God outside space and time.

Metaphysics, with theology, is eliminated as literally meaningless because what it characteristically proffers as propositions are not genuine propositions at all. The need to be clear about what are genuine propositions arises from the fact that we are misled by the surface appearance of statements in metaphysics into thinking they express propositions; but we know they do not express propositions because they do not say anything whose truth or falsity can be determined in the only two ways possible: by their being analytic or by their being empirically verifiable. Metaphysics is disposed of not because it is false, but because it is composed of statements which are largely nonsense; it may appear to be composed of propositions – statements that can be true or false – but really it is composed of statements incapable of being either true or false because their truth or falsity cannot be established even in principle by the only two ways possible. If we are to say that any of the statements of metaphysics is literally meaningful, then it must be translatable into statements that are analytic or empirically verifiable. However, if a statement is analytic, it tells us nothing about the world, and if it is empirically verifiable, then it ceases to be a metaphysical statement at all, but merely becomes part of the body of scientific theory testable by observation. Neither translation is congenial to the metaphysician who wishes to contend that his statements both say something about the world – are factually significant – and cannot be settled by empirical verification; but it is impossible, Ayer argues, that both these conditions can be simultaneously satisfied. Indeed, metaphysics often claims to speak of the world behind or beyond the world as it appears. Either a statement says something about the world, in which case it is empirically verifiable, or a statement says nothing about the world; no statement can be about the world and not be empirically verifiable. Therefore metaphysics, which purports to produce truths and refutations of falsehoods about the nature of the world or reality in statements which are empirically unverifiable, is impossible; it produces only literal nonsense. Metaphysics makes only literally meaningless assertions and raises spurious questions; it is, in short, composed of meaningless pseudo-propositions which have the appearances of genuine propositions. It follows that there can in reality be no genuine disputes between metaphysicians: if "*p*" is a metaphysical statement, it is literally meaningless, but then "not-*p*" is also meaningless.

Logical positivism holds that all *a priori* propositions are analytic and, although necessary, are necessary only because they are factually empty: they say nothing about the world, but reveal only the conventional meanings of words. All *a posteriori* propositions are synthetic and contingent, but they are, whether true or false, factually informative: they say something about the world. Contrary to the view of a philosopher such as Kant, there can be no *a priori*, necessary propositions that are synthetic. These considerations can be summarized in the following diagram:

	Analytic/tautological /necessary	Synthetic/contingent
a priori	A	B
a posteriori	C	D

All genuine propositions – that is to say, all propositions – fall into either, but not both, of the shaded areas: *A* and *D*. No propositions fall into the unshaded areas: *B* and *C*.There are therefore only two classes of genuine propositions:

A: *a priori*/analytic/necessary.

D: *a posteriori*/synthetic/contingent.

All statements that fail to fall into the classes *A* or *D* are not propositions at all; they are incapable of being true or false – they are not literally meaningful – although they may be meaningful in some other way.

Thus, in so far as metaphysics does contain literally meaningful propositions, it consists either of analytic propositions, which tell us nothing about the world, whose truth or falsity can be determined *a priori*, or synthetic propositions, which do purport to tell us something about the world, whose truth or falsity can be determined only *a posteriori*. There is no special class of metaphysical propositions which are at once *a priori* and tell us something about the world: no facts can be known *a priori*.

All the statements of logic, mathematics and geometry express non-empirical, non-factual, propositions, that are *a priori* valid and necessary in virtue of their being analytic or tautologies: their truth depends solely on the meaning of the symbols of which their statements are composed. They are also devoid of factual content; the reason such truths are necessary is just that they do not make any assertions about the world that could be confuted or confirmed by the evidence of experience. We do not have to suppose, in order to explain our *a priori* knowledge of necessary truths, that the truths refer to some realm of entities transcending experience. All *a priori* analytic truths – including those of logic, mathematics and geometry – are not *about* anything at all, but simply reflect the meaning we have chosen to give to linguistic signs.

Philosophers such as Kant have argued that there is a special class of propositions which are *a priori* synthetic and necessary. Kant accepted that propositions such as "All bachelors are unmarried" are analytic, necessary, their denial implying a contradiction; the concept of the predicate is implicitly contained in the concept or definition of the subject, so to assert that someone is a bachelor, but not unmarried, is a logical contradiction. Such propositions, Kant agreed, tell us nothing about the world. However, Kant thought that the propositions of arithmetic and geometry were at once *a priori* and synthetic.

He then felt obliged to construct an elaborate philosophical system in order to explain how this was possible. How could a proposition which is synthetic, so that its denial does not entail a logical contradiction, be true, and be known to be true, *a priori*? It appeared to Kant that arithmetical propositions such as $7+5=12$ were known *a priori*, and were necessary truths, and yet were *synthetic* because it was possible to think of $7+5$ without thinking of 12. Ayer argues that this is a purely psychological point. Kant's explanation for our knowledge of synthetic *a priori* truths is that they characterize the form we impose on the matter of sensation and so are valid for the world only as it appears. Ayer thinks such an explanation quite unnecessary: the truth of $7+5=12$ and the *a priori* knowledge of that truth depend entirely on the conventional definition of the terms in it, and it is thus quite independent of empirical evidence or, *a priori*. The same argument applies to geometrical truths; such truths are not a description of physical space, they merely unravel whatever definition of the terms we started off with. Logical propositions such as "Either p or not-p" are true regardless of any facts of experience and depend for their truth entirely on the meaning of the signs composing them; they are tautologies because they always come out true regardless of what propositions are substituted in them provided the substitution is done uniformly. It follows that such analytic propositions, although necessary, are trivially true or devoid of factual content. The proposition "either it is raining or it is not raining" tells us nothing whatsoever about the weather, and is true independently of whatever the facts about the weather are; its truth excludes nothing at all.

If it is the case that all *a priori* propositions are analytic, how do we explain the usefulness of logic, mathematics and geometry, and their ability to surprise us? The explanation lies entirely in the limitations of our intellect. In the case of complex analytic propositions we are, as a matter of fact, intellectually incapable of seeing at once all the consequences of the definitions we adopt. To an intellect of sufficient power, the complex propositional theorems of logic, mathematics and geometry would be of no more interest than "$A=A$" is to us. The interest for us of analytic propositions is that we cannot always see immediately everything that our definitions imply.

This brings us to what for Ayer is the function of philosophy. Philosophy cannot determine the nature of reality, as metaphysics would suggest. Any proposition concerning the nature of reality would be a factual scientific or common-sense proposition whose truth or falsity could be established only by the test of experience and not by philosophy as such. The function of philosophy, once it is demonstrated that metaphysics is literally meaningless, is analysis and clarification. Analysis is a branch of logic and consists of giving precise definitions of concepts, or presenting the logical consequences of definitions, of terms used in science and common sense; thus all the propositions of philosophy are analytic. The function of philosophy is to translate talk of one sort into logically equivalent talk of another sort, an activity which has purely linguistic significance. Philosophy itself can produce no new factual knowledge about the world but can only deduce the logical consequences of propositions whose truth or falsity, if they are not analytic – and so devoid of factual content – is determined by the facts.

It is important to establish more exactly what is meant by empirical verifiability in order to determine which non-analytic statements are propositions. Such propositions must in all cases be capable of being verified or falsified by experience. It is necessary, however, to make two sets of distinctions here:

(a)   verification in practice
(a´)   verification in principle
(b)   "strong" or conclusive verification
(b´)   "weak" or probabilistic verification.

In both cases Ayer says he adopts the more liberal of the two alternatives, (a´) and (b´). The reason for this is that (a) would entail denying as literally meaningful all sorts of empirical propositions because we could not in fact verify them. Thus the proposition "There are mountains on a particular planet on the other side of the galaxy" is not a proposition which I could in fact verify; perhaps it never will be verified; nevertheless we know what *would* verify the proposition; we can conceive of certain logically possible observations which could *in principle* be made which would verify or falsify the proposition. There would be an inevitable tendency for (a) to lead to solipsism whereby my possible knowledge extended only as far as propositions describing my actual private experiences. Adopting (b) would also prove or exclude too much, for no empirical proposition can be *conclusively* verified or falsified; empirical observations can only render the truth or falsity of a proposition more or less probable. One reason for this is that, whatever empirical proposition we take, the conclusion or import we draw from observations relevant to determining the truth or falsity of the proposition will always depend on assuming the truth of certain other propositions describing the circumstances of the observation. But then the truth or falsity of these other propositions describing the initial conditions of the empirical test could themselves, if they are factually significant, be tested by experience, and so on. Also most of the propositions of natural science of the form "All *A* is *B*" would be rendered literally meaningless if we adopted (b) because we could not even in principle examine what is an open infinite class of cases; there may always be cases we have not examined, and there is no way of demonstrating that there are not such cases. In short, Ayer thinks all empirical propositions are *hypotheses* because there is no way of absolutely confirming or refuting such propositions.

Ayer admits that empirical hypotheses do not confront experience singly, but only as part of a system of propositions. Thus if an observation appears to verify or refute a given hypothesis, it is always logically possible for us to refuse to admit to the significance of the observation by modifying the other hypotheses that gave the observation its significance as evidence of a particular sort. Take the proposition "All trees have leaves"; suppose we test the truth or falsity of this proposition by making observations; whatever observations we make, they always depend on certain other empirical hypotheses connecting the observation and the proposition under test; for example, that we are not suffering from an illusion, or we have correctly identified something as a leaf. Some of the logical positivists argued that there is a class of isolated "basic propositions" about which it is impossible for us to be mistaken, and which can be conclusively confirmed or refuted by experience because they refer only to immediate experience. Ayer initially thought that any factually significant proposition involves using general classificatory terms (such as "red") which it is always possible to misapply, and so no factual proposition can be conclusively verified or refuted, since we can always find out we have made a mistake in the light of further evidence.

Thus, according to "weak" verifiability (b´), a genuine proposition – a statement capable of being true or false – if it is not analytic, is an empirical hypothesis the truth or falsity of which experiences could, in principle, render more or less probable. The purpose of formulating scientific theories is essentially predictive and pragmatic: it is therefore the very meaning of rational behaviour that we adopt those theories and methods which function to enable us to anticipate and control the course of our experiences. The function of theories, and the purpose of testing them, is to produce theories which are more efficient instruments for describing and anticipating experiences. Whether a theory will be successful in this way can be revealed not by *a priori* argument but only by its success in practice, but it is always logically possible that it may fail in cases we have not observed.

The "weak" verification principle thus states that all literally meaningful non-analytic statements are in principle verifiable by being rendered more or less probable by propositions which describe specific experiences; all other statements, apart from analytic ones, are literally meaningless. So all statements which are not analytic propositions and cannot be verified by experience are literally meaningless: they do not express a proposition at all. The verification principle gives a criterion for distinguishing the literally meaningless from the literally meaningful.

The attempt to give a precise formulation of empirical verifiability leads Ayer into difficulty. Ayer's initial version of the "weak" verifiability principle is: a non-analytic statement is a genuine factual proposition – and thus not literally meaningless – if we can deduce from it, along with certain other statements describing the conditions under which relevant observation could take place, some experiential proposition which refers to actual or possible experience (sense-contents), which cannot be deduced from those other statements alone. This formulation is, however, faulty as it excludes nothing as a literally meaningful proposition. If N is any statement you like, even one that is meaningless or metaphysical, and O is an experiential proposition, then O is deducible from [(if N then O) and N], without being deducible from O alone. This means that N would, by the criterion, be verifiable and hence a literally meaningful proposition even though it can be any statement at all. If we say that the "other statements" must be themselves factually significant, then we have got no further, since distinguishing factually significant statements was the point of the criterion, and we cannot assume we can distinguish which statements are factual. Ayer tries to rectify this fault, but he does not succeed in discovering a precise formulation that includes and excludes just what he wants.

One way of avoiding such problems would be to adopt the "strong" verification principle (b). In this case it is not just a matter of some empirical evidence being deducible which would be favourable or unfavourable to the truth of a proposition. "Strong" verification demands that the whole content of empirical or factual propositions, when fully analyzed, be expressible in wholly experiential propositions or observation-statements. Indeed, sometimes Ayer does seem to be working with the "strong" verifiability principle, whereby any genuine non-analytic proposition must, if we are to understand it, be translatable into propositions which describe only actual or possible experiences: sense-contents. A statement is then a factually significant proposition if and only if it can be completely defined as a logically equivalent set of purely experiential propositions which entails the original proposition and is entailed by it; the two statements are thus identical. The literal meaning of any factual proposition is then no more or less than a set of propositions describing some actual (categorical) or possible (hypothetical) experiences. The thinking behind this is that understanding the meaning of factually significant statements involves having, at least in principle, access to experiencing the factual conditions under which the proposition which expresses the statement would be true; that is, experience in principle of the truth-conditions of a proposition is required to understand the literal meaning of the statement it expresses. All factually significant propositions, such as "I am now sitting in front of a table", are abbreviations for a complex of propositions describing sense-contents alone. If any part of a statement appears to refer to something that is not even in principle a feature of actual or possible experience, then we can be sure that that part of the statement is without factual significance, and is meaningless unless it is analytic: that part is literal nonsense, what we say is literally "sense-less". Only by expressing a non-analytic statement using symbols which wholly stand for sense-contents are we able to make literally intelligible *what* it is we are talking about.

It is surely this "strong" notion of verifiability that leads Ayer to various forms of philosophical analysis and reductionism. Such analyses are epistemological and are ontologically neutral. We find this reduction at work, for example, in his analysis of the concepts of a material object and of causation. In the case of material objects Ayer is led to phenomenalism: statements about material objects, if they are meaningful at all, must be wholly translatable into experiential propositions which do not mention material objects; what we mean when we talk about "material objects" is nothing more than some set of actual or possible sense-experiences. Such a translation defines "material object". This disposes of the problem of the existence of the external world arising from our making inferences from propositions concerning our experiences to propositions referring to material objects, because there is no gap in the end between experiences and material objects: to talk of material objects is just to talk of certain ordered collections of actual or possible experiences, and the set of propositions describing particular sense-contents is identical to a proposition describing a material object. The same analysis applies to causation. Ayer agrees with Hume that "*C* causes *E*" is not a logical relation: if "*C* causes *E*" is a non-analytic, factual, proposition then to assert *C* occurs but deny *E* occurs is never a logical contradiction. To say that "*C* causes *E*" is to say no more than that "whenever *C*, then, under certain circumstances, *E*"; there is nothing further in our experience, and indeed nothing further at all, to which the concept of the "necessary connection" of *C* and *E* could correspond. Causality amounts to no more than the definition "invariable association in a potentially infinite number of possible cases". Generally, to avoid talking literal nonsense one must specify what feature of actual or possible experience the talk describes.

The "self" is also not meaningfully identifiable with any non-experiential soul or mental substance, but is, like a material object logically constructed out of sense-contents. The way in which we think of the minds of others presents problems, however, because we have in principle no access to their sense-contents, but only to their behaviour. This produces an incoherent asymmetry whereby the ascription of mental states to myself is phrased in "mental" sense-contents, whereas its ascription to others is phrased in "physical" or "behavioural" sense-contents.

Logical positivism has a dilemma. The problem with adopting "strong" verifiability is that although it excludes statements that Ayer wishes to regard as literally meaningless, it also excludes statements he would wish to regard as meaningful. Ayer came to think later that the complete reduction of propositions about material objects to sense-contents was not possible, because no finite set of propositions referring to sensory experience was ever logically equivalent to a statement referring to a physical object. No finite set of observation-statements can give the necessary and sufficient conditions which would constitute the truth that X is a physical object, since further, logically possible evidence – further experiences – may show we must have been mistaken. So no finite set of propositions referring to sense-experiences can conclusively verify the proposition that X is a material object. Hence the problem with "strong" verifiability is that it implies that most, perhaps all, of the statements of natural science are meaningless. The problem with "weak" verifiability is that although plausibly it permits the statements of science and common sense as literally meaningful, factual, propositions, it fails to exclude those statements which Ayer wishes to regard as metaphysical and meaningless.

Take, for example, the statement "God exists": the same consider-ations apply to "God does not exist". Ayer wants to say that such an assertion is literally meaningless rather than false. But it is not excluded by the "weak" verification principle, for someone might admit that a particular experience was evidence for or against the existence of God – thereby qualifying "God exists" as a literally meaningful proposition – without thereby having to admit that what is meant by "God" and "His existing" is wholly exhausted by those evidential experiential propositions. Only by adopting the "strong" verification principle is there hope of identifying "God exists" as literally meaningless and so eliminating it. However, no sophisticated religious believer is likely to admit that what he means by God existing is nothing more than some actual or possible sense-experi-ences – for example, the observed intricateness and orderliness of nature – even if he might admit it as evidence of God's existence.

Ayer's analysis of apparent ethical and aesthetic statements – "statements of value" – concludes they are not genuine propositions at all; they are without literal meaning. They are not factual synthetic statements, but rather *expressions* of feelings of approval or disap-proval, which may affect others so they feel the same way. Value statements are not about anything – they do not even describe the fact that there is a subjective psychological state which constitutes a feeling – rather, they are an expression *of* feeling, akin to a cry of pain or grunt of satisfaction. Expressions of value are therefore neither rational nor irrational: they are just a piece of non-rational behaviour. Since value statements are incapable of truth or falsity, then no two value statements can conflict. If we argue with someone over value, it must be over what are the facts concerning the situation which prompted our feeling.

A further problem that arises with the "verification principle" which lies at the heart of logical positivism is the logical status of the principle itself. For the statement "Every genuine proposition must be either analytic or empirically verifiable" appears itself to be neither analytic nor empirically verifiable, in which case it is self-defeating and the "verification principle" is literally meaningless and incapable of truth or falsity. Logical positivism is not the first or the last philosophy to saw off the branch on which it is sitting. One response to this is to say that the principle is not a statement, but a prescriptive rule which we ought to adopt. But the problem with that is there is no way of showing why the rule should be adopted.

Popper

Karl Raimund Popper was born in Vienna in 1902. Although his parents were Jewish, they were baptized into the Protestant Lutheran Church before their children were born. The circumstances in which he was brought up were bookish and intellectual. His father was doctor of law of the University of Vienna and, as well as practising as a lawyer, he was also a scholar. With this background Popper began reading early about philosophical, scientific and political matters. In 1918 he enrolled at the University of Vienna and sampled a wide range of lecture courses, but concentrated his attention on mathematics and physics. After university he taught mathematics and physics in secondary schools. During this time he took a keen interest in left-wing politics, although his later work was greatly concerned with the totalitarian dangers of socialist and Marxist mass collectivization and of the belief in inevitable laws of historical development. His resistance to doctrines claiming access to final truths and dogmatism led him to favour individualism and piecemeal evolutionary social change rather than grand revolutionary change, also tentative solutions to social problems against a background of the greatest possible freedom for the expression of opinion and criticism which is characteristic of an open society. The chief culprits attacked by Popper are Plato, Hegel and Marx.

Popper had contacts with the logical positivism of the Vienna Circle, but he was never a logical positivist, and instead became one of its critics, despite a common interest in the methods of science. The root of Popper's criticism was that questions of meaning were of relatively little importance; what concerned him was the status of theories and their testing. The logical positivists held that, apart from the propositions of logic and mathematics, all literally meaningful statements were empirical and scientific. Popper never held that all non-logical statements that were not scientific were meaningless.

Popper's "criterion of demarcation" was, unlike the logical positivists' criterion, concerned with the distinction not between the meaningful and the meaningless but between science and non-science. Non-science includes pseudo-science, which consists in intellectual activities that claim to be scientific, but are not.

Before the Second World War, Popper left Austria, and from 1937 to 1945 he taught philosophy at the University of New Zealand. He came to England in 1946. He remained on the outside of philosophical activities as practised in both Oxford and Cambridge, and received greatest intellectual sustenance from those who were not primarily philosophers such as the art historian E. H. Gombrich and the economist and political theorist F. A. Hayek. In 1949 Popper was made Professor of Logic and Scientific Method at the London School of Economics; and this position he held for the rest of his university career. He was knighted in 1965. Popper's work has been enormously influential in the philosophy of science, and on the methodology of the social sciences.

It is possible to identify three important connected strands of thought in Popper's philosophy: (a) the solution of the problem of induction, (b) the problem of demarcating science from non-science, (c) the importance of maximizing criticism and maintaining a "critical attitude" as essential for rationality and vital for the growth of knowledge.

The essential nature of philosophy involves the critical questioning of fundamental assumptions that we might otherwise take for granted; this is obviously connected with point (c). Points (a) and (b) are also connected with this because it has been thought that what distinguishes science from non-science is the inductive method: the extent to which the truth of its propositions is derived from and justified by their origin in the facts of experience. The ideal picture that this inductive model of science evokes is its beginning by collecting pure or presuppositionless observations which give the facts, in a passive, unprejudiced, neutral manner; then from the repetition of these observations certain patterns begin to emerge which lead to the framing of universal hypotheses connecting particular observed phenomena; these hypotheses are then, by further experimental tests, proved true, or at least confirmed as highly probable. The aim is to pick out, from the many features repeatedly observed, the necessary and sufficient conditions for the event to be explained; that is, the aim is to identify the cause of the event by identifying that feature of the situation that is always present when the event to be explained occurs and is never present when the event to be explained does not occur.

Popper argues, with others, that there are at least two major problems that such a view of science encounters.

(i)   The first problem is that there are no presuppositionless, neutral, raw observations free of theoretical content. All observation involves some identifying, and therefore theory-loaded, idea of the nature of the thing observed that already determines and presupposes the kind of thing observed, which therefore necessarily pre-empts any conclusion derived from observation. To observe at all necessarily involves theoretical presuppositions about what we are observing. We always when observing observe something *as* a so-and-so which carries with it theoretical implications which often take us beyond the bare content of the observation. For example, the assertion "Here is a glass of water" carries with it theoretical assumptions about the behaviour of entities denoted by "glass" and "water", assumptions with implications beyond the evidence of present observations; indeed, Popper says that such a statement is unverifiable, because the universal law-like behaviour implicit in denoting terms such as "glass" and "water" is not reducible to any finite class of experiences. Another point is that when we identify two events as a repetition of the same event, we are necessarily picking out some respect in which they are similar, and ignoring other respects in which they differ; they must differ or they would not be two distinct events. Observations, to be possible at all, always involve the selection, implicitly or explicitly, of certain of the features of our environment and the rejection of others; the possible range of things we could make note of is infinite, so we are forced to be selective. What we choose to observe is guided by theoretical interests.

(ii) The second problem is that of inductive inference; Popper characterizes this as "Hume's problem". In valid deductive reasoning it is not possible for the premises of the argument to be true and the conclusion false; necessarily if the premises of a valid deductive argument are true, then the conclusion is true. To assert the premises and deny the conclusion of a valid deduction is to contradict oneself. A deductive argument involves the claim that the premises present conclusive grounds for its conclusion. Thus if it is the case that "All men are mortal" and "Socrates is a man", then "Socrates is mortal". Inductive arguments are not conclusive in this way: the premises can be true, yet the conclusion false.

The theories of science are characteristically universal propositions of the form "All *A*s are *B*s" which go beyond the evidence of experience; the proposition does not follow from any finite number of observations of *A*s and *B*s – which give propositions of the form "Some *A*s are *B*s" – for there is no logical contradiction involved in the assertion that the next observed *A* will not be a *B*. From this it follows that no universal scientific proposition can be proved to be true. Scientific laws always transcend experience. The inference from experience to universal laws, or more generally to unobserved instances, is neither a logically valid deductive argument nor an inference that could be justified by experience, for the argument from "inductive inferences have worked in the past" to therefore "inductive inferences will work in the future" is itself an inductive inference, so any such attempted justification would be circular. An inductive inference could be made valid on the assumption that regularities or uniformities observed in the cases we have observed hold in cases we have not observed. But this assumption is not a logical *a priori* truth such that its denial implies a contradiction or such that it can be justified by experience. We might say that uniformities have been found to hold in all cases we have observed, therefore uniformities will hold in cases we have not observed; but that evidence from cases we have observed can be evidence for cases we have not observed is exactly what the uniformity principle justifies, so such evidence cannot be used to justify the uniformity principle itself.

It will not help to fall back on probability, for we can still ask why we think the observation of certain cases should even make more probable events we have not observed. We can say further that no finite number of observations can make a universal statement of the form "All *A*s are *B*s" more probable by the frequency theory of probability; the class of examined cases is always finite, and the class of unexamined cases is potentially infinite, so that the probability of the universal statement "All *A*s are *B*s" will always approach zero. Even if we restricted the range of our general statement, we could still not be sure that the next, ninety-ninth out of a hundred, *A* will be a *B*, on the basis of observing past *A*s and *B*s, since "*A* and not-*B*" is never a logical contradiction.

Popper rejects induction both as a fruitful method of formulating scientific theories, and as a logic for justifying theories. He claims to have solved the problem of induction, but he does not so much solve it as sidestep the problem; he does not give or seek a justification for induction, rather he substitutes a different scientific methodology that is independent of induction, but does the same job as induction in allowing us rationally to prefer one theory to another on empirical grounds. Popper maintains the empiricist principle that it is only by observation and experiment that we may rationally decide to accept or reject scientific theories. Such decisions cannot be justified *a priori*. This leads on to the heart of Popper's philosophy, and the idea that what distinguishes science from non-science is not induction as a method or a justificatory logic, but that science consists of theories which are both logically self-consistent and such that they can *in principle be falsified or refuted*. Popper uses the terms "hypotheses", "conjecture", "theory" and "scientific law" interchangeably. The logical basis for this is quite simple, and derives from the deductive principle of *modus tollens*:

If *p* then *q*,

not-*q*
_____

therefore, not-*p*.

Roughly this says that if asserting *p* entails asserting *q*, and *q* is false, then *p* is also false. We can substitute in this formula, *H*, standing for some universal scientific hypothesis, for *p*, and *e*, standing for an observation-statement, for *q*. The observation-statement *e* is *deduced* from *H*. We then have the following.

If *H* then *e*,

not-*e*
_____

therefore, not-*H*.

The essential point to notice is that this indicates a logical asymmetry between verification and falsification: while it is the case that no finite number of observations can ever prove the truth of a universal scientific theory, logically only one case is required to contradict a theory's universal assertion in order for it to be falsified or refuted. What is distinctive about scientific theories is not that they can be proved true, or even made more probable, but that they are testable, that is, they can be falsified. So from the universal proposition "All *A*s are *B*s" (*H*), we can deduce the proposition that "It is not the case that some (even one) *A* is not a *B*" (*e*); if we observe "Some (at least one) *A* is not a *B*" (not-*e*), then it follows purely as a matter of deductive logic that "All *A*s are *B*s" is false (not-*H*). The assertion "All swans are white" is falsified by the observation of a single non-white swan which entails that "Not all swans are white". Thus a theory is falsifiable if and only if there is some observation-statement deducible from it, which, if false, would falsify the theory. A genuine scientific theory must exclude some logically possible state of affairs by specifying more or less exactly what the state of affairs will be: it must not be compatible with all logically possible evidence. More exactly what is deducible from a scientific theory is at least one "basic statement" which is a potential falsifier; such a statement will be a singular observation-statement that refers to some publicly observable event. This excludes pure existential statements of the form "Some *A* is a *B*" from being scientific because they are untestable; no possible evidence can ever refute them as there is, so to speak, always somewhere we have not looked.

Popper was impressed by the contrast between the theories of Marxism and Freudian psychoanalysis on the one hand, and Einstein's theories on the other. According to Popper, Marxists and Freudians saw everywhere confirmation for their theories, whereas Einstein made an effort to formulate a very specific observable prediction which followed from his theory concerning the bending of light, which, if it failed to be upheld by observation, would have refuted the theory. What is at issue here is not the psychological fact, if it is one, of the reluctance of Marxist and Freudian defenders to admit evidence refuting their theories, but rather the nature or logical structure of Marxist and Freudian theories themselves which rendered them immune from falsification. Popper's suspicion was that Marxist and psychoanalytic theories were only "confirmed", and seemed to explain everything, because they were, through reasons of vagueness or devices designed to explain away counter-evidence, irrefutable. Such theories are anathema to the proper critical scientific attitude. That is not to say that Marxist and Freudian theories were meaningless, or even that what they said was untrue, rather the theories were not scientific in that they were highly untestable, that is, difficult, if not impossible, to falsify. The theories were constantly hedged around with caveats or qualifications, so that apparent counter-evidence was no longer a deducible consequence of the theories. For Popper this indicates that the holders of these theories were not adopting the proper critical scientific attitude. But far from pre-scientific myths being meaningless, Popper says they can often be modified to form the basis of later scientific theories and so become testable by experience.

A further point concerns a comparison of Newton's and Einstein's theories. Popper argues that despite the fact that Newton's theory can be massively confirmed by observation, this is not enough to establish its truth. He holds the view that discrepancies emerged in Newton's theory, between its predictions and observations, which led to the development of Einstein's competing theory despite the enormous confirmation of Newton's theory.

Having explained the *logic* of Popper's philosophy of science, it is necessary to distinguish this from the *methodology* or practice of falsificationism. While the logic of falsification is quite simple, the methodology is a good deal more complex. This arises because, although it is clear what would, logically speaking, constitute the refutation of a scientific theory, determining whether a theory is in fact refuted is quite a different matter. Not only is it the case that there are various reasons why it is difficult to determine if a refutation has taken place, but Popper also acknowledges that there are various ways in which an apparent refutation can always be avoided. These considerations require that we adopt certain *methodological rules* so as to maximize the possibility of scientific progress, although there is no method that can guarantee it.

There are various problems that arise in attempting the actual falsification of a theory by critical discussion, observation and experiment.

(i) It is always possible to doubt that the observation we have made is correct – we may have made an observational error.

This introduces the problem of the empirical base: if we cannot be certain of the truth of the observation-statements we use to test our theories, we cannot be certain our theories are refuted by them. Popper admits that there are no indubitable observation-statements; all observation-statements themselves have some theoretical content and are open to further testing. But this does not lead to a vicious infinite regress, because although all empirical statements are potentially testable, they can be provisionally or conventionally held as true, and so used to test or falsify theories for which they are potential falsifiers. If they are doubted, further tests can always be carried out. There are no ultimate empirical foundations.

(ii) This problem concerns the fact that scientific theories are always tested in groups. In testing any theory it is necessary that we describe the initial conditions by a set of auxiliary hypotheses; that is, certain other theories are involved which act as assumptions concerning relevant circumstances of the test; these also give the falsifying significance to the observation deduced from a theory. For example, in making an observation we might assume that light travels in a straight line. Thus the falsifying *modus tollens* formula becomes more complex.

If $(H+h)$ (hypothesis + auxiliary hypotheses), then e,

not-e

therefore, not-H.

Strictly speaking, all we can say in this complex situation is that some element in the totality $(H + h)$ is refuted – is shown to be false – and that need not be the theory H under test, but could instead be one or more of the auxiliary hypotheses h. What can be said here is that the auxiliary hypotheses are themselves open to testing.

(iii) Closely connected with point (ii), it is always possible to adopt *ad hoc* hypotheses so as to evade refutation. By *ad hoc* hypotheses is meant hypotheses adopted for no other purpose than to avoid refutation. For example the theory "All bread nourishes" can be immunized against refutation by the example of some poisonous bread in France by tacking on to the proposition "All bread nourishes" the expression "except in France". Another *ad hoc* method of evading refutation is simply to define away apparent counter-evidence; thus if "All As are Bs" is presented with the evidence of an A that is not a B, it can be said that if we seemed to observe an A that was not a B, then it could not have been an A that we observed at all; this makes being a B part of the identifying definition of an A. So we might say a non-white swan is not a swan at all.

The adoption of *ad hoc* hypotheses and definitional man-
oeuvres Popper regards as intellectually dishonest. We must
therefore adopt some methodological rules so as to avoid
adopting *ad hoc* hypotheses. Partly this is achieved by the
methodological principle that if we modify a theory with the
addition of some new hypotheses so as to avoid refutation,
there must be some consequences that can be deduced from
the original theory and the new additional hypotheses that
were not deducible from the original unmodified theory. In
other words, the additional or modified hypotheses must form
a new hypothesis which is testable in some way the original
hypothesis was not: they must be independently testable. Thus
we reject as *ad hoc* "All bread nourishes, *except in France*", since
it has no new testable consequences which are not also a test
of "All bread nourishes"; the reverse is not the case, since
there are testable consequences of "All bread nourishes" which
are not also testable consequences of "All bread nourishes,
except in France".

It is clear that some hypotheses are more testable or falsifiable than
others. The theory that "All planets move in loops" (H_1) is less
falsifiable than "All planets move in ellipses" (H_2), because H_1 is less
specific about what evidence would refute it. To put it another way,
H_1 excludes less than H_2: its truth is compatible with a far greater
range of possible observations. H_2 not only says that the planets move
in closed loops, but also specifies the exact kind of loop that is
involved. Thus we can say that all the observations that would falsify
H_1 would falsify H_2 but some observations that would falsify H_2 would
not falsify H_1; if the planets moved in anything but ellipses, H_2 would
be false, while as long as they still moved in some kind of loop H_1
would be true. Popper expresses this point by saying the greater the
information content of a theory, the more falsifiable it is: it tells us more
about the way the world *is* by excluding as being the case more
logically possible states of affairs. The information content increases
with the set of statements which are incompatible with the theory.

Popper also notes that the falsifiability and the information content
of a theory are in inverse proportion to its probability. The information content of a tautology – for example, "Either it is raining or it is
not raining" – is zero, and its probability is at the maximum of 1. The
probability of H_2 ("All planets move in ellipses") being true is far less
than the probability of H_1 ("All planets move in loops") being true
because the class of potential falsifiers of H_1 is a proper subclass of the
potential falsifiers of H_2. For example, "The planets move in a straight
line" would falsify both H_1 and H_2, but "The planets move in a circle"
would falsify H_2 but not H_1 because a circle is a kind of loop.

Popper's overall position is then that we make progress in our
knowledge, and approach the truth, by a process of trial and error.

Popper gives the following evolutionary view of the growth of scientific knowledge:

$$P_1 \rightarrow TT_1 \rightarrow EE_1 \rightarrow P_2$$

Here P_1 designates a problem, for which we propose the tentative theory TT_1; we then try to eliminate false theories by testing them severely and subjecting our theory to critical discussion, EE_1; then P_2 is the problem-situation as we emerge from our attempted solution to our problem, and so on. Science makes progress by conjecture and refutation; we learn from our mistakes. We start with problems, not with neutral observation: that is, we start with the failure to explain some phenomenon. No mere observation constitutes a problem; we have a problem only in the light of some existing theory which fails to explain an observation. We try to solve the problem not by proposing the most probable theory – for more probable theories have less information content – but by proposing bold conjectures or guesses which, because they are highly specific and precise in what they say about the world, are highly falsifiable; we can then test these theories in severe and crucial tests. The tests are severe because what the theory entails is incompatible with a very wide range of possible observations. Intuitively we can see that the severity of a test will increase with its improbability. A new theory will be bold and improbable (unlikely) and its tests severe because it involves rejecting part of the background knowledge of scientific theories of its historical time. For example, Einstein's theory was bold relative to the theoretical background assumptions of its time because it contradicted the background assumption of its time that light travels in straight lines.

It is significant that in Popper's falsificationism the *source* of a scientific theory is totally irrelevant to whether it is scientific or not. A theory is scientific if and only if it is falsifiable; it is quite unimportant whether the theory arises from laboratory observation or an inspirational blow on the head. One method might as a matter of fact be more fruitful as a means of producing good theories than another; but that is irrelevant to the question of whether a statement is scientific or not, and, if it is scientific, how good a scientific theory it is. Science has no mechanical method by which it can make progress; Popper's philosophy gives free rein to imaginative bold speculation. Good science requires just as much imagination as any of the arts. Popper says we do not in fact come to the world as passive or neutral observers, but are born with certain natural expectations or dispositions that operate in the same way as consciously constructed theories. Indeed all animals are in their behaviour acting out innate solutions to problems. But while these innate "theories" might be psychologically *a priori*, that does not mean they are *a priori* valid. The main difference between man and other animals is the extent to which man can allow his theories to die rather than dying himself; man can adopt new theories rather than hanging on to his theories and dying with them. One sees the point of this in considering the way a wasp unremittingly batters at a glass window and so "fails to solve" the "problem" of escaping.

Normally we will not be in the situation of testing one theory in isolation, but will have to choose between a number of competing theories. Even if we find an observation that falsifies a theory we will not reject it unless we have some better theory with which to replace it. Indeed, Popper's methodological rules demand that we do not hastily reject a theory after a single falsifying instance, but only after frequent and rigorous falsification has taken place, and we have a better theory with which to replace it. The choice between competing theories should be made in the following way: theory T_2 should be preferred to T_1 if T_2 solves all the problems that T_1 solves and it solves the problems T_1 failed to solve (that is, where T_1 was refuted), *and* it offers solutions to some additional problems about which T_1 says nothing, thus allowing the further possibility for refutation. To put it another way, we should choose the theory that explains all the previous theory explains, explains what the previous theory failed to explain, and offers an explanation for further phenomena not explained by the previous theory. The satisfaction of these conditions effectively rules out our new theory being merely the old theory plus some *ad hoc* hypotheses which serve only to avoid the apparent refutations or failures.

Popper's philosophy of science can be summarized in the following way. Knowledge progresses by proposing bold explanatory theories, that is, explanations with a high information content that are highly falsifiable, by subjecting those theories to severe and crucial tests and by the replacement of falsified theories by better theories. We can be said to replace a theory by a rationally preferable, better theory, even if the old theory has not been *conclusively* falsified, when the new theory, provided it has not been falsified, is able to explain all that the old theory explained, and things the old theory failed to explain, and offers as well explanations for things for which the old theory offered no explanation. That is, the better theory T_2 will contain T_1 as an approximation. If any falsification of T_1 would be a falsification of T_2, but not vice versa, then T_2 is rationally preferable to T_1 provided T_2 has not been falsified. This means we choose the theory which is more falsifiable – has more information content – provided that theory has not been falsified. We can make our assessment of theories only from the position of the current historical state of critical discussion.

If a theory survives continuous attempts to falsify it by severe tests, it can be said to be highly *corroborated*. That is *not* to say its truth has been conclusively established, or even made more probable. The corroboration of a theory at a certain time is essentially a report on its degree of testability, the severity of the tests to which it has been subjected, and the way it has stood up to those tests. The corroboration of a theory will increase with its falsifiability, provided it is not falsified, because the more falsifiable it is the more severe the tests it can potentially survive. It can then be subjected to further severe tests. Popper is quick to deny that corroboration reintroduces the notion of induction, for he says that the corroboration accorded to a theory does not say anything about its reliability in the future or anything about its future performance. The less the probability of a theory, the higher its degree of potential corroboration can be. A less probable theory can pass more severe tests and so can be more highly corroborated. A theory that has been well corroborated can be *provisionally* accepted. If there is more than one theory covering the same ground, it is rational to choose the best corroborated theory because that has been most severely tested. This again gives an account of rational preference between theories: T_2 is preferable to T_1 if T_2 survives all the tests T_1 survives, survives the tests T_1 fails, and goes on to explain further facts which are testable consequences of T_2, and if T_2 has not yet been refuted.

It is clear from Popper's position that we can never establish that a theory is true. He says that we can never "know" in the sense of conclusively establishing a theory to be true so that there is no possibility of our being mistaken. In this sense Popper is a fallibilist: we can never be certain that we have found the truth. All our theories are conjectures or guesses which are open to testing; we can then perhaps say that some conjectures are better than others because they have stood up to tests better.

Since we are interested in the truth we shall be interested in eliminating a theory which we discover to be false, for that way we might hit upon a theory that is true. Popper is absolutely clear in distinguishing whether a theory *is* objectively true or false as a matter of correspondence, or failure of correspondence, with facts (p is true if and only if it corresponds to the facts), from our *knowing* if p corresponds to the facts. Popper takes from the logician Alfred Tarski (1902–83) the definition of truth: "'p' is true if and only if p". Every unambiguous statement is either true or false, and there is no third possibility; but determining *when* a proposition corresponds to the facts is quite a different matter, and Popper thinks we are never in the position to say that we have established or justified the truth of a theory. However, the correspondence definition of truth can act as a regulative principle: it is something we can aim at and get nearer to. Indeed, as the corroboration of a theory increases, it is reasonable to conjecture that we are getting nearer the truth. The extent to which a theory approaches the truth Popper refers to as its *verisimilitude*. Popper derives the notion of verisimilitude from the information content of a theory: the content of a theory T is all those propositions entailed by it. The content of T can then be divided into its truth-content (the class of all true statements entailed by T) and its falsity-content (the class of all false statements entailed by T). The verisimilitude of T is its truth content – minus its falsity – content. Assuming that theories T_1 and T_2 are comparable, then T_2 has greater verisimilitude than T_1 if its truth-content is greater than T_1, but its falsity-content is less than T_1, or the falsity-content of T_2 is less than T_1 but the truth-content of T_2 is greater than T_1. If more true statements, but not more false statements, follow from T_2 than T_1, then T_2 is nearer the truth.

If T_2 entails all the true statements entailed by T_1, and T_2 entails some true statements not entailed by T_1, and T_2 does not entail more false statements than T_1, then it is reasonable to say that T_2 is nearer the truth than T_1: T_2 has greater verisimilitude even if it is false. Thus we can rationally prefer T_2 to T_1 if we are in pursuit of the truth even if T_2 is false, provided that the falsity-content of T_2 is not too great.

The verisimilitude and the degree of corroboration of a theory are connected. If we compare the corroboration of two theories and determine that all the tests passed by T_1 are also passed by T_2, and that T_2 passes some tests that T_1 does not pass, and that T_2 does not fail more tests than T_1 failed, then it is rational to prefer T_2 to T_1 because T_2 can be conjectured to have greater verisimilitude: it is nearer the truth. T_2 will be more testable than T_1: it will have a greater information content; it will say more about the way the world is. Although we have not established the truth of T_2 – indeed, as we are fallible, it is likely to be false – we can express a *rational preference* for T_2 as being better corroborated than T_1 and nearer to the truth than T_1. T_2 is more testable and survives more tests than T_1.

From Popper's acceptance of the correspondence theory of truth it can be seen that he is a metaphysical realist. He thinks that our theories, if true, refer to a reality which is independent of mind and our theories. However, he agrees that such metaphysical realism does not take us very far except as a regulative idea, for we still have to determine when our theories correspond to things as they really are. We cannot "look around" our theories to reality, but can only take to be reality what our best theories in the light of current *critical* discussion and testing say reality is. Popper thinks it unlikely that we will ever discover "the truth" about the world. Popper is opposed in science to instrumentalism, which asserts that scientific theories do not refer to real entities which explain the course of our observations, but are rather useful devices which posit whatever is required – without maintaining its reality – for predicting accurately the course of our experience. On this view scientific laws are rules rather than truths. Popper also opposes essentialism, which maintains that we can discover an ultimate reality in terms of which everything else is explained. This attitude he sees as stultifying to the pursuit of ever better explanations. Popper takes a middle course in which science is a genuine attempt to explain some real state of affairs which is known or assumed to be true by some other real state of affairs that is unknown and requiring discovery, the truth of which can be tested independently of the phenomena to be explained; but there is no end to the depth to which we can progress in pursuit of explanations.

When Popper talks about "knowledge" he is not referring to finally established, or justified, truths. He also emphasizes that when he talks about "knowledge" he is talking about knowledge in the *objective sense*. He intends by this to make a distinction between any person's subjective knowledge and objective knowledge as it is formulated in language and existent in books and journals in libraries and research institutions open to public inspection and testing. Scientific knowledge is objective in this sense. Objective logical relations exist between statements which are formulated in language, regardless of whether anyone is actually aware of them or not. What individual scientists believe is relatively unimportant compared to the objective growth of knowledge. The error of what Popper terms "belief philosophy" is that it tries to see knowledge as an especially sure kind of belief.

Popper, in fact, makes a distinction between three interdependent worlds: World 1 is the physical world; World 2 is the subjective mental world; World 3 is the objective world of theories, mathematics, literature, art, and the like, within which there exist objective logical relations – objective, that is, in being independent of the awareness of individual minds. The objects of World 3 are developed by World 2 minds, often in response to problems perceived in World 1; but once formulated, they have an objective status transcending the intentions of the individual. Yet it is knowledge in the subjective sense – what the individual person can know – on which traditionally philosophy has concentrated, the notion being that it is only from what an individual mind can really know that any further knowledge claims can be justified. Yet most human knowledge in the objective sense is not known by anyone in the subjective sense. Human knowledge, especially scientific knowledge, almost entirely consists of knowledge without a knowing subject. Popper's World 3 has some similarities to Plato's realm of objective Forms; however, a vital difference is that Popper's World 3 is by no means fixed, but constantly changes and develops as knowledge grows and progresses through the critical examination of the knowledge we already have.

CHAPTER ELEVEN

Linguistic philosophy: Wittgenstein

After the publication of the *Tractatus logico-philosophicus* in 1921, Wittgenstein abandoned philosophy because he thought that the *Tractatus* gave a definitive solution to all the problems of philosophy. During the following years, however, owing to various influences, including conversations with other philosophers, he came to think that the *Tractatus* was seriously flawed. This led not merely to an attempt to rectify the faults in the position expounded in the *Tractatus* in a piecemeal fashion, but eventually to the development of a new philosophical outlook. Wittgenstein returned in 1929 to Cambridge where he taught and wrote copiously; but no work other than the *Tractatus* was published in his lifetime apart from a short article which he almost immediately repudiated. However, soon after Wittgenstein's death in 1951, a work appeared that he had been preparing for publication, the *Philosophical investigations*; and it is this that contains the most considered and polished statement of his later thought.

There are, however, some common concerns and connections between the earlier and later philosophies. The most obvious of these are the concern with language, the drawing of linguistic boundaries, and the idea that we are led into philosophy and philosophical problems through misunderstanding the nature of language. We should not "solve" the problems of philosophy in their stated form, or on their face value, but should first see whether the problems are a result of our being fundamentally misled by language. Wittgenstein wishes to jolt us out of the traditional way of approaching philosophical problems, not so as to provide yet more in the way of "solutions", but so that we may look at the problems themselves in a manner whereby we see why they do not require such "solutions". Much philosophy rests on a confusion about the way language acquires its meaning, and many philosophical problems are really pseudo-problems or are misconceived.

Wittgenstein also opposes the idea that philosophy is a kind of super-science in either its methods or its problems. He objects to the picture of philosophy as being just like science except for the fact that it pushes the search for explanations and justifications deeper, presenting philosophical theories and hypotheses. If we examine carefully the matters discussed in philosophy, we will discover something peculiar and illegitimate about them, and in the later philosophy this will be manifest chiefly in comparing the use of language in philosophy with other uses.

In the *Tractatus* philosophical or metaphysical propositions are ruled out all at once in virtue of their involving meaningless linguistic signs. Since philosophical propositions do not conform to what is *essential* to a proposition being meaningful, they cannot be meaningful. There is an essential way that propositions are meaningful: it is supposed that propositions are meaningful because of something they all have in common; that is, if, and only if, certain conditions are met can a linguistic expression or sign be said to be meaningful. There are necessary and sufficient conditions that any linguistic expression must satisfy if it is to be meaningful; if it fails to satisfy these conditions, then a putative linguistic expression or proposition is meaningless. The essential condition for meaningfulness given in the *Tractatus* is the picturing relation with the world: a genuine proposition is an arrangement of names that pictures a possible fact and is ultimately constituted out of names whose meanings are the objects they stand for in the world. That the propositions of philosophy do not satisfy the essential condition means that philosophy and its "problems" are disposed of in one blow as meaningless.

The *Philosophical investigations* involves a very important shift in approach. If anything binds together the later philosophy, it is *anti-essentialism*. Essentialism amounts to the view that the reason for regarding a group of distinct things as of the same kind is that they have a distinguishing set of features shared by all and only members of that group. Thus we might define an "automobile" as "a self-propelled vehicle suitable for use on a street or roadway". Wittgenstein opposes essentialism generally, and in particular in the attempt to demonstrate that there must be some single way that all instances of meaningful language ultimately have their meaning, which therefore explains or accounts for the meaningfulness of the whole of language. There is no essential feature in virtue of which all language is meaningful. The key to the later philosophy is perhaps the attack on essentialism in general, and about meaning in particular. One attempt to give an account of the essence of language – that language consists ultimately of names of objects – is given in the *Tractatus* itself. A *part* of language may consist of names of objects, but it is not the essence – defining common feature – of all language.

The anti-essentialism of the *Philosophical investigations* has far-reaching consequences. It may seem that in rejecting the view that language has an essential way of being meaningful Wittgenstein is giving up all hope of disposing of philosophical problems in virtue of their expression being meaningless. In a sense this is true, although an expression might be meaningless in virtue of not being meaningful in *any* of the different ways it might be meaningful. However, anti-essentialism cuts both ways: it has the consequence that there is no way of dismissing philosophical expressions as wholly meaningless because they do not satisfy what is essential for meaningfulness, but it also has the consequence that because there is no single universal way that expressions are meaningful, there is no way of claiming that philosophy concerns itself with the one true, correct, or real meaning of expressions as opposed to the vagaries of their meaning outside philosophy – for example, their ordinary meaning. That there is no single universal criterion for meaningfulness suggests that all philosophical talk cannot be dismissed as wholly meaningless; but it also entails that there is no universal hidden, but perhaps discoverable, standard of meaningfulness in virtue of which one meaning could be picked out as the true meaning which takes precedence over other meanings in other contexts.

It is important to bear in mind the revolutionary nature of Wittgenstein's later thought. The attempt to fit his later thought into the philosophical tradition will result only in distortion and fundamental misunderstanding. There is a great temptation to take Wittgenstein as presenting new solutions and theories for traditional philosophical puzzles; but if we do this we misunderstand what he is about, and come away with a diminished view of his achievement because, viewed as traditional philosophy, what he says may seem deeply unsatisfactory and even beside the point. The later work offers ways of stopping before we begin to step on the road that leads to the traditional problems of philosophy by revealing something about how language acquires its meaning. If this is to be consistent it must avoid philosophizing as it is traditionally thought of. For this reason some have said that in his later thought Wittgenstein is not doing philosophy at all; indeed, Wittgenstein says that his philosophy is "one of the heirs of the subject which used to be called 'philosophy'". The point is that it is possible to talk *about* philosophy without *doing* philosophy in the traditional sense.

Wittgenstein is adamant that he is not putting forward philosophical theories or explanations, but rather assembling reminders as to the actual use of language. Some have argued that the assembling of reminders of actual usage of language in different contexts is without philosophical significance; but this objection assumes that there is something beyond, or other than, the employment or function or use of language in particular contexts, in virtue of which it acquires its meaning, and from which *the* true meaning could be determined independently of the use in particular contexts. If there were something beyond, and other than, the actual concrete usage of language in different contexts which determined the essential meaning of expressions, then we might ignore the usage in different contexts and concentrate on the real essential meaning of expressions. Wittgenstein argues that there is nothing hidden beyond the meaning involved in the exact description of the usage of expressions in different contexts which would give the real meaning; and there is nothing in common between the various usages in different contexts which we could pick out as the essential meaning of words and concepts.

The negative part of Wittgenstein's project is to show why none of the ways that have been suggested in which language essentially has meaning are correct. There have been various suggestions as to how language essentially has its meaning: for example, terms get their meaning ultimately by naming objects, or by ostensive definitions whereby we are shown examples of what terms mean, or by the association of terms with mental images or ideas. When a feature or set of features is suggested as necessary and sufficient for meaning, Wittgenstein cites instances where these features are not present, and yet we still regard the language as meaningful. The positive part of the project is to describe the different ways that expressions are used in different contexts, which is the same as showing the various meanings that expressions can have.

The *Philosophical investigations* aims to make explicit that philosophy involves using language in ways that are *different* from their normal employment, also that philosophy does not pick out some essential core meaning of expressions. One aim of the later philosophy is not primarily to correct philosophical language, but to show that philosophical usage is radically different from ordinary usage; in that case, what we mean by certain expressions in a philosophical context will be different from what we mean in an ordinary context; and there is no external standard to which we could refer to establish which of the various meanings in different contexts is the only correct one. The generation of many of the problems of traditional philosophy – for example, scepticism – relies on supposing that the meanings given to the concepts studied are the correct ones, or at least that talk of *the* single correct meaning makes sense.

In traditional philosophy there is the semblance of an attempt to solve problems and really get to the bottom of matters, whereas really there are, in different areas, always frameworks and presuppositions which keep the problems alive – indeed keep them as problems – while in other contexts outside philosophy such "problems" do not even arise.

One of the chief characteristics of traditional philosophy is to seek ultimate explanations and justifications beyond the point at which they can make sense and even arise. That this is not manifestly impossible is only because we do not really take such a step, but bracket off some area in virtue of which the philosophical problems can be stated and solutions offered. For example, in applying universal Cartesian doubt to discover the indubitable foundations of knowledge, we omit to doubt the meaning of the words used to express the universal doubt, without which questions of doubt and knowledge would not arise at all. The supposedly universal doubt of the Cartesian sceptic inconsistently assumes that we know the meaning of the language in which the processes and arguments leading to such doubt are expressed. The later philosophy of Wittgenstein makes these implicit assumptions explicit, and thereby demonstrates that our seeking after ultimate explanations and justifications outside contexts within which they can arise is impossible or nonsensical. There cannot be such explanations for they would either involve something further that would itself require explanation – although this may not be immediately apparent – or step into an area where the request for explanation does not arise. One of Wittgenstein's slogans is that "Explanations come to an end". The import of this is that there comes a point at which our attempts to explain and justify have to stop, and beyond which the question of justification can no longer arise. But we do not stop at something that finally explains all the rest, we stop at something which cannot be given further explanation: at the perimeter of the framework within which asking the questions in that context makes sense. Explanation has to stop and we have to be content with a *description*.

This does not mean that in the special sciences, such as physics, we cannot explain one thing in terms of another, and push this procedure to profound depths. Philosophy asks certain kinds of questions that sometimes look like questions in the special sciences, but they are not; they often seek to question the very framework in which providing explanations and solving problems could make sense, and so they go beyond the point where explanations can be given or are required. If we do not notice differences in the meaning of the expressions we use in different contexts, we will be tempted to think that we are doing exactly the same kind of thing in each context. If we are explaining X, we can do so in terms of a, b, c; and we can perhaps further explain a, b, c. In explaining anything we are involved in a web of interrelated elements which are used in explaining one another; but it makes no sense to try to step outside everything, and ask for an explanation of the whole thing. Explanations of why something is so require contexts within which asking for explanations makes sense. Eventually we will reach a point at which to ask for explanations in a given context has to end: further explanations will fail either because they are question-begging, or because they involve something further that itself requires explanation. There is in any case no framework of explanation accounting for or justifying the practices of all other explanatory frameworks, although the frameworks may be logically interconnected. And even if there were such a super-framework, it would also require explanation. This important idea applies to meaning: expressions have meaning in their use in various contexts, and it makes no sense to ask what is their real meaning stripped of what would be said to justify their meaning as employed in various actual contexts.

Moreover, what philosophy is concerned with is seeking logical *justifications* or *reasons*, not, as in the sciences, causal explanations. It is of course possible to give logical justifications or reasons for what we do or say in various contexts; but traditional philosophy often seeks justifications or reasons in ways and in contexts, or outside all contexts, where we can no longer provide them. It seeks to answer the question of what rational justification we have to go on, as we have been doing in certain contexts beyond the point at which such justifications need or can be given; and the attempt to do so merely generates philosophical conundrums which further entangle the philosopher in fruitless theorizing. For example, Wittgenstein himself in the *Tractatus* sought to give an ultimate reason for the meaningfulness of language in terms of its consisting of names of simple or unanalyzable objects.

That there are sometimes *causal* explanations for why we do what we do is not in dispute; but to give a causal explanation is not to say we are *justified* in doing what we do. I might, for example, believe it to be true that $1,574 \times 6,266 = 9,862,684$, and give a causal explanation for having this belief as resulting from a sharp blow on the head received while a child; but that would not give any justification for the belief that the multiplication is true or should be thought so by others. What we require is a justification for the belief that the multiplication is true in terms of some appropriate evidence from which the conclusion can be seen to follow logically or by which it is supported. For example: this was the result I got with my pocket calculator. We might go on further and ask why we believe the calculator reliable. Again we are asking for the evidence we have used, from which the conclusion follows, to be displayed; we are not asking for a causal explanation. An appropriate answer to the question would not be in terms of my brain being in a particular causally produced state, or my being brought up in a particular way, for that would not give us a reason for believing the calculator reliable. I may judge that p is true; a causal explanation for my making that judgement could be given; but that would not answer the question of whether I had a valid reason for thinking p true; for that I would have to present evidence for judging p true; and that would involve some kind of appropriate *logical* connection between the evidence or reasons and the conclusion that p. To suggest otherwise is to confuse causal power and logical validity. I can be causally determined to arrive at a conclusion without the conclusion rationally following from any available evidence; conversely a conclusion may rationally follow from the available evidence without any causal process guaranteeing that I draw it. An example of the latter case is someone saying, "But after all this evidence, you can't say that", followed by the quip "I just did".

Wittgenstein's point is that the giving of reasons or justifications must come to an end, and what we can use as evidence or justification must be available to us to use as evidence or justification, and not be something hidden. But such justification must reach something that does not require further logical justification, and beyond which the seeking of logical justification becomes senseless. At this point we hit bedrock. This line of thought applies, for example, to the justification of belief. In the same way an explanation or an account of the meaningfulness of language must come to an end with something available to us which can be given in explanation, with reference to which we can justify or give reasons for the meanings that words and other linguistic expressions have, but beyond which no further justification is required or can be given.

This attempt to stand completely outside the totality of the patchwork of contexts – it might be pictured as a collection of many overlapping circles – in which justification can be given, and to give reasons for everything at once, is prevalent in the various areas of philosophy. We find it in the area of giving an account of how language gets its meaning and also in the area of what we can be said to know. We are seeking to answer the question of what rational justification we have for saying that certain words have a meaning, and what right we have to say that we know certain things. What justification have we for saying that certain words have, or have not, a meaning? What justification have we for saying we understand the meaning of a word? What justification have we for saying that we do, or do not, know some particular truths? Again, that there are necessary causal conditions for our making claims (such as having brains, having been born, etc.) is not in dispute; nor does what Wittgenstein says rival such causal accounts. What is at issue is whether we can give logical justifications for such claims; we require evidence that in some way supports the truth of the conclusions, and not just a causal explanation for why we in fact make those claims.

Wittgenstein replaces essentialism about meaning with what might be termed linguistic instrumentalism: an account of the phenomenon of language eventually ends at a description of what we do, and the meanings of the concepts language involves can be explained or justified as being the way they are only from within language, not by something else that lies beyond or behind language. Wittgenstein says in the *Philosophical investigations* "Think of the tools in a tool-box . . .

The functions of words are as diverse as the functions of these objects." Wittgenstein shows how the attempt to justify the meaningfulness of language as a whole fails, because the use of factors outside language always presupposes some linguistic competence, and so does not succeed in grounding the *whole* of language. He also shows that such external ultimate justification is not in any case required for meaningful language.

The negative side of Wittgenstein's work attacks various attempts to justify the meaning that expressions have in virtue of something extralinguistic that purports to give a complete explanation or justification for language having the meanings and concepts it has. If the view opposed by Wittgenstein were established, we might discover the real meaning of expressions beyond their meanings acquired and justifiable within certain contexts. The accounts of language that Wittgenstein opposes involve giving a single unified account of how all language ultimately gets its meaning; it is supposed that all the various manifestations of language have an essence, or single logic, in virtue of which its expressions ultimately have or acquire their true meaning. Three cases Wittgenstein considers are as follows:

(a) the theory of the *Tractatus*
(b) ostensive definition
(c) mentalism.

(a) The heart of the *Tractatus* theory is that whatever the surface appearance of language, on analysis it consists entirely of names which mean the objects for which they stand. There is an obvious problem with the *Tractatus* view that the ultimate constituents of language are names, and the meaning of a name is its object: the problem is that Wittgenstein was unable to give any examples of simple names or objects of the required indestructible unchanging simplicity which would guarantee the meaningfulness of language. If the objects named are complex and hence capable of destruction, and the object is the meaning, then the meaningfulness of language cannot be assured. Moreover, if the objects are hidden and not available readily for us to use in any justification of what we mean, it is difficult to understand in what sense they can be said to explain the meaning of words or be used to justify our understanding of their meaning. Also, naming is merely one of a multitude of functions language can perform and is an activity that presupposes an understanding of what naming something is.

(b) If we are asked to give the meaning of a word we might give some kind of account of its meaning in words in a verbal definition; but this would be of any use only if we understood the meaning of the words used in the given definition. Some have thought that if this process is not to go on indefinitely and language is to talk about the world, not just words, we must step outside language. This is said to be done through ostensive definitions – that is, by showing. If we take the word "dog" for example, we might learn the meaning of the word through someone uttering the word "dog", in the presence of a dog, and perhaps pointing at the dog. Such understanding of the meaning of words could then be used to build up verbal definitions within language. Wittgenstein does not question that such ostensive teaching of language takes place. What he objects to is the idea that such teaching is sufficient to underpin our understanding of language as a whole. Ostension is systematically ambiguous, so we must understand the significance of, or what is intended in, the situation in which ostensive definitions are given, and such understanding is not accounted for by ostension itself. For us to understand that we are meant to be learning a general name like "pencil", and not a particular name like "Fred", already presupposes some linguistic understanding – in this case the distinction between particular and general names – not accounted for by mere ostension. For this reason ostensive definitions cannot be the ultimate explanation for how language gets its meaning, for ostensive definitions leave some linguistic understanding unexplained; they do not explain how we get from no language at all to some language. Children and foreigners learn some aspects of language by ostensive definition; but such ostension works only because they already have some linguistic understanding.

(c) Another view is that to understand the meaning of a word involves associating it with a mental image or idea in the mind. Insuperable difficulties arise for this view even if we set aside the obvious objection that what an image of, say, justice would consist in is entirely baffling. Suppose we try to use this theory to explain our understanding of the word "red". I come across an object and I am deciding whether or not to call it red. The mentalistic account suggests that what happens is that I call up the image I have of red, compare it with the colour of the object, and decide whether they are the same; if they are the same the object is correctly called red. But how is this to be done? It is no use my merely *having* the image of red; I must be able to call up the correct image. However, being able to call up the right image involves recognizing which image, among others, is that of red; but such recognition was exactly what we set out to explain. My ability to call up the right image is not explained by my comparing it with another image, because how am I to call up the correct image in that case? Wittgenstein is not denying that we do sometimes use images, and that we may use them to identify things; what he denies is that the reference to images can be the foundation for our understanding of all language, for it already presupposes the kind of understanding it was meant to explain.

Wittgenstein generally objects to the idea that understanding the meaning of a word is constituted by being in some kind of special mental state. The meaning of words does not rest on our mentally intending a meaning. If we say, "Alan understands what is meant by a crescendo", we are not supposing that there must be thoughts running through Alan's head which constitute this understanding. If this were the case we would say that he ceases to understand what it means when he is asleep or distracted by some other thought. Mental processes are neither necessary nor sufficient for many other cases, such as "knowing", "remembering", "believing".

Wittgenstein's aim is not to deny that many of the ways which are mistakenly proposed as accounting for or explaining the meaning of language as a whole could not be used to account for or explain what we mean within parts of language; what he denies is that there is a single unified account or explanation in terms of something external to language as a whole. This means that the answer to the question "What justifies the meanings and concepts we have in our language as a whole?" is "Nothing does". There is no standard external to the *agreed use* of an expression in the language by which our usage can be further justified. The question cannot be answered any other way because any justification would already involve understanding and taking for granted that we did understand the meaning of certain expressions and concepts. So there is nothing outside all language which gives such a total or complete justification for language being as it is.

This complements Wittgenstein's denial that he is presenting overarching justificatory philosophical theories about language or indeed about any other philosophical matter. By posting reminders of the diversity and multiplicity of the uses of language, he hopes to show that such overarching theories cannot be produced.

It may be thought that if we correctly call a collection of things or activities by the same name, then they *must* have something in common in virtue of which they are things or activities of that kind; they must have a set of features which they, and only they, share; they must have an essence. Such an essence could be characterized by a definition which gives necessary and sufficient conditions or features for being a particular kind of thing: necessary because anything of that kind must have those features; sufficient because anything with those features will be of that kind – so something is an X if and only if it satisfies a certain set of conditions or has a certain set of features. Wittgenstein thinks this is a mistake. If we try to define a concept in this way, we will be unable to give conditions that are at once both necessary and sufficient. Wittgenstein asks us to consider games, and points to the difficulty involved in giving the essence of games: something that they all have in common in virtue of which they are all games. There is no such essence. There are of course resemblances; but there is no single defining set of features that runs through them all. We characterize them all as games in virtue of a series of various overlapping resemblances; these Wittgenstein calls "family resemblances" and likens to the way that we notice various resemblances between members of the same family.

In the case of language, what we have is not a common defining essence across all uses of language in virtue of which we count something as language, but "a complicated network of similarities overlapping and criss-crossing" between various linguistic activities. There is also a network of logical relations between different linguistic activities which enables us to speak of the whole system of *language* as such.

In the *Tractatus* there was a single essential nature to language and a single boundary between sense and nonsense; in the later philosophy of the *Philosophical investigations* we have a patchwork of related languages with internal boundaries – and although they may change, the ignoring of them produces confusion – the sum total of which constitutes our whole language. Wittgenstein refers to the variety of kinds of ways that language can be used and the functions it can have as "language-games". Outside the boundary of *all* language-games collectively, we do not have language at all, but nonsense.

Wittgenstein is not denying that we can lay down special technical definitions, in science, say; but this is not the way words acquire meaning or their meaning is understood in ordinary language. Once we begin to use a word or concept in normal contexts the definition will break down, and be outgrown, as we extend the application of the concept.

The notion of "family resemblance" applies to the characterization of language itself. Wittgenstein draws an analogy between language and games, and so refers to language-games. But the resemblance between games and language is only partial. He uses the term language-game sometimes to apply to parts of actual language, sometimes to restricted or different imaginary languages, and sometimes to the whole of human language. He is of course concerned not with any particular human language (like English or German), but rather with features of human language in general. Examples of language-games Wittgenstein gives are, among others, giving and obeying orders, describing, storytelling, joking, asking, praying, speculating. Each language-game has a "grammar" which describes, but does not explain, the possible ways that concepts can be combined within the game. We are making a grammatical, not an empirical, point, if we say, "Every measuring rod has a length"; its denial would be ungrammatical, and it is impossible in a different way from a physical impossibility.

Wittgenstein's position is that there is nothing that underlies the whole of language which explains its meaning. Language forms a patchwork of logically related activities which, unlike games, more than merely resemble one another: they are interrelated. Thus we may *order* someone to answer a *question*. The justification for saying that words have a certain meaning does not reside in some single mode of justification and cannot reside in something postulated that is hidden from view beyond language. What justifies the meaning of a word, so far as it *can* be justified, to be of any use to us in giving a justification, must not be something hidden (as the *Tractatus* suggests) but something open to view. If we are to give a logical justification for a word having a certain meaning, it must be in terms of features that are open to view and not hidden. What is hidden is not available to us, and so could not be used in giving a justification of our understanding of the meaning of linguistic expressions. What is available to view is the various ways that language is *used* or employed in different contexts. If we want to give the meaning of a word, the best we can do is to *describe the use* of the word in various contexts; eventually there is no further justification for the use we can give. Ultimately we describe, saying: *that is* how we use it.

If we were asked, "How many goals have been scored in this chess game?", the question would not pose a problem which needs to be solved on its face value, like "How many goals have been scored in this football match?"; rather, we would explain the rules of chess, and that "goal" is "ungrammatical" (in Wittgenstein's sense of the term) in this context. So it is with language-games; propositions are ungrammatical in involving words transferred from a context in which they have a use to a context where they are inappropriate, that is, they have no use. Many philosophical problems are a result of not noticing the transference of a word from one context where it has a use to another where it does not have a use. For example, we may transfer talk of "mechanism" or "object" in a physical context to the context of talk about minds. We produce nonsense by trying to transfer talk outside any and all linguistic frameworks.

It is important to note that Wittgenstein is not giving a "use theory of meaning", as if the use *explains* the meaning; the use in various contexts just *is* the meaning; meaning and use are identical. There is no single feature common to all the various uses to which language can be put; there is a multiplicity of uses. It is not as if the meaning of a word were one thing and its use another; a word gets its meaning in its being used in particular ways. Ultimately the meaning of a word does not determine its use; rather, the use of a word is its meaning; and without a certain sort of use the word does not have a meaning which could determine its use.

However, not every difference in use entails a difference in meaning, so is it right to identify meaning and use? What is involved here are matters of degree; we do not have to suppose that expressions which we regard as having the same meaning must have identical common uses which are *the* use; that would be to revert to the kind of essentialism Wittgenstein rejects; all that we need suppose is that there is sufficient overlap in use for us to say the meaning is the same. Analogously it is perfectly correct to say a mallet and a plane are both carpentry tools because of what is done with them and the contexts in which they are used, even though their use is not identical. If the uses to which a word was put failed to overlap at all, we would say that we have a word with different meanings, for giving a description of how we would use the word in various situations is what the meaning of the word amounts to. If words failed to overlap by the criteria (whatever they turn out to be) which determine their correct application – that is, uses that are recognized by others – we would then be likely to say that the words each had a different meaning. That a word has a meaning at all depends on there being *some* agreement in use. But the point at which a change of meaning occurs is not necessarily clear-cut. Here Wittgenstein gives up the *Tractatus* requirement of definiteness of meaning.

A good analogy is with money; something becomes money through the way it is used. That something is money consists in what people are willing to do with it, such as take it in exchange for goods and services as virtually everyone else is willing to do. It was soon found to be unnecessary for coins to be made from gold or even to be backed by gold. It is not something intrinsic to the coin which constitutes its being money. If this is doubted we have only to think of the way cigarettes became money during the Second World War and at other times; cigarettes being money was a matter of the way they were used.

To understand the meaning of a word is to be able to participate in using the word appropriately in a language-game. To use a word or other linguistic expression in a language-game is in turn to be involved with using language in a certain "form of life" – certain natural activities and behaviour which arise from human needs, interests and purposes. Language is autonomous in the sense that its justification must lie within it, but is nevertheless evolved from human practices and human needs. At the basic level it is agreement in these practices – the agreement as to how to go on – that makes meaningful language possible but does *not* justify that meaning. That is, the form of life is not what justifies our saying that certain words have such-and-such a meaning; but that we naturally go on in certain ways is what makes agreement in use – hence meaning – possible. The form of life is what we have to "accept as given"; it involves the most basic features of the human condition which stem from the fundamental facts about human nature and the world, "the common behaviour of mankind". That certain fundamental things are unavoid-able features of human beings, and that we share needs and interests, is what enables agreement as to ways of going on in certain situations to get going in the first place. These common needs and interests and our agreement to go on naturally in certain ways are what makes agreement as to use possible. That these ways of going on are often unavoidable means that they are not open to choice; they are not arbitrary; they are simply what we do in a given situation, and lie beyond being justified or unjustified. It is possible that we could go on differently, but in fact in certain ways we do not: we agree.

We can no more ask for rational justification for the givens of human life, or say that they are unjustified, than we can ask for a rational justification – rather than a causal explanation – for a tree falling on us. Rational justification, once we have exhausted all the ways in which we can justify our doing something in such-and-such a way, must come to an end in a description. To lay to rest our philosophical search for ultimate foundations, we have to come to see that certain of our human activities – for example, deriving one proposition from another – are ultimately groundless and not justified, but *also* that they are not the kinds of activities that can be further grounded or justified; therefore their lacking such a grounding is not a deficiency in those activities. Such ways of going on are neither justified nor unjustified, rather they are fundamental facts about human nature and the way humans agree to go on in various situations. That there is no rational justification does not show that what we do is irrational or confused, it could be simply non-rational: what we do. In this it is possible to see some similarity between Hume and Wittgenstein: they agree that rational justification has its limits, and what we are left with are the most basic things that human beings cannot help doing; and it now makes no sense to ask for rational justification for matters that are not a product of reasoning at all.

The possession of our most basic concepts – such as inferring, recognizing, assent and dissent – is not something that can be further explained or justified, because any explanation would *presuppose* those concepts or some others. There is a great diversity of practices or language-games and each involves basic concepts which it is senseless to question; it is senseless because without taking those concepts for granted as "given", the kinds of justifications that take place within the language-games could not even arise. Having these concepts means we can take part in the language-game or practice; but if one does not have them, then the possession of those concepts cannot be further justified by anything else within the language-game, for that would already involve accepting the basic concepts the language-game involves. If the use of expressions within two practices is sufficiently different – that is, there is little or no overlap in use – then it is not that we disagree in our judgements involving these concepts; rather, we are simply saying something else. Wittgenstein says the practice, or language-game, and the form of life of which it is a part, is given. It is not given in the sense of being a self-evident logical foundation; it is given in the sense that there is no further justification for the whole practice, for justification only makes sense within practices. The form of life which involves a language-game is neither reasonable nor unreasonable. That is not to say that up to a point the normally accepted bedrock of a language-game cannot alter, but there are limits, for beyond a certain point we will say not that we are dealing with a different linguistic practice, but rather that we are not dealing with a language at all. If we cannot identify any part of some behaviour as manifesting the possession of any of our concepts – such as assent and dissent – then we will say that what we are witnessing is not language at all.

It might be thought that the meaning of a word could be finally settled and justified as being such-and-such by citing a rule for its use. We can first note there is no such rule-book for ordinary language; but even if there were it would not help. Any rule can be interpreted in an indefinite number of ways. Suppose I am asked why I interpret a rule in a certain way. I could go on to cite a further rule which says how the original rule is to be interpreted. But suppose I am then asked why I interpret the further rule in a certain way. Eventually this process must come to an end and I will have exhausted all justifications; I will have to say: "This is what we do", which gives a description, not a justification. It makes perfect sense to say that one can act correctly, in accordance with a rule – follow a rule – even though one can give no justification for why one acts that way and interprets it thus. Following a rule amounts to acting in a customary way in specific cases. In the end it is not rules that determine the meaning of words but use of words that determines the rules for use that we might formulate; the rules for use do not exist prior to what we do with the words in the language. That a certain rule can be "interpreted" – substituting one rule for another – in a certain way eventually depends upon there being an agreed natural particular way of going on, perhaps after some kind of natural response to training. Some examples will illustrate these points.

(i)   We might give a justification for saying X is red by comparing X against a colour-chart. How would we know that what we had identified on the chart as red was red? We might say it was because "red" was printed there. But how would we know we were using the chart correctly? A mental colour-chart would have the same problem. We have reached bedrock; we have the capacity to identify the colours of things thanks to the way we naturally respond to certain training. No rational justification can be given as a whole for our adopting classification by colour-concepts.

(ii) Suppose we asked someone to accept the simple logical theorem *modus ponens*: "If *p* then *q*, *p*, therefore *q*". Here "*p*" and "*q*" stand for any propositions you like. What further justification could be given of this? If a person cannot see this, then it is not clear how we could go on to offer further justification as to why, given "(if *p* then *q*) and *p*", he should logically infer "*q*". The person has parted company with us even before the game of logic begins; he is playing a different game. Even if something further could be offered in justification, we would have to come to an end in a natural way of going on. For a rule does not say of itself how it must be interpreted.

(iii) Wittgenstein gives the following example. Suppose we are given the following table or schema where the letters can be used as orders as to how we should move about:

$a \rightarrow$
$b \leftarrow$
$c \uparrow$
$d \downarrow$

We are then given an order, *aacaddd*. We look up in the table the arrow corresponding to each letter; we get:

Suppose someone read not straight across the table but diagonally instead? Thus he or she would proceed to read the table according to the following schema:

And there are many other possible schemata. What could we do? Construct another table on how to read the first? But this cannot go on indefinitely; eventually one simply has to gather or catch on to what is wanted, and no further justification can be given, for *any* rule can be variously interpreted.

We cannot be compelled to do logic and use language in a certain way unless we already take for granted a framework within which disputes about the correct way of going on can arise. The meaning of the rules is generated by the way they are used; we then impose the

rules upon ourselves. We eventually exhaust reasons, and we have
then no reason to follow a rule as we do; that there is such a thing as
"following a rule" depends on there being some customary ways of
going on, for whatever re-expression we give we eventually have to
stop at some agreed way of acting which cannot be further re-
expressed.

What we count as "doing the same thing" each time we apply a
rule will itself be relative to a framework. Our being inside practices
and frameworks takes for granted or depends on human beings acting
in natural sorts of ways in certain circumstances – human beings
having certain natural ways of responding or reacting; this, logically
speaking, gets the practice or framework off the ground. *Within* these
practices disputes can arise. No rule can *force* you to go on in a certain
way; no logical deduction means you *must* accept the conclusion if
you accept the premises. Lewis Carroll in his essay "What the Tortoise
said to Achilles" anticipated this point by showing that the attempt to
justify all rules of inference, or the process of inference itself, leads to
an infinite regress because each attempt will involve a further
inference.

This does not mean that necessary truths such as those of mathematics and logic depend for their truth on facts about human nature;
what depends on facts about human nature is our possessing and
understanding the concepts required for disputes over whether
something is true or proved within mathematics and logic to arise at
all.

To show whether I understand a word I can give a definition of it;
but such definitions cannot go on for ever. Eventually I will have to
show that I can use words appropriately in given contexts or
practices. The meaning of words and other linguistic expressions is a
matter of public or communal agreement to use those words and
linguistic expressions in particular ways – ways that can, with care,
be described. I can be said to understand the meaning of a word if I
can use it in agreed ways. If I start to use it in some other way that
differs sufficiently from the agreed usage, it will be doubted that I
understand the meaning of the expression at all.

It might be thought that talk of communal agreement involves a
kind of relativism about truth, as if it were the case that if enough
people agree that something is true, it is true. But this is a mistake.
Wittgenstein is concerned with a more fundamental kind of agreement: without our participation in a framework, so that we understand the meaning of its basic concepts, the question of truth or falsity
has not yet arisen. But there is no way one can make someone
participate in the framework in the first place. We cannot force
someone to answer the question "Is this checkmate?" if they cannot,
or will not, play chess. The agreement which is relevant here is one
of meaning, not of truth. If an agreement or disagreement over the

truth or falsity of a statement is possible, then we must mean the same by the statement. That we mean the same will be determined by agreement in use. Take the statement that "*x* is *F*"; that two people can be in disagreement as to the truth of this statement presupposes that the meaning of "*F*" for the two people is the same; whether it is the same is established by how the two people use or apply "*F*" in particular contexts. Disagreement as to whether "*x* is red" is true or false presupposes an agreement over what we mean by "red".

This brings us to Wittgenstein's "private language argument". Wittgenstein argues that language is communal in nature: it depends upon agreement in use within a community. If it were possible to construct a logically private language then this would refute Wittgenstein's view. We must note that such a case must be *logically* private, so that it is impossible for anyone else to understand the language; that is, it must be untranslatable into any other language. Such a case is where we supposedly give names to our private sensations by a sort of "inner" ostensive definition; by this is meant the association of a word with a private mental image which is then the meaning of the word. This is a special case of the meaning of a word being the object for which it stands. Suppose that I keep a diary, and write down "*S*", intending it to stand for a certain sensation; I then aim to write down "*S*" on subsequent occasions when the sensation occurs. How can I tell that I am applying "*S*" correctly on subsequent occasions? One suggestion might be that I could call up from memory the original sensation and check that in applying "*S*" to my current sensation I am applying it correctly. But how do I know that I have called up the right sensation from my memory? Do I go on to check that memory against a further memory? But in that case I have got no further, as the same problem would arise. Without there being some kind of independent objective check as to whether I am applying "*S*" correctly, we cannot speak of being correct or incorrect at all, since there is no distinction between merely seeming right and being right. No consequences follow from my applying the word in one way rather than another; it cannot clash with any established use; and so it is not proper to speak of "*S*" being correctly or incorrectly used. Hence, "*S*" has not been given a meaning; a logically private naming of sensations is not possible. This may imply that no logically private language is possible.

The philosophical import of Wittgenstein's views derives to a large extent from two important connected ideas:

(I)   That there is no essence to language: there is no single way that words and other linguistic expressions acquire their meaning by reference to something external to language.

(II) That the meaning of a word and other linguistic expressions varies with their use in particular contexts or practices.

These two points together have the effect of undermining much of traditional philosophy and its problems. They attack the idea that philosophy can establish and study the true or real meaning of certain words which express concepts. There is no independent absolute standard from which the question of *the* correct meaning could be judged or arise, since words and other linguistic expressions have meaning only in their use in actual or concrete human practices. If we attempt to step outside all cases where an expression is actually used, then it ceases to have any meaning, and the question of a meaning being correct does not arise.

Traditional philosophy tends to claim that it is examining the real meaning of "knowledge", and other concepts, as opposed to their meaning in ordinary usage. But there are no grounds for claiming that the philosophical meaning is superior. The sceptic claims that we do not have knowledge in situations where it is perfectly obvious that according to ordinary usage we do have knowledge – but it is in ordinary usage that the meaning of "knowledge" is established; therefore the sceptic's meaning of "knowledge" is different.

Wittgenstein is not saying that the ordinary usage of these concepts is unalterable. The point is that there is no way of establishing that a term has only one correct meaning, disregarding the meaning arising from the ordinary employment of the term. If a term ceases to be applied in any of the cases where it normally has a use, then we will say that it has at least altered its meaning. To argue that this fact is philosophically unimportant relies on the idea that there is some single correct meaning of words which is their true meaning established in all cases by something other than their actual function or use. Philosophers use words in ways different from their ordinary use. Wittgenstein posts reminders that words do have other than philosophical uses and that if philosophers uses the words in ways they would never be used in ordinary contexts, then he must mean something different by them. Concepts have different meanings in different contexts, and no one context can claim to be superior to the rest in giving the single correct meaning of the concept. The denial of this supposes that there is more to the meaning of a word or linguistic expression than the description of how it is used, functions, or is applied in a given context; it supposes that somehow, behind the description of how an expression is used, there is something else by which we can identify its real or essential meaning. The view that posits something else giving the real meaning of a term beyond the meaning resulting from a term's actual agreed use is the view that Wittgenstein rejects.

What becomes of the traditional problems of philosophy? Why does Wittgenstein have so little to offer in the way of traditional philosophical solutions? The answer to this is that Wittgenstein's account of language means that many of the traditional problems of philosophy disappear as problems. The problems we are referring to are such as "our knowledge of the existence of the external world", "our knowledge of the existence of other minds", "that we cannot really know that someone is in pain, but can only infer it from their behaviour"; and such problems involve concepts such as "knowledge", "being", "object", "I", "proposition", "name". Given that traditional philosophy cannot claim the right to say it has identified the true or real meaning of these terms, Wittgenstein makes explicit the fact that they have a use in circumstances in which there are no problems of the sort characterized by philosophy. There is a perfectly good sense in which we do know whether other people have minds, and whether they are in pain, and we can describe the circumstances in which we employ the words involved. If it is said that we do not really *know* in such cases, then we must say, precisely because there is an attempt to exclude the use of "know" in circumstances central to establishing its use and hence its meaning, that "know" must be being used in a different sense from normal. The meaning of a concept such as "know" is its use in appropriate circumstances; therefore it makes perfect sense to say that we know in those circumstances. There is nowhere beyond a description of actual agreed use from where we could say that it is wrong to speak of knowledge in those cases. If we do not mean by "knowledge" what we mean in cases where "knowledge" is most normally used, then what do we mean by it?

What the sceptical position is supposed to show is that correctly establishing the satisfaction of the criteria of application of a term "X" does not show that anything actually corresponds to the theoretical or ontological assumptions that are normally involved in the application of "X". The sceptic about knowledge does not doubt that we in fact clearly distinguish cases of knowing from not-knowing in the sense of consistently applying "know" in certain circumstances and withholding it in others; but this fails to show that the cases where we are linguistically correct (by the normal criteria of our language) in applying "know" can be justified as cases of knowing. The reply to this is that if the cases in which we normally use the word "know" are not what we *mean* by "know", then it is not clear what the sceptic can mean when he says that in ordinary cases we do not "know". The sceptic must mean we do not "<know>" (giving some special sense to this word), which is to construe "know" independent of its ordinary use. But then the proposition "I know in circumstances *abc*" cannot be logically contradicted by the proposition "You do not <know> in circumstances *abc*". Otherwise it would be like saying that "I fight in circumstances *abc*" is logically contradicted by the proposition "You do not jump in circumstances *abc*". We may also take the view that if the sceptic fails to pick up on publicly established criteria for the usage of terms, then he does not mean anything at all by "<know>", since it has no use. And even if he does give a new meaning to "<know>" (perhaps by definition, or by indicating the criteria which have to be satisfied for its use), the onus is on the sceptic to show why it is that we should accept his radically different use (hence different meaning) as the one that should be satisfied before anything can count as knowing instead of the one we all normally accept.

CHAPTER TWELVE

Recent philosophy

By "recent philosophy" is here meant philosophy since roughly 1945. Some of the most significant figures of this period have already been looked at in some detail in earlier chapters. There will be no attempt here to discern the detail of trends or tendencies in recent philosophy; but it can at least be said that recent philosophy is extremely diverse in its interests and approaches. So in covering the period from 1945 to the present day in a single chapter I will cite some of the more prominent names and state briefly what they stand for. There is, no doubt, room for disagreement over which figures should be selected and which omitted; there is no question of this choice being definitive. The people mentioned are discussed in chronological order according to their date of birth, and main works by the philosophers mentioned are given in the bibliography.

Gilbert Ryle

Gilbert Ryle (1900–76) was part of a philosophical movement that held that many philosophical problems arose from a misunderstanding and misuse of ordinary language. One of the ways in which such misunderstandings arise is through what Ryle calls "category mistakes", whereby we mistakenly take a concept to refer to a certain kind of entity. Generally this leads to mistaken ontological commitments, that is, to the existence of all sorts of entities which we are misled into supposing exist owing to the way we misunderstand our language. Ryle applies this view to his theory of mind: his opposition to mind as a ghostly object-like substance. We take the term "mind" to refer to some special, albeit ethereal, kind of *thing*. But the mind is not any kind of thing; it is not a thing at all; rather, to talk of mind is to refer to certain kinds of behaviour and dispositions to behave. This has led to Ryle's views being dubbed behaviourist; but this is a label he rejects as indicating a misunderstanding of his views.

Nelson Goodman

Nelson Goodman (1906–) is a philosopher with a background in mathematical logic. His overall philosophical conclusions have led him to a form of relativism, but a relativism within "rigorous restraints". Goodman's argument is that there can be no way of choosing between different versions of the world by a direct comparison with a world that is independent of all versions – all descriptions and depictions – for there can be no such "world". What we aim at in world-views is not truth – that would tend to lead us to the construction of a trivial disconnected inventory; rather, our view or "world-making" always involves simplification and abstraction where what is important is "rightness", which seems to consist of correctness of "fit" within a world-view. The choice between different systems or world-views introduces a battery of criteria; but it is questionable whether these criteria, if they are given determinate content only within systems, can avoid irrational relativism.

W. V. O. Quine

W. V. O. Quine (1908–) is a philosopher much of whose earlier work was in the philosophy of mathematics and mathematical logic. Quine agrees with Russell that ordinary language requires "regimentation" into a clearer logical language which makes the minimum of ontological presuppositions so that we do not find ourselves committed, merely because of the grammar of the language we use, to assuming the existence of various entities. Linguistic expressions such as names, whose meanings seem to presuppose the existence of the objects to which they refer, can be replaced by descriptions whereby it becomes a matter of fact whether anything actually satisfies those descriptions. Quine has also attacked the analytic/synthetic distinction, and the view that there is an absolutely non-theoretical basic language which refers to immediate experience. Quine replaces this view with a holistic theory of meaning and knowledge: the sense and epistemological standing of a statement can only be assessed in relation to its position and entrenchment in the whole system of statements which is present knowledge, which Quine identifies as "the whole of science". Statements about the external world answer to or confront experience as a whole; we can always hang on to any statement we like as true provided we are willing, so as to maintain consistency, to make big enough changes elsewhere in the system.

J. L. Austin

J. L. Austin (1911–60), like Ryle, thought that philosophical problems tended to arise from a misunderstanding of language. Unlike Ryle he did not attempt to replace the systematic philosophies which arose from what he saw as the inattention to fine distinctions of language with a systematic philosophy derived from a view of language purged of such inattention. Austin supposed that philosophy and logic were too ready to ignore the subtle discriminations present in ordinary language. This led to the careful study of shades of meaning manifest in linguistic usage which would be not only a way of avoiding philosophical error but also of interest in its own right.

Stuart Hampshire

Stuart Hampshire (1914–) has put forward a theory of language and knowledge which is relativistic in that the system of concepts which we bring to talk about the world is not absolute or fixed, but depends upon the special interests we bring to the world as human beings and as agents in the world. We cannot detach ourselves as disembodied spectators and so achieve a disinterested view of the world. He rejects the view that the more we know about the causes of our actions the less free we will become; on the contrary, it is the essence of our existence as human beings always to be able to stand back from knowledge of our situation, no matter how detailed, and decide what we then want to do.

Donald Davidson

Donald Davidson (1917–) has been notably influential on certain parts of analytical philosophy in recent years. Much of his work has centred on the philosophy of language, and the implications of this work for various other areas of philosophy, such as the philosophy of mind. In the philosophy of mind he argues for an "anomalous monism" where, although each mental event is identical with a physical event, there are no strict law-like connections between the two different sorts of descriptions of events.

P. F. Strawson

P. F. Strawson (1919–) has been one of the chief opponents of the idea that logic somehow represents in an ideal form the structure of ordinary language. Strawson's investigations into the informal logic of ordinary language led him to what he called "descriptive metaphysics", which aims to lay bare the most basic features of the conceptual system we actually have; that is, those features of our conceptual system which are a historically unchanging core; this is to be contrasted with "revisionary metaphysics", which aims to change or replace the conceptual structure we actually have with a better one. It is from these considerations that Strawson's project has been seen as having an affinity with the Kantian one of making manifest the common core of conceptual presuppositions logically required for our talk about the world; however, in Strawson's case the aim is the less ambitious one of identifying the logical requirements relative to *our* conceptual system, that is, the concepts logically presupposed by our conceptual system, not by any conceptual system whatsoever. For example Strawson concludes that the possibility of a world in which we re-identify various categories of kinds of particular things depends upon the category of material bodies in space and time. Strawson has also written against the correspondence theory of truth: the function of saying "p is true" is not to describe p as having some special relation with the world, but rather to say that one confirms or endorses p.

Thomas S. Kuhn

Thomas S. Kuhn (1922–) was trained as a physicist and has been extremely influential in the philosophy of both the physical and social sciences; in this respect he is second only to Popper. His chief thesis involves suggesting that science is not the tidy rational enterprise it is sometimes represented as being by philosophers. Scientists most of the time engage in "puzzle-solving" or "normal science" within a set of currently unquestioned assumptions about the world which forms a "paradigm" or world-view. The "anomalies" presented by experience are in normal science accommodated within the assumptions defining the paradigm. But eventually the anomalies become too troublesome. The choice of paradigms, the revolutionary movement between them being called a "paradigm shift", is difficult to justify rationally because the standards of rationality, methodology, and what constitutes good evidence are determined within each paradigm. Many have seen Kuhn's view as an admission of relativism because of the rational incommensurability of paradigms, and as an undermining of the rationality of science.

Paul Feyerabend

Paul Feyerabend (1924–) is a philosopher whose training was originally in theoretical physics. His main work has been in epistemology
and the philosophy of science. The chief outcome of his work has
been to criticize the view that there is something called "the scientific
method", and thus to release human investigations into the nature of
the world from the presupposition that there is only one rational way
of going about such investigations. There is no pure way of describing
the world independently of conceptual and theoretical assumptions,
which leaves us with the possibility of there being a variety of
conceptual systems between which there can be no means of adjudi-
cation ultimately independent of all theoretical assumptions. This has
led to a view of Feyerabend as a methodological anarchist. But his
position is best described as that of a democratic relativist which, he
suggests, frees inquiry from the shackles of supposing there is only
one correct method of understanding the world.

Michael Dummett

The two most important aspects of Michael Dummett's (1925–) philosophical doctrines are his search for a systematic theory of meaning
and his anti-realism. The knowledge we display of the meaning of
expressions is based on the implicit knowledge of linguistic principles,
and it is the function of a theory of meaning to bring these to light.
The proposition central to the notion of anti- realism is the assertion
that there are certain classes of statements which are not determinately true or false independently of our means of knowing which they
are. This amounts to a denial of the principle of bivalence which says
that any statement must be determinately either true or false
regardless of whether we can know which it is.

Richard Rorty

Much of Richard Rorty's (1931–) recent work has been concerned
with examining the nature of the philosophical enterprise itself. This
has led him to question the presuppositions that lie behind much of
what he identifies as the philosophical tradition. The philosophical
approaches that are chiefly criticized are analytical philosophy and
continental phenomenology; philosophy in these traditions he sees as
a kind of dead end where there is no possible way of adjudicating
between different views. In particular Rorty suggests that the central
error of the philosophical tradition of which he is critical is the

attempt to hold a mirror up to nature in which is reflected the nature of the world in a way that is ahistorical, spectatorial, and independent of any perspective. But we cannot escape our historical and human perspective. Rorty advocates that we replace traditional "systematic" philosophy, which aims at timelessly true foundations (represented by such figures as Descartes, Kant, Husserl, Russell), with "edifying" philosophy (represented by such figures as Heidegger, Wittgenstein, Dewey, Sartre), whose central job is the freeing and facilitation of dialogue between different areas of human inquiry in the historical context in which they find themselves.

John R. Searle

Much of the work of John R. Searle (1932–) has been in the philosophy of language, but he has also done important work in the philosophy of mind and the philosophical implications of artificial intelligence. Central to Searle's work in the philosophy of language is that of "speech acts" (which partly develops the pioneering work of Austin), which are distinguished by their point or purpose; expressions with similar content fall into different types of speech act depending on what is done with them: whether they are orders, promises, pleas, descriptions, predictions and the like. Searle aims to produce a taxonomy of speech acts.

Saul Kripke

Saul Kripke (1940–) is a philosopher trained in mathematical logic; his work in modal logic has led him to revive a form of essentialism and reintroduce the concept of natural or metaphysical necessity. Necessity is said, especially by empiricists and logical positivists, only to hold among the propositions of mathematics, logic and semantic truths (such as "All bachelors are unmarried"), not among objects or events in the world, and all propositions concerning the actual nature of the world are contingent. Kripke thinks mistaken the view of some philosophers that the *a priori* and the *a posteriori*, and the necessary and contingent, are, respectively, coextensive. The distinctions belong to different philosophical domains: knowledge and metaphysics. There are, Kripke argues, necessarily true statements which cannot be known to be true merely through understanding the meanings of the terms involved, but can be known only through experience *a posteriori*. In particular there are expressions that Kripke calls "rigid designators", which name the same individual in every possible world in which that individual exists, and which form identity statements, such as "The Morning Star is identical with the Evening Star", which are necessary but knowable only *a posteriori*. He reintroduces essentialism: the notion that particular objects and kinds of objects have necessary properties: that is, those properties something must have to be just *that* object or *that sort* of object.

BIBLIOGRAPHY

The aim of this bibliography is to give guidance as to where to go for further reading on matters dealt with in this book. The bibliography, although large, does not pretend to be exhaustive; indeed its being exhaustive would defeat the object of selecting what seems most helpful. I have included only books and not articles that appear in philosophy journals. It should also be pointed out that what is listed are only works in English. Often the publication date given is the date of the individual copy I have consulted. Where necessary the original publication date is also given in brackets immediately after the title.

General works

This section of the bibliography lists some general works on philosophy and its history. Sometimes the items mentioned are reference works that are not meant to be read right through.

Of general works on the history of philosophy, Frederick Copleston, *A history of western philosophy*, 9 vols. (New York: Image Books, 1964), is long but very useful. Another valuable work on the history of philosophy, which is accessibly in one volume, is D. J. O'Connor (ed.), *A critical history of Western philosophy* (London: Macmillan, 1985, first pub. 1964). Works that jointly cover the history of philosophy from about 1840 to recent times are John Passmore, *A hundred years of philosophy*, 2nd edition (London: Penguin, 1966), and John Passmore, *Recent philosophy* (London: Duckworth, 1985).

The following are general introductions to philosophy. The most elementary introduction is Martin Hollis, *Invitation to philosophy* (Oxford: Blackwell, 1985). Another accessible introduction is Robert C. Solomon, *The big questions: a short introduction to philosophy*, 3rd edition (New York: Harcourt Brace Jovanovich, 1990). Brief and good is John Cottingham, *Rationalism* (London: Paladin Books, 1984), which is more general than its title might suggest. A fine introduction with plenty of detailed philosophical discussion is James W. Cornman, Keith Lehrer, and George S. Pappas, *Philosophical problems and arguments: an introduction*, 3rd edition (Indianapolis: Hackett Publishing Company, 1987). There is also A. C. Ewing, *The fundamental questions of philosophy* (London: Routledge, 1951); this book has the merit of being beautifully written. A classic work is Bertrand Russell, *The problems of philosophy* (Oxford: Oxford University Press, 1967, first pub. 1912), and a book written in the same philosophical spirit is A. J. Ayer, *The central questions of philosophy* (London: Penguin, 1976). A longer general work is

Anthony Quinton, *The nature of things* (London: Routledge, 1973).

An excellent introduction to modern philosophy, which deals with problems rather than philosophers, is Anthony O'Hear, *What philosophy is* (London: Penguin, 1985). Two other books complement this: Ted Honderich and Myles Burnyeat (eds), *Philosophy as it is* (London: Penguin, 1979) which contains a collection of important recent articles by leading modern philosophers, and Ted Honderich and Myles Burnyeat (eds), *Philosophy through its past* (London: Penguin, 1984), which contains important articles on past philosophers.

A useful thing to have by one in reading any work of philosophy, and by no means to be despised, is a good dictionary of philosophy, such as Antony Flew (ed.), *A dictionary of philosophy* (London: Pan, 1984). A helpful reference source on philosophy is J. O. Urmson and Jonathan Rée (eds), *A concise encyclopedia of Western philosophy and philosophers*, new edition (London: Unwin Hyman, 1991). A collection of essays on the central concerns of philosophy is G. H. Parkinson (ed.), *An encyclopedia of philosophy* (London: Routledge, 1989). A very valuable and rich reference source of massive size is Paul Edwards (ed.), *The encyclopedia of philosophy*, 8 vols. (London: Collier Macmillan, 1967).

Logic and philosophical logic have always been important in philosophy, if sometimes only implicitly, but they have become increasingly important in a more explicit way since the beginning of the twentieth century. Good logic books are Irving M. Copi and Carl Cohen, *Introduction to logic*, 8th edition (London: Macmillan, 1990); E. J. Lemmon, *Beginning logic* (Surrey: Thomas Nelson, 1971); Howard Kahane, *Logic and philosophy* (Belmont, California: Wadsworth, 1990); W. Hodges, *Logic* (London: Penguin, 1977). On philosophical logic there are Susan Haack, *Philosophy of logic* (Cambridge: Cambridge University Press, 1978) and A. C. Grayling, *An introduction to philosophical logic* (London: Duckworth, 1990).

Presocratic Greek philosophy

There is no substitute in the study of Presocratic philosophers for actually examining the surviving fragments of their thoughts and comments by those who had access to the original works. The most convenient collection of translated Greek texts is Jonathan Barnes (tr. and ed.), *Early Greek philosophy* (London: Penguin, 1987). Another collection, including both the original Greek and the translation with some valuable commentary, is G. S. Kirk, J. E. Raven and M. Schofield (eds), *The Presocratic philosophers*, 2nd edition (Cambridge: Cambridge University Press, 1983).

The most recommendable single-volume work on Presocratic philosophy in general is Edward Hussey, *The Presocratics* (London: Duckworth, 1972). W. K. C. Guthrie, *A history of Greek philosophy*, vols I, II, III (Cambridge: Cambridge University Press, 1962, 1965, 1969) is humane, scholarly, and full of good sense, as well as being a pleasure to read; it is a work that aids greatly a deeper understanding of the Presocratics. A classic work, in places rather dated, is J. Burnet, *Early Greek philosophy*, 4th edition (London: A. & C. Black, 1930).

There are useful collections of essays in David J. Furley and R. E. Allen (eds), *Studies in Presocratic philosophy* (London: Routledge, 1970, 1975) and A. P. D. Mourelatos (ed.), *The Presocratics* (New York: Anchor Books, 1974).

A comprehensive analysis is Jonathan Barnes, *The Presocratic philosophers*, vols. I, II, 2nd edition (London: Routledge, 1982). This work critically applies the techniques of modern philosophy to the ancient texts; it is not a flowing guide, but more of a philosophical dissection – in consequence it is frequently difficult.

The intellectual backdrop to the period preceding the Greeks of Ionia is described in a classic work: Henri Frankfort (ed.), *Before philosophy* (London: Penguin, 1949).

A poetic exposition of the scientific and moral consequences of the ancient atomist tradition, written at a time when Greece had become part of the Roman Empire, is Lucretius, *On the nature of the universe* (London: Penguin, 1976).

Greek philosophy

Plato

The works of Plato take the form almost entirely of dialogues of great literary merit, concerning a wide range of philosophical problems; most have Socrates as the central figure. The authenticity and chronology of the works are open to scholarly dispute, but some matters are more or less settled, and it helps to divide the works into three periods. The chronological order within these periods is, of course, even more difficult to determine.

Early Period: *Apology, Crito, Laches, Charmides, Euthyphro, Hippias Major* and *Minor, Protagoras, Gorgias, Ion.*

Middle Period: *Meno, Phaedo, Republic, Symposium, Phaedrus, Euthydemus, Menexenus, Cratylus.*

Late Period: *Parmenides, Theaetetus, Sophist, Politicus, Timaeus, Critias, Philebus, Laws.*

There is a shift in philosophical emphasis between the periods from ethical through metaphysical to epistemological concerns, but it is only a shift; Plato's philosophical interests are integrated.

It is usual to refer to places in the works of Plato by the title of the work followed by standard numbers that appear in the margin of most editions. These numbers, in fact, derive from the page numbers of the 1578 Stephanus edition, and the numbers are followed by a letter (a–e), which divides each page into approximately equal segments. Central to understanding Plato are the *Republic*, Book 5, 472c to Book 7, 541b, and also the *Phaedo*. Other dialogues of great importance are the *Symposium, Theaetetus, Sophist*; although any such selection must to some degree be arbitrary. Many of Plato's works appear in excellent editions as Penguin Classics. An almost complete collection is E. Hamilton and H. Cairns (eds), *Plato: collected dialogues* (Princeton: Princeton University Press, 1961). Special mention should be made of the classic F. M. Cornford, *Plato's theory of knowledge*

(London: Routledge, 1960), which is an annotated edition of the *Theaetetus* and *Sophist*; some of Cornford's views, however, are not uncontroversial: see the commentary by Robin Waterfield in Plato, *Theaetetus* (London: Penguin, 1987). Another good edition with a lengthy and helpful introduction is Myles Burnyeat and M. J. Levett, *The Theaetetus of Plato* (Indianapolis: Hackett Publishing Company, 1990). A major controversy concerning the *Theaetetus* is over the relation of Plato's theory of Forms to that work. Whatever the result of this debate, it can be argued that it makes good sense to read the *Theaetetus* in conjunction with those dialogues where the doctrine of the Forms receives exposition, such as the *Phaedo, Republic*, and *Sophist*.

The secondary literature on Plato is vast. Of central importance is the ever readable and illuminating W. K. C. Guthrie, *A history of Greek philosophy*, vols. IV, V (Cambridge: Cambridge University Press, 1975, 1978). On Socrates see W. K. C. Guthrie, *Socrates* (Cambridge: Cambridge University Press, 1971), and the detailed Gregory Vlastos, *Socrates: ironist and moral philosopher* (Cambridge: Cambridge University Press, 1991). A fresh and clear general introduction to Greek thought is Terence Irwin, *A history of Western philosophy: classical thought*, vol. I (Oxford: Oxford University Press, 1989). Introductory works on Plato are R. M. Hare, *Plato* (Oxford: Oxford University Press, 1982); Frederick Copleston, *A history of philosophy*, vol. I, Part I (New York: Image Books, 1962); G. C. Field, *The philosophy of Plato* (Oxford: Oxford University Press, 1969); J. E. Raven, *Plato's thought in the making* (Cambridge: Cambridge University Press, 1965); David J. Melling, *Understanding Plato* (Oxford: Oxford University Press, 1988).

There are other more difficult and analytical works: Norman Gulley, *Plato's theory of knowledge* (London: Methuen, 1962); I. M. Crombie, *An examination of Plato's doctrines*, vols. I, II (London: Routledge, 1963); Nicholas P. White, *Plato on knowledge and reality* (Indianapolis: Hackett Publishing Company, 1976); J. C. B. Gosling, *Plato* (London: Routledge, 1973). There is also R. C. Cross and A. D. Woozley, *Plato's Republic: a philosophical commentary* (London: Macmillan, 1964). Other important works are A. E. Taylor, *Plato: the man and his works*, 7th edition (London: Methuen, 1960); G. Vlastos (ed.), *Plato*, vols. I, II (New York: Doubleday, 1971); J. N. Findlay, *Plato: the written and unwritten doctrines* (London: Routledge, 1974).

Aristotle

Most of the writings of Aristotle, which were often in the form of dialogues, are lost; the bulk of the considerable amount that remains is notes for lectures; there are also lecture notes made by pupils. Perhaps the central work for understanding Aristotle's views on epistemology and metaphysics is the *Metaphysics*. But other works are also important: *Categories, De interpretatione, Prior analytics, Posterior analytics, Physics*. The best selection of the works of Aristotle in English is J. L. Ackrill (ed.), *A new Aristotle reader* (Oxford: Clarendon Press, 1987). The complete works in English are found in J. A. Smith and W. D. Ross (eds), *The works of Aristotle translated into English*, 12 vols. (Oxford: Oxford University Press, 1912–52). There is also Jonathan Barnes (ed.) *The complete works of Aristotle*, revised Oxford translation, 2 vols. (Princeton: Princeton University Press, 1984).

The most accessible introductory books on Aristotle are Jonathan Barnes,

Aristotle (Oxford: Oxford University Press, 1982); J. L. Ackrill, *Aristotle the philosopher* (Oxford: Oxford University Press, 1981); and A. E. Taylor, *Aristotle*, revised edition (New York: Dover Publications, 1955). W. D. Ross, *Aristotle*, 5th edition (London: Methuen, 1953) is better used as a reference book than read right through.

With regard to longer works it is necessary to be selective. A special mention must be made of W. K. C. Guthrie, *A history of Greek philosophy*, vol. VI (Cambridge: Cambridge University Press, 1983). An important work is G. E. R. Lloyd, *Aristotle: the growth and structure of his thought* (Cambridge: Cambridge University Press, 1968). Lucid and insightful is Marjorie Grene, *A Portrait of Aristotle* (London: Faber and Faber, 1963). Other excellent works are J. H. Randall, *Aristotle* (New York: Columbia University Press, 1960); Henry B. Veatch, *Aristotle* (Bloomington: Indiana University Press, 1974); J. D. G. Evans, *Aristotle* (Brighton: Harvester Press, 1988).

Medieval philosophy

The most accessible collection of excerpts from medieval writers is Arthur Hyman and James J. Walsh (eds), *Philosophy in the Middle Ages* (New York: Harper and Row, 1967); among other items this includes extracts from works by Augustine, Aquinas and Ockham.

There are several general books on medieval thought. The most purely philosophical in approach is Frederick Copleston, *Medieval philosophy* (London: Methuen, 1972). There is also David Knowles, *Evolution of medieval thought*, 2nd edition (London: Longman, 1991); Gordon Leff, *Medieval Thought: St Augustine to Ockham* (London: Penguin, 1958). Much longer, but a fine work of scholarship, is Etienne Gilson, *History of Christian philosophy in the Middle Ages* (London: Sheed and Ward, 1955). Substantial collections of essays are A. H. Armstrong (ed.), *The Cambridge history of later Greek and early medieval philosophy* (Cambridge: Cambridge University Press, 1967) and Norman Kretzmann, Anthony Kenny, and Jan Pinborg (eds), *The Cambridge history of later medieval philosophy* (Cambridge: Cambridge University Press, 1982).

Augustine
The quantity of Augustine's writing is huge, but it is also rather repetitive – there are too many works to list here individually. His writings fall into three forms: sermons, treatises, and letters. There is a selection of Augustine's works in W. J. Oates (ed.), *Basic writings of Saint Augustine*, 2 vols. (New York: Random House, 1948), and Vernon J. Bourke (ed.) *The essential Augustine* (Indianapolis: Hackett Publishing Company, 1974). The two best known works by Augustine are R. Pine-Coffin (tr.), *Confessions* (London: Penguin, 1961) and H. Bettenson (tr.), *The city of God* (London: Penguin, 1984).

Discussions of the specifically philosophical content of Augustine's thought are rather thin on the ground. Most helpful as a starting point is Frederick Copleston, *A history of philosophy*, vol. II, Part I (New York: Image Books, 1950), and the essay by R. A. Markus, "Augustine", *A critical history of Western philosophy*, D. J. O'Connor (ed.) (London: Macmillan, 1985, first pub. 1964). A work devoted to Augustine which deals with him in philosophical depth is Christopher Kirwan, *Augustine* (London: Routledge, 1989); but some may find inappropriate his dedicated application to Augustine of the methods of modern analytical philosophy. There is also R. A. Markus (ed.), *Augustine: a collection of critical essays* (London: Macmillan, 1972). Another work on Augustine is Henry Chadwick, *Augustine* (Oxford: Oxford University Press, 1986); but this is mostly theological in its concerns.

Aquinas

The quantity of Aquinas' writings is gigantic. Anthony Kenny, in his book on Aquinas, illustrates this fact by pointing out that just one relatively minor work by Aquinas, like the *Disputed questions on truth*, alone represents more than half of the total of all the surviving works of Aristotle. Aquinas achieved this magnitude of work partly by dictating to secretaries. Lack of space prohibits the listing of all of the works of Aquinas individually. The best known works are the two massive *Summae: Summa contra gentiles*, printed in 5 vols. as, A. C. Pegis, J. F. Anderson, V. J. Bourke, C. J. O'Neil (tr.), *On the truth of the Catholic faith* (New York: Random House, 1955–57) and *Summa Theologiae*, 60 vols., Blackfriars English edition (London: Eyre and Spottiswoode, 1963–75), which appears in a one volume version, *Summa theologiae: a concise translation*, Timothy McDermott (ed.) (London: Methuen, 1991). Other works vital to understanding Aquinas are: *Quaestiones disputatae*, on a variety of philosophical and theological subjects, and *De ente et essentia*. An accessible selection from the works of Aquinas is Christopher Martin (ed.), *The philosophy of Thomas Aquinas: introductory readings* (London: Routledge, 1989). Useful selections of Aquinas' works are A. C. Pegis (ed.), *Basic writings of St Thomas Aquinas*, 2 vols. (New York: Random House, 1945), and the even more compressed collection in one volume, A. C. Pegis (ed.), *Introduction to Saint Thomas Aquinas* (New York: Random House, 1948).

Aquinas has perhaps received more attention than any other medieval thinker; much of this is, however, concerned with theological matters. A fine philosophical guide to Aquinas is Frederick Copleston, *Aquinas* (London: Penguin, 1955). Also excellent, more recent, but not so comprehensive, is Anthony Kenny, *Aquinas* (Oxford: Oxford University Press, 1980). Kenny has also edited a collection of critical essays on Aquinas; but many of these are quite technical and difficult: Anthony Kenny (ed.), *Aquinas* (London: Macmillan, 1970). A clear introductory essay is Knut Tranøy, "Aquinas", *A critical history of Western philosophy*, D. J. O'Connor (ed.), (London: Macmillan, 1985, first pub. 1964).

Ockham

Ockham is generally regarded as the most important philosopher of the fourteenth century, and the last of the great scholastic philosophers. As with the other philosophers of the Middle Ages, Ockham was a theologian first and a philosopher second. Christian doctrine was largely fixed; it was the unalterable framework within which one worked, although it was a system of belief capable of some reinterpretation. Ockham's contribution to philosophy is to be found among his theological and logical works. The most important works, from a philosophical point of view, are: *Commentary on the sentences, Summa logicae* and *Quodlibeta septem*. The best introductory selection of Ockham's own writings is Philotheus Boehner and Stephen F. Brown (tr. and eds), *Ockham: philosophical writings*, revised edition (Indianapolis: Hackett Publishing Company, 1990); this has Latin/English facing text.

Comprehensive works on Ockham are Gordon Leff, *William of Ockham* (Manchester: Manchester University Press, 1975) and Marilyn McCord Adams, *William Ockham*, 2 vols. (Notre Dame, Indiana: University of Notre Dame Press, 1987); it should be pointed out, however, that both these works are massive. A good place to start is with the article by Ernest A. Moody, "William of Ockham", *The encyclopedia of philosophy*, Paul Edwards (ed.) (London: Collier Macmillan, 1967). There is also Ruth L. Saw, "Ockham", *A critical history of Western philosophy*, D. J. O'Connor (ed.) (London: Macmillan, 1985, first pub. 1964). An accessible secondary source is Frederick Copleston, *A history of philosophy*, vol. III, Part I (New York: Image Books, 1964); in this Copleston devotes a good deal of space to Ockham. A more specialized work, but dealing with what some regard as the most important part of Ockham's thought, is Ernest A. Moody, *The logic of William of Ockham*, 2nd edition (London: Russell and Russell, 1965).

Rationalism

Descartes

The works of Descartes that are central to an understanding of his philosophy are: *Meditations on first philosophy; Objections and replies; Discourse on the method; Principles of philosophy; Rules for the direction of the mind*. The best and most accessible place to start is with the *Meditations*; these should be read in conjunction with the *Objections and replies*. A good collection is Margaret D. Wilson (ed.), *The essential Descartes* (New York: Mentor Books, 1969); this also contains a helpful introductory essay. Another excellent collection is John Cottingham, Robert Stoothoff, Dugald Murdoch (tr. and eds), *Descartes: selected philosophical writings* (Cambridge: Cambridge University Press, 1989). The best comprehensive version of Descartes' works in English is John Cottingham, Robert Stoothoff and Dugald Murdoch (tr. and eds), *The philosophical writings of Descartes*, vols. I, II (Cambridge: Cambridge University Press, 1987).

There are many excellent books on Descartes' philosophy. Very helpful and detailed is Bernard Williams, *Descartes: a project of pure enquiry* (London: Penguin, 1978). Another good work is John Cottingham, *Descartes* (Oxford: Basil Blackwell, 1986). There is also Anthony Kenny, *Descartes* (New York: Random House, 1968). A short introduction is Tom Sorell, *Descartes* (Oxford: Oxford University Press, 1988). There is also Margaret Wilson, *Descartes* (London: Routledge, 1978). A collection of essays is Willis Doney (ed.), *Descartes* (London: Macmillan, 1968).

Spinoza

The *magnum opus* central to an understanding of Spinoza is the *Ethics*, originally written in the universal language of scholarly exchange, Latin.

This he began in 1663, and finished in 1675; a wise caution meant that it remained unpublished until after his death. In 1663, Spinoza began an exposition of Cartesian metaphysics titled *Principles of Cartesian philosophy*, which set it out in the form of geometric proofs; but it is clear that he is critical of what he expounds. Early indications of Spinoza's philosophy are found in the *Treatise on the improvement of the understanding*, begun in 1661, but left unfinished, and also, in draft form, *A short treatise on God, man and his well-being*, completed around the same date. He also published anonymously in 1670 the *Theologico-political treatise*, which advocated religious tolerance; its author was soon identified, and the work was banned in 1674; it was the last work published in his life-time. At his death Spinoza was working on a *Tractatus politicus*.

The definitive English edition of Spinoza's works on metaphysics and epistemology, including the *Ethics*, is Edwin Curley (tr. and ed.), *The collected works of Spinoza*, vol. I (Princeton: Princeton University Press, 1985). A handier version of the *Ethics*, with a much improved translation thanks to revisions by G. H. R. Parkinson, is Spinoza, *Ethics* (London: Everyman, 1989); this also includes very helpful extensive annotations by Parkinson. Also available but an unreliable edition is Spinoza, *On the improvement of the understanding, Ethics, Correspondence*, R. H. M. Elwes (tr.) (New York: Dover, 1955).

The best book to start with is either Stuart Hampshire, *Spinoza* (London: Penguin, 1987) or Roger Scruton, *Spinoza* (Oxford: Oxford University Press, 1986). Other relatively easy introductions are Edwin Curley, *Behind the geometrical method: a reading of Spinoza's Ethics* (New Jersey: Princeton University Press, 1988), and Henry E. Allison, *Benedict de Spinoza: an introduction* (New Haven: Yale University Press, 1987). Works of greater difficulty that apply sharp critical analysis to Spinoza are R. J. Delahunty, *Spinoza* (London: Routledge, 1985), and Jonathan Bennett, *A study of Spinoza's Ethics* (Cambridge: Cambridge University Press, 1984).

Leibniz
Leibniz never systematically put all his ideas into a *magnum opus*, so in studying him we have to rely on his many concise essays, which are often of great clarity. The best shorter collection, containing the most important works, is G. H. R. Parkinson (ed.), *Leibniz: philosophical writings* (London: Dent, 1973). A more extensive collection is Leroy E. Loemker (ed.), *Gottfried Wilhelm Leibniz: philosophical papers and letters*, 2nd edition (Dordrecht: D. Reidel, 1969). Very useful is Nicholas Rescher, *G. W. Leibniz's Monadology: an edition for students* (London: Routledge, 1991). Also useful is Robert Latta (tr. and ed.), *Leibniz: the monadology and other philosophical writings* (Oxford: Oxford University Press, 1971); this contains annotations and an exposition of Leibniz's philosophy.

An excellent introduction to Leibniz, which also goes quite deep, is Nicholas Rescher, *Leibniz: an introduction to his philosophy* (Totowa, New Jersey: Rowan and Littlefield, 1979). A more general and shorter introduction is G. Ross MacDonald, *Leibniz* (Oxford: Oxford University Press, 1986). A book of characteristic meticulousness is C. D. Broad, *Leibniz: an introduction* (Cambridge: Cambridge University Press, 1975). A work with scholarly attention to detail is Stuart Brown, *Leibniz* (Brighton: Harvester Press, 1984). A classic, although difficult, work is Bertrand Russell, *A critical exposition of the philosophy of Leibniz*, 2nd edition (London: Allen & Unwin, 1937). An important work is G. H. R. Parkinson, *Logic and reality in Leibniz's metaphysics* (Oxford: Clarendon Press, 1965). An fine work that treats Leibniz in depth is Benson Mates, *The philosophy of Leibniz* (Oxford: Oxford University Press, 1986).

Empiricism

An important general, but difficult, work on the philosophers considered in this chapter is Jonathan Bennett, *Locke, Berkeley, Hume: central themes* (Oxford: Oxford University Press, 1971).

Locke
Fortunately, most of Locke's views on epistemology and metaphysics are contained in one work: John Locke, *An essay concerning human understanding*. This went through many editions. The best and most complete edition now available of the *Essay* is Peter Nidditch (ed.), *An essay concerning human understanding* (Oxford: Oxford University Press, 1975). But there are also handier abridgements that are quite adequate for the general philosophical reader: A. D. Woozley (ed.), *An essay concerning human understanding* (Glasgow: Fontana, 1977), and John W. Yolton (ed.), *An essay concerning human understanding* (London: Everyman, 1985); the former has the advantage of a longer and highly informative introduction.

There are several introductions to Locke's philosophy. Accessible and helpful is R. S. Woolhouse, *Locke* (Brighton: Harvester Press, 1983). Another useful general work is D. J. O'Connor, *Locke* (New York: Dover, 1967). Two longer classic works of a general nature are Richard I. Aaron, *John Locke*, 3rd edition (Oxford: Clarendon Press, 1971), and James Gibson, *Locke's theory of knowledge and its historical relations* (Cambridge: Cambridge University Press, 1917). A substantial study is Michael Ayers, *Locke*, vol.I: *Epistemology*, vol.II: *Ontology* (London: Routledge, 1991). More specialist works of importance are John W. Yolton, *Locke and the compass of human understanding* (Cambridge: Cambridge University Press, 1970), and Peter Alexander, *Ideas, qualities, and corpuscles: Locke and Boyle on the external world* (Cambridge: Cambridge University Press, 1985). There is also John W. Yolton, *Perceptual acquaintance from Descartes to Reid* (Oxford: Blackwell, 1984). There are valuable collections of essays on Locke, particularly, I. C. Tipton (ed.) *Locke on human understanding* (Oxford: Oxford University Press, 1977); also J. L. Mackie, *Problems from Locke* (Oxford: Oxford University Press, 1987), and C. B. Martin and D. M. Armstrong, *Locke and Berkeley* (London: Macmillan, 1969). The definitive work on Locke's life is Maurice Cranston, *John Locke: a biography* (Oxford: Oxford University Press, 1985).

Berkeley
The two central works for understanding Berkeley's philosophy are *A treatise concerning the principles of human knowledge* and *Three dialogues between Hylas*

and Philonous; and fortunately neither of these is very long. But other significant works are *An essay towards a new theory of vision*, *De motu*, and the collection of short notes, *Philosophical commentaries*. These, and other works, are handily collected in one volume: George Berkeley, *Philosophical works*, M. R. Ayers (ed.) (London: Everyman, 1983). Another single volume collection is George Berkeley, *The principles of human knowledge: with other writings*, G. J. Warnock (ed.) (London: Fontana, 1975). There is also George Berkeley, *Principles of human knowledge and three dialogues*, Roger Woolhouse (ed.) (London: Penguin, 1988). Berkeley's works are found complete in A. A. Luce and T. E. Jessop (eds), *The works of George Berkeley, Bishop of Cloyne* (London: Nelson, 1948-57).

There are several excellent works on Berkeley. The best short introductory work is J. O. Urmson, *Berkeley* (Oxford: Oxford University Press, 1982). An excellent longer but more difficult work is George Pitcher, *Berkeley* (London: Routledge, 1984). Other works of high quality are: G. J. Warnock, *Berkeley* (London: Penguin, 1969); Jonathan Dancy, *Berkeley: an introduction* (Oxford: Basil Blackwell, 1987); A. C. Grayling, *Berkeley: the central arguments* (London: Duckworth, 1986). There are valuable collections of articles in John Foster and Howard Robinson (eds), *Essays on Berkeley* (Oxford: Clarendon Press, 1985), and C. B. Martin and D. M Armstrong, *Locke and Berkeley: a collection of critical essays* (London: Macmillan, 1969). The definitive biography is A. A. Luce, *The life of George Berkeley, Bishop of Cloyne* (Edinburgh: Nelson, 1949).

Hume

The two major works by which Hume's philosophy must be judged are *A treatise of human nature* and the somewhat later *Enquiries concerning human understanding and concerning the principles of morals*. The *Treatise* made relatively little impact at its first appearance; thinking this due to the manner of presentation Hume recast his ideas in the *Enquiries*. The relation between the two works is complex; what can be said is that there are differences both of style and of some philosophical substance.

There are several good editions of Hume's *Treatise* available: *A Treatise of Human Nature*, L. A. Selby-Bigge (ed.) (Oxford: Clarendon Press, 1968); *A Treatise of Human Nature*, Ernest C. Mossner (ed.) (London: Penguin, 1984); *A Treatise of Human Nature*, D. G. C. Macnabb (ed.) (Glasgow: Fontana, 1987); and for the Hume *Enquiries*, 3rd edition, L. A. Selby-Bigge (ed.), revised by P. H. Nidditch (Oxford: Clarendon Press, 1975).

Of books on Hume, excellent introductions are Terence Penelhum, *Hume* (London: Macmillan, 1975) and D. G. C. Macnabb, *David Hume* (Oxford: Basil Blackwell, 1966). A useful short work is A. J. Ayer, *Hume* (Oxford: Oxford University Press, 1980). A book of fundamental importance for the interpretation of Hume's philosophy is Norman Kemp Smith, *The philosophy of David Hume* (London: Macmillan, 1941). A fine work treating Hume in depth is Barry Stroud, *Hume* (London: Routledge, 1977). More specialized works are John Passmore, *Hume's intentions*, 3rd edition (London: Duckworth, 1980); Robert J. Fogelin, *Hume's skepticism in the Treatise of Human Nature* (London: Routledge, 1985); David Pears, *Hume's system: an examination of the first book of his Treatise* (Oxford: Oxford University Press, 1990). A collection of essays is V. C. Chappell (ed.), *Hume* (London: Macmillan, 1968).

The definitive biography of Hume is E. C. Mossner, *The life of David Hume*, 2nd edition (Oxford: Oxford University Press, 1980).

Transcendental idealism

Kant

Kant's own thoughts on epistemology and metaphysics are contained in two main works: Immanuel Kant, *Prolegomena to any future metaphysics that will be able to present itself as a science* (Manchester: Manchester University Press, 1971), and Immanuel Kant, *Critique of pure reason* (London: Macmillan, 1976), which is the authoritative English translation by Norman Kemp Smith containing both the 1781 and 1787 editions of the *Critique*.

There are many good books on Kant in English. Good introductory accounts are Frederick Copleston, *A history of Western philosophy*, vol. VI, Parts I, II (New York: Image Books, 1964), Roger Scruton, *Kant* (Oxford: Oxford University Press, 1982); John Kemp, *The philosophy of Kant* (Oxford: Oxford University Press, 1979). Stephen Körner, *Kant* (London: Penguin, 1977), gives a lively critical overview. Also useful is A. C. Ewing, *A short commentary on Kant's Critique of Pure Reason* (London: Methuen, 1938). Norman Kemp Smith, *A commentary to Kant's Critique of Pure Reason* (London: Macmillan, 1923) is valuable as a detailed guide through the *Critique of Pure Reason*. C. D. Broad, *Kant: an introduction* (Cambridge: Cambridge University Press, 1978), is a detailed, clear, illuminating study. A helpful work is Ralph C. S. Walker, *Kant* (London: Routledge, 1978). There is also H. J. Paton, *Kant's Metaphysics of Experience*, 2 vols. (London: Allen & Unwin, 1936). A comprehensive guide is Paul Guyer (ed.), *The Cambridge Companion to Kant* (Cambridge: Cambridge University Press, 1992). Books that go considerably beyond being expositions are: P. F. Strawson, *The bounds of sense* (London: Methuen, 1978), and Jonathan Bennett, *Kant's Analytic* (Cambridge: Cambridge University Press, 1966), *Kant's Dialectic* (Cambridge: Cambridge University Press, 1974); Strawson is ultimately sympathetic, Bennett is highly analytical. A detailed study is Paul Guyer, *Kant and the claims of knowledge* (Cambridge: Cambridge University Press, 1987). Another work worth studying is W. H. Walsh, *Kant's Criticism of Metaphysics* (Edinburgh: Edinburgh University Press, 1975). Ernest Cassirer, *Kant's life and thought* (New Haven: Yale University Press, 1981), fills in the intellectual background and origin of Kant's ideas.

Later German philosophy

Hegel

Hegel's philosophical works are characteristically long and difficult; his output is large, but the most important items are mentioned here. Of major importance are: Hegel, *The phenomenology of spirit* (also known as *The phenomenology of mind*), A. V. Miller (tr.) (Oxford: Oxford University Press, 1977); *Lectures on the philosophy of history*, J. Sibree (tr.) (New York: Dover, 1956); *Science of logic*, A. V. Miller (tr.) (London: Allen & Unwin, 1969);

Philosophy of right, T. M. Knox (tr.) (Oxford: Clarendon Press, 1942). Giving an overall picture of his philosophy is Hegel, *Encyclopedia of the philosophical sciences*, which is published in three parts, Part I: *Logic*, W. Wallace (tr.) (Oxford: Clarendon Press, 1975), Part II: *Philosophy of nature*, A. V. Miller (tr.) (Oxford: Clarendon Press, 1970), Part III: *Philosophy of mind*, A. V. Miller (tr.) (Oxford: Clarendon Press, 1971). Useful is the edited collection of excerpts from Hegel's works, M. J. Inwood (ed.) *Hegel: selections* (London: Macmillan, 1989).

There are quite a few good guides to Hegel's philosophy. An excellent overall exposition of Hegel's philosophy, notable for its clarity and orderly approach, is W. T. Stace, *The philosophy of Hegel* (London: Macmillan, 1924). A good short general introduction is Peter Singer, *Hegel* (Oxford: Oxford University Press, 1983). Another introductory work is Richard Norman, *Hegel's phenomenology: a philosophical introduction* (Brighton: Sussex University Press, 1976). An important work is Ivan Soll, *An introduction to Hegel's metaphysics* (Chicago: University of Chicago Press, 1969). A helpful collection of essays is M. J. Inwood (ed.) *Hegel* (Oxford: Oxford University Press, 1985). Large works on Hegel are Charles Taylor, *Hegel* (Cambridge: Cambridge University Press, 1978), and the analytical examination by M. J. Inwood, *Hegel* (London: Routledge, 1983). There is also J. N. Findlay, *Hegel: a re-examination* (London: Allen & Unwin, 1958). A useful companion while reading Hegel is M. J. Inwood, *A Hegel dictionary* (Oxford: Blackwell, 1992).

Nietzsche

The works of Nietzsche are unconventional when regarded as philosophical works; they contain an enormous variety of literary styles: arguments, narratives, aphorisms, metaphors, polemics and hyperbole. Indeed, the pluralism of Nietzsche's style can be seen as an attempt to distinguish himself from traditional philosophy so that he is understood as marking the beginning of a new philosophy. The following lists some of the most important of Nietzsche's works, in roughly chronological order of their creation, written between 1872 and 1888.

The birth of tragedy, Walter Kaufmann (tr.) (New York: Vintage Books, 1966); *Human, all too human*, R. J. Hollingdale (tr.) (Cambridge: Cambridge University Press, 1988); *Daybreak*, R. J. Hollingdale (tr.) (Cambridge: Cambridge University Press, 1982); *The gay science*, Walter Kaufmann (tr.) (New York: Vintage Books, 1974); *Thus spoke Zarathustra*, R. J. Hollingdale (tr.) (London: Penguin, 1980); *Beyond good and evil*, Walter Kaufmann (tr.) (New York: Vintage Books, 1966); *On the genealogy of morals*, Walter Kaufmann and R. J. Hollingdale (tr.) (New York: Vintage Books, 1969); *Twilight of the idols*, R. J. Hollingdale (tr.) (London: Penguin, 1982); *The antichrist*, R. J. Hollingdale (tr.) (London: Penguin, 1982); *Ecce homo*, R. J. Hollingdale (tr.) (London: Penguin, 1979); *The will to power*, Walter Kaufmann and R. J. Hollingdale (tr.) (New York: Vintage Books, 1968). There is also Nietzsche's *Nachlass*, which consists of large numbers of fragmentary notes.

A good place to start reading Nietzsche is the selective compendium R. J. Hollingdale (tr. and ed.), *A Nietzsche reader* (London: Penguin, 1977). There are convenient collections of Nietzsche's works: *Basic writings of Nietzsche*, Walter Kaufmann (tr.) (New York: Random House, 1968) contains *The Birth* of Tragedy, Beyond Good and Evil, On the Genealogy of Morals, The case of Wagner, Ecce homo; The portable Nietzsche, Walter Kaufmann (tr.) (New York: Viking Press, 1954) contains Thus spoke Zarathustra, Twilight of the idols, The antichrist, Nietzsche contra Wagner.

It is important to note that there are significant divergences of interpretation over Nietzsche. Of works on Nietzsche that are philosophically deep there are Alexander Nehamas, Nietzsche: life as literature (Harvard: Harvard University Press, 1985); Arthur C. Danto, Nietzsche as philosopher (New York: Columbia University Press, 1980); Richard Schacht, Nietzsche (London: Routledge, 1983). A valuable study is Maudemarie Clark, Nietzsche on truth and philosophy (Cambridge: Cambridge University Press, 1990). There is also Gilles Deleuze, Nietzsche and philosophy (London: Athlone Press, 1983). An excellent collection of essays designed to aid the reading of Nietzsche is Robert C. Solomon and Kathleen M. Higgins, Reading Nietzsche (Oxford: Oxford University Press, 1988). A more general work is Walter Kaufmann, Nietzsche: philosopher, psychologist, antichrist, 4th edition (Princeton: Princeton University Press, 1974). An interesting study is Ruediger H. Grimm, Nietzsche's theory of knowledge (New York: Walter de Gruyter, 1977); it unfortunately leaves quotes from Nietzsche untranslated. Also good is John T. Wilcox, Truth and value in Nietzsche: a study of his metaethics and epistemology (Michigan: Michigan University Press, 1974). The best account of Nietzsche's life, and one that also gives some idea of his philosophy, is Ronald Hayman, Nietzsche: a critical life (New York: Oxford University Press, 1980).

Analytical philosophy

The best general introduction to the subject of this chapter is perhaps J. O. Urmson, Philosophical analysis (Oxford: Oxford University Press, 1967). But it should be noted that Urmson's point of view is a critical one.

Russell

A complete list of Russell's works would be very long. Much of Russell's early intellectual activity was concerned with technical aspects of mathematics and mathematical logic, although some of this had philosophical import. This work is partly found in The principles of mathematics, 1st edition 1903, 2nd edition (London: Allen & Unwin, 1937), and culminates in the monumental work Russell completed with A. N. Whitehead, Principia mathematica, 3 vols. (Cambridge: Cambridge University Press, 1910–13). There is also Russell, Introduction to mathematical philosophy (London: Allen & Unwin, 1919). The list below is of the works whose emphasis is philosophical. Russell changed some of his views over his lifetime; the best introduction to his philosophy is Bertrand Russell, My philosophical development (London: Allen & Unwin, 1959) read in conjunction with the relatively early work, Bertrand Russell, The problems of philosophy (1912) (Oxford: Oxford University Press, 1978). In order to gain a balanced view of Russell's work it is necessary to consult his later thoughts on the central questions of philosophy in An inquiry into meaning and truth (1940) (London: Penguin, 1965) and Human knowledge: its scope and limits (London: Allen &

Unwin, 1948). Other works by Russell of importance are *Our knowledge of the external world* (1914) 3rd edition (London: Allen & Unwin, 1926); *Mysticism and logic* (1917) (London: Penguin, 1954); *The analysis of mind* (London: Allen & Unwin, 1921); *The analysis of matter* (London: Allen & Unwin, 1927); *An outline of philosophy* (London: Allen & Unwin, 1927); *History of Western philosophy* (London: Allen & Unwin, 1945); *Logic and knowledge* (London: Unwin Hyman, 1956).

As to works on Russell, good is A. J. Ayer, *Russell* (London: Fontana, 1972) and A. J. Ayer, *Russell and Moore: the analytical heritage* (London: Macmillan, 1971). Longer and more detailed is R. M. Sainsbury, *Russell* (London: Routledge, 1979). A detailed and sometimes difficult work is David Pears, *Bertrand Russell and the British tradition in philosophy* (London: Fontana, 1972). There is also a collection of essays, P. A. Schilpp (ed.) *The philosophy of Bertrand Russell* (New York: Tudor Publishing Company, 1951). A valuable collection of essays which pay due attention to Russell's later work is C. Wade Savage and C. Anthony Anderson (eds), *Rereading Russell: essays on Bertrand Russell's metaphysics and epistemology* (Minnesota Studies in the Philosophy of Science, vol. XII) (Minneapolis: University of Minnesota Press, 1989).

Wittgenstein

That Wittgenstein appears in two separate chapters in this book (Chs 8 and 11) reflects the distinction between his earlier and later philosophies. All of Wittgenstein's books, apart from the *Tractatus logico-philosophicus* of 1921, were published after his death, when many of his papers and notes were compiled into books. His earlier philosophy is found in Wittgenstein, *Tractatus logico-philosophicus* (1921), D. F. Pears and B. McGuinness (tr.) (London: Routledge, 1974), which in the hardback edition has facing German text. There is also an earlier translation, *Tractatus logico-philosophicus*, C. K. Ogden and F. P. Ramsey (tr.) (London: Routledge, 1955), which has facing German text and was checked by Wittgenstein. Also useful is Wittgenstein, *Notebooks 1914–1916*, G. H. von Wright and G. E. M. Anscombe (tr. and eds) (Oxford: Basil Blackwell, 1979).

In listing books on Wittgenstein for Chapter 8 there is some overlap with books appropriate to the bibliography for Chapter 11 on Wittgenstein because several books deal with both the early and late philosophy in one work.

Of works on Wittgenstein's thought in general a fine introduction is Anthony Kenny, *Wittgenstein* (London: Penguin, 1973). Also useful as general introductions are: A. C. Grayling, *Wittgenstein* (Oxford: Oxford University Press, 1989); David Pears, *Wittgenstein* (Glasgow: Fontana, 1977). Other works which consider Wittgenstein's thought as a whole are: R. J. Fogelin, *Wittgenstein*, 2nd edition (London: Routledge, 1987); David Pears, *The false prison: a study of the development of Wittgenstein's philosophy*, 2 vols. (Oxford: Clarendon Press, 1987, 1988); Derek Bolton: *An approach to Wittgenstein's philosophy* (London: Macmillan, 1979); P. M. S. Hacker, *Insight and illusion*, 2nd edition (Oxford: Oxford University Press, 1987). An enormous collection of essays is found in Stuart Shanker (ed.) *Ludwig Wittgenstein: critical arguments*, vols. I–IV (London: Croom Helm, 1986).

Works specifically on the early philosophy are: H. O. Mounce, *Wittgenstein's Tractatus: an introduction* (Oxford: Basil Blackwell, 1981); Erik Stenius, *Wittgenstein's Tractatus* (Oxford: Basil Blackwell, 1960); Max Black, *A companion to Wittgenstein's Tractatus* (Cambridge: Cambridge University Press, 1964); G. E. M. Anscombe, *An introduction to Wittgenstein's Tractatus* (London: Hutchinson, 1959). A valuable collection of essays is I. M. Copi and R. W. Beard (eds), *Essays on Wittgenstein's Tractatus* (London: Routledge, 1966).

Biographical information is contained in Norman Malcolm, *Ludwig Wittgenstein: a memoir* (London: Oxford University Press, 1962) and B. F. McGuinness, *The young Wittgenstein* (London: Duckworth, 1988). The most complete biography is Ray Monk, *Ludwig Wittgenstein: the duty of genius* (London: Cape, 1990). There are general assessments of Wittgenstein and articles on his philosophy in K. T. Fann (ed.), *Ludwig Wittgenstein: the man and his philosophy* (Sussex: Harvester Press, 1978).

Phenomenology and existentialism

Husserl

Husserl wrote a large amount; although there is a standard edition in German of his output, the various English translations present one with a rather bewildering array of works. The quantity of Husserl's work partly reflects the extent to which he constantly rethought and reformulated his views. Perhaps the best concise introduction is Husserl, *The idea of phenomenology*, William P. Alston and George Nakhnikian (tr.) (The Hague: Martinus Nijhoff, 1964). There is also the relatively short work, Husserl, *The Paris lectures*, Peter Koestenbaum (tr.) (The Hague: Martinus Nijhoff, 1985). Both of these contain helpful introductory essays by the translators. There is an extremely concise introduction to phenomenology prepared by Husserl which originally appeared as "Phenomenology" in the *Encyclopaedia Britannica*, 14th edition, 1929; it is reprinted in an improved translation in Peter McCormick and Fredrick A. Elliston (eds), *Husserl: shorter works* (Notre Dame: University of Notre Dame Press, 1981); this includes other shorter essays by Husserl. Of his longer works perhaps *Ideas: a general introduction to pure phenomenology*, W. R. Boyce Gibson (tr.) (London: Allen & Unwin, 1931) gives the best notion of his phenomenology. Of the other longer works the most important are Edmund Husserl, *Logical investigations* (First pub. 1901, revised 1913) 2nd edition, J. N. Findlay (tr.) (London: Routledge, 1970); *Cartesian meditations*, D. Cairns (tr.) (The Hague, Martinus Nijhoff, 1973); *The crisis of European sciences and transcendental philosophy*, David Carr (tr.) (Evanston: Northwestern University Press, 1970). There is also the short work, Husserl, *Phenomenology and the crisis of philosophy: philosophy as a rigorous science and philosophy and the crisis of European man*, Quentin Lauer (tr.) (New York: Harper and Row, 1965).

An excellent introduction to Husserl and to phenomenology in general is David Stewart and Algis Mickunas, *Exploring phenomenology*, 2nd edition (Athens, Ohio: Ohio University Press, 1990). Another general introduction is Michael Hammond, Jane Howarth and Russell Keat, *Understanding phenomenology* (Oxford: Basil Blackwell, 1991). Of longer, more detailed studies of Husserl most helpful are David Bell, *Husserl* (London: Routledge, 1990) and J. J. Kockelmans, *A first introduction to Husserl's phenomenology* (Pittsburg: Duquesne University Press, 1967). There are also useful collections of essays in J. J. Kockelmans (ed.), *Phenomenology: the philosophy of Edmund Husserl and its interpretation* (New York: Double Day, 1967); Frederick A. Elliston and Peter McCormick (eds), *Husserl: expositions and appraisals* (Notre Dame: University of Notre Dame Press, 1977); E. Pivčević (ed.), *Phenomenology and philosophical understanding* (Cambridge: Cambridge University Press, 1975). A large classic work which covers the whole history of phenomenology is Herbert Spiegelberg, *The phenomenological movement*, 2 vols., 2nd edition (The Hague: Martinus Nijhoff, 1971). An advanced study of phenomenology is Josef Seifert, *Back to "things in themselves"* (London: Routledge, 1987). Some intellectual connections between continental phenomenology and analytical philosophy are explored in Harold A. Durfee (ed.) *Analytic philosophy and phenomenology* (The Hague: Martinus Nijhoff, 1976)

Sartre

The most substantial single philosophical work of Jean-Paul Sartre is *Being and nothingness: an essay on phenomenological ontology* (1943), Hazel E. Barnes (tr.) (London: Methuen, 1977). Other philosophical works are Sartre, *Imagination* (1936), Forrest Williams (tr.) (Ann Arbor: University of Michigan Press, 1962); *The transcendence of the ego: an existentialist theory of consciousness* (1936) Forrest Williams and Robert Kirkpatrick (tr.) (New York: Noonday Press, 1957); *The psychology of the imagination* (1940), Bernard Frechtman (tr.) (London: Methuen, 1972); *Existentialism and humanism* (1946), Philip Mairet (tr.) (London: Methuen, 1948); *Literary and philosophical essays*, Annette Michelson (tr.) (London: Hutchinson, 1968). There is also considerable philosophical substance in Sartre's novels and plays; a good example, once one sees the philosophical points it is making, is Sartre's novel *Nausea* (1938) (London: Penguin, 1976).

There are several excellent works on the philosophy of Sartre. A fine lucid introduction is Arthur C. Danto, *Sartre* (London: Fontana, 1975). A helpful work is Mary Warnock, *The philosophy of Sartre* (London: Hutchinson, 1972). There are also Peter Caws, *Sartre* (London: Routledge, 1984); A. R. Manser, *Sartre* (London: Athlone Press, 1966); Marjorie Grene, *Sartre* (Washington DC: University Presses of America, 1983). Those who wish to tackle Sartre's *Being and nothingness* may find helpful Joseph S. Catalano, *A commentary on Jean-Paul Sartre's Being and Nothingness* (Chicago: Chicago University Press, 1980). There is a collection of essays on Sartre in P. A. Schilpp (ed.) *The philosophy of Jean-Paul Sartre* (La Salle, Illinois: Open Court, 1981). On Sartre's interlinked life and work there are Ronald Hayman, *Writing against: a biography of Sartre* (London: Weidenfeld and Nicolson, 1986) and Annie Cohen-Solal, *Sartre: a life* (London, Minerva, 1991).

Some of the thinkers often identified as existentialist, apart from Sartre, are Søren Kierkegaard (1813–55), Karl Jaspers (1883-1969), Gabriel Marcel (1889–1973), Martin Heidegger (1889–1976). Perhaps the core figures are Heidegger and Sartre, despite the unhappiness they expressed about the label "existentialist".

For a general introduction to existentialism the best is the lucid and engaging David E. Cooper, *Existentialism* (Oxford: Basil Blackwell, 1990). Another useful work is Mary Warnock, *Existentialism* (Oxford: Oxford University Press, 1970). A useful brief survey is Alasdair MacIntyre, "Existentialism", *A critical history of Western philosophy*, D. J. O'Connor (ed.), (London: Macmillan, 1985, first pub. 1964). Helpful both in charting the intellectual emergence of existentialism and in its account of existentialism itself is Robert C. Solomon, *From rationalism to existentialism* (New York: University Press of America, 1972). An interesting and accessible collection of essays is Robert C. Solomon, *From Hegel to existentialism* (Oxford: Oxford University Press, 1987). There are expositional essays on the major philosophers often regarded as existentialist in H. J. Blackham, *Six existentialist thinkers: Kierkegaard, Nietzsche, Jaspers, Marcel, Heidegger, Sartre* (London: Routledge, 1961).

Logical positivism and falsificationism

Ayer

The chief work for the study of Ayer in the period of his adherence to logical positivism is A. J. Ayer, *Language, truth and logic* (1936, revised edition 1946) (London: Penguin, 1975). This provides a beautifully clear introduction to the central tenets of logical positivism in general, although there were some important differences within the logical positivist movement. The revised edition in 1946 contains a new "Introduction"; this would be more appropriate as an appendix as it involves replies to criticisms of the first edition and rethinking, which in some cases produces modification of the original doctrines; it is sensible to read the "Introduction" after the main body of the text.

Those wishing to understand Ayer's later thought when he moved away from logical positivism should consult, among his other works, A. J. Ayer, *The problem of knowledge* (1956) (London: Penguin, 1964) and *The central questions of philosophy* (1973) (London: Penguin, 1977); also two collections of essays, A. J. Ayer, *Metaphysics and common sense* (London: Macmillan, 1969) and *The concept of a person* (London: Macmillan, 1973). There are also several other important works by Ayer.

A useful collection of essays on Ayer's logical positivism is Barry Gower (ed.) *Logical positivism in perspective: essays on Language, Truth and Logic* (London: Croom Helm, 1987). For a detailed work discussing Ayer's philosophy in general see John Foster, *Ayer* (London: Routledge, 1985); the excellent first chapter of this book is devoted to Ayer's logical positivism. There is also a collection of essays dedicated to Ayer with replies by him: G. F. Macdonald (ed.), *Perception and identity* (London: Macmillan, 1979). Another substantial collection of essays is Lewis Hahn (ed.), *The philosophy of A. J. Ayer* (La Salle, Illinois: Open Court Publishing, 1992).

Among the central figures in the logical positivism movement were Morris Schlick (1882–1936), Rudolf Carnap (1891–1970), Otto Neurath (1882–1945), Friedrich Waismann (1896–1959); the influence of the group was considerable.

The best introductory book on logical positivism in general is Oswald Hanfling, *Logical positivism* (Oxford: Basil Blackwell, 1981); there is also a collection of readings, Oswald Hanfling (ed.), *Essential readings in logical positivism* (Oxford: Basil Blackwell, 1981). Another collection is A. J. Ayer (ed.), *Logical positivism* (Glencoe, Illinois: Free Press, 1959). Although not all by followers of logical positivism, a valuable collection of essays relevant to logical positivism is Herbert Feigl and Wilfred Sellars (eds), *Readings in philosophical analysis* (New York: Appleton-Century-Croft, 1949).

Popper

Since the publication of his first major work Popper's outlook has been remarkably consistent and unified. His work has mainly concentrated on epistemology, philosophy of science and political philosophy. Probably the best introduction to his thought is Karl R. Popper, *Conjectures and refutations* (1963), 4th edition (London: Routledge, 1972), read in conjunction with his interesting intellectual autobiography, *Unended quest*, 4th edition (London: Routledge, 1992). The origin of much of the later thinking of Popper is contained in *Logik der Forschung* (1934), translated as *The logic of scientific discovery* (1959) (London: Hutchinson, 1977). His ideas are elaborated in *Objective knowledge* (Oxford: Clarendon Press, 1979). Popper's views in the philosophy of mind are in a work he wrote with John C. Eccles: *The self and its brain* (New York: Springer International, 1977). Popper's arguments in political philosophy are intimately connected with his epistemology and are found in *The open society and its enemies* (1945), 2 vols (London: Routledge, 1966) and *The poverty of historicism* (1957) (London: Routledge, 1961). With the general subtitle *From the Postscript to The Logic of Scientific Discovery* three volumes of Popper's work have appeared: W. W. Bartley III (ed.), *Realism and the aim of science; The open universe: an argument for indeterminism; Quantum theory and the schism in physics* (London: Hutchinson, 1982–83). Also there is Karl R. Popper, *In search of a better world: lectures and essays from thirty years* (London: Routledge, 1992).

There are several excellent books on Popper's thought. A good short introduction is Bryan Magee, *Popper* (London: Fontana, 1982). More extensive and detailed are Anthony O'Hear, *Popper* (London: Routledge, 1980) and T. E. Burke, *The philosophy of Popper* (Manchester: Manchester University Press, 1983). There is also a collection of critical essays by various authors in P. A. Schilpp (ed.) *The philosophy of Karl Popper*, 2 vols (La Salle, Illinois: Open Court, 1977); this includes replies to critics by Popper.

Popper's views, especially on the nature of rationality, philosophy of science and epistemology, can be better understood in relation to others working in these areas, including those critical of his views and those who present alternative positions. Excellent books on these matters are, Anthony O'Hear, *An introduction to the philosophy of science* (Oxford: Oxford University Press, 1990); A. F. Chalmers, *What is this thing called science?*, 2nd edition (Milton Keynes: Open University Press, 1982); W. Newton-Smith, *The rationality of science* (London: Routledge, 1981). A work with a more historical approach is Derek Gjertsen, *Science and philosophy: past and present* (London: Penguin, 1989).

Linguistic philosophy

Wittgenstein
The work central to understanding the later philosophy of Wittgenstein, published posthumously in 1953, is *Philosophical investigations*, G. E. M. Anscombe and R. Rhees (eds) (Oxford: Basil Blackwell, 1974). Ludwig Wittgenstein, *The blue and brown books*, R. R. Rhees (ed.) (Oxford: Basil Blackwell, 1975), can perhaps be used as something like an introduction to his later thought. The most important of his other later works are: *On certainty*, G. E. M. Anscombe and G. H. von Wright (eds) (Oxford: Basil Blackwell, 1979) and *Zettel*, G. E. M. Anscombe and G. H. von Wright (eds) (Oxford: Basil Blackwell, 1967). Other works are *Remarks on the foundations of mathematics*, G. H. von Wright and R. Rhees (eds) (Oxford: Basil Blackwell, 1978); *Philosophical remarks*, R. Rhees (ed.) (Oxford: Basil Blackwell, 1975); *Philosophical grammar*, R. Rhees (ed.) (Oxford: Basil Blackwell, 1969).

As was stated in the bibliography for Chapter 8, many books on Wittgenstein deal with both the earlier and later philosophy together; those books dealing with Wittgenstein's philosophy as a whole are listed in the bibliography to Chapter 8.

There is significant divergence of interpretation over the later philosophy. An excellent work on the later philosophy is Oswald Hanfling, *Wittgenstein's later philosophy* (London: Macmillan, 1989). Other important works are Norman Malcolm, *Nothing is hidden: Wittgenstein's criticism of his early thought* (Oxford: Basil Blackwell, 1986) and E. K. Specht, *The foundations of Wittgenstein's late philosophy* (Manchester: Manchester University Press, 1967). There is also S. Kripke, *Wittgenstein on rules and private language* (Oxford: Basil Blackwell, 1982). Collections of essays on the later philosophy are George Pitcher (ed.) *Wittgenstein: the philosophical investigations* (London: Macmillan, 1968) and Alice Ambrose and Morris Lazerowitz (eds), *Ludwig Wittgenstein: philosophy and language* (London: Allen & Unwin, 1972). An extremely detailed study of the *Philosophical investigations* is found in the three volumes, G. P. Baker and P. M. S. Hacker, *Wittgenstein: meaning and understanding* (Oxford: Basil Blackwell, 1980, 1983); G. P. Baker and P. M. S. Hacker, *An analytical commentary on Wittgenstein's Philosophical Investigations* (Oxford: Basil Blackwell, 1980); P. M. S. Hacker, *Wittgenstein: meaning and mind* (Oxford: Basil Blackwell, 1990).

Recent philosophy

There is no real substitute, in studying recent philosophy, for reading the works of recent philosophers themselves. A selection of the works by the philosophers mentioned in Chapter 12 appears below. The bibliographies appear in the same order as the philosophers occur in Chapter 12. I have restricted myself to books; there are, of course, many articles in journals which are unmentioned.

There are some general works relevant to the study of recent philosophy. The later chapters of John Passmore, *A hundred years of philosophy*, 2nd edition (London: Penguin, 1966) have material on recent philosophy, and this work is carried on in John Passmore, *Recent philosophy* (London: Duckworth, 1985), which is the best general survey of recent philosophy. There is also A. J. Ayer, *Philosophy in the twentieth century* (London: Allen & Unwin, 1982). A useful collection of essays by recent philosophers – including Hampshire, Davidson, Strawson, and Kripke – is found in Ted Honderich and Myles Burnyeat (eds), *Philosophy as it is* (London: Penguin, 1979). Books that concentrate on philosophical problems as they are addressed by recent philosophy are: Anthony O'Hear, *What philosophy is* (London: Penguin, 1985); A. R. Lacey, *Modern philosophy* (London: Routledge, 1982); Jonathan Dancy, *Introduction to contemporary epistemology* (Oxford: Blackwell, 1985).

Gilbert Ryle: *The concept of mind* (1949); *Dilemmas* (1954); *Collected papers 1929–1968* (1971).

Nelson Goodman: *The structure of appearance* (1951); *Fact, fiction and forecast* (1955); *The languages of art* (1968); *Problems and projects* (1972); *Ways of worldmaking* (1978).

W. V. O. Quine: *Methods of logic* (1962); *From a logical point of view* (1953); *Word and object* (1960); *The Ways of Paradox and other essays* (1966, revised edition 1976); *Ontological Relativity and other essays* (1969); *Philosophy of logic* (1970); *The web of belief* (1970); *The roots of reference* (1974); *Pursuit of truth* (1990).

J. L. Austin: *Philosophical papers* (1961); *Sense and sensibilia* (1962); *How to do things with words* (1962).

Stuart Hampshire: *Spinoza* (1951, revised edition 1987); *Thought and action* (1959); *Freedom of the individual* (1965, new edition 1975); *Modern writers and other essays* (1972); *Freedom of mind* (1972); *Two theories of morality* (1977).

Donald Davidson: *Essays on action and events* (1982); *Inquiries into truth and interpretation* (1985).

P. F. Strawson: *Introduction to logical theory* (1952); *Individuals* (1959); *The bounds of sense* (1966); *Logico-linguistic papers* (1971); *Subject and predicate in logic and grammar* (1974); *Freedom and Resentment and other essays* (1974); *Skepticism and naturalism: some varieties* (1985); *Analysis and metaphysics: an introduction to philosophy* (1992).

Thomas S. Kuhn: *The Copernican revolution* (1957); *The structure of scientific revolution* (1962, enlarged edition 1970); *The essential tension* (1977).

Paul Feyerabend: *Against method* (1975); *Science in a free society* (1978); *Philosophical papers: Realism, rationalism, scientific method*, vol.I, *Problems of empiricism*, vol.II (1981); *Farewell to reason* (1987); *Three dialogues on knowledge* (1991).

Michael Dummett: *Frege* (1973); *Elements of intuitionism* (1977); *Truth and other enigmas* (1978); *The interpretation of Frege's philosophy* (1981); *Frege and other philosophers* (1991); *The logical basis of metaphysics* (1991).

Richard Rorty: *Philosophy and the mirror of nature* (1979); *Consequences of pragmatism* (1982); *Contingency, irony, and solidarity* (1988); *Objectivity, relativism and truth: philosophical papers I* (1990); *Essays on Heidegger and others: philosophical papers II* (1991).

John R. Searle: *Speech acts: an essay in the philosophy of language* (1969); *Expression and meaning* (1979); *Intentionality* (1983).

Saul Kripke: *Naming and necessity* (1972, republished 1980); *Wittgenstein on rules and private languages* (1982).

INDEX

172, 173, 175; *see also* noumena
time 165–6, 168
transcendent 168
transcendental 165
transcendental deduction 166,
169–70
transcendental idealism 171–2
understanding 166, 175
Kepler, Johannes 157
Kierkegaard, Sren 220, 328
knowledge
by acquaintance 210
by description 210
empiricism on 74–5, 114–16
limits of 117–18, 125, 127
rationalism on 74–5, 114–16
Wittgenstein on 222, 302–4
Kripke, Saul 310–11
Kuhn, Thomas S. 308

language
limits of 221
meaning as use 285, 286, 287,
289, 293–6, 297–8, 300–1,
302–3
misleading nature of 198, 204–7,
284
ideal 205, 212, 214
ordinary 204, 206, 214
private 301
language-game (Wittgenstein) 294–8
Lebenswelt (Husserl) 245
Leibniz, G. W. xi, 101–13; *see also*
79, 88, 158, 160–2, 164, 262
accidents 107
analytic 102, 107–9, 111
a posteriori 164–5
appearance 105, 107, 109, 110,
111, 112–13
a priori 103, 113
atomism 106
basic principles of 102–3
Cartesianism 101, 104
causation 109
complete concept 107, 110, 112
determinism 107–8
essence 107
freedom 111–12
God 103, 106, 107, 108, 109, 110,
111, 112
existence proof 106–7
identity of indiscernibles 102,
103–4, 110
individuals 104

inesse principle 102, 112
labyrinth of the continuum 105–6
life of 101
logic 102
mind/body problem 111
monads 105–7, 108, 109, 110,
111, 112
nature of 106–7, 109
levels of 111
true substances 105
necessitarianism 108
necessity 108
phenomena bene fundata 107
possible worlds 102, 103, 107,
108, 109, 110, 111, 112
pre-established harmony 109
principle of non-contradiction
102
principle of perfection 102–3
principle of sufficient reason 102
reality 103–4
science 112–13
space 110, 107
Spinoza 101, 104, 105, 107
substance 104–10, 113
substantial form 104
time 107, 110
truth 102
contingent/necessary 103
of fact/of reason 103
well-founded phenomena 107,
110
Leucippus xi, 5, 15, 18–20, 21
Locke, John xi, 116–28; *see also* 66,
72, 129, 133–4, 135, 137 141, 158
aim of his philosophy 117
a posteriori 120 127
a priori 119, 120, 127, 128
Berkeley 124
Boyle 116, 124
causation 128
corpuscles 116, 123–4, 125
empiricism 119–20
essences
nominal 122, 125
real 125
experience
reflection/sensation 119
God 119, 123, 124, 126–7
hierarchy of certainty 127
Hume 128
ideas 120–1
abstract 122
agreement and disagreement of

Index